The Dissemination of News and the Emergence of Contemporaneity in Early Modern Europe

Edited By
BRENDAN DOOLEY
University College, Cork

ASHGATE

© Brendan Dooley and the contributors 2010

All rights reserved. No part of this publication may be reproduced, stored in a retrieval system or transmitted in any form or by any means, electronic, mechanical, photocopying, recording or otherwise without the prior permission of the publisher.

Brendan Dooley has asserted his right under the Copyright, Designs and Patents Act, 1988, to be identified as the editor of this work.

Published by
Ashgate Publishing Limited
Wey Court East
Union Road
Farnham
Surrey, GU9 7PT
England

Ashgate Publishing Company
Suite 420
101 Cherry Street
Burlington
VT 05401-4405
USA

www.ashgate.com

British Library Cataloguing in Publication Data
The Dissemination of news and the emergence of contemporaneity in early modern Europe.
  1. Communication, International–History–16th century. 2. Communication, International–History–17th century. 3. Press–Europe–History–16th century. 4. Press–Europe–History–17th century. 5. Communication–Social aspects–Europe–History–16th century.
  6. Communication–Social aspects–Europe–History–17th century.
  I. Dooley, Brendan Maurice, 1953–
  302.2'094'09031—dc22

Library of Congress Cataloging-in-Publication Data
The dissemination of news and the emergence of contemporaneity in early modern Europe / Brendan Dooley [editor].
  p. cm.
  Includes index.
  ISBN 978-0-7546-6466-6 (hardcover : alk. paper) 1. Newspaper publishing—Europe—History. 2. European newspapers—History. 3. Press—Europe—History. 4. Communication—Europe—History. I. Dooley, Brendan Maurice, 1953–
  PN5110.D57 2010
  079.4—dc22
                                                                              2009040616

ISBN 9780754664666 (hbk)
ISBN 9781409402138 (ebk)

Printed and bound in Great Britain by
MPG Books Group, UK

Contents

List of Figures vii
List of Tables ix
List of Contributors xi
Preface: Brendan Dooley xiii

Introduction 1

PART 1   JOINING TIME AND SPACE: THE ORIGINS

1   Philip of Spain: The Spider's Web of News and Information 23
    Cristina Borreguero Beltrán

2   News Networks between Italy and Europe 51
    Mario Infelise

3   The Early German Newspaper—A Medium of Contemporaneity 69
    Johannes Weber

PART 2   TIME, MOTION AND STRUCTURE IN EARLY MODERN COMMUNICATIONS

4   The Birth of Maria de' Medici (26 April 1575): Hearsay, Correspondence, and Historiographical Errors 83
    Alessio Assonitis

5   Making It Present 95
    Brendan Dooley

6   Contemporaneity in 1672–1679: the Paris *Gazette*, the *London Gazette*, and the *Teutsche Kriegs–Kurier* (1672–1679) 115
    Sonja Schultheiß-Heinz

7   "The Blowing of the Messiah's Trumpet": Reports about Sabbatai Sevi and Jewish Unrest in 1665–67 137
    Ingrid Maier and Daniel C. Waugh

PART 3 INTER-EUROPEAN SPACES AND MOMENTS

8   Handwritten Newsletters as Interregional Information Sources in Central and Southeastern Europe   155
Zsuzsa Barbarics-Hermanik

9   Between the French *Gazette* and Dutch French Language Newspapers   179
Charles-Henri Depezay

10   Antwerp and Brussels as Inter-European Spaces in News Exchange   193
Paul Arblaster

11   Offices of Intelligence and Expanding Social Spaces   207
Astrid Blome

PART 4 NEW METHODS AND APPROACHES

12   Narrating Contemporaneity: Text and Structure in English News   225
Nicholas Brownlees

13   Historical Text Mining and Corpus-Based Approaches to the Newsbooks of the Commonwealth   251
Andrew Hardie, Tony McEnery and Scott Songlin Piao

Epilogue   287

Index   *291*

List of Figures

0.1	Giuseppe Mitelli, 'Agli appassionati per le guerre' (to those passionate about the wars), Bologna, 1690. Biblioteca dell'Archiginnasio di Bologna	4
0.2	The Creation of News Texts	12
0.3	News Stories in Transition	15
5.1	Tracing back Antwerp newspaper copies found in Florence	113
13.1	An original page from *The Perfect Diurnal*. British Museum	255
13.2	Clustergram Output for the Matrix shown in Table 13.2	261
13.3	Visualization of the Clustergram in Figure 13.2	261
13.4	Clustergram for Major Series of Periodicals	264
13.5	Distribution of Minimum Similarity Scores for Candidate Derived Texts	267
13.6	Crouch Summary Report for ModIntell171#2 as Candidate Derived Text, WPostWood171 as Candidate Source Text	269
13.7	Crouch Weighted Score for ModIntell171#2 as Candidate Derived Text, WPostWood171 as Candidate Source Text (overall score: 0.188)	270
13.8	Crouch Alignment Table for ModIntell171#2 as Candidate Derived Text, WPostWood171 as Candidate Source Text	271
13.9	Weighted Score Output for ModIntell171 as Candidate Derived Text, WPost171 as Candidate Source Text (overall Score: 0.364)	275
13.10	Weighted Score Output for ModIntell171 as Candidate Derived Text, WPostWood171 as Candidate Source Text (overall score: 0.872)	276

List of Tables

1.1	Charge and data presented by Juan de Tassis. 6 July 1589, A.G.S., C. and J.H., Leg. 257	40
1.2	The accounts of Juan de Tassis from 1595–1607. A.G.S., G.A. 3rd época, Leg	41
12.1	Margin captions in *Mercurius Britanicus* (10–17 June 1644)	245
13.1	Details of the Data	254
13.2	An Example Text Comparison Matrix	260
13.3	Matrix for Major Series of Periodicals	264
13.4	Distribution of Scores across the Whole-Corpus Matrix	266
13.5	Sample Comparisons at Different Levels of Scoring	266
13.6	Sentence-by-Sentence Breakdown of Correspondences between ModIntell171#2 and WPostWood171	272
13.7	Extract from Corpus Metadata	274
13.8	Matrix for Wood and Horton's Newsbooks of 4 and 5 April 1654	275
13.9	Variation in the Discussion of Scottish Deaths in the Battle against Cooper	279
13.10	Scores < 0.9 from the Matrix Column for FScoutHorton171	281
13.11	Scores < 0.9 from the Matrix Column for FScout173	281

List of Contributors

Paul Arblaster currently teaches at the Facultés Universitaires Notre-Dame de la Paix, Namur, Belgium.

Alessio Assonitis is the Research Director of the Medici Archive Project in Florence, Italy

Zsuzsa Barbarics-Hermanik teaches Early Modern and Southeast European History at University of Graz, Austria.

Astrid Blome is a researcher at the research institute "Deutsche Presseforschung" and teaches in Bremen University.

Cristina Borreguero Beltrán teaches Early Modern History at the University of Burgos, Spain.

Nicholas Brownlees teaches English Language and Linguistics in the University of Florence, Italy.

Charles-Henri Depezay received his doctorate from the University of Orleans, France.

Brendan Dooley teaches Renaissance Studies in the Graduate School of Arts and Social Sciences at University College Cork, Ireland.

Andrew Hardie teaches Linguistics at Lancaster University.

Mario Infelise teaches Modern History at the University of Venice.

Tony McEnery teaches English Language and Linguistics at Lancaster University.

Ingrid Maier teaches Russian Language and Literature at the Uppsala University, Sweden.

Scott Songlin Piao is a Researcher in the Computing Department at Lancaster University.

Sonja Schultheiß-Heinz teaches Early Modern History at the University of Bayreuth.

Daniel Waugh teaches history in the University of Washington, Seattle.

Johannes Weber teaches Modern German Literature at the University of Bremen.

Preface

Brendan Dooley

What is contemporaneity? As understood by the authors of this book, it is the perception, shared by a number of human beings, of experiencing a particular event at more or less the same time. It is not simply a crowd phenomenon, since the observers in question may be out of sight or earshot of one another and still imagine themselves as a group. Depending on the scale of the event and the size of the group, it may have important consequences from a social, cultural and political standpoint. At the very least, it may add to a notion of participating in a shared present, of existing in a length of time called "now." Distributed over a certain geographical space or spaces, it may contribute to individuals' sense of community, or their identification with one another. With good reason, anthropologists and historians have identified it as a hallmark of modernity. Although it is as familiar to modern-day humans as the news in the media, we believe it has a history—a history dating back to early modern times. That was when the first world-wide communications networks emerged; and in spite of the frequent delays, shifting borders, linguistic barriers, unreliable carriers and differences in the reckoning of time, Europeans began to share a knowledge of one another and of events in the world taking place in the present. Already in the seventeenth century, something of what happened in Venice was known in Strassburg, events in Palermo were on the pages of papers in Augsburg. People could have a concept not only of living within a European social space, a European theater of political, social and economic reality, but of knowing what was going on in many parts of it contemporaneously. They also might begin to apprehend a differentiation within Europe, along East/West and perhaps North/South lines. The emergence of contemporaneity may have helped form the basis for the much more widespread and deeper sense of contemporaneity that was to emerge later on.

But how was contemporaneity experienced in the early modern period? How indeed was it distinguished from other perceptions of time and place? What were the stages in its development and diffusion? How can the historian trace it? The authors of these essays share the conviction that the answers are to be found largely within the history of news and news publications; and accordingly, they focus a diverse array of methods, in some cases developing new historiographical approaches, using a wide variety of sources, centered in a myriad of geographical locations.

Contemporaneity was made possible by uniting time and space. If uniting time and space was a challenge in the sixteenth and seventeenth centuries, it may occasionally be so still today. And the effort of building a project based in England, Germany, France, Italy, Belgium, Spain, Sweden and the USA has required the combined effort of many, including the contributors, who have all supplied far more than just their texts. In addition, we would like to thank Lara Fleischer, Anne Heyer, David Lucker, Catalin Moscaliuc, Barbara Marti Dooley and all the others who have made the text editing a lighter task. Uros Urosevic provided precious research assistance when time was particularly scarce; Mitul Jain supplied technical support. Thanks also to the Presseforschung unit of the University of Bremen, located within the Bremen Staats- und Universitaatsbibliothek, and especially Holger Böning, for support and hospitality. Finally, we would particularly like to thank Jacobs University in Bremen, supplier of a true *locus amoenus* for our collaborative endeavors on two occasions, in December 2006 and 2007, when our research group met to discuss many of the issues presented in this volume, and in between these times, when it hosted the invisible academy of our collective communications over two years.

The coordination of our endeavors has supplied us with a further confirmation of something we always knew but that is sometimes forgotten in current discussions of education reform—namely: furnishing the conditions for the creation and communication of knowledge is the highest purpose of the modern university.

Florence, Italy, July 2009

Introduction

This volume explores how new methods of communication in the sixteenth and seventeenth centuries generated new notions about the layout of Europe and the pace of change that helped build a sense of contemporaneity. With respect to standard histories of journalism, this is a special vantage point. We are aware that studies on the communication system in single countries in the early modern period are already numerous. The dynamic and somewhat chaotic reality of the English press of the seventeenth century is already fairly well known, along with the various attempts by information entrepreneurs to evade repeated efforts by crown and parliament to rein it in.[1] The wide variations between the centers of the Continental press have been brought to light, from the French model of a centralized official system (the *Gazette*) accompanied by a lively black market of titles published abroad, to the complex polycentric realities in Germany and Italy.[2] The institutional and commercial setting of news production has been examined in some detail.[3] News entrepreneurs have been identified; their relations with local governments have been elucidated. Printed news in most places is now viewed in connection with what is known about the manuscript transmission

---

[1] C. John Sommerville, *The News Revolution in England: Cultural Dynamics of Daily Information* OUP 1996; Joad Raymond, *The Invention of the Newspaper: English Newsbooks 1641–49* (Oxford: Clarendon Press, 1996, with new preface, 2005).

[2] Bob Harris, *Politics and the rise of the press: Britain and France, 1620–1800* (London: Routledge 1996); Gilles Feyel, *L'Annonce Et La Nouvelle. La Presse De l'Information En France Sous l'Ancien Regime (1630–1788)* (Oxford: The Voltaire Foundation, 2000); C. Berkvens-Stevelinck, H. Bots, P.G. Hoftijzer, eds, *Le Magasin De L'Univers – The Dutch Republic As the Centre of the European Book Trade* (Brill, 1991); Johannes Weber, "Avisen, Relationen, Gazetten. Der Beginn des europäischen Zeitungswesens," in *Bibliotheksgesellschaft Oldenburg. Vorträge – Reden – Berichte*, ed. H. Brandes and W. Kramer, No. 20 (Oldenburg: BIS 1997), pp. 34 ff.; Johannes Weber, "Der große Krieg und die frühe Zeitung. Gestalt und Entwicklung der deutschen Nachrichtenpresse in der ersten Hälfte des 17. Jahrhunderts," *Jahrbuch für Kommunikationsgeschichte*, ed. H. Böning, A. Kutsch and R. Stöber, vol. 1 (Stuttgart: Steiner 1999), p. 26; Jean Sgard, ed., *Dictionnaire de la Presse 1600–1789*, 2 vols (Paris: Universitas 1991).

[3] In addition to the bibliographies of the articles in this book and those by Sabrina Baron, Michael Mendle, Thomas Schröder, Otto Lankhorst, Jean-Pierre Vittu, Paul Arblaster, Henry Ettinghausen, and Paul Ries, in Brendan Dooley and Sabrina Baron, eds, *The Politics of Information in Early Modern Europe* (London and New York: Routledge, 2001); see also Johannes Weber, "Kontrollmechanismen im deutschen Zeitungswesen des 17. Jahrhunderts. Ein kleiner Beitrag zur Geschichte der Zensur," *Jahrbuch für Kommunikationsgeschichte*, ed. H. Böning, A. Kutsch and R. Stöber, vol. 6, 2004, pp. 56–73.

of news.[4] We propose to draw together some of the threads of this research and pull them in a new direction, toward a study of local and international news flows, with a special regard for cross-boundary transmission and reception. Our ultimate object of study is the perception, shared by a number of human beings, of experiencing a particular event at more or less the same time. Often our approach will involve comparing content to reveal the paths of stories as they moved from place to place among various audiences, suggesting the potential for contemporaneity.

But first of all, a small clarification. We are well aware that the experience of contemporaneity in the sixteenth and seventeenth centuries was far different from the one to which Hegel appears to allude in a famous passage in his notebooks. "The morning newspaper reading is a kind of realistic morning prayer," he said, presumably in Jena between 1803 and 1806. He goes on: "One orients one's attitude against the world and toward God, or else vice versa. Both give the same security, because one thus knows where one stands."[5] Unlike in the early nineteenth century, news reading in the early modern period was not yet a daily ritual, offering certainties of a secular sort, somehow parallel to the theological certainties offered by religious rituals. And readers were not yet in such great numbers; nor were they so frequently reminded of the existence of other human beings practicing the same secular ritual at the same time and sharing the same news events. The impact of this shared experience would only later contribute to building the imagined communities that were, according to Benedict Anderson, the cultural and social vehicles of the developing nation-states.[6] Yet there is no denying that already in the early modern period people began to formulate in their minds a concept of the world shared with others, within the same time and space and within a basically secular context.[7]

---

[4] The updated bibliography now includes: Mario Infelise, *Prima dei giornali. Alle origini della pubblica informazione* (Roma-Bari: Laterza, 2002); Johannes Weber, "Daniel Hartnack – ein gelehrter Streithahn und Avisenschreiber am Ende des 17. Jahrhunderts. Zum Beginn politisch kommentierender Zeitungspresse," *Gutenberg-Jahrbuch*, 1993, pp. 140–58.

[5] G.W.F. Hegel, *Dokumente zu Hegels Entwicklung* (Stuttgart-Bad Cannstatt: Frommann, 1974), p. 360.

[6] Benedict Anderson, *Imagined communities. Reflection on the origin and spread of nationalism* (London and New York: Verso, 1981).

[7] For an early approach to the theme, Martin Welke, "Gemeinsame Lektüre und frühe Formen von Gruppenbildungen im 17. und 18. Jahrhundert: Zeitungslesen in Deutschland," in *Lesegesellschaften und bürgerliche Emanzipation. Ein europäischer Vergleich*, ed. Otto Dann (Munich: Beck 1981), pp. 29–53. In addition, Daniel Woolf, "News, history and the construction of the present in early modern England," in Brendan Dooley and Sabrina Baron, eds, *The Politics of Information in Early Modern Europe* (London and New York: Routledge, 2001), pp. 80–118. Paul Hunter, "'News and new things': Contemporaneity and the early

Indeed, contemporaneity appears to have been an object of some reflection at the time, even as a kind of secular ritual, if we are not reading too much into an illustration engraved by Giuseppe Mitelli in Bologna in 1690 and dedicated to "those who are passionate about the wars" [Fig. 0.1]. Here we see a group of people in some street or square with Bologna's famed porticoes in the background, gathered around one in spectacles who appears to be reading the news—the typical title, "aviso" does not distinguish a printed from a manuscript sheet. Around the speaker persons from various professions react to the story by expressing their dismay, or even their disbelief, in reference to what they hear. "It cannot be," says one; and another, "yes it is." On the right hand side we see a Frenchman and a Spaniard in characteristic garb, locked in combat. The dedication of the engraving is the clue to what is going on here. The two fighters obviously refer to "the wars" about which certain people are "passionate," the wars that are the object of the story being read. The specific struggle in question would be the War of the League of Augsburg that pitted Bourbon against Habsburg in the struggle over the succession to the Palatinate.

The group of listeners on the left represents those persons who are attentive to the news in the bounded space of a single city, and who experience the succession of time in terms of a succession of non-religious events—no ecclesiastic, in fact, is portrayed. The story reaches all members of the crowd simultaneously. On the right we have the story itself that is transpiring in another space, perhaps many miles away. Those on the left hand side are experiencing the story as though it were in their own space. And in spite of the distance, the reader and listeners on the left may have the sensation of sharing something not only with each other but with the Frenchman and the Spaniard. In fact, one of the listeners between the two areas of the page joins the right hand space to his, declaring "what folly." As we will see, the new means of communication made possible the sharing of a perceived present across small, medium and large distances, at the various levels of family, neighborhood, village and wider world, encouraging a critical apprehension of events.

To be sure, time and space were not unproblematic concepts when Mitelli drew; and any concept of contemporaneity is severely strained, if we take into account the separation between, say, Flanders, where the fighting in Mitelli's drawing is supposed to be taking place, and Bologna, where the imagined audience may have been. Two to three weeks was not an usual wait for information to get from there to here. We must not forget Fernand Braudel's resounding description of "Distance, le premier ennemi"—distance, the primary enemy of

---

English novel," *Critical Inquiry* 14 (1988): 493–515; and by contrast, Stephen Kern, *The culture of time and space, 1880–1918* (Harvard University Press, 1983).

Figure 0.1   Giuseppe Mitelli, 'Agli appasionati per le guerre' (to those passionate about the wars), Bologna, 1690. Biblioteca dell'Archiginnasio di Bologna

early modern society. He went on to say, "Today we have too little space, the world is shrinking around us. In the sixteenth century there was too much. Only with great difficulty (so he said) can we understand the notion, at the time, of an "unlimited space" and its effects on daily life—indeed, "every activity" he says "had to overcome the obstacle of distance."[8] And the lag times he cited (based on Pierre Sardella's survey of manuscript newsletters) are still workable averages for the period between the sixteenth and seventeenth centuries: for news traveling longer distances, say, to Venice, from Alexandria in Egypt (55 days), or from Constantinople (34 days), from London (43 days)—although Milan might be three days or less away, depending on the importance of the story.

If the time lag due to distance could to some degree be overcome, time itself imposed yet other obstacles to contemporaneity. To be sure, we should suppose that only insignificant misunderstandings might result from the contrast between the North European 12-hour clock beginning at noontime, and the Italian system of considering sunset as the first hour of a 24-hour day, with the resulting slight seasonal and geographical variations. Dramatic differences on the other hand derived from the multitude of calendars currently in use around Europe.[9] Not all areas adopted the reform decreed by Pope Gregory XIII in 1582, although the centuries-long slippage caused by an inaccurate calculation of the length of the solar year in the Julian calendar was hard to ignore. Those who agreed to shave 11 days from the calendar one time only, introducing the leap-year system to avoid future inconsistencies, remained seriously out of sync with those who did not. And in the months after October 1582, when the reform went into effect, even those whose confessional differences did not stand in the way, did not all change immediately—creating disagreements between towns in the same general area. Indeed, until the eighteenth century, news readers had to remember not only that England and Italy were generally many days apart, but that 22 January in, say, the Duchy of Prussia, might be 11 January in, say, the Duchy of Westphalia, until 1610, when Prussia changed, with the Principality of Minden remaining behind until 1688. Reckoning of the New Year was subject to different traditions from place to place. In France as well as in the Low Countries, Germany and much of Italy, no Gregorian reform was required to force observance of the first of January. On the other hand, nothing could persuade the Venetians to move the Venetian New Year two months back from the date inherited from the Roman

---

[8] Fernand Braudel, *The Mediterranean and the Mediterranean world in the age of Philip II*, tr. Sian Reynolds (New York: William Collins and Sons and Harper and Row, 1972), part 2.1.1, pp. 355–63. Concerning commercial correspondence note also Michael North, *Kommunikation, Handel, Geld und Banken in der Frühen Neuzeit* (Munich, Oldenbourg: 2000).

[9] Fritz Bünger, *Geschichte der Neujahrsfeier in der Kirche*. Göttingen 1911; Hermann Grotefend, *Zeitrechnung des deutschen Mittelalters und der Neuzeit*. 3. Bände, 1891–98.

Republic, the 1 March. In Tuscany, England and Scotland, on the other hand, the Julian New Year, 25 March, continued to prevail, while Russia began the year on the day of the Creation (1 September). So gaining a sense of exactly when things were happening was no simple matter—in fact, it was a skill that went along with travel and every other form of intercity and interstate communication.

Hiram Morgan has offered some interesting reflections on the possible day-to-day significance of the clash of calendars, from the standpoint of soldiers on the field of battle. The occasion he has in mind is the Battle of Kinsale, the last major episode in the English conquest of Ireland during the Nine Years War in the time of Elizabeth I. Spanish reinforcements had just arrived to help the Irish; from their point of view and that of the Irish, the battle was taking place on 3 January 1602, by the Gregorian calendar. From the English viewpoint however the battle was occurring on on 24 December 1601, according to the old Julian calendar that would be in force until 1751. Among the many pressures on fighters' morale, he suggests, the difference in date, especially in the case of a special date such as the vigil of a feast day, is not to be taken lightly. Indeed, "The trapped English army was yet to have its Christmas dinner and indeed was unlikely to have any if it did not win. On the other hand, the Irish had celebrated Christmas and New Year."[10] Many disadvantages beset the struggling Irish; perhaps this one too.

For pinpointing the exact moment of a particular occurrence, typical early modern newspapers were not much help. They were usually made up of compilations of many stories cobbled together from manuscript newsletters or other newspapers, each story bearing the date of the original source, often in the original style of dating, which might be different from the style used where the story was being read, and different from the styles in still other stories drawn from other sources. Consider the following example, from *Several Proceedings OF STATE AFFAIRS In England, Scotland and Ireland. With the Transactions of the Affairs in other NATIONS*:

> We have received a confirmation of the retreat of the Turkish fleet at Constantinople, where the general Bashaw hath made his peace though for a while he was under a cloud. The report is, that having presented to the young Emperor a young Virgin of extraordinary beauty, who is of the Greek Nation, that thereupon he was received into favour, and the young Maid like to be his chief Favourite.

---

[10] Hiram Morgan, "The Pope's new invention: the introduction of the Gregorian calendar in Ireland, 1583–1782" (unpublished paper at "Ireland, Rome and the Holy See: History, Culture and Contact," a UCC History Department symposium at the Pontifical Irish College, Rome, 1 April 2006).

The report is dated Venice, 11 February 1653. Compare this to a report, obviously based on the same information, in the Hamburg-based *Sambstägige Zeitung*:

> The previous Turkish general on the sea has obtained grace and pardon. He is said to have brought to the Turkish Emperor a very beautiful young Greek girl, and the latter had the luck to become the sultana and wife of the Emperor.[11]

This report is dated 20 January 1654. Now, Venice has a different dating system both in regard to the year and in regard to the days of the month, both in respect to England and in respect to Hamburg. The English journalist wrote down the date on the original source without any comment. The Hamburg journalist appears to have corrected for the year. Did he also correct for the day of the month? We do not know.

Finally, current notions of geography in any one place might stand somewhat in the way of precisely conceptualizing where those in another place could be, who presumably experienced events within the same time frame. We are inclined to take for granted the local city plan engraved on our minds from the multiplicity of such images in our midst, or the familiar classroom globe or Mercator's projection, however vaguely remembered, and modified through time by economics, politics and war, that forms the backdrop to our sense of "here" or "there." Already in the sixteenth century printed maps began to circulate more widely, permitting a basic visualization of space relations.[12] Certain city maps, such as Jacopo de' Barbari's map of Venice, attained a remarkable degree of accuracy already by 1500; and maps showing the relations between various parts of Europe were widely available. However, the best images were often costly, and images in general differed greatly in quality. For most people local space was probably experienced in terms of directions to the major parts of town; and the nearest approximation of a universally accepted world picture was a series of mental vectors leading out from home toward the major centers (Paris, Rome, London, perhaps Constantinople) where news originated. The further from home one got, in fact, the more fantastic the picture might be. Consider the struggle on the Continent to situate the major locations involved in the Spanish

---

[11] "Der Türckische gewesene General zur See hat Gnad und Perdon erlangt. Dieser sol dem Türckischen Käyser eine überaus schöne Griechische junge Tochter mitgebracht/ und diese das Glück gehabt haben/daß sie Sultane und des Käysers Ehegemahlin worden." Report dated 20 January 1654, Venedig, in *Sambstägige Zeitung 1654, Hamburg*.

[12] Consider the essays in David Buisseret, ed., *Envisioning the City: Six Studies in Urban Cartography*. Kenneth Nebenzahl, Jr., Lectures in the History of Cartography (University of Chicago, 1998). David Woodward, *The History of Cartography*, Volume 3: *Cartography in the European Renaissance* (University of Chicago, 2007).

Armada story, when a certain "Hylandia," maybe a corruption of the Scottish "Highlands," is given as one of the Orkney Islands.[13]

In spite of the strains on contemporaneity, increasing quantities of news were indeed transmitted, uniting times and spaces and generating commentary on topics of civil interest. Mitelli's etching illustrates not just the origin and spread of news but the origin and spread of rumor in a society where rumor plays an important role. Mitelli would not even have had to be aware of the voluminous early modern literature on rumor in order to notice what was going on all around him.[14] For news traveled fast at the very local level within an early modern city; and individuals could surely visualize themselves in a context where many people were talking about the same thing. Such a notion, "that many people are talking about the same thing and are aware of this"—this is the sense of contemporaneity.

However, to appreciate the spread of news and rumor across time, we move from the synchronic form of the drawn image to the diachronic form of the written narrative. We are in Naples in 1647, when public rumors began with written news, causing, in this case, a major upheaval (now most closely associated with the name of one of the leaders, a certain Masaniello). And if we consider that public awareness may have historically played an emancipatory role, in respect to oppressive powers, it is no wonder that the sense of contemporaneity, in some work, has been associated with the notion of a public sphere outlined years ago by Jürgen Habermas.[15] In the account by Alessandro Giraffi, a Neapolitan jurist writing about the Masaniello revolt at the time when it took place, rumor not only joins areas that are wide apart geographically, but also joins different internal zones of one of the two or three cities in Europe with a population of 100,000 or more. Whether Giraffi was aware of the full significance of the story he was telling is hard to say—but at least, concerning this last aspect, namely, the impact of news on the circulation of rumor, his insight exactly corresponds to what we might expect, if our hypothesis is correct.[16]

---

[13] See my chapter below.

[14] Concering rumor and the literature about it in sixteenth- and seventeenth-century Italy, see my *The social history of skepticism: Experience and doubt in early modern culture*, Baltimore: Hopkins, 1999, Ch. 1. For Britain, consider Adam Fox, *Oral and Literate Culture in England 1500–1700*, Oxford Studies in Social History (New York: Oxford University Press, 2000).

[15] For instance in Daniel Woolf, "News, history and the construction of the present in early modern England," p. 81.

[16] Alessandro Giraffi, *Ragguaglio del tumulto di Napoli* (Venice: Baba, 1647), Prologue, translated in Dooley, ed., *Italy in the Baroque* (New York: Garland, 1995), pp. 242ff. The long-term causes of the revolt are analyzed by Rosario Villari, *The Revolt of Naples*, tr. James Newell

That spring, Giraffi narrates, the new Spanish viceroy of Naples introduced a new fruit tax. This was not liked, and there was murmuring. In June, for similar reasons, an insurrection took place in the city of Palermo against the Spanish viceroy of Sicily, led by an artisan named Giuseppe d'Alessi. And here is how Giraffi explains the reaction in Naples, a reaction of a large portion of the community, to information, which Giraffi perceives as being shared by many in the same space at the same time:

> Boldness and also envy increased with the news of the success of the revolution of Palermo and most of Sicily except for Messina. There the people had obtained tax relief by force of arms from the viceroy of that kingdom, the Most Excellent Lord the marquis of Los Velez, who afterwards granted a general pardon for all excesses. And these decrees circulated everywhere. ... The people of Naples, allured and encouraged by the example of the neighboring kingdom, grew very anxious to attain the same goal, saying, "What? Are we less than Palermo? Are not our people, if they unite, more formidable and combative than them?"

But that is not all. Giraffi also explains how shared information joined the various parts of Naples into a single community. Consider the following:

> It came to pass that in the royal city of Naples and its dependent suburbs a multitude of the common people, much burdened by the gabels and especially unable to tolerate any longer that upon fruit, made the situation known on several occasions to the Most Excellent Lord the duke of Arcos, viceroy of that kingdom. He heard the public cries and lamentations of all the women, children and men of Lavinaio and other popular areas as he passed through Piazza del Mercato to go to the church of the Carmelites ... for his devotions to the most holy Virgin of the Carmine. Even the archbishop, the Most Eminent Cardinal (Ascanio) Filomarino and others petitioned him to remove the said gabel. At last on a Saturday, as His Excellency went to the said church, he heard people whispering words that were almost threatening and that presaged the riots later to come; and he promised

---

with the assistance of John Marino (Cambridge: Polity Press, 1993), p. 89, and Antonio Calabria, *The Cost of Empire: The Finances of the Kingdom of Naples in the Time of Spanish Rule* (Cambridge: Cambridge University Press, 1991). The ritual aspects of the revolt are analyzed by Peter Burke, "The Virgin of the Carmine and the Revolt of Masaniello," *Past and Present* 99 (1983): 3–21. In addition, useful information was drawn from Aurelio Musi, *La Rivolta di Masaniello nella scena politica barocca* (Naples: Guida, 1989). The constitutional issues are examined by Pier Luigi Rovito, "La rivoluzione costituzionale di Napoli (1647–48)," *Rivista storica italiana* 98 (1986): 367–462; and the spread of the revolt in Idem, *La rivolta dei notabili* (Naples: Jovene, 1988).

to remove the gabel. He returned to the palace in such fear that, from then on, not only did he avoid the church of the Carmine, but he prohibited the usual celebration of the solemn feast of St. John the Baptist, in order to prevent such a multitude of people as there are in Naples from assembling in one place.

Giraffi provides the means for readers at the time and for us to imagine our way into this city and to observe the collective behavior of people in the various neighborhoods:

In the meantime, the people got more and more impatient and kept grumbling about the delay in the concession of the promised favor until one night they set fire to the toll house in Piazza del Mercato, where the said gabel was collected (this has been said to have actually occurred twice) And from time to time very vicious invectives, full of popular grievances and of fiery protests against the public officers, were posted in the most public places of the city.

In the event, the ultimate consequences are dramatic: a community is not only formed; the crescendo of criticism crosses the threshold into outright rebellion.

But at this point we have gone about as far out as we dare to go in the direction of community formation and expression as seen from the vantage point of contemporary history writing. We now move on to the world of everyday journalism. Consider an excerpt from the Gazette of Turin in 1661 claiming readers were "impatient" to hear the upshot of "the news written two or three times from Paris" in August 1661, about a battle between the Spanish and the Portuguese[17]—a reference to a recent episode in the continuing independence struggle of Portugal from Spain. The gazette writer is addressing the reader, and whether or not these expressions are mere banalities cooked up in the imagination of the writer is not the point. They nonetheless imply a sense of shared interests—although we cannot be sure with whom. Perhaps the writer has in mind the group of some 250 readers who subscribed to the gazette, along with perhaps 10 or 20 times that number who actually saw these sheets as they passed from hand to hand. Is he thinking about a community within Turin alone, or within the duchy of Savoy, or a virtual community spread thinly among elites distributed across wide spaces? Whatever our answers to these questions are going to be, clearly writers and readers shared a desire for information and a desire for closure as a story broke and developed, sometimes in a seemingly inconclusive way, and the day to day or at least (at this time) week

---

[17] Enrico Jovane, *Il primo giornalismo torinese* (Turin: Di Modica, 1938), p. 47; in addition, concerning the Turin journal, Bellocchi, *Storia del giornalismo italiano*, 3: 39–43.

to week sharing of this experience could only have reinforced the sense of people moving as a group simultaneously through time—which is the essence of the idea of contemporaneity that we have been trying to put across.

For characterizing the present shared by people separated in space, much depended on the news sources available. For foreign news, compilers of the printed newspapers borrowed stories from each other as well as from the relatively costly manuscript newsletters that originated in diplomatic and commercial circles and by the sixteenth and seventeenth centuries had become a genre in themselves, circulating far and wide across Europe. An example in the newspaper from Bologna was apparently based upon a newsletter from Venice circulated within the papal court in Rome (and we do not know where else). Here is the version in the newspaper:

> We hear from Venice that after the success written about in the Bernissa campaign, the Turks in the land of S. Cassiano in the Venetian domain killed five persons who were sick, and took some fifty others prisoner, and brought away around 20 cows. ... Since the place is noteworthy regarding its location, being on a hill in between two rivers, it was believed that the Venetians were about to fortify themselves there, since five iron pieces [=cannon] were found.

The newsletter underlying the story is preserved in the same file in the Vatican Archives as the newspaper version, and there the story is identical, although a city is referred as "Bernizza" in the newsletter becomes "Bernissa," a place called "Cassiano" becomes "S. Cassiano," "twenty-five cows" become "twenty," and there is a speculation at the end of the newspaper version, regarding a possible Venetian fortification.[18]

The following article in an English newspaper entitled *Italy, Germany, Hungaria, Bohemia, Spaine and Dutchland*, which circulated in London in 1621, was presumably based on a Dutch coranto (still not identified).

> From Venice the 6 of July 1621: On Sunday at night, certain men with Shippes well appointed, set upon the Ship called the Toro Negro, that lay richly laden to sayle to Constantinople, and having slaine the Massaro, and cast him overboard, and taken certain Balles laden with cloath of gold, silke and some Chests of Rials of Plate, they set fire on the Ship, whereby the great Gally called Balby, that lay not farre from it, was also fired, and much spoyled: there are five men taken that were Actors therein...

---

[18] The texts are to be found in Rome, Biblioteca Apostolica Vaticana, Ottob. latini 2450, c. 97r, and c. 101v.

The coranto in turn evidently offered a word for word translation of a story in a Venetian newsletter available to the Florentine court, which is now in the Medici papers at the state archive—only the number of accomplices in the newsletter story of the burning of the ship is raised from three to five, perhaps based on new information acquired within three days later.[19]

A basic schematization of the possible dynamics in the creation of news texts is as follows:

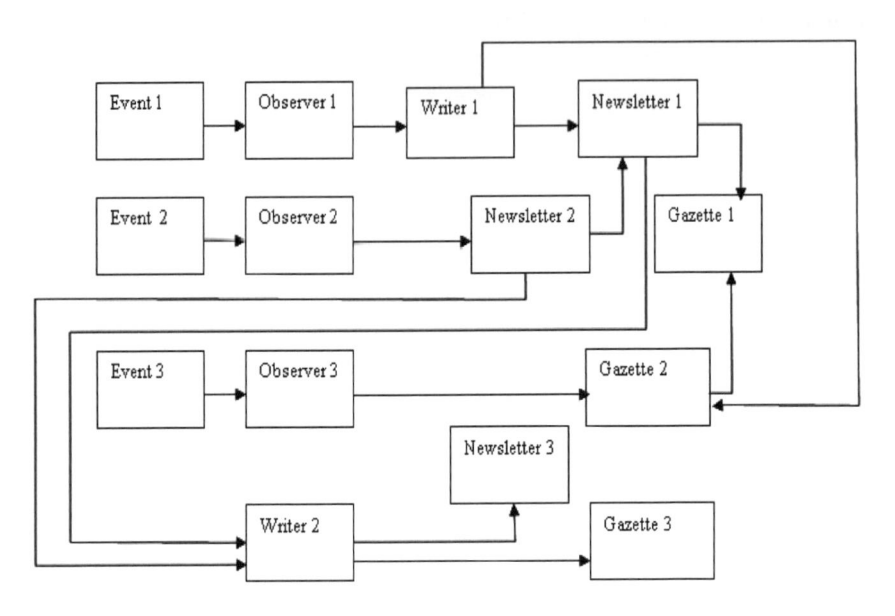

Figure 0.2   The Creation of News Texts

The diagram proposes three interlinked models for the development of news stories based on several cases. Event 1 is observed by Observer 1, who conveys the information to Writer 1, who writes for Newsletter 1 as well as Gazette 2. Gazette 1 utilizes information from both Newsletter 1 and Gazette 2. Event 2 is observed by Observer 2, who is the writer of Newsletter 2, upon which Newsletter 1 is partly based. Event 3 is observed by Observer 3, who is also the

---

[19] Florence, Archivio di Stato, Mediceo del Principato, filza 3088a, c. 3v: "Di Venezia li 3 luglio 1621 ... Sabbato notte in questo porto sendo andati alcuni con una Peota armati alla nave nominata Toro Negro, che carica di diverse riche merci stava di partenza per Cost.li, salitisi sopra uccisero il Massero, gettandolo in acqua, et poi levarono delle palle di pannine doro, e di seta, dando fuoco ad essa nave che nell abbruggiarsi si accese anco fuoco nel Gran Galione Balbi, che si fracassò ieri vicino, mettorno il tutto abbruggiato ... già sono stati presi 3 imputati complici al tal maleficio."

writer of Gazette 2. Finally, Writer 2 compiles his Newsletter 3 and Gazette 3 on the basis of material drawn from Newsletters 1 and 2. Other permutations and combinations are likely. The key role often played by local postmasters in this network is taken into account in our model in the persons of Writers 1 and 2.

Some of the more serious variations between different sources could have imposed yet another challenge to the formation of a shared present, as in the following examples comparing the English and German reporting on the ongoing attempts by the Dutch Republic to seize Portuguese portions of South America. A report in *The Faithful Scout* dated 11 May 1654, had this to say about action in Bahia: "From Paris it is certified, That the Portugal Ambassador has received audience of his Majesty, to whom he imparted the joyful Tidings of a Victory obtained by the Portugal fleet against the Hollanders in Brazil; and of the taking of Reclif and about 40 other Towns and Castles from them." The article in a Hamburg paper, dated "Cologne, 5 May 1654" and claiming to draw upon an English source received by way of Antwerp, speaks not of 40 towns, but of 40 ships being involved[20]—indeed, we may doubt the likelihood that there were so many as 40 cities to take. Yet another English version of the same story gives a totally different reference to the same event, counting 28 forts and 65 ships.[21]

Yet another example was Emperor Ferdinand IV's propositions to the States of Bohemia in 1654, closing one of the last chapters in the Thirty Years War. They were recounted in detail in a report dated "Prague 18 April 1654" published in the Hamburg *Sambstägige Zeitung*, and reduced, in *The true and Perfect Dutch Diurnal OF SEVERAL PASSAGES and PROCEEDINGS, Of and in Relation to the STATES of HOLLAND*, 20 May, from twelve to nine. All the articles are virtually identical, beginning with the injunction to propagate the Catholic faith. In the Enlgish version, the original points five and six, stipulating the maintenance of the Imperial forces in Bohemia and the release of back pay to disbanded solders, are mixed together and renumbered as five. The original number ten, regarding the continuation of immunity from prosecution for war-related crimes, and number eleven, regarding the payments to be made by the countship of Glatz, are completely left out.[22] Were these modifications made by the editor of the paper, or

---

[20] *Cöllen Sambstägige Zeitung 1654* (printed in Hamburg).

[21] *Several Proceedings OF STATE AFFAIRS In England, Scotland and Ireland. With the Transactions of the Affairs in other NATIONS*. Monday 20 May [1654].

[22] Here is the text from the Hamburg paper: "Den 13. dieß seyn die Herrn LandStändt in grosser Anzahl/zu dem außgeschriebenen Land Tag erschienen/ darauff Käyserl: Praeposition abgelesen worden/ besteht in folgenden Puncten: I. Die Catholische Religion im Land alles eyffers fortzusetzen. 2. St. Josephs Fest gleich andern heil: Landes Patronen zu Celebriren. 3. zu bey Hülff ihrer Käyserl: Mayest: Hoffstadt/Ambassadorn Residenten Unterhaltung/ auch Ungarischen GränzHäuser Versehung Fortificirung haltbahrer Plätz/ Verschaffung

were they based on yet another version borrowed from somewhere else? Only the original text of the negotiation could reveal the answer with certainty.

In the next and final example, variations in a story about a possible Turkish assault on Italian ports that appeared in different versions in two German papers, possibly drawn from the same third party source (in this case, a report from Venice dated 24 April) or drawn from each other—we cannot be sure—show contrasting styles of presentation.

| That thus, not without reason, it is feared that the Turks in that region are preparing a dangerous strike on the Italian coast, Naples, Sicily, or Malta.[23] | ... For this reason all the seaports of Christendom were on the alert, and the two islands of Sicily and Malta were particularly prepared for an attack.[24] |

In this case, the actual elements of this story appear to be the same, except for the mention of Naples in the text on the left, which is not present in the text on the right, and the involvement of all of Christendom, which is not present in the text on the left.

Instead of exploring more examples, we move back to the realm of generality, and here are hypothetical routes of three versions of the same story, originating in Constantinople, which changed slightly as it moved from place to place (versions 1a, 1b, amongst others).

The graphic could be further complicated by indicating possible interconnections between versions, such that, for instance, a version 2a, available in Milan, may draw upon version 1a, circulated in Genoa, for its variation from the standard version 2.

---

eines Vorrahts Munition und anderen Käyserl: Außgaben ein Summa Gelds zubewilligen / wie nicht weniger. 4. die noch haltende KriegsVölcker/ wie bißhero/ ferners zu verpflegen. 5. da aber davon etliche abzudancken/ die Gelder darzu anticipirn. 6. frembde Saltzeinfuhr/ ohne Entrichtung der Gebühr abzustellen. 7. ohne Bewilligung keinen Saliter auszuführen. 8. die Ein:vnnd Zufuhr der frembden bösen und Türckischen wol darauß untüchtige Tücher gemacht werden/ abzustellen. 9. die ElbeSchifffahrt bis auff Praag zu vollziehen. 10. wie das Moratorium wegen der Schulden zu prolongiren. 11. die Graffschafft Glatz bey vorigen LandsBeytrag/ des zwantzigsten Theils / oder dessen gegen Nohtturrft zu deliberiren. 12. was bey vorigen Land Tagen beschlossen/annoch werckstellig zu machen. Seithero hero seyn die HerrnStände töglich darüber zu raht gefahren / vnd wird der Schluß vavon erwartet."

[23] *Europaische Mittwochentliche Zeitung* 18, 3 Mai 1671, report dated 24 April: "... das also nicht ohne Ursache gefürchtet wird die Turcken von dannen auß einer gefährlichen Auschlag auff die Italienische Cüsten/ Naples/ Sicilien oder Malta vorhaben ..."

[24] *Wochentliche Ordinari Post-Zeitung* 18, report dated Venedig 24 April: "... deswegen man in allen Seeporten der Christenheit sehr allert ist/ und die beide Inseln Sicilien und Malta auff einen Angriff vor andern sich in guten bereitschaft halten."

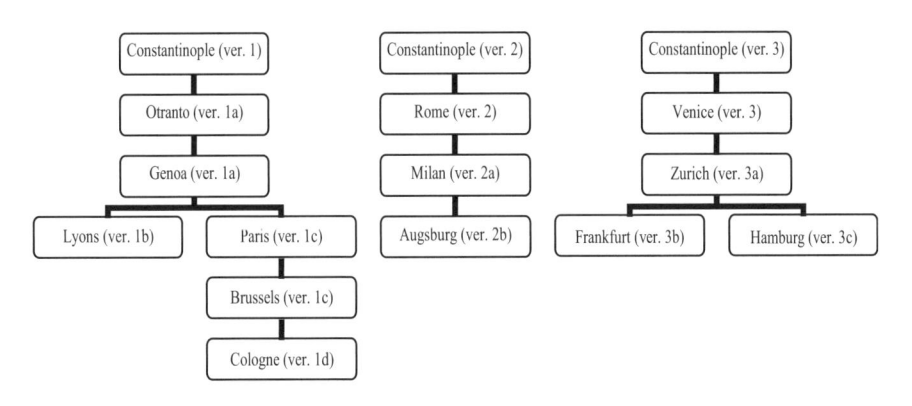

Figure 0.3   News Stories in Transition

The number of possible examples showing the vagaries of news transmission across time and space is almost infinite. Rather than adding to the ones already offered, in order to introduce our concept of contemporaneity and the ways and means of investigating it, we now turn to the chapters in this book. And to investigate the concept we have assembled a highly heterogeneous group of researchers in various locations ranging from Florence to London, and including literary historians, cultural historians, military historians, media historians, a librarian or two and some social scientists. In trans-disciplinary fashion, we wish to focus the skills and methods of all these fields on a set of related problems—not necessarily to come to a solution, but certainly to see what the questions are and what the procedures for answering them might be. Accordingly, the volume is divided into four parts: the first, "Joining Time and Space," concerning the basic genres of communication ranging from letters to newspapers; the second part, "Time, Motion and Structure," investigating the actual networks joining times and spaces across Europe; the third, "Inter-European Spaces and Moments," examining a number of case studies; and finally, "New Methods," introducing techniques and technologies that aid in this research.

And to demonstrate the communications mechanisms of the early modern period at their height, where better to begin than in late sixteenth-century Spain? King Philip II, as Cristina Beltran shows in her chapter, found that consulting up to date information about occurrences all over his reign and formulating appropriate responses could be a matter of life and death. With thousands of letters and other handwritten communications coming in regarding foreign wars, matters in the colonies, important dynastic concerns and whatever else, Philip sought to deploy his communications system to bring about action on multiple fronts. Yet the task of achieving an understanding of what was being communicated and formulating hundreds of responses per day may have strained to the limits his procedure of behaving "like a spider in his web." The abundance of information could have a paradoxical effect, such that an individual, even a king, could experience difficulty in attempting to defeat all barriers of time and space, and therefore engage everywhere contemporaneously—no matter how "grand" his strategy might be. Mario Infelise reminds us that within the early modern scheme of information, newsletters played an important part. The roots (he shows) go back to fourteenth- and fifteenth-century commercial correspondence. Since information was a commodity, privately circulated among buyers and sellers, control was difficult and the connection with politics was always problematic.

The emergence of the specific genre of the printed newspaper, which Johannes Weber traces to the Alsatian town of Strasbourg in 1605, marked a major step toward creating more widespread and uniform habits in regard to information. The genre rapidly spread, and just in the German-language area alone, the number of emulators in every major city was regarded as remarkable at the time. Already in the first sheets the pattern was set of including a mix of local and foreign political news. Considering the prevalence of details regarding war and conflict around Europe, one could imagine that contemporaneity, even at this level, led in the direction of political awareness, and eventually, a public sphere. In Weber's view, the newspapers had more potential to bring this about than the typical one-off publications of the pre-newspaper era, even if such publications reached some of the same audiences and contained similar information.

Both the letter and the newspaper functioned within a system of communication that had been developing in tandem with territorial states and capitalist enterprise; and in Part Two we try to outline the basic elements of this structure. Brendan Dooley focuses on the particular case of Giovanni de' Medici, a warrior, diplomat and informer, reporting from the Flanders front between the sixteenth and seventeenth centuries. Rendering the realities of a battle was no simple matter, then or now. Giovanni's efforts to give the Medici grand dukes, first his half-brothers Francesco and Ferdiando and then his nephew Cosimo II, the impression of being present with him on the field, demonstrate the strengths and weakness of a system built over centuries. Alessio Assonitis examines the creation and circulation of news and rumor concerning a single typical item of general interest: namely, the birth of Maria de' Medici, the future queen of France. Pressure for notification concerning the birth was made all the more extreme, due to the previous failure of Johanna of Austria and Francesco de' Medici to produce a male heir to the newly minted Tuscan grand dukedom. With expectations raised to fever pitch, true and false reports competed for attention, to such a degree that the confusion has affected even the modern historiography on the dynasty.

Among the inhabitants of particular cities, the so-called "offices of intelligence" (*bureaux d'adresse*), studied by Astrid Blome, were designed to facilitate exchange of knowledge and information of all sorts. First conceived in France in the sixteenth century, such offices, centered in a store front or private home, claimed to answer a wide variety of purposes ranging from the personal to the political. Famously, activities of this sort helped launch the information-purveying career of Theophraste Renaudot, later editor of the Paris *Gazette*. In England they were associated with such names as John Drury and Samuel Hartlib, drawing upon the model for a knowledge clearing-house set out in Francis Bacon's *New Atlantis*. When these schemes referred to knowledge about matters of current interest to many citizens, they could reinforce the sense of sharing the moment of contemporaneity in a similar fashion to the reading of news publications.

Zsuzsa Barbarics points out that in Central and Southeast Europe, the handwritten newsletter remained the vehicle of choice largely because the press was underdeveloped. And taking into account such sources, we find that these regions were far more closely connected to the more familiar markets and cultures of Western Europe than was previously thought. Indeed, the depth and breadth of the tradition of newsletter writing and copying suggests a constant and voluminous flow of foreign news permitting the elite to gain a sensation of being aware of the dynamics of a wide world context at any particular moment.

The third part of our book opens with comparisons of foreign news coverage across regions and linguistic territories. Sonja Schultheiss-Heinz gives an account of news reporting in three specific texts: the French *Gazette*, the London *Gazette*, and the Nuremberg *Teutsch Kriegs-Kurier*, mainly in regard to a single event: the abduction of a French agent named Fürstenburg in Holland during the War of Devolution. If readers in the three publishing areas of these papers had the impression of experiencing the same event at the same time, they were right; although their experience may not have been uniform. Schultheiss-Heinz reminds us that the details of an event follow an itinerary from the place of action to the reader, along which modifications both in fact and interpretation may occur. In this case, reporting tends to reflect the official line in each country, with the English favoring Holland, the Germans showing hostility to France, and the French demonstrating indignation.

Charles Depezay explores an international news exchange between France and the Netherlands, whereby the French elite gained information on the same events from a variety of sources reflecting different outlooks. Published in Paris and closely monitored by the royal government, the *Gazette* propounded an "official" view. From 1688, a time when Louis XIV's frequent wars excited a more insistent demand for information, the Amsterdam-based *Gazette d'Amsterdam*, founded by Claude Jordan and Jean Tronchin Dubreuil, was smuggled into France for circulation among the same audience as the *Gazette*. It propounded an alternative view, not hostile to the government. Also available on the black market was an openly anti-French paper, founded by Jean-Alexandre de La Font in 1677, and called the *Gazette de Leyde*. According to Depezay, the development of a shared awareness regarding French involvement in European affairs helped build the kind of critical public that the monarchy sought, diffidently and tentatively, to engage in its own support.

Many circumstances combined to give particular cities of Europe a privileged position within the developing network of news transmission; and this was nowhere truer than in the Low Countries. Paul Arblaster accordingly shows how local interests and international politics determined the relative roles of Brussels and Antwerp. Easily equal to Brussels as a news entrepot at the end of the sixteenth century, Antwerp eventually recedes to the background because of royal strategies favoring the Tassis family organization of letter carriers (and their Habsburg monopoly) as well as because of competition from other larger centers across Europe.

Of course, not all information that circulated along the expanding news routes was about wars and dynastical affairs; nor did it appeal exclusively to the rational critical viewpoints of the readers. Ingrid Meyer and Daniel Waugh explore the circulation of news, stemming from Russia, regarding the presumed Messiah Sabbatai Sevi, which became a Central European sensation in the years 1665–67. The effects of this news on Jews and Christians may well have been to reinforce a sense of community within each group, while at the same time to create greater differentiation between them, through stereotyping and through contrasting inclinations regarding the credibility of the stories.

Opening the final section on new methods and approaches, Nicholas Brownlees applies media discourse analysis to the English pre-Civil War corantos. Textual structures or styles of narration, he finds, were the syntactical bearers of the varied content transmitted by the physical vehicles of the newspaper or newsbook. Indeed, study of the structures in English news reporting from 1620 through 1640 reveals a striking change. In the early pre-Civil War period the writing tended to express the writer's detachment and objectivity, evincing a simple unproblematic conveying of material, upon which the reader might draw to form an idea of contemporaneity. Later writing on the other hand tended to emphasize the writer's position as an interpreter or even observer of events, one who, like the reader, attempts to make sense of contemporaneity. Finally, Andrew Hardie Tony McEnery and Scott Songlin Piao illustrate analytical procedures within the Lancaster corpus of newsbooks covering the years 1653–54. Their database allows rapid comparisons of single news stories across eleven publications. Approaching their results from the standpoint of corpus linguistics, they are able to locate interrelationships between different versions of a story, suggesting conclusions regarding editorial practices and ideologies. Extending this approach to other times and places would provide a broad panorama of news available to be shared at any particular juncture.

PART 1
Joining Time and Space: The Origins

CHAPTER 1
Philip of Spain: The Spider's Web of News and Information

Cristina Borreguero Beltrán

Introduction

Fifteen years after the death of Philip II, a scribe named Alonso Gascón de Cardona writing from the Far East to the Spanish court described empires so fabulous that they had to be seen to be believed: "The further you travel and the more you see, the buildings, the people and other such things, the more you can lend credence to the old novels about chivalry, knights and magic spells."[1]

Merchants, monks, soldiers and scribes such as Alonso Gascón de Cardona were slowly establishing world-wide networks through which news could travel as quickly as these new worlds were discovered. Despite their limited oral and written skills these privileged spectators sought to communicate all that they had seen, heard, touched, tasted, and smelled. This veritable universe of new experiences and sensations conveyed in their letters and tales was rapidly made known throughout the Old Continent. However, it soon became necessary to send specialists—cosmographers and scientists—to explore and study the hitherto unknown regions. These men not only transmitted their feelings about these newly discovered lands but also very real data as knowledge of these lands would be necessary to govern them well. Any European sovereign who could understand the reality and the nature of these hitherto unknown peoples and territories would eventually be able to establish his power and influence over them.

The challenges faced by the Spanish crown, which had extended its dominion across the oceans, were immense. The task of governing Asiatic subjects—Hindus, Filipinos—from the antipodes by imposing and consolidating sovereign authority over territories and populations of different races and creeds required continuous effort to understand and delve deeper into the reality of these worlds. Only a well-organized communications system would ever permit government over these lands and cultures, the existence of which was only slowly dawning on Europeans.

---

[1] Emilio Sola Castaño, *Libro de las maravillas del Oriente lejano* (Madrid, 1980), p. 17.

Much of the historiography has portrayed Philip II as a spider at the center of his web. This metaphor highlights the sedentary nature of the monarch, who ruled from the heart of Castile. This comparison, however, unquestionably hides another aspect: the monarch was able to put together a communications network reaching around the world that enabled his sovereign authority to be consolidated and his influence to be extended throughout the transoceanic territories of Spain's empire.

This chapter begins with a description of the information infrastructure or communications network developed under the reign of Philip II. It then moves on to examine the temporal and geographical conditions that shaped those networks. Finally, it discusses and examines the consequences of a series of measures taken by the monarch in an effort to professionalize those networks.

The Communications Network in Europe

Philip II inherited territories that were scattered across Europe and, more than any other sovereign, needed a solid infrastructure for collecting information which he deemed essential for the governance and the security of his estates and for consolidating his pre-eminence in Europe. No sovereign could secure continuous influence over European affairs without being able to gather accurate information at just the right moment on the intentions of European potentates and on their most closely guarded secrets.

Various factors contributed to the spinning of the spider's web that Philip began to weave across Europe from north to south. One cannot forget that the monarch knew the Old Continent well. He had started his apprenticeship from an early age thanks to the letters of his father, Charles V. When at the age of 16 the prince was left as governor of the peninsula under instructions from his father, the governmental structures that ruled at a distance required a reliable communications system between the father in his European court and the Spanish court of the son.

Already by 1505, the flow of communications set up by Philip I, who arrived in Castile from Flanders, was fairly reliable. The new king had contracted a courier service with the Tassis family between Spain and the Low Countries. Although peninsular Spain already had a long-standing postal service, especially in Aragón, Catalonia, and Valencia, the contract with the Tassis family meant the incorporation of Castile into the European postal organization of the house of Burgundy. The route crossed France from north to south and had a considerable number of relay stations.[2] In those first years of the sixteenth century, this system of stations was a real step forward in communications.

The coronation of Charles as King of Spain in 1516 and as Emperor in 1519, allowed the Tassis family to extend their services as a total monopoly in Spain, Italy, Germany, and France.[3] It was a diplomatic postal service for the exclusive use of the Emperor from his residences at Innsbruck, Verona, Valladolid, Rome, and Naples to support his diplomacy, but it also served as a vehicle of instruction and advice from a traveling father to a son being educated in the heart of Castile.

Later, the Emperor decided that his son should travel to meet him in Brussels. Philip II's journey through Europe added to his education as it taught him firsthand the geography of the Western Mediterranean basin, the center and North of Europe, and the North Sea. Above all, it introduced him to the towns and peoples of Europe and he undoubtedly also learnt from the art, painting, architecture, and military defenses; all of which gave him useful experience concerning the transit routes, distances, and slowness of communication within Europe. Philip II was out of Spain for eight years but from 1559 until his death

---

[2] Cayetano Alcazar, "Los orígenes del correo Moderno en España," *Revista de la Biblioteca, Archivo y Museo del Ayuntamiento de Madrid* (1928): 168–87. Jaime Ascandoni Rivero, "El correo durante el reinado de Felipe II" in Enrique Martínez Ruiz (coord.), *Felipe II, la ciencia y la técnica* (Madrid, 1999), pp. 253–74.

[3] By Royal Decree of 28 August 1518, Charles V conferred the title of Post Master General on the brothers Bautista Mateo and Simón de Tassis and agreed on a series of clauses that were the basis of later postal contracts:

> That only they may send out foot messengers or couriers and pay them the due amounts for their journeys; the post master retains sole rights, and a fine of 100,000 *maravedis* shall be imposed on those who carry such documents without license. The post master can employ those couriers he sees fit for the royal service, but only after they have sworn an oath; the death penalty will be imposed on anyone who performs such a service without being duly appointed and all his possessions shall be seized by the royal treasury. The property of the post master will be exempt from taxes and other council charges and neither may he be detained or arrested for non-payment of debts...

However, guidance was given on action to be taken in serious cases:

> Couriers shall be supplied with the provisions and mounts necessary for their journeys, and paid the just amount and no more according to the calculations of the post master along with other supplies for the safety and immunity of themselves and their households....

The instructions went on to say that:

> they may employ arms for the defense of their persons both in the court and throughout the kingdom, and that they shall not be ordered to surrender their arms ....

Information contained in the Itinerary of the posts within and without the realm. (Madrid, 1988) Facsimile of the original of 1761, fol. VIII.

the monarch never left the peninsula again. Thus, the only link between the monarch and many of his subjects was the postal service. This explains why the king attributed such importance to correspondence and, in general, to all written documentation that passed through his office.

Routes and Distances

The positive results of the service provided by the Tassis family maintained the communications system established by Charles V. Governance of the Low Countries, Milan, and Naples—at anywhere between 1,500 and over 2,000 km by land from Madrid[4]—required an efficient communications system between such scattered territories. It was operated from the offices of the Secretary of State, a sort of universal office that managed the business of running the territories of the Spanish crown. But the pressure of political events in Europe meant that the information network had to be reinforced and the Tassis family experimented with safer routes that ran north to south across Europe.

In the Monarch's Italian territories the well-known old Roman–Spanish route was still in use, which started in Madrid and passed through Zaragoza, Barcelona, Narbonne, Montpellier, Nîmes, Avignon, Genoa, Pisa, Florence, Siena, Viterbo and Rome.

Given the political circumstances, there were only three routes to the Low Countries that could be maintained, the most direct of which crossed France via Lyon. Aware of its importance, Charles V had agreed with Francis I of France to respect the secrecy of the diplomatic mail from both states which was allowed to pass freely through their territories during peacetime. In more troubled times, the route through Barcelona, Genoa and the North of Italy was used and finally, the Atlantic route was also used whenever possible.[5] These were never alternative routes as they were all used simultaneously whenever possible to ensure safe delivery of the dispatches.

The sensation of great distances in Europe, due as much to geography as to the slowness of communications, worsened considerably during the winter months. At the beginning of the sixteenth century, the agreement with the Tassis family stated that a dispatch from Brussels to Paris—some 308 km—should take 44 hours in summer and 54 hours in winter. In addition:

---

[4] The distance today from Madrid to Brussels by road is 1,500 km, to Amsterdam 1,700 km, to Milan 1,728 km and to Naples 2,200 km.

[5] Henry Kamen, *Felipe de España* (Madrid, 1997), p. 26.

- From Brussels to Innsbruck should take five-and-a-half days in summer and one more in winter.
- From Brussels to Toledo, 12 days in summer and 14 in winter.
- From Brussels to Granada, 15 days in summer and 18 in winter.

In 1517, the Tassis family agreed on reductions in the journey times:

- From Brussels to Paris, 36 hours in summer and 40 in winter.
- From Brussels to Innsbruck, five days in summer and six in winter.
- From Brussels to Blois, 50 hours in summer and 60 in winter.
- From Brussels to Lyon, three-and-a-half days in summer and four in winter.
- From Brussels to Rome, ten-and-a-half days in summer and 12 in winter.
- From Brussels to Naples, 14 days in winter.
- From Brussels to Burgos, seven days in summer and eight days in winter.[6]

The average speed the messengers had to maintain to meet these targets was between 5 and 7.7 km per hour.

The only way to make the postal service move faster was by increasing the effort invested in the journey. This was done by paying incentives to the couriers. Those who managed to cover 10 leagues—55 km—in a day received two-and-a-half *reales* a day. Those who covered 15 leagues in a day—83 km—were given one-and-a-half ducats and four ducats were given to anyone who beat the record of 20 leagues—110 km—in a day.

Despite these incentives given to the operators of the postal service, the sensation of distance and slowness within the European continent and between the subjects and the allies of the Spanish monarch and the king persisted. This feeling was even stronger in those territories which were far removed from the main hubs of the communications network: "Because of the distance from here to where Your Majesty is—wrote Terence O'Neill to Philip II from Ireland— we can not do our business as often or as well as we would were we closer to the Court."[7]

Two factors forced Philip II to give fresh impetus to communications: on the one hand, the rapid increase in private mail and on the other, political pressure, which forced the monarch to place numerous ambassadors and agents at strategic points throughout Europe.

---

[6] Alcazar, "Los orígenes del correo Moderno en España." See also Juan Ignacio Fernández Bayo, "El Correo en España," *Historia y Vida*, 19 (1986): 4–10.

[7] Archivo General de Simancas (A.G.S.) Estado (E.), Legajo (Leg.) 492: Terence O'Neill to Philip II. Donegal, 4 April 1597.

Progress in Communication: the "Ordinary" Postal Service

Private correspondence spiraled, mainly as a result of the conquest and colonization of the Americas. Soldiers, scribes, and missionaries who left their families on the other side of the Atlantic increasingly felt the need for a regular and fast communications system to keep them in contact with their families and homes. The need for a public communications service was also voiced.

Up until this time, personal correspondence had come second to the royal mail. However, in cities such as Medina, Valladolid, and Burgos, certain families privately began to contract such services independently of the monarch, as did traders and banks. The convergent needs and interests of the monarch, of traders, and of the general public led to the same system being used for dispatches from different quarters. If the previous system meant paying one messenger for one letter or dispatch, then with the new system the same messenger could carry several letters, with obvious economic advantages for all concerned.

Thus a more modern postal service was born, known as the *ordinary* service, a permanent means of communication which facilitated the constant and regular flow of information. The new postal service was accompanied by a series of measures put in place to improve the system. Stops were established every 4 leagues on the itineraries to make it easier to rest and take refreshment and a number of houses with stables destined for this purpose were supplied with fodder and provisions. These houses, which were under the special protection of the sovereign and had the royal shield on their facades, were inhabited by people in charge of the relay posts who bore the title of "masters of the resting places." The billeting of troops, for example, was forbidden in such places and a fresh horse was always kept ready for the couriers. Apart from these lodgings for rest, offices were also set up in towns along the routes, assisted by a post master and two, four, or eight dispatch riders. A pool of horses was maintained in Brussels, Antwerp, and other important cities, to avoid any eventual shortages and to dispatch special mail.

But the most significant advance in this new system was the frequency of deliveries, necessary for the organization of the post as a public service. The Tassis family took charge of the management of the ordinary service that left the court bound for Brussels, Rome, and Lisbon and returned by the same routes. Besides these services, express or special post in emergencies had to be organized by the sender, as well as all those which linked up with the routes of the ordinary service.

From 1560 an ordinary postal service between Madrid and Brussels began to operate, leaving the court and the city of Brussels on the first day of each month, which became fortnightly later on. The land route passed through Burgos, Miranda de Ebro, Vitoria, Tolosa, Rentería, Irún, Fuenterabbía,

Hendaya, Bayona, Castets, Lesperon, Burdeos, Poitiers, Orleans, Angerville, and finally Paris. Here the dispatch riders left mail for the ambassador and picked up any letters for the governor of the Low Countries and for the ambassador in London. From Paris, the route took them to Roye-sur-Matz, Cambrai, Valenciennes, Tubize, and Brussels. Brussels was the most important communication center in the North of Europe as it was the headquarters of the postal network directed by Juan Bautista de Tassis. After Brussels, Antwerp was the second most noteworthy nucleus of communication since it had been assigned the service between the Low Countries and London. In 1590, correspondence from the duke of Parma in the Low Countries with the Spanish court regularly involved about two letters a month.[8] This ordinary post took between 17 and 22 days on the Lyon–Barcelona route, a little more than the time stipulated by Tassis in his contracts.

The ordinary postal service that carried correspondence to the Spanish embassy in London left Antwerp and took the Scheldt to Ghent, and from there followed the old trade route that connected the continent to England: Ghent, Bruges, and Ostend, to Calais where there was a special boat service to ensure that the mail crossed the channel to Dover. After the peace of Cateau–Cambresis the crossing was re-established and operated between Dunkirk and Dover. Disembarking at this port, the dispatchers went on to Canterbury, Sittingbourne, Rochester, Gravesend, and then to Greenwich and on to London. The return journey was down the Thames from Greenwich to Gravesend. Using this system, a letter could be sent from Brussels to London in less than five days.

Towards the east, the ordinary post with Italy used sea transport, although the land route remained open. The fleet of galleys in Genoa became the safest way to transport between Barcelona and Genoa.[9] The ordinary post from Italy via Genoa began with a service that left the court every 15 days and the offer of this public service was spread throughout Madrid in the form of "notices that were put up in public on most street corners of this city."[10]

---

[8] The letters from the Duke of Parma were dated 14 March 1590, 24 March 1590, 4 May 1590, 19 May 1590, 20 May 1590, 1 June 1590, 24 June 1590. "On February 17, I received there those duplicates of those of the 30th January." A.G.S., E. Leg. 598, f. 44: the Duke of Parma to the king. Brussels, 4 April 1590.

[9] Philippe Montoya, *Les Reines de la Méditerranée. Les galères au service de L'Éspagne en Méditerranée Occidentale, 1570–1621* (Toulouse, 1995), p. 115.

[10] A.G.S., S.P., Leg. 78.

The European Spider's Web

The establishment of the ordinary postal service not only made private communications easier, but it also increased the flow of political and diplomatic information. At the same time as the means of communication improved, so too did the numbers of people posted throughout strategic locations in Europe at the service of the Spanish crown. Philip II had an army of ambassadors, representatives, and agents who, amongst their other duties, were expected to correspond regularly with the court; viceroys, and ambassadors had to inform the king of events at least once a week. This led to a real upsurge in information flowing towards the center of the spider's web.[11]

At the same time, Philip II obliged his ambassadors, governors, and agents to set up regular exchanges of correspondence between each other, further adding to the circulation of news around Europe. In 1580, when Philip II appointed Juan Bautista de Tassis as his representative to France, his instructions clearly stressed the duty of the representative to maintain correspondence with the governors of Flanders, Margaret of Parma and Alessandro Farnese, the viceroys of Naples and Sicily, the governor of Milan, the ambassadors in Rome, Germany, Venice and Genoa, the viceroys of Aragón, Catalonia, and Navarre, and the Field Marshal of Guipúzcoa, to advise them—the instructions said textually—"of anything of which they should take heed for the wellbeing and safety of the Spanish dominions."[12]

This correspondence between ambassadors, representatives, and governors wove new routes around those already in existence. Correspondence between Rome and the Low Countries and between Rome and Paris went through Viterbo, Siena, Florence, Bologna, Mantua, Trent, Brixen, Innsbruck, Ausburg, Reinhauser, Namur, and Brussels. Another route also branched out from Bologna, going through Modena, Reggio, Parma, Piacenza, Alessandria, Turin, Chambery, Lyon, Melun, and on to Paris. In the establishment of these routes, the Franche-Comté (the "Free County" of Burgundy) was of great strategic

---

[11] Generally, this diplomatic correspondence had a similar structure. Ambassadors and agents always made reference to the last post sent and received, such that this information allowed for confirmation or otherwise of the receipt of all previous dispatches. Secondly, they explained their rapid replies or, on the contrary, delays due to poor communications, bad weather, or periods waiting for further news. Thirdly, they set out all of their administrative problems, lack of funds, shortage of staff, and lack of court news, and difficulties of all types in the exercise of their functions. Lastly, they always sought to supply all possible information concerning the movements of the enemies of the Spanish crown.

[12] C. Pérez Bustamante, "Las instrucciones de Felipe II a Juan Bautista de Tassis," *Revista de la Biblioteca, Archivo y Museo*, 19 (July 1928): 241–59.

value in maintaining relationships between Flanders, Italy, and Austria, in the midst of military difficulties. In contacts with the Habsburg domains, Innsbruck emerged as the great center of Central European communications.

To assure his lines of communication with Austria, in addition to the ordinary post that was often overwhelmed, Philip II employed personal messengers with increasing frequency, who were sent by court and by his ambassadors and even by the Emperor. Francisco de Paredes was one of the most outstanding envoys to perform the service between the two Habsburg courts during the years 1565–73.[13] In the winter of 1586 he took 47 days on the return journey, managing to reduce this time to 32 in the autumn of 1570, taking 19 days to get there, and 13 to return to Madrid, which constituted a real record. On the majority of his trips, Paredes, like many other messengers, traveled north as far as the duchy of Alba in the Low Countries and, on his return from Austria, crossed France to pick up or leave mail for the ambassador in Paris, Francés de Alava. However, on other trips he chose the route that went through Genoa.

Among the messengers at the service of the Emperor who also performed important services for Philip II, one of the most exemplary was Gil Gerin, better known as Giles. His professionalism and safety led the monarch to charge him with other tasks, amongst which, that of taking the marriage papers together with the gift of diamonds to Philip's future wife, Anne of Austria. The notes of his trips between 1564 and 1570 are numerous. He normally took about 25 days to make the journey from Vienna to Madrid and back again. Just crossing France took about five days; in 1570, he took an average of 17 days to travel between Spira and Madrid. Thanks to the Emperor's messengers, communications between Austria–Flanders–Paris–Madrid were relatively fluid, which also aided communication between Margaret of Parma and Philip II who were able to keep in touch without excessive difficulty.

Savoy was considered to be a state of great relevance for communications with Italy, strategically and politically. The king set up an embassy which was in constant contact with the Spanish court along the two available routes by land and sea. In 1590, the ambassador Josepe de Acuño regularly sent his dispatches by sea, which still represented the fastest route to Barcelona,[14] but he also sent

---

[13] See Colección de Documentos Inéditos (C.O.D.O.I.N.). España: vol. CI, CIII, CX. Collected letters of the Duke of Alba: vol. II, p. 459.

[14] A.G.S., E., Leg. 1271, f. 16: Letter from Josepe de Acuña to the king. Nice, 15 August 1592: "On the second of this month I dispatched a letter to Your Majesty on a frigate from Barcelona whose owner is named Bernadino Morel and I included the copy of the dispatches of the 8, 10, 17 and 21 July and in view of the good prevailing weather I trust that they will have arrived so long as no ship has cut them off."

missives by land, taking advantage of any messenger travelling on the old Roman route,[15] or sending post to Lyon to connect up with the Flanders route.[16]

Rome was the nerve center of the lines of communication within Italy, being the headquarters of embassies close to the Pope. In 1590, the Spanish ambassador in Rome, the Count of Olivares, had to maintain intense correspondence not only with Madrid but also with Brussels and Paris, which forced him to use highly trustworthy messengers:

> Many of the dispatches I have sent to Your Majesty since I have been in this post have been in the hands of Mateo Balbano de León, and I have also sent him dispatches so that any couriers who pass through from other parts or at the service of other ministers may carry them to Your Majesty. Likewise, to Flanders or Paris, those letters which it has been necessary to write to the Duke of Parma and don Bernadino de Mendoza (ambassador in Paris) and he has conscientiously delivered the documents to me from many different parts. The same messenger has sent news by the ordinary service of what is happening and of what he has heard from others that on occasions has served me well...[17]

In the South of Italy, Naples became the communications hub with the Central and Eastern Mediterranean. News from Constantinople and Berbería arrived there via Malta from whence it arrived in Spain via the fleet at Naples.[18] In 1590, the viceroy of Naples, at the time the Count of Miranda, tried to send as much news as possible concerning the movements of the Constantinople fleet and the problems in Persia.[19] Communications between these two peninsulas was

---

[15] A.G.S., E., Leg. 1271, f. 39: Letter from Josepe de Acuña to Francisco de Idiáquez. Nice, 3 August 1592: "With the mail I dispatched to His Majesty on the 21st of last month I wrote to His Majesty, the copy of which I am sending by sea. Since that date I have received no letter from His Majesty although two dispatches for Italy from His Majesty have indeed arrived."

[16] A.G.S., E., Leg. 1271, f. 52: Letter from Josepe de Acuña to the king. Nice, 28 May 1592: "I have written of private things in this letter, concluding it with everything I deem necessary to relate to Your Majesty and accordingly I am sending it by mail to Lyon so that this dispatch may leave as soon as possible. If it has not arrived in four days, I will send another by special post."

[17] A.G.S., E., Leg. 1092, f. 51: The Count of Olivares to the king. Rome, 23 September 1590.

[18] The fleet at Naples comprised some 23 galleys, of these the royal galley was normally entrusted with the transport of mail. See Montoya, "Les reines de la Mediterranée," p. 39.

[19] "Things in Berbería are still unsettled and, according to the reports, Morabut, the head of the insurrectionists with a band of people is near Tripoli, which could mean that the

especially difficult in the winter, when storms and bad weather forced the ships to shelter in the harbor. The mooring documents of the galleys specified that from 15 November to 15 March the ships were docked because of storms which made sailing more dangerous. Delays in the arrival of the galleys from Naples due to adverse weather conditions were the object of great anxiety both in Naples and on the peninsula.[20] In good weather, the regularity of communications made it possible to deal with matters in 23 or 25 days.

Communications with Naples were not, however, limited to maritime channels. They also linked up with the ordinary post to Italy by land and, in emergencies, the express or special post. For important matters, the king even used all the means of communication available to him simultaneously. One of the most peculiar cases was the dispatch that Philip II sent to the ambassador to inform him of matters relating to the affairs of Antonio Pérez, urging delivery "in safe hands and as rapidly as possible, one with the ordinary service, another with the first special post and a third to go on the galleys."[21]

Communications with the East of Europe were much slower and more difficult. The distance seemed to grow despite the efforts of the ambassador in Prague, Guillén de San Clemente, to send the king all possible notifications and news concerning affairs in Poland, Sweden, and Muscovy.[22] Post from Prague to Madrid was very slow and extremely unsafe, "it was some surprise that the mail is never lost, so unsure are the roads along which it must travel," wrote the ambassador in 1589; "this must explain why letters of mine have not arrived."[23] It was also unpredictable as, on occasions, they could take more than five months to reach Spain, only to arrive at the court in Spain almost in shreds.[24] The ambassador used everything in his power to send his reports, from the

---

Turks send out another army there this summer, which would force us to be on our guard for whatever might happen." Letter from the Count of Miranda to the king. Naples, 14 April 1590. A.G.S., E., Leg.1092, f. 15.

[20] A. G. S., E., Leg. 1092, f. 3: Letter from the count of Miranda to the king. Naples, 5 January 1590.

[21] A.G.S., E., Leg. 1092, f. 79.

[22] On 9 May 1598, the ambassador sent news of the wedding of the Princess of Sweden to Maximilian of Poland to Spain and informed the king of the appointment of an envoy to the Emperor of Muscovy. A.G. S., E. Leg. 696, f. 130: letter from Guillén de San Clemente to the king. Prague, 9 May 1589.

[23] Letter from Guillén de San Clemente to Juan de Idiáquez. Prague, 22 August 1589. A.G.S., E., Leg. 696, f. 130.

[24] This happened with the two letters sent 27 October 1589, but which didn't arrive until 4 April of the following year. A.G. S., E., Leg. 696, f. 13: mail from Guillén de San Clemente to the king. Prague, 27 October 1589.

dispatchers sent by the Emperor to any messenger who was headed towards the West: "If king Maximilian of Poland sent a gentleman of his to Your Majesty I would indeed make use of him and write longer reports."[25] The unpredictable character of mail coming from the East was confirmed when the letters sent with this gentleman arrived at the Spanish court in a record time of 34 days.

The Communications Network on the Peninsula

The postal service with Italy, the Low Countries, and the rest of Europe required a peninsula link from and to Madrid, the center of the web. Madrid was considered:

> ... the heart of Spain ... being in the middle, and because the seaports are all more or less within a reasonable distance, so necessary for the rapid dispatch of His Majesty's armadas to all his Kingdoms, to fight against the enemy, since it is becoming easier and easier to send mail from Madrid every day.[26]

Thanks to the management of Tassis, the monarch came to have an extraordinary network of messengers "coming and going" to the court, who covered all the routes at all hours of the day and night in search of the addressees. As from July when the king moved to *San Lorenzo del Escorial* leaving his central administration in Madrid, the monarch relied on a daily postal service to Madrid, which made the journey several times a day if necessary. Nor was the flow of mail interrupted when the king moved to *Campillo* at the beginning of October, and some weeks later to *El Pardo*.[27]

The routes which left Madrid were radial. In 1589, fixed routes were established for general dispatches consigned to specific locations.[28] The king's mail was to be delivered by hand.

---

[25] A.G.S., E., Leg 696, f. 64: letter from Guillén de San Clemente to the king. Prague, 4 October 1589.

[26] Pérez de Herrera, "Speech to his Royal Highness the Catholic King Don Philip our Lord, in which he begged the king to consider the many qualities and the greatness of the city of Madrid, to consider honouring the city with a city wall and other things that he proposed, such as it deserving to be the permanent Court and assistant of the great Monarch," in Alfredo Alvar Ezquerra, *Felipe II, la Corte y Madrid en 1561* (Madrid, 1985), p. 40.

[27] The king owned a few little palaces and retreats, situated between the fertile lands of the river Tajo and the Guadarrama mountain range: Aranjuez, Aceca, Vaciamadrid, Madrid, El Escorial, Campillo, Monasterio, Fuenfría, El Pardo, and, finally Valsaín, Ibid, p. 39.

[28] A.G.S., G.A., Leg. 266, f. 40–50: Routes which dispatchers must take out of Madrid, 1589.

Let a messenger go directly to Tarragona with a document from his Majesty for the governor of Castile, Field Marshal of the Spanish Galleys, and should he not have arrived there with the returning galleys, then the messenger shall remain in Tarragona until his arrival, where he must hand over the said document. If the Field Marshal has already passed through Tarragona, then the messenger must follow him along the coast to Denia to give him the said document.[29]

Making use of the Madrid–Seville–San Lucar–Gibraltar route, dispatches were also sent to North Africa using any ship ready to sail.[30] Philip had outstanding agents in the north of Africa who supplied him with information on all of the movements of the North-African sheiks and any news of interest that might occur on these coasts. One of the most active was the Moroccan agent, Baltasar Polo, who was well informed of the news that arrived at its ports about the incursions of Sir Francis Drake.[31] He used all the means of communication open to him to keep the Spanish court informed. The most frequent method that allowed him to send news to the court was on the Portuguese galleons from India.[32]

In the east of the peninsula, Lisbon was the center of maritime communications for the Atlantic. Through its port, the Spanish court received information from Europe and America as well as India. Here the court obtained information on the exercises of English privateers in Atlantic waters, Irish attempts to wrest control of their island from the English, and the interests of overseas subjects

---

[29] A.G.S., G.A., Leg. 225, Book of departures. List of where the royal mail had to be taken (1588).

[30] "From the nearest route I will send another courier to Malaga with a document from His Majesty for the suppliers of his Armadas there, to whom another two documents from His Majesty: one for Antonio de Tejeda, Mayor of Melilla and the other for Diego de Vera, Mayor of the Peñón, that they be sent in the first vessel available."

[31] On 13 April 1595, Baltasar Polo wrote to the court explaining that his last letter had been sent on 30 November 1594 and that he had not written since awaiting the following news: "Merchant ships and English ships which have arrived at these ports confirm that Sir Francis Drake is ready to sail with one hundred and forty ships: the king having asked me if I knew of this news and knew where they were bound, all I could answer was that I only knew what the English had said and that it seemed to me that they all wanted to get their hands on as much as possible of the great treasure that Your Majesty has ordered be assembled in Havana, but that they all knew that when Your Majesty ordered it to be sent to Spain, it would be with so much protection that neither those enemies nor many more would be enough to take it." Baltasar Polo to the king, Morocco, 13 April 1595. A.G.S., E., Leg. 492.

[32] A.G.S., E., Leg. 492: Baltasar Polo to the king. Morocco, 20 July 1595: "That afternoon I took to Sheik Ruttb the two letters from Your Majesty, one having come by way of the Portuguese Crown which only concerned the rescue of three noblemen who had been taken prisoner […] and I gave him both letters which he gracefully received."

arriving on the galleons from India. In order to channel all this information to the court, the Tassis established an ordinary post that linked up Madrid and Lisbon (some 644 km) in five days.

Efficiency and Cost

Thus, the Spanish crown had set up a magnificent infrastructure of routes, with an exceptional number of relay posts and messengers. But this was still not enough to create a truly efficient system, as communications posed many other problems. The greatest of these were delays, but there were also problems of insecurity, lack of immunity, loss and confiscation of dispatches, and above all the financial cost.

Philip II began a merciless fight against the slowness of the service and even dreamt of an aerial postal service. Firstly, to try to speed up the service, he imposed a demanding work load on the Secretary of State. "Today we have received the post dispatched there," wrote Antonio de Eraso. "This post must be quickly read and dealt with."[33] On 16 June, the Count of Miranda and ambassador of Naples wrote to the king asking him whether he should keep the *tercios* of Italians. The letter was received by the monarch on 11 July after a journey of 25 days. The surprising thing was not Philip's reply, ordering him to conserve the *tercios* of Italians, but the speed with which the consultation was resolved and the date of the letter, signed by the king on 12 July, the day after it had been received! On 4 August, Miranda received the reply to his question and acted immediately on the decision, such that the matter was wound up in little more than a month and a half.[34]

At the same time, the monarch tried to make the postal service more flexible. On 17 January 1583 he established the "Way in which letters shall be dispatched," the most significant policy for the post. Among other rules, mail had to be "held up as little as possible" in order to avoid delays. The decree was well accepted: "It appears to us a good order and for our part (on many occasions) they have been held up for some hours and besides His Majesty will save much money and will be better and more quickly served."[35] Likewise, the regular departure of the ordinary meant that ambassadors and agents had to make their replies more quickly. Lack of punctuality had its price; if the information was not ready in time to be sent by the ordinary post then it had to be sent by special delivery at the expense of the sender.

---

[33] A.G.S., G.A., Leg. 115, f. 229: Antonio de Eraso to Gómez de Santillán, 12 July 1581.

[34] A.G.S., E., Leg. 1092, f. 3: Letter from the count of Miranda to the king. Naples, 5 January 1590.

[35] A.G.S., G.A., Leg. 141, f. 191: Gómez de Santillán to Antonio de Eraso. Seville, 23 January 1583.

The safety and secrecy of the mail was another of the great challenges facing the postal service. Couriers were fairly frequently assaulted and wounded by the enemies of the Spanish crown. The best way to prevent this was to avoid the dangers by choosing alternative less-trodden routes. "Much news concerning England and even Flanders, I cannot send to your Majesty because many days letters do not arrive as the routes are so dangerous."[36] Robbers, apart from the wounds they inflicted on the couriers, intercepted and stole the mail, compromising the interests of the crown. It was not difficult to relieve the couriers of their load as letters were normally transported in packets wrapped in cloth and placed in wooden boxes or in leather bags bearing the royal coat of arms.

Insecurity was greatest in France where the mail service suffered repeated setbacks. The quickest route between Flanders and Madrid crossed France, but since French territory was often divided by religious disturbances, the immunity of the couriers could never be guaranteed. In 1567, for example, couriers lived through awful times, when they were forced to use the German routes. Chantonnay, Philip's ambassador in Paris, regretted having sent ten cards and five duplicates to Madrid between 4 April and 11 May 1562 and not having received any replies. The area around Poitiers was well known for attacks on foreign couriers and for the attacks by the Huguenots on messengers sent by the French court. In that same decade, ambushes in that region had become endemic: in January 1560, a messenger was wounded; in August 1562 and in 1567 others were robbed and, more serious still, in August 1568, the Spanish courier, Villota, was murdered twelve leagues south of the city. The attempts of a Spanish captain, traveling from Poitiers to Madrid, to retrieve the stolen diplomatic mail were in vain.[37] Another problematic region for messengers in the service of the Spanish crown was the city of Orleans. In 1562, queen Catherine of France ordered that all mail should pass through this city. Chantonay was firmly opposed to this proposal because it meant that all couriers traveling north would have to pass through the unprotected region of the Loire, and he doubted the queen's ability to guarantee complete security. It soon seemed like madness to risk sending a messenger across France.

---

[36] A.G.S., E., Leg. 598, f. 128: Letter from the Duke of Parma to Philip II. Corbel, 21 October 1590.

[37] The Spanish captain Salazar arrived at the post at two o'clock in the morning when the unfortunate Villota had already been murdered together with the French messenger. Salazar's interest in recovering the stolen dispatches took him to Poitiers to inform the Bishop of the occurrence: "because he would give orders that the dispatches cross over to Spain in the hands of good messengers." Salazar continued on his way and once in Madrid wrote up his report on 8 September. John B. Allen, *Post and Courier Service in the Diplomacy of early Modern Europe* (The Hague, 1972), pp. 90–93.

In order to try and assure insofar as was possible the immunity of messengers in their journeys across Europe on foot, by horse, by cart, or by boat, they were issued with a sovereign passport to aid them in their travels across foreign lands; special mail couriers, who occasionally carried secret documents to Spain's ambassadors in London, were given an additional English passport.

Amongst the measures taken to confirm delivery of the dispatches, addressees were obliged to give or sign a delivery receipt and send it back with the same courier or at the first opportunity. The senders would write several copies of the letter of dispatch and send them by different routes and with each new mail a copy of the previous one was also sent. Up to five copies of the same letter were written by the Duke of Parma to the king in January 1590, probably due to the need to assure delivery to the court of an urgent petition for money.[38] Thanks to this procedure, information always arrived sooner or later at the court even though some of the copies may have been intercepted. Foreseeing this contingency, a system of codes was developed to make state plans or any other important information inaccessible to the enemy. The key to the code was altered as it was often discovered that the enemy had successfully deciphered it. In 1590, the Duke of Parma wrote to the king explaining that he had not sent the duplicate of a previous letter "as he did not dare to send it in the code since he had been advised that the first letter had been intercepted in France."[39] Urgency, security and codes required the work of skilled professional people—scribes and messengers, experts in coding and decoding, translators amongst others—at the service of the Secretary of State, who were able to decipher the coded information intercepted from other sovereigns and undertake translations of the abundant correspondence sent to the monarch from the most distant parts of the globe.

The inviolability and confidentiality of mail was explicit in the contractual agreements between the crown and the Tassis family. These agreements stipulated that the couriers be upright men, scrupulous in the performance of their duty. In the report of the post master of Portugal, Juan de Monte, this inviolable trait of private correspondence as one of the rights of the individual was already clear:

> I am reluctant to complain about the problems Govea has caused me recently by holding up my mail and "losing" documents of whose receipt I had been advised Neither do I like to complain about other letters which have been opened and letters of friends which have been opened to see if there were any letters of mine

---

[38] A.G.S., E., Leg. 598, f. 1–5: Letter from the duke of Parma to Philip II. Vinçe, 8 January 1590.

[39] A.G.S., E., Leg. 598, f. 14: Letter from the duke of Parma to Philip II. Brussels, 17 January 1590.

in the same package. This is damaging and prejudicial to the general good of the Republic. Taking away our natural and civil rights simply will not do. It cannot be done anywhere where there is a postal service. Every individual has a right to give and to send his letters whenever he pleases.[40]

The professionalism of Philip II's European postal system was proven on many occasions, when it was seen that the monarch received both more complete and more detailed information than any other European potentate. This was evident in dealings with the French ambassador Fourquevaux at the Spanish court (1562–72) who often found himself at a disadvantage because the king knew about events in France before he himself did. On 15 October 1569, Philip II "with a smile on his lips" announced to Fourquevaux in an audience that the royal French armies had won a great victory over the Protestants (in Moncontour, near Poitiers, 3 October). The news had first reached him in a letter written on 7 October by a Spanish agent in Lyon and the official confirmation of the victory arrived on 21 October thanks to a letter sent by the Spanish ambassador in France written on 6 October, whereas Fourquevaux received the news from his own government days later.[41]

But this professionalism was acquired at a cost to the crown. The service set up by the Tassis family depended on a monthly sum of money paid in advance by the Royal Treasury to cover the costs of horses, mules, and messengers. Before leaving, the courier received a sum from the treasury and upon his return the corresponding payment order was made out according to the time taken. More often than not the funds were advanced by the Tassis family and then the royal treasurer reimbursed the amounts paid out.[42] Generally speaking the money issued was inferior to the total expenditure in the month. The Tassis had to pay the necessary money in advance and then present a memorial of total expenditure before it was reimbursed. Despite the professional service and esteem in which the family was regarded by the king, the crown was often slow to pay its debts to the postal service. In 1582, the Royal treasury owed:

---

[40] A.G.S., G.A., Leg. 148, f. 151: Juan del Monte recounts the abuses of the courier Manuel de Govea.

[41] Geoffrey Parker, "Philip II, knowledge and power," *Military History Quarterly*, XI.1 (Autumn, 1998), 104–11 (Spanish translation in J.M. de Bernardo Ares (ed.), *El Hispanismo Anglonorteamericano: aportaciones, problemas y perspectivas sobre Historia, Arte y literatura españolas*, II (Córdoba, 2001), pp. 1085–1104; expanded Spanish version published in P. Navascués Palacio (ed.), *Philippus II Rex* (Madrid, 1998), 17–55.

[42] For all these services, the Tassis had received 11,000 gold *ducados* from the Emperor each year, 6,000 in Spain, 4,000 in Naples and the remaining 1,000 in Flanders, A.G.S., Consejo Real, Leg. 170.

562,000 maravedis for the journeys of couriers and the Post Master General requests payment of this sum and on occasion has been obliged to delay the dispatch of mail for want of money. We beg His Majesty to order that these 562,000 maravedis be taken from the coffers to pay for these journeys and for those dispatches that are sent out each day, the amount that your Majesty orders be withdrawn as the pay of the Couriers cannot be delayed, as they are poor, needy people.[43]

Each month Tassis sent a list of expenses to the Treasury Council for the payment of his debts. This was accompanied by a memorial insisting "that he had spent in the four months of this year (1588) more than ten thousand *ducados* and, not having received more than three thousand, had suffered financially."[44] In 1589, the sum paid out in the first five months of the year, was of 3,375,000 *maravedis*, but expenses amounted to 5,170,125 *maravedis*, as can be seen in the following table.

Table 1.1   Charge and data presented by Juan de Tassis. 6 July 1589, A.G.S., C. and J.H., Leg. 257

Funds received by the Royal Mail	Maravedis
January	750,000
February	750,000
March	750,000
April	750,000
May	375,000
TOTAL:	3,375,000
Expenditure in these Months	
January	341,375
February	964,500
March	874,875
April	1,043,625
May	1,545,750
TOTAL:	5,170,125
TOTAL OWED:	1,795,125

As from 1595, the accounts presented by Juan de Tassis became much more detailed. At the same time as recording each journey and its cost, he recorded the

---

[43] A.G.S., G.A., Leg. 123: José de Sotillo to the secretary Juan Delgado. Seville, 7 February 1582.

[44] A.G.S., Consejo y Juntas de Hacienda, C. and J.H., Leg. 247: Memorial presented by Juan de Tassis. 7 May 1588.

name of the person in charge of carrying the correspondence and his position (courier, foot messenger or other) and also explained the system of transport used and the addressees in the listings of the journeys. When a dispatch was sent "at speed" or "express" this meant by the fastest means possible, in other words by horse covering 30 leagues (about 150 km) in 24 hours; this extra speed added to the cost of the journey.

During the last few years of the reign of Philip II, expenditure on the postal service remained more or less stable between 7 and 8 million *maravedis*. However, in later years, the cost shot up, reaching 19 million *maravedis* in 1605.

Table 1.2   The accounts of Juan de Tassis from 1595–1607. A.G.S., G.A. 3rd época, Leg

Year	Total expenditure in maravedis
1595	7,090,726
1596	8,071,288
1597	7,635,523
1598	7,891,924

Expenditure on the postal service accounted for the "domestic" expenses, which was only one part of the court's expenses, which exceeded 500,000 *ducados* per annum during the reign of Philip II. From 1590 to 1600, the income of the crown was roughly 10 million *ducados* a year, five of which were spent wholly on the costs of war. The other five were to cover periodical costs of a non-defensive nature and among these figured not only the costs of the court or the "domestic" costs but also pensions and bonuses for civil servants, old soldiers and their families, artists and others.[45] Thus, it may be seen that the cost of the postal service represented only a relatively small, albeit significant part of the costs of the monarchy that were rising relentlessly.

Other Means of getting Information

Apart from the ordinary post, there were other channels of information that Philip II used when he saw fit.[46] When the king wished to collect accurate first-hand information, or perform specific tasks, he sent his own emissaries or agents. These representatives became real spokespersons for the king and champions, upon their return to the court, of any favor or need of the distant subjects or

---

[45]   Robert A. Stradling, *Europa y el declive de la estructura imperial española, 1580–1720* (Madrid, 1983), pp. 59–60.

[46]   These require much more study and analysis.

allies of the monarch. At the same time, their missions led to the exchange of information and ensured communication between the king and the vassals or allies in question. The support lent by Philip II to the Irish Catholics required as much reliable information to be gathered as possible on their situation and that of the island, to which end the king sent out emissaries who gave him precise information upon their return:

> His Majesty ordered a dispatch to be sent to Ireland which was entrusted to the services of Antonio de Cisneros who reports the following: that he found O'Donnell and the rest of those who followed the catholic party in very good spirits and they declared themselves most happy to hear the news that the armada was ready to sail to their aid and they made promises to die or defend themselves with the help of God at least until the beginning of June.[47]

To the official news was added the unofficial news that came to the king's ear from any person who sent news or arrived with news at the court: occasional travelers, captives and freed prisoners, commercial agents and others. Merchants maintained their own communications networks which served as a pipeline for political and commercial information; at the same time, the official messengers often picked up important information along the way which was added to the general flow of news.

Apart from the spy network, which requires a separate study, other significant sources of information were the clientele of ministers. The case of Eraso is considered one of the most exemplary because of the number of agents he had left at his service in Flanders after his stay in the Low Countries. Jerónimo de Curiel, Fernández de Zamora, and Juan López Gallo informed him of affairs relating to public finance and the Agustin monk, Lorenzo de Villavicencio kept him up to date with events that had occurred since his departure. All of them regularly passed on dramatic or juicy missives to Madrid with first-hand information concerning the situation in these territories.[48]

Communications with India and America

While the Spanish crown had an unprecedented information network in Europe managed by the Tassis family, a world-wide service was being set up

---

[47] A.G.S., E., Leg. 492, f. 1597.
[48] Francisco Javier de Carlos Morales, "El poder de los secretarios reales: Francisco de Eraso," in José Martínez Millán (ed.), *La corte de Felipe II* (Madrid, 1994), pp. 107–48.

and extended directly by the central administration for communication with the overseas empire. This maritime communication not only served to transmit news between various continents but also to consolidate the government of the Spanish monarchy thousands of kilometers away, at times in parallel with commercial transactions and at other times via private maritime journeys, which all led to improvements in inter-continental communications.

In 1580, the Portuguese colonial empire was incorporated into the Spanish empire, which for Philip II meant new dominions and spheres of influence around the Indian Ocean, which entailed new lines of communication. Communications as regular as those already established with India had to be maintained with the government of the Portuguese colonial territories in Malacca and Macao, and the use of these and other channels meant abundant correspondence in Portuguese soon began to arrive at the court in Spain.

The Portuguese had established regular communications between the Asiatic territories and the peninsula via a convoy of galleons that left Lisbon every year en route to Goa, the capital of Portuguese India. Philip used this system, known as the Portuguese route, to inform his new Asian subjects of the incorporation of Portugal into the Spanish crown. From that moment, the galleons became the umbilical cord of the metropolis with its Portuguese colonies and the lifeline through which the court in Madrid could deal with its affairs relating to the Indian viceroy, located in Goa, and other authorities belonging to the Portuguese territories.

One of the viceroy's duties was to send an annual general report describing all that had taken place during that time in those remote territories: "Over the last years I have written at length to Your Majesty concerning all that takes place here in this state. I will continue to keep you informed of all that happens and of all that I do."[49] Together with the general report, he used to send other letters about private matters or in answer to orders or petitions made by the king.[50]

The annual convoy, made up of some five vessels, arrived in India in September and left again in December after the autumn rains. So all the correspondence addressed to the court or to individuals had to be ready by these dates. It is significant that all the letters are dated at the end of November or beginning of December.[51] Those who wished to send letters to Spain from other cities had

---

[49] A.G.S., S.P., Book 1551, f. 81m, a general letter from Duarte Meneses, viceroy of India, Goa, 6 December 1587.

[50] "Replying jointly to what Your Majesty has asked me in this year's letters and in other more personal letters as I deem is warranted by affairs."

[51] All the correspondence sent in the annual galleon of December 1587 was dated between 23 November and 11 December. Ibid., f. 9.

to make haste and fleets of small vessels arrived in time for the departure of the galleons, normally around mid-December. The voyage that circumnavigated Africa following the Portuguese route lasted about ten months and for the court was the primary means of communication with those territories.

But there were also other means of communication with the Iberian Peninsula that could be used whenever the need arose. The so-called second route began by ship from India to the port of Ormus, at the entrance of the Persian Gulf, and then continued on by land by any means available. The so-called third route, the least used, reached the Iberian Peninsula after sailing across the Red Sea to Cairo and from there across the Mediterranean to Naples or Genoa where it linked up with the ordinary post.[52] Although some information was sent by the first two routes in duplicate, the second and third were rather less frequent, needing special protection, particularly the route which linked up with the strategic situation of Ormus. Insecurity in the area led the viceroy to insist on Philip II sending experienced captains to defend these strategic posts:

> I have informed Your Majesty on previous occasions of the importance for these states and for their postal service of selecting captains with the qualities necessary to lead certain forces, ... these forces are those of Ormus, firstly, Mozambique, Ceylon. Malacca and Andaman where Fernando Meneses Vello is now posted, but they are insufficient, are too lax and are utterly unused to this region.[53]

The land route, as the route to Ormus was known, was a more risky adventure than the others and the foot messengers who used this route recompensed the dangerous crossing by requesting regal favors in return for the services performed.

The defense of Spanish–Portuguese interests in the area forced the king to pay close attention to the movements of these peoples and their governors, their aims, battles, and confrontations, which gave rise to correspondence full of varied and exotic news arriving on Philip II's desk from the Asian world. "I have news of Equebar," writes the viceroy of India, "who is involved in wars with the Tartars and is building fortifications in certain passes, and there are also movements in Cambodia led by king Zinho Mudafar and his allies."[54]

---

[52] "At the beginning of last April I wrote to Your Majesty via El Cairo using an Italian courier, and at the end of the same month I sent mail from here to Julián de Costa via the Ormus route [...] I was moved to do this after the loss of the ship which I have related at length in another letter...." Ibid., f. 70.

[53] Ibid., f. 23.

[54] Ibid., f. 23.

Apart from troops in strategic locations, Portuguese commercial interests also required the maintenance of a large fleet in the Indian Ocean to control the coasts in this region:

> By last year's vessels, the viceroy of India again writes, explaining how he sent Martín Alonso de Mello with a large armada to the coast of Melinde to prevent the movement of the Turks and suppress the rebellion of some kings in the area [...] Don Martín Alonso then went on to Ormus where he found Basora to be causing no trouble, nor did the Jizaros (Arabian soldiers) or Arabs have any intentions to stay in the region since the expectations of the Turks had improved greatly in Persia following the death of the son of the Shah.[55]

The regularity of annual communication with the metropolis granted a certain freedom of movement to the viceroys and governors to take governmental decisions, although by naming the successor in advance, the king tried to forestall the contingency that arose when a viceroy had to be replaced without the king's authorization. When the viceroy of India, Duarte Meneses, died in 1588, the new governor, without waiting for the galleon, sent an Armenian with the news by the Ormus route, explaining that he was temporarily taking over until the king appointed another person. In December, with the departure of the galleon, he again sent a general letter to the king informing him once more of the events of May.

The arrival of the galleon in India with news from the Iberian Peninsula was awaited with great anticipation each year: "At the end of September of this year, this city of Bacay received news from Your Majesty with great rejoicing."[56] It was known that the journey was no easy task. The vessels had to overcome a great many dangers before reaching their destination.[57] Even greater difficulties faced land couriers who dared to cross Asia to the far west of Europe. This line of communication, which was successfully covered by various messengers, confirms, more than any other feature, the unprecedented web-like extent of the Spanish monarch's communications network. The tale of the courier Jorge Antonio de la Cruz is extremely illustrative. His three journeys on foot from Goa to the Spanish court and back during the reigns of Philip II and Philip III clearly show the extension of the Spanish empire throughout the world. Upon arrival in Genoa, the messenger–adventurer was the object of a thorough identification procedure, as they wrote from Genoa:

---

[55] Ibid., f. 34.

[56] Ibid., f. 188.

[57] On its return journey to the peninsula in 1586, the galleon lost one of its ships, the *Reliquias*, causing great alarm because of the large amount of information it was carrying.

> He is one of Your Majesty's couriers and carries correspondence from the viceroy of India for the king of Spain. He is 50 years old, is well built and strong and a native of Goa. He was educated in Ormus where he studied arts under the Jesuits and thus he learnt Latin which he speaks very well; since Ormus is a trade centre where there are merchants from many nations he also learned other languages; Chaldean, Persian, Turkish, Moorish, Greek, Italian, and Spanish and even the Indian language which is his native tongue, which means he can circulate freely everywhere.[60]

After this identification process he was questioned about his journey to Genoa and it was explained that:

> From Goa he came to Ormus, always by land, walking by day and most of the night. He took two months to complete the journey, about 500 leagues, which are 1,500 Italian miles …. He spent 4 days in Ormus and with the permission of the governor he continued on his journey back to Persia where he was received by the king of Persia in Ispahan (Isfahan) … He travelled across this region to the Caspian sea which is a distance of 500 leagues always by horse, oxen or dromedary by which means he sometimes covered 30 leagues. He boarded ship in Abescum and travelled 180 leagues to Sobran where he disembarked, and walked to the Black Sea, the sea of the Turks, and from there overland passing through Anatolia to Constantinople. There he took a French ship to Malta, from whence he went on to Sicily, was received by the viceroy, and then left for Naples. He continued by land to Rome where he was presented before the Catholic ambassador to the Pope whose feet he kissed …. He arrived in Genoa on the 20th August …. He said that two other messengers left Goa at the same time as him, with copies of the letters and that he had done this journey safely three times both coming here and returning to Goa.[58]

This account depicts the lines of communication that Philip II was obliged to employ to govern the old Portuguese colonies thousands of kilometers away. Given the enormous areas they covered, communication with Asian lands was costly, slow and, above all, unpredictable. Only on a few occasions was the service surprisingly fast, such as the first time the monarch used it to communicate his succession to the Portuguese crown. His letters dated 7 November 1580 in Badajoz, arrived in Goa on the 1 September 1581, just ten months later, and in Malacca on the 23 November. When these letters arrived in Macao, in March

---

[58] Godofredo Ferreira, *Account of a letter which came from the East Indies, leaving the city of Goa on 1 January 1608 and arriving at the city of Genoa on 20 August, transcription of a manuscript from the Ajuda Library in Lisbon* (Lisbon, 1953).

1582, the news of the succession of Philip had already reached them via Mexico and Manila.

The Pacific route via the Philippines and Acapulco, also known as the Manila Galleon or the Acapulco Ship, has been studied in depth. Its existence dates from 1566, two years after the discovery of the return journey from America making the most of favorable winds blowing from the east on the 27th parallel. Andrés de Urdaneta's[59] journey in 1564 connected Acapulco with the island of Guam (Mariana Islands) and Manila on a journey that used to take between 50 and 60 days.

The return to Manila, taking advantage of the so-called "return wind" was longer, between four and six months, due to the direction of the currents that carried ships towards the north.[60] The discovery of the return winds allowed the establishment of a regular line that maintained trade and communications between Spain–Mexico–Philippines and China up until 1815. The galleons left Acapulco towards February, arriving in Manila at the end of April or beginning of May and after a period in the Philippine capital left again in June, entering the port of Acapulco in December of the same year. The whole voyage lasted about nine months. In 1587, after the convoy of galleons had been attacked by Cavendish, Philip II ordered it to take the express route to reach Acapulco in the shortest time possible.

Once in Acapulco, goods and correspondence were transported from the Pacific coast, crossing Mexico by land, to Veracruz on the Atlantic coast. Once at Veracruz, bound for Seville, the mail was taken on board the *pataches* or mail boats, small rapid crafts that were not allowed to transport passengers, merchandise, or any other kinds of goods other than mail.[61] On the first voyage, the correspondence took just over eleven months to reach Madrid from the Philippines.

The departure of mail boats to New Spain soon became more regular. They normally left Seville (and Cadiz later on) at the beginning of January in groups of two bound for Veracruz with only one stopover at Puerto Rico to take on water. They stayed in Veracruz for two months, after which they sailed to Cadiz with a stopover at Havana. The following two ships left at the end of March or at the beginning of April, the third two on 15 June and the last two at the beginning

---

[59] The first voyage consisted basically of sailing from Acapulco in a southeasterly direction to reach the 12th parallel north and following this west taking advantage of the northeasterly trade winds.

[60] The return journey consisted of going in a northeasterly direction making the most of the Kuro–Shivo currents and the southeasterly winds from the Asian continent until the parallel 40º north where the ships headed east until Cape Mendocino in upper California, from where they sailed southeast along the coast to Acapulco.

[61] These news ships dated from the reign of Charles V who established them on 27 October 1525.

of November; periods which had the most favorable weather for these types of vessels. The crossing to Veracruz took about 30 days.[62] From 1561, the dangers of the crossing led to the ships sailing in a convoy of armed merchant vessels en route to India, returning to their ports of origin with the happy news of the arrival of the fleets.

The duration of the Atlantic voyage and its inherent dangers caused disruption and changes in government. In 1583, Diego de Menéndez complained to the king about not having been received as governor in Puerto Rico because the certificate of his appointment had been lost in a captured mail boat.[63] Private affairs and business were also affected by the distances between the metropolis and the colonies:

> Last year Your Majesty favored me with a reply to my letter requesting the granting of a license to go to this realm to do important business for the king as well as personal affairs. Your Majesty forwarded me to the viceroy Don Duarte who having died could do nothing, which leads me to make the same request to Your Majesty once more.[64]

Despite all the difficulties, news and the king's orders always reached even the most remote cities, albeit occasionally with a delay of one or two years.[65] The news of the defeat of the Great Armada finally reached Goa in November of 1589: "We have learned through the governor of Goa, Manuel de Sousa Coutinga, of the disastrous outcome of the Armada which Your Majesty sent with such affection and zeal to England."[66]

---

[62] Francisco Garay Unibaso, *Correos marítimos españoles* (4 vols, Bilbao, 1987), vol. 1 and 3.

[63] A.G.S., G.A., Leg. 144: "The title has not reached me [...]. I beg Your Majesty to send copies. I presented my letter to Your Majesty in council and requested that I be received by the governor. Juan Melgarejo who is currently the governor obstructed me and seeing his will the aldermen agreed with him." Diego de Menéndez to the king, Puerto Rico, 3 April 1583.

[64] A.G.S., S.P., Leg. 1551, f. 792.

[65] In November 1588, the letters from Goa reflected their unawareness of what had happened to the Spanish Armada: "From this year's vessels we know that the greatness of Your Majesty allows almighty God to grant you a long life to increase and govern your kingdoms and states and vassals in the east." A.G.S., S.P., Leg. 1551, f. 792, Don Enríquez to the king, Goa, 16 November 1588.

[66] 24 November 1589. A.G.S., S.P., Leg., 1551, f. 798.

Conclusion

The Spanish crown's centripetal communications systems provided Philip II with an unprecedented supply of information. The communications network that fanned out around the globe enabled him not only to exercise governance at a distance of thousands of miles, but also for the king to exercise his power, while the crown gained fame and prestige, which was upheld by a myriad of ambassadors and agents in the service "of the good and of the growth of the His Majesty's royal crown."

Philip II had at his disposal a mass of information, but at the same time, as suggested by Geoffrey Parker,[67] he suffered from an overabundance of information which threatened to overwhelm him. He was supplied with more data than a single mind could cope with. It remains to be proven whether this excess was one of the causes that led to the failure of the prudent king's great strategy.

Hundreds of letters and orders left the Spanish court day and night to destinations all over the world, and sooner or later their arrival would normally lead to the orders being complied with and put into effect thousands of kilometers away.

In the opposite direction, thousands of letters on the most diverse affairs arrived on Philip II's desk from almost everywhere in the world. Some letters, from sheiks, kings, and sultans, even made specific mention of vassalage to King Philip II.[68] Along with the many missives that reached his court from the far flung corners of his realms, came gifts such as pearls and precious stones, which clearly bear testimony to a monarch on whose communications infrastructure it was thought that the sun would never set.[69]

---

[67] Geoffrey Parker, *Felipe II: conocimiento y poder*. Paper presented in Burgos, 15 September 1997.

[68] Amongst the most significant are those entitled "Letter from your serf and loyal vassal sheik Ayocte, son of the king of Tuxaxa" and from the king of Cuco and the mountains known as Cidramar, a kinglet from the north of Africa, who "has written to me notifying me of his desire to develop a friendship with Your Majesty, because he says his father was a friend of Your Majesty's father, the emperor." A.G.S., S.P., Book 1551, fol. 161.

[69] A.G.S. E., Leg. 492: "Who gave two letters, one for Your Majesty and the other for the princess with a green stone that he says is estimated to be worth 2,000 escudos." Julio Felipe Romana to the king.

CHAPTER 2

News Networks between Italy and Europe

Mario Infelise

For a number of centuries, or at least from the fifteenth to the eighteenth, European political information took the material form of handwritten newssheets in which political and military news, likely to be of public interest, were collected periodically. Hence a market for information originated and developed over a long period of time, characterized by manual reproduction, which, as we shall see, had considerable advantages over printed forms. Printed gazettes became widespread from the first decades of the seventeenth century; but in the period under examination here these were entirely dependent upon the handwritten versions.[1]

The Genesis of Handwritten Newsletters

It is likely that the news-sheet emerged and evolved as an offshoot of mercantile information. It is well-known that the great merchants of the thirteenth and fourteenth centuries enjoyed broad networks of contacts and held systematic correspondence with one another. The impressive archive belonging to the Prato merchant Francesco Datini (1335–1410), comprising 140,000 letters from 285 different European and Mediterranean cities is clear evidence of the systematic nature of these contacts.[2] This correspondence did not however merely convey commercial or economic items connected with the mutual relationship between

---

[1] On the handwritten journalism and on the circulation of information in Early Modern Europe see Mario Infelise, *Prima dei giornali. Alle origini della pubblica informazione* (Roma–Bari: Laterza, 2002) and *Cultural exchange in Early Modern Europe*, III: *Correspondence and Cultural Exchange in Europe*, edited by Francisco Bethencourt and Florike Egmont (Cambridge: Cambridge University Press, 2007), especially the articles of M. Infelise, Z. Barbarics and R. Pieper, F. Trivellato.

[2] Jérôme Hayez, "L'archivio Datini. De l'invention de 1870 à l'exploration d'un système d'écrits privés," *Mélanges de l'école française de Rome. Moyen Âge*, CXVII/1 (2005): 121–91. On economic information between the Middle Ages and Early modern periods: M. Infelise, "La circolazione dell'informazione commerciale," in Franco Franceschi, Richard A. Goldthwaite, Reinhold C. Mueller (eds), *Il Rinascimento italiano e l'Europa*, IV: *Commercio e cultura mercantile* (Treviso–Costabissara: Fondazione Cassamarca, Angelo Colla, 2007), pp. 499–522.

the writers but, in the normal course of exchanging information, included news concerning the great political events of the time. Already in 1419 Antonio Morosini had written from Venice to Biagio Dolfin, the Republic's Consul in Alexandria, Egypt, on the subject of events occurring at that time in Europe, using a form which not far different from the one which actual political news-sheets were to assume in later times. What is more, the public oral divulgation of the contents of newsletters of this kind appears to have already been common practice.[3]

In the course of the fifteenth century in other areas, indeed, we begin to hear more frequently of news-sheets aimed expressly at keeping readers regularly abreast of political and military events. Dispatches from ambassadors to the Italian courts in the second half of the fifteenth century often make reference to passages taken from letters from merchants and other correspondents which were put together and sent with a certain regularity. Among the papers of the Duke of Ferrara in the State Archive in Modena there are sheets from the period, which carry headings such as "A copy in several chapters of news in letters from Bruges starting 7th and ending 31st December [1464]," "Summary of letters from France [1495]" and "Summary of letters from Rome," below which follows random news of a general political kind, gathered from various sources.[4]

The Newsletter System

In the same years we begin to hear of professional compilers of such news-sheets. Between 1470 and 1480 the Florentine Benedetto Dei maintained an extensive web of contacts with prominent figures of his age to whom he wrote succinct reports in a style not dissimilar to that of the papers in the Modena archive.[5] Of merchant stock, Dei as a young man had performed political duties of modest importance. These involved gathering secret information in favor of Florence and against Venice. In the middle years of his life he traveled at length throughout the Mediterranean, venturing along the Sahara desert roads as far as Timbuktu and also living in Constantinople, gaining along the way a wide experience of the

---

[3] Georg Christ, "A Newsletter in 1419? Antonio Morosini Chronicle in the Light of Commercial Correspondence between Venice and Alexandria," *Mediterranean Historical Review*, 20 (2005): 35–66.

[4] "Copia de più capitoli di novele in littere da Brugia. Comenzata a 7 e finita a 31 de dicembre [1464];" "Summario de lettere di Francia [1495];" "Sommario de lettere da Roma." Archivio di Stato di Modena, *Cancelleria ducale, avvisi e notizie dall'estero*, 1–3.

[5] On Benedetto Dei see the article by R. Barducci in *Dizionario Biografico degli Italiani*, vol. 36 (Roma, Istituto dell'Enciclopedia Italiana, 1988) pp. 252–3; Paolo Orvieto, "Un esperto orientalista del 400: Benedetto Dei," *Rinascimento*, 20 (1969): 205–75.

Italian colonies in the Levant. On his return to Italy he was able to take advantage of the extraordinary network of relationships he had built up and maintained in the course of his busy life, lending himself as a systematic informant concerning anything going on. Hence he would assemble all the relevant news he was able to gather and set it out all in one in multiple handwritten copies, scores of which he would send off to correspondents all over Italy in exchange for an agreed sum.

This system went on to improve in the course of the sixteenth century. In cities such as Rome and Venice professional writers at the hub of an articulated network of correspondence drew up news-sheets which put together events gathered both from letters and other news-sheets received by post as well as news they wrote themselves. The resulting compilations were then reproduced in quantity at copyists equipped for that very purpose. Once ready they were sent to Italy and Europe by postal couriers whose arrival and departure led to dates of issue becoming more regular. At the same time the reorganization and consolidation of postal services began to guarantee delivery times.

Halfway through the sixteenth century the system had become defined in its general outline. Certain large European cities tended to take on the role as centers of production and circulation of such writing. These were cities where there was a convergence of wide networks of political, diplomatic, religious, and commercial relationships like, for example, Rome and Venice in Italy, Paris in France, Cologne and Frankfurt in Germany, Antwerp in Flanders, and Amsterdam in Holland. In these cities a veritable market for information grew up, wherein various professionals competed with one another, all able to offer their own written works to anyone able to afford them—especially ambassadors, who used the sheets to write the dispatches they had to send back to their respective courts (although subscribers also included great churchmen, nobles, and merchants).

In a city such as Venice a market of this kind was centered around the offices of the scribes and all those who made copies for a living. Although many often went no further than the passive reproduction of news-sheets drawn up by others, the most organized managed to set up veritable information agencies. Through the postal services, they received correspondence and other news-sheets from abroad, and to these they added a local section, put together for the most part by gathering any news that might emanate from centers of power where couriers and dispatches arrived from all parts of Europe and the Mediterranean, but also drawing on news filtered through the network of merchants and ships arriving in port.

At the end of the sixteenth century, the taking root and consolidation of this new profession led also to the fixing of names for the folios containing news. In Italian the most usual term between the fifteenth and sixteenth centuries was the generic *avviso* (notice), which did not however distinguish between the object and its content. A German *avviso* could be at one and the same time a news-sheet carrying various *nuove* (news) coming from Germany or, more simply, a single piece of news from Germany. In Venice the term *reporto* was widely used with the same meaning, which was then carried to England as the word *report*. Consequently *reportista* (reporter) was synonymous with a compiler of newsletters or gazettes. In Rome from the mid-sixteenth to the end of the seventeenth century, the expression *menante* enjoyed great favor to denote a writer of handwritten work. Around 1560 the word *gazzetta* began to be recorded but seemed for many decades to be primarily a term belonging to the spoken language to refer to those news-sheets without any great credibility which might circulate in the city. The definition given to the term by John Florio in his Italian–English dictionary *A Worlde of Wordes* of 1598 (a work sensitive more to common usage and expressions of dialectal origin than to educated usage) is most significant; under the Italian entry for the plural form *gazzette* there is a precise definition: "the daily newse or intelligence written from Italie, tales running newes." Florio records another two connected terms: the verb *gazzettare* meaning "to write or report daily occurencees one to another, to tell flying tales" and the profession of *gazzettiere* defined as "an intelligencer or such as have daily occurrences."[6] However it was evidently in those very years that the use of such sheets began to spread beyond court circles so that in the second edition of 1611, Florio added to the previous definition of *gazzettiere* the words "flim flam tales that are daily written from Italie, namely from Rome and Venice." The role of the *gazzettiere* himself was also changing. He ceased being an "intelligencer" and became simply a "writer or reporter of gazettes."[7] It must be of further significance that towards the end of the sixteenth century Francis Bacon in his own correspondence uses the Italian term *gazzetta* rather than a matching English term or the anglicised word "gazette."[8]

John Florio's definitions well illustrate the ambiguities surrounding these works, which from being secret information documents read in seats of power were turning into newsletters written for a public readership. The gazetteer, originally part copyist and part spy and in any case dealing only in court circles, ambassadors' chancelleries, and prominent figures in European capitals, managed increasingly to forge new relationships with a widening readership, allowing the formation of a veritable market for information.

---

6   John Florio, *A Worlde of Wordes* (London: Blount, 1598), p. 145.
7   John Florio, *Queen Anna's New Worlde of Wordes* (London: Bradwood, 1611), p. 205.
8   Francis Bacon, *The Letters and the Life* (London: Longman, Green, Longman and Robert, 1862) vol. II, p. 32, letters to Antony Bacon 15 and 20 May 1596.

A Profession is Born

Yet what were the daily tasks of a professional gazetteer in the seventeenth century? We can gain an insight into the ordinary routine of a *studio di reporti* (literally a "report studio"), to use an expression common in Venice, from documents left by Giovanni Quorli, a gazetteer who was very active in Venice immediately after the middle years of the seventeenth century. His news-sheets enjoyed wide circulation in Europe and were also taken up fairly systematically in the pages of printed gazettes.[9]

There are few biographical details available on Quorli. Born at the start of the century in some territory of the Papal States, he gained experience in writing news-sheets in Florence, where it was said he had been banned. He had a son, engaged in the Rome Curia, who enjoyed a certain reputation as the author of a confutation of Paolo Sarpi's history of the Council of Trent, which came out before the confutation by Sforza Pallavicino.[10]

Giovanni Quorli lived in Venice between 1652 and 1668 where he ran a gazette newsroom, often using false names as cover. In this period he did not work alone but had Venetian partners who lent a hand in running the office. Around 1655 records show he was in partnership with Ferigo Steffanino, a priest of the San Cassiano church and well known as pro-empire and anti-Venetian and whose news-sheets also circulated in France. Quorli later worked in partnership with another gazetteer, Paolo Angelelli, to whom he left the running of the office in 1668 when, for reasons which are unclear but inevitably connected to his profession and the nature of his news-sheets, he was forced to leave Venice in all haste. Certainly, in abandoning Venice he had no time to put his affairs in order; thus, from the pair's correspondence in subsequent years we gain many insights into the organization and running of a gazetteer's newsroom.

The office had a good number of clients spread around Europe. Every week Quorli would supply around 60 subscribers with 245 news-letters chosen from those of Venice, Paris, Rome, Milan, London, Vienna, and Cologne. The first pages were drawn up originally by the gazetteer, who wrote them after frequenting the Venetian patricians and those areas of the city, such as St Mark's Square in front of the Doge's Palace, where dispatches arrived from ambassadors throughout Europe. The other news was compiled on the basis of handwritten or printed gazettes received from all over Europe, purchased in cash or acquired in exchange from those very same contacts. The clientele was

---

[9] On Quorli see Infelise, *Prima dei giornali*. The documents quoted are in Venice, Archivio di Stato, *Avogaria di Comun*, Miscellanea civile, b. 233, fasc. 13.

[10] Filippo Quorli, *Historia concilii tridentini ex eademmet historia confutata adversus Petrum Suavem Polanum* (Venice: Ercole Tommaso Montini, 1655).

inarguably prestigious. It counted illustrious members of the highest German imperial nobility such as the Prince of Brunswick, the Count of Auersperg, foreign minister to Emperor Leopold I, the Count of Windisch–Graetz, Vice-Chancellor of the Empire, the Counts of Liechtenstein, Lodron, and Colloredo, as well as Prince Lobkowitz. There were also prince-bishops such as Maximilian Heinrich of Bavaria, elector and archbishop of Cologne, and Wenzelaus von Thun, bishop of Passau, and important diplomats such as Count Franz von Pötting, the imperial ambassador to Madrid. Noble Italian families were certainly present and came mostly from the area of the Paduan plain. These included the Duke of Mirandola as well as the Serbelloni, Martinengo, and Sarego families. There were also prominent Spanish functionaries such as Sebastián de Ucedo, secretary of war to the governor of Milan, and also heads of the postal service such as Baron Tassis and Marquis Manzoli di Modena, not to mention other names more difficult to identify but mostly German. Around half the clients, comprising the most illustrious, demanded the complete set of sheets, and for this they paid a subscription of 30 ducats a year. Lesser clients made do with a selection, in some very rare cases limited to a single series, at a minimum cost of 5–10 ducats. According to Quorli's calculations, the cost of running the office amounted to 11 ducats a week, 572 a year, and was made up of the cost of buying foreign news-sheets, the payment of writers employed, postal charges and office rental. Gross income reached 1,179 ducats without counting those who paid in kind in quite contrasting ways, including those giving in exchange certain foreign news-sheets, those making an undisclosed "gift" or granting more or less "special" favors, perhaps a barrel of wine or, like the Count of Sissa, "three pairs of hose." After customs duty 590 ducats would have been left.

Overall income was not negligible and well beyond the average salary of a master glass maker of the time. Concerning the accuracy of this figure there were, however, divergent opinions. Paolo Angelelli, Quorli's partner, who wished to slim down the value of the company while negotiations were taking place for the splitting of the partnership, remarked that the business was not profitable; for while it was true that clients were many, they were not always prompt in the payment of their subscriptions. If everyone had paid regularly, profit could have reached 350 ducats but the figure remained hypothetical. Besides, the gazetteer had very few means available to obtain what was owed for services rendered.

Such figures were therefore only theoretical. As mentioned above, they presupposed prompt payment and continued subscriptions. However the collection of money owed was not always simple and the means to do so barely existed, to the extent that it was not always worthwhile to abruptly cut off all ties to illustrious defaulting subscribers. As Angelelli wrote: "We meet resistance in collecting debts." Subscription renewals took place at the start of the New Year.

At Christmas subscribers were sent a letter wishing them glad tidings and at the same time were reminded of the expiry of their subscription. At times this delicate approach was not enough. For six years from 1663 Count von Pötting received news-sheets weekly and around 20 other publications in Madrid without ever bothering to pay for them. Quorli had often enjoined von Pötting's relatives in Vienna to help and the latter sent back encouraging replies but it was not enough to persuade the diplomat to pay the 150 *ongari* balance of the total account, to the point that Quorli was forced to threaten that he would withdraw his services.

Sixty subscribers was a high figure. Other *reportisti* were able to survive with a more limited client base. However, the smaller the number of clients, the greater importance each single subscriber came to have, especially in terms of income. This gave rise to fierce competition between those *reportisti* who were able to furnish the same service at the same level. Indeed these *reportisti* very frequently accused one another of stealing clients and of unfairly copying gazettes. Even the loss of one single client could upset the company. Some years after the events surrounding Quorli, another *reportista,* Giambattista Marchesati, who used to supply news-sheets to very well-known clients such as the Savoy Court, the historian Girolamo Brusoni and high prelates of the Roman Curia, on hearing the news that Cardinal Flavio Chigi no longer intended to purchase his sheets, tried to make the illustrious client take pity on him by writing to Chigi that "that occupation is the sole provider for my poor dwelling with mother and sister."[11]

The importance of each single subscriber depended also on the high unit cost of each subscription. Investigating the costs of newsletters is, however, a delicate operation because of the fragmentary nature of the data available and the difficulty of comparing values that are never homogeneous. The conditions of sale are rarely made public in their entirety and even when certain data are available it is not always possible to take all variables into account; some of these such as postal charges might make a considerable difference. The annual fee to subscribe to Quorli's news-sheets was of five ducats for each series. Most clients however took out a subscription for all seven sheets that the gazetteer had to offer, at a total cost of 30 ducats a year. It is difficult to make comparisons with other situations. The cost of handwritten gazettes could vary widely according to the hand involved and their overall reliability. In 1670 Giovanni Quorli wrote from Florence to admonish his partner in Venice for spending as many as 16 doubloons for a newsletter packed full of "back-stabbing and spicy fact" when he was able procure for 25 *giullii* the same news-sheet that the Venetian

---

[11] Biblioteca Apostolica Vaticana, *Archivio Chigi. Corrispondenze*, 32, fols. 419–21, letters of September 1685. On Marchesati Venice, Archivio di Stato, *Inquisitori di Stato*, 452, 22 February 1678; 566, 5 and 19 July 1677.

ambassador had bought from the Pope and all "pondered subject matter, good and political." Aside from the quality, the cost could also depend on direct negotiations between gazetteer and client. The latter might supply other news or goods in order to pay less or as an alternative to money changing hands. Between 1594 and 1640 the Republic of Lucca paid between 15 and 50 Lucca *scudi* a year to *reportisti* providing news. The figure depended on the gazetteer's reputation. Lucio Aresi, a "most capable news writer" from Venice able, according to Fulvio Testi, to "penetrate the darkest and most deeply concealed things," provided his reports to Lucca for 50 *scudi* while being tempted to offer his services to the Duke of Modena in return for two goblet plates worth 35 ducats. In addition to the annually agreed fee, a sort of honorarium was made at the end of the year which, going by Luca Assarino's words in writing to the Great Chancellor of Lucca about sending his secret notices, was customary for all Europe's reporters.[12] In 1701 the Duke of Mantua paid six ducats for a six-month subscription to the Venetian gazette by Antonio Minummi and between 1709 and 1710 the Duke of Modena sent six doubloons to Pietro Donà for a presumably similar gazette.[13]

Beyond the variations between one publication and another, subscription costs were in any case always kept high to the extent that they were beyond the reach of a middle-class readership. The 30 ducats a year which most of Quorli's clients were willing to spend were as many as ten more than the average rent of a dwelling in Venice. Yet popular enjoyment of the gazettes did not depend on subscription costs. The publication of each news-sheet was followed, after some delay, by further copies and city-dwellers could partake without significant inconvenience by means of public readings. Evidence for this is widespread; it is suffice to say the writer Secondo Lancellotti wrote that the great thing about gazettes was that they allowed one to find out about the world's affairs while spending nothing.[14]

In addition, the copy offices ended up becoming centers of collection, reproduction and distribution for products connected with information which it was not advisable to send to the printers for reasons of censorship. Indeed political production and becoming versed in the art of politics itself required other instruments. For this reason a good copy office, beyond drawing up its weekly gazettes, was able to supply on commission a catalogue of fairly broad writings on different subjects, although generally speaking of a political or

---

[12] Infelise, *Prima dei giornali*, p. 41.

[13] Mantua, Archivio di Stato, *Archivio Gonzaga*, 1584, 28 May and 10 December 1701; Archivio di Stato di Modena, *Cancelleria. Estero. Ambasciatori, agenti e corrispondenti dall'estero*, Venezia, 138, 14 September 1709, 8 November 1710.

[14] Secondo Lancellotti, *L'hoggidì, overo gl'ingegni non inferiori a' passati* (Venezia: Valvasense, 1681) vol. 2, p. 352.

satirical nature. For example there was great demand for Venetian ambassadors' reports in which there was a most lively trade in Italy and Europe, kept alight by the reputation these reports enjoyed, a reputation we witness still today through the large amount of contemporary copies held in libraries throughout the world. Despite these texts being long and complex and despite oft-repeated bans, there was always lively trade in them and, shortly after their presentation to the Council, they ended up on sale in the copy offices and not even then in a particularly secretive fashion. From the last decades of the sixteenth century, this was normal business with vast international ramifications. Copies were quickly made and were shortly after distributed to correspondents in Italy and abroad. In March 1665 the gazetteer Benedetto Giuliani was offering Pietro Basadonna's Rome report of a few months previously. He used this opportunity to present a long list of other reports from Rome, Spain, France, and Germany, "all marvelous," at "so much a page," both for old ones and those "right up to date."[15] When one did not succeed in obtaining an original text rapidly enough, the problem was dealt with by the none-too-strict practices of reporters and book sellers. In 1662 and 1664 an apocryphal report from Rome by Angelo Correr enjoyed wonderful success between Amsterdam and London. This had nothing to do with the original and ended up being printed beyond Italy, first in Italian and then in the course of a few months translated into French, Latin, and English.

The range of tasks performed in a gazetteer's office meant that the owner or partners paid different employees to carry out different duties. The documentation left by Quorli also enables us to unearth evidence to understand the inner workings of the office and relationships with the office's employees and clients. Apart from the owner, the office was the place of work of a manager and a fair host of copiers whose job it was to materially reproduce the gazettes. The presence of such a labor force meant that the gazetteer had to take care of a number of issues. It was necessary to maintain the secrecy of the portfolio of clients and the integrity of the texts in order to avoid unfaithful employees stealing texts or subscribers' names. The general rule was to have confidence in no one. "Do not trust anybody," was Quorli's advice to the manager of his copy office, Paolo Angelelli, while explaining how to produce and send the newsletters. The manager had to write the original gazette which was then handed to the copyists who reproduced it. However, the addresses of the recipients were to be written only by the owner, who in this way could check the work of his copyists, who were sometimes led to lighten the weight of the news-sheets. The illegal reproduction of written work brought even greater risks. In order to protect the

---

[15] Mantua, Archivio di Stato, *Archivio Gonzaga*, 1574, 7 March 1665.

long-term value of news-sheets, the gazetteer had to check their circulation and make unauthorized copying more difficult. Here again it was unwise to trust employees. Hence it was not beneficial to let a copyist work on an entire text or allow it to be copied outside the office. In any case it was always good practice for the owner to keep the beginning to himself. The same applied to the dispatch of the batches of documents, which never should be entrusted to third parties.

Linked to these issues were certain graphic and stylistic points to which the purchasers showed themselves particularly sensitive. The writing had to be legible without effort. Loyal customers became irritated by changes in handwriting and or by any that was too "minute." Antonio Minummi reached the stage of having to justify the illness of his usual copyist to the Duke of Modena, who was vexed by an unfamiliar passage written by the copyist's replacement.[16] It was also best to write in large letters so, as Quorli put it "Germans and the elderly might understand." Nor should spelling neglected, as reports often contained too many mistakes.

Quorli's practical suggestions for the writing of news-sheets were added to the current advice on the style to be adopted in letters of news. This advice was also to be found in treatises for secretaries and followed models which were by then well established. A dry, essential style had characterized this form of writing from its origins. The passage of time had barely altered the principal requirement of clarity and concision which, at the height of the seventeenth century, lay in stark contrast to the Baroque models of literary prose. Writing on current affairs demanded simplicity and efficacy and must not fall into the slovenliness for which it was often reproached. It had no foolish ambition therefore to "delight with poetic license" but rather a need to lay out the facts "with sentences in brief." Ettore Scala, one of the many compilers of historical–geographical reports of the period's ongoing wars, used material of this kind as his primary source and felt obliged to beg the forgiveness of his readers for using "words not of the Crusca" taken hastily from "the most recent notices of a Germanic reporter."[17] He justified this recourse not by "accident of the pen" but by "current usage." The statement of facts had therefore to be "clear, significant and ordered," thanks also to "one's own turn of phrase," that is to say using habitual terms "having the strength and faculty to express and represent." In order to facilitate clarity it was necessary to divide the subject up into "distinct items" based on the model of the life of Caesar of Suetonius.[18] The writer Tommaso Costo was insistent on this very point as "it is an annoying and awkward thing … when a

---

[16] Mantua, Archivio di Stato, *Archivio Gonzaga*, 1584, 29 April 1702.
[17] Ercole Scala, *L'Ungheria compendiata* (Venice: Pittoni, 1687).
[18] Panfilo Persico, *Del segretario* (Venice: Combi e La Noù, 1662), pp. 186–95.

letter containing many items is written as uninterrupted prose."[19] Digressions, repetitions, and superfluous words were to be avoided. The same care was to be taken over the formal layout. It was a sound idea to eliminate abbreviations; and where corrections were made, these had to be evident and not concealed ("never shave a page's surface but rather score out and write above"). In the case of letters made up of several pages it was best to number them and not enclose them one inside the other; when they referred to events occurring at different times "the day should be marked in the margin." The language used should create no difficulties. Notices from abroad, when not already in Italian, were translated. Those gazetteers with subscribers abroad did not let this issue worry them for they sent them the same newsletters they sent to their local client. If anything, it was the task of the recipient to make a version in the local language.

Returning to Quorli, we gain an idea from his papers of the caution required in writing drafts. In particular it was important to avoid "items from Venice you might be hanged for" and "items from Rome leading to the Inquisition." Experience suggested being very wary of the Venetian political authorities and the need to maintain good relations with the magistrates of the *Inquisitori di Stato*. Placing in the gazettes unverified or unwelcome news might determine an immediate summons either by the *Inquisitori* or by the heads of the Council of Ten, which could end in expulsion from the state. However, it was not always possible to resolve the issue by simply ignoring a piece of news, especially when it was on everybody's lips around the city. Every gazetteer was aware that this was one of the risks of the job and that he had to maneuver between the need for rapid information and the danger of conveying news that was better not to write. This fine line was not easy to keep when, as often occurred, it was necessary to choose between keeping silent and thus disappointing the clients or trusting unconfirmed rumors and running the risk of being contradicted.

Care needed to be taken too in personalizing the newsletters. One of the reasons not to be discounted for the long survival of the handwritten system of information lay in the flexibility and the ability to adapt quickly to the demands of each client. There were those who required numerous gazettes to be put together while others, for reasons also of economy, desired less information or only selected news items. Quorli was well aware of the need to protect the interests of the illustrious clients he served; and the necessity to avoid spreading news that these same clients would not appreciate was part of this. For someone with political responsibilities, building a bond with a *reportista* enjoying wide circulation for his newsletters was also a way of preventing any damaging news from reaching Europe. This bond implied a guarantee which a good gazetteer

---

[19] Tommaso Costo, *Lettere* (Venezia: Barezzi, 1602), p. 370.

had inevitably to sustain. The Vice Chancellor of the Empire, the Count of Windisch-Graetz, was one such client. He would buy seven weekly gazettes for the usual 30 ducats. It would not have been appropriate to write "an article against him" in the Milan gazette. Quorli concluded by saying that "One must be warned against writing anything prejudicial against those we serve." Quorli's advice was in some ways the counterpart of the "institution," ("necessary for a happy life"), then widespread in the courts of Europe, according to which it was vital "to treat with kid gloves the news gatherers and writers who carry on their trade in the houses and courts of princes so that they might praise you and also expect praise themselves in public." Even though gazetteers were often vile and despicable people, a good courtier would do well to take into account their ability to influence others.[20]

From Script to Print

Over the whole period of time under consideration, the material form of the handwritten gazette underwent little change. Its constituent parts, graphic layout, and the criteria for presenting subjects in order remained identical to the extent that they were taken up wholesale in the first printed versions of the seventeenth century. The gazette opened with a heading comprising the date and the place where the news was gathered. There followed a series of brief paragraphs written in the most essential terms possible and laid out in random order which was not that of the origin of the news. The material was not reworked unless in the most superficial of ways. Re-working was minimal and usually, if there no political demands, was conditioned only by the size of the page.

Form and Structure

As research stands, it is not easy to go further than these considerations. Comparisons with and systematic checking of entire series of handwritten gazettes is indispensable in order to reconstruct and the paths and transformations which news underwent in passing from one gazette to another. From this perspective it would in fact be useful to be able to examine the main series of gazettes held in the archives and libraries of Europe. Indeed only a wide document base would allow us to reconstruct the phenomenon in all its

---

[20] Biblioteca Apostolica Vaticana, *Ottob. lat. 2246, Raccolta fatta in diverse corti dell'Europa d'avvertimenti et instruttioni necessarie per poter ben vivere in quelle*, fol. 190v.

complexity. Handwritten and printed gazettes carried texts which were never attributed to a single author. As we have seen, they were always the result of progressive modification which led to radical transformation in the course of their progress. Hence each text and each news-sheet were the result of different input by several writers, some deliberate and some less so, mainly as a result of the system of handwritten reproduction and of the haste with which every gazetteer had to act, given that couriers were always departing and arriving and with the inevitable delays. In addition, only drawing a truly European picture will allow us to see the span of the network in its entirety and to pick out the places which at different times served as a connecting point for more limited local networks. Again, the lack of a catalogue of similar material prevents us from finding out about other mechanisms linked to their function. Hence we can still say little about the evolution and transformations of the texts, about the languages prevalently in use, about translations from one language to another and about the inevitable linguistic and cultural transfers determined by this massive, systematic production of written texts.

It is difficult, therefore, to go much beyond hypotheses. A starting point might be to consider the structure and organization of the gazette. Generally speaking, the size is variable. In contrast to most printed gazettes which were conditioned by the size of a printing sheet, handwritten sheets could come in different sizes. The work of Quorli himself and his price list show that his gazettes were of various sizes according to the demands of the client. Indeed it is true that it was very often convenient to stay within the four sheets of a half-folio folded once. On average each side of a sheet could contain the equivalent of 1,700–1,800 letters. The resulting four pages could therefore hold around 6,800–7,200. Each news-sheet, introduced by place and time (for example Venice, 29 May 1610), was divided into a series of reports reaching the editing office from other localities. The former were referred to in Italian as *capitoli* (chapters) or *bollettini* (bulletins). Every "chapter" was in its turn headed by further dating and also often carried the means by which the information was delivered: "from Paris, on the 27th of this month, we have …;" "Particular letters from Prague dated the 15th state …;" "On Saturday at around 10 pm a special courier from Turin arrived."

It would be very useful in understanding the characters and styles of composition to check the gazettes drawn up by a single copy-shop and to compare them with others originating in the same city, just as it would be interesting to follow a news item through its successive phases. At the current time nothing of this kind is possible. Yet we may gain some ideas by examining certain Venetian gazettes which were very likely born in the same copy-shop. The Venetian state archive holds, in certain rare cases, different copies of a news-sheet dated the same day. For example five copies remain of one dated 29 May 1610; it is as well a news-sheet of considerable importance because it contains the news of the assassination in Paris of King Henry IV and this fact allows us to make some additional remarks.[21]

The first of the five *avvisi* contains 13 *capitoli*. In order of presentation we find news from Prague contained in undated "particular letters," from Nancy dated 7 May, from Florence on the 15th, from Milan giving news from Spain dated 19 April, from Genoa on the 15th, from Vienna on the same day, from Prague again on the 17th, from Paris on the 14th, arriving by special courier, and again from Milan dated the 26th. There were also two items of news gathered in Venice, probably written by the gazetteer himself. It seems clear that the writer, used to writing one newsletter a week, wrote the edition as the reports arrived in Venice and worked until Saturday, which was both closing and publication day. It happens, therefore, that we very often find two *capitoli* from the same place but with different dates, as we have seen in the cases of Prague and Milan. In addition, comparison with other reports of the same day allows us to see that each *capitolo* was the result of a single work of composition, a sign that at the origin there was a single editorial team. This does not mean that the texts were absolutely identical. There were obvious variations in spelling, particularly in the case of foreign place names. Single words could also change, either because they were misunderstood in one of the editings or else deliberately altered. The cutting of parts of news items could also occur, here too by accident in the copying stage when it was thought necessary to shorten a text for reasons of space. In any case, in order to reduce the length of a *capitolo*, whole parts were cut (a chapter, a parenthesis or an entire paragraph). This was never achieved by summary or abridgement. The outcome of such changes could lead to heavy distortion of the original item, and omitted words and other misunderstandings might produce a version barely recognizable compared to the original. In the five gazettes under examination, the chapters are laid out following the same order. Yet here too there can be variations. One *capitolo* might be skipped while another might be brought forward or inserted later, probably the outcome of how the copying had been organized. We may presume that on occasion the copy manager personally dictated the text. Other times, while he was engaged in writing or checking correspondence he had received, he would try to speed up the copying process by circulating around the copy shop the previously-written chapters on separate sheets, leading therefore to an imperfect matching of the order in which news was presented.

---

[21] Venice, Archivio di Stato, *Inquisitori di Stato*, 704.

Further remarks can be made from the *capitolo* on the assassination of Henry IV of France. The king had been wounded on the evening of 14 May 1610 in Paris. Death occurred several hours later in the course of the night. The extraordinary news of his attack obviously reverberated immediately around the French capital. The Venetian ambassador Antonio Foscarini found out straightaway and even before learning of the king's demise he began to draw up a dispatch which was finished at the very moment that death was announced. The dispatch was immediately directed to Venice by special courier. On the same date of 14 May, Foscarini sent a further dispatch with news of the arrest of the assassin and the proclamation of the new king. That same day other dispatches for Venice were sent, from the Court to the French ambassador and to Cardinal Giovanni Dolfin. All these missives arrived in Venice at the same time on Saturday 22 May, when the gazette due for publication that day had been closed and was ready for circulation. The dispatch to the Senate was registered in the records office the following day. However, in the meantime, other letters had certainly reached Venice via Turin and Milan. The news appears therefore for the first time in the gazette of 29 May with details which do not exactly coincide with those of the dispatch sent to the Senate, a sign that gazetteers had access to sources of information which were different from those of the Venetian government's official ones. It is therefore indicative of this multiplicity of sources that four of the five gazettes carry the same text while the fifth published a much longer and more detailed article bearing nothing in common with the preceding four. This leads us to think that the courier delivering Foscarini's urgent dispatches on the evening of 22 May had delivered other totally independent letters; therefore there must have existed more or less stable communication channels between the compilers of Paris and those of Venice. Indeed the chapter opens with a series of details on these very sources and couriers and reminds readers that the news of the death of the king had been given directly by Paris as well as by the Venetian ambassador to the Senate and by the Court to the French ambassador and to Cardinal Dolfin. It is also fairly credible that there was direct contact between gazetteers. From these sources probably came further news not contained in Foscarini's hasty, whirlwind dispatch. These sources gave details on the assassination, the coronation of Louis XIII and contained hypotheses on the political developments following the attack with even a brief but eloquent piece praising the late sovereign.

The Reading Public

These varieties of text suggest some conclusions regarding audience effect. It was quite normal that readers compared each other's information. It was a common scenario of urban life of the times, especially at moments of political tension. From the shops of the *reportisti* the news-sheets and news reached common meeting places such as pharmacies and sellers of spirits, each with their own regular customers, where animated discussion followed on from an often public reading. It is natural that different news-sheets on the same events ended in fierce debate. It was these same news-sheets that gave rise to "conventicles and entanglements among the hotheads" which sometimes ended up with hundreds arguing in St Mark's Square, followed by "insults," "blows with a stick," and "slaps and punches." This for example happened on 19 December 1676 between two elderly common people, Berto, a "fruit seller in *calle della testa*" and another "shopkeeper." As an informer to the Venetian state inquisitors wrote: "They punched each other over the subject of the capture of Melisso of which there were different accounts."[22] There were "uproarious scuffles" after every battle in Europe or the Mediterranean. Abbot Frugoni, who was an acute critic of the urban life of those years, made the point that:

> Everyone had their own ideas and when a gazetteer's article took a particular line it became a riotous excuse to come to blows for each test his mettle. It was war upon war; they skirmished more with their wheeling tongues than the soldiers had done with their sharpened swords ... They sometimes grabbed each other and decided battles with their fists, deaths by injury and set up camp by abuse.[23]

In the France of the thirties, the support given by the monarchy to the *Gazette* of Theophraste Renaudot, consisting of the banning of foreign printed and handwritten news-sheets, was part of a plan aiming to establish a sort of centralization of the flow of information into the country in order to avoid unrest of this kind. In his preface to the first issue, the French gazetteer pointed out the advantages that a news-sheet such as his could confer on government and private citizens. The former could benefit in stopping false rumors from stirring

---

[22] Venice, Archivio di Stato, *Inquisitori di Stato*, b. 566, 19 December 1676.

[23] Ognuno la raccontava a suo genio e quando il testo del novellista favellava in favor di quel foglio servia di bandiera spiegata per azzuffarsi al cimento. Si facea una guerra sopra una guerra; e si scaramucciava più con le lingue caracollanti che non havean fatto i soldati con le spade affilate ... S'acciuffavan tal volta e decidean co i pugni le pugne, con le ferite le morti e con le contumelie i campeggiamenti. Francesco Fulvio Frugoni, *Del cane di Diogene* (Venice: Bosio, 1687), 4, pp. 90–92.

up domestic sedition while the latter could gain information which previously could only be sought with uncertainty and great effort.[24] The printed gazette therefore should be seen as part of an ambitious and complex policy to bolster the absolutist structures of power. Within the remit of this plan, the standardization of information, in the same way as censorship, became an extraordinary means to shepherd and control the opinions of the subjects of a large national state. As we know, the plan worked but only up to a certain point. The multiplicity of handwritten sheets in circulation and their extreme variability provide cues for constant debate up to and throughout the eighteenth century. As Gregorio Leti remarked in 1666: "Princes have introduced [the gazettes] to allow their peoples to know of their vigilance in maintaining the state" but however "People read them as they are written but interpret them as they wish and most often turn good into evil but not evil into good."[25] It was these very news-sheets which were bringing change to the conditions for exercising power. If in the past a prince could care nothing of the opinions of his subjects and busy himself with government policy, the introduction of information news-sheets induced him to worry about how certain forms of behavior might be interpreted on paper. This change was of no little account. For Leti, the people, who up to then were taken up only with their own private concerns, were on the way to turning themselves "from a people into a prince, from unlearned into educated, from simpleton into shrewd and from obedient into disobedient."[26] Hence the institution of the court of public opinion was not long in coming.

---

[24] Gilles Feyel, *L'annonce et la nouvelle. La presse d'information en France sous l'ancien régime (1630–1788)* (Oxford: Voltaire Foundation, 2000), p. 1319.

[25] "I principi l'hanno introdotte per far sapere a' popoli la loro vigilanza nella conservazione dello stato; i popoli le leggono come sono scritte, ma l'interpretano come loro piace et il più sovente fanno del bene male, ma non già del male bene." [Gregorio Leti], *Dialoghi politici o vero la politica che usano in questi tempi i prencipi e repubbliche italiane per conservare il loro stati e signorie* (Roma: Francesco Moneta, 1666). pp. 241–89.

[26] "Il popolo dall'altra parte che prima non haveva l'occasione d'esercitar lo spirito in tante chimere e fatasticherie che si trovano nelle gazzette, se ne stava otioso, pensando ogni uno alla cura della sua casa, non a quella del suo prencipe, ma chimerizando e fantasticando è divenuto di popolo prencipe, d'ignorante virtuoso, di semplice scaltro e d'ubbidiente disubbidente."

CHAPTER 3

The Early German Newspaper—A Medium of Contemporaneity

Johannes Weber

Johann Carolus and his Invention

This chapter concerns the early, printed, periodical German Newspaper and its historical origin.[1] Let us first define our terms: an early modern newspaper is a bound printed object with a moderate number of pages, which appears at brief periodical intervals, at least once per week. It can be bought by anyone for relatively little money and transmits the latest news from around the world and all fields of interest. In the fall of 1605, for the first time, publications with this definition reached the public. Our evidence is a petition by Johann Carolus, a young book dealer, newspaper writer, and print shop owner from Strasbourg (Straßburg), addressed to the city council in December of that year.[2] In it, he asked for the *Freyheit* to produce weekly newspapers. *Freyheit* was then a synonym for "privilege"—this means: Carolus wanted the exclusive local right, or monopoly, for the printing of newspapers in Strasbourg. Although the city council rejected his petition, from their reply we can learn about the professional and material conditions that enabled Carolus to publish a periodical newspaper for the first time. Before becoming a commercial printer of newspapers, Carolus bought the weekly arriving *avise* (handwritten newspapers or newsletters), copied them by hand and forwarded them to a limited group of subscribers in return for money. We include the main text of his petition here, for its intrinsic interest in regard to the inquiry in this book:

---

[1] A comprehensive account of the subject is: Johannes, Weber, "Straßburg 1605. Die Geburt der Zeitung," in *Jahrbuch für Kommunikationsgeschichte*, ed. H. Böning, A. Kutsch, R. Stöber, vol. 7, Stuttgart 2005, S. 3–26.

[2] The petition was found in 1985 by George Kintz and Martin Welke; compare Johannes Weber, "Zum 350. Geburtstag der Tageszeitung am 1. Juli 2000," in Arnulf Kutsch u. Johannes Weber, *350 Jahre Tageszeitung. Forschungen und Dokumente* (Bremen, 2002), p. 14. Publication of the petition was by Johannes Weber, "Unterthenige Supplication Johann Caroli / Buchtruckers. Der Beginn gedruckter politischer Wochenzeitungen im Jahr 1605," in *Archiv für Geschichte des Buchwesens* (Frankfurt am Main, 1992), vol. 38, p. 259.

Whereas I have hitherto been in receipt of the weekly news advice and, in recompense for some of the expenses incurred yearly, have informed and advised yourselves every week regarding an annual allowance. Since, however, the copying has been slow and has necessarily taken much time, and since, moreover, I have recently purchased at a high and costly price the former printing workshop of the late Thobias Jobin and placed and installed the same in my house at no little expense, albeit only for the sake of gaining time, and since for several weeks, and now for the twelfth occasion, I have set, printed and published the said advice in my printing workshop, likewise not without much effort, inasmuch as on each occasion I have had to remove the formes from the presses. As, however, it is now a cause of concern to me that other book printers here would likewise wish to undertake to print and publish the advice and news papers, at small profit to themselves though to my own great harm and disadvantage, and would not, moreover, preserve the news papers as they come here from all parts but would soon make additions and augmentations and seek to cause one to be better than the other and thus easily sow confusion and corruption. Seeing, however, that I have hitherto printed the advice without any additions, and propose to continue to do the same, and moreover am the first here to have done so, which has caused me special expense, effort and labour, since the starting of any such task, however small, is what is most difficult and cannot happen without expense, whereas it would be to my considerable disadvantage were such news papers to be printed and published by others. In order, however, that I may have some recompense from the effort and labour I have undertaken, and that your Graces may continue to receive the news papers without any additions, and that I shall not thereby be subject to interference from others. Accordingly, I submit to your Graces my humble and most earnest request that you graciously grant me such a privilege and freedom with regard to the ordinary news papers aforesaid, and that you acknowledge and declare by judicial decree that the other book printers, book keepers and book sellers, on pain of a stated monetary fine established at your Graces' discretion, shall not set or print the weekly ordinary advice for ten years, either for themselves or in the names of others, but shall be wholly and entirely forbidden from doing so, although as regards any advice that they may receive extra ordinary I do not request that they be debarred therefrom; and I undertake, in order that your Graces may be able to see that I shall print the said advice without any additions and not otherwise than in the manner in which it has been written and received, to submit and deliver to your chancellery, weekly and without fail, four printed copies of the said news papers; and, seeking in this and in every other way humbly to do your Graces' service, and desirous of hereby commending myself to your Graces, and likewise humbly confident of a favourable reply, I am Your Graces' humble and obedient citizen, Johann Carolus, Printer of books.[3]

---

[3] Johannes Weber, "Straßburg 1605. The Origins of the Newspaper in Europe." In: *German History. The Journal of the German History Society*, vol. 24, Nr. 3, 2006, pp. 409–11. The article is a translation of the article at note 1 above.

Sources of News

The professional copying of newsletters was of course nothing new in the German-speaking area. The practice had emerged together with the developing postal infrastructure during the sixteenth century, which ensured the regular transportation of news. Mounted *Ordinari-Post* riders sent by the imperial postmasters belonging to the Thurn und Taxis family concern originally carried exclusively diplomatic correspondence. Soon the same riders began carrying private correspondence and newsletters containing mainly political news of public concern.

German-language newsletters originated partly from "informants" who had direct access to political events and used their information to earn extra money, and partly from local postmasters who added news from their administrative district to the routing slips that accompanied the sealed mail. These slips originally contained only information about the mailbag's contents; in Germany, they were called *avisi*, corresponding to the term *avise* for the handwritten newsletters.

Through their activities in the exchange of news local postmasters acquired a key role in the flow of information across regions. Some postmasters used their positions close to the sources of information to create their own handwritten newsletters and offer them for sale to a range of subscribers. The first printed "postal newspapers" of the seventeenth century, for example in Frankfurt, Berlin and Hamburg, originated this way.

Other postmasters were satisfied with the still lucrative role of intermediaries; they gave the newsletters arriving regularly from several places to professional scribes known as *Zeitunger* or *Novellanten*. These scribes then combined the news material from the various letters into letters of their own, made multiple copies and sold them independently. During the last decades of the sixteenth century, a number of scribes were active in entrepôts like Augsburg, Cologne and Nuremberg.[4] One might even say that these scribes were the precursors of modern press agencies.

Carolus' activity as a purveyor of newsletters in Strasbourg was thus not unusual untile he acquired a printing press in 1604. The purchase of such an item indicates that he was as well acquainted with its usage as he was with his profession as a scribe. Hence Carolus combined a knowledge of contemporary communications with a knowledge of printing. As noted in his petition, he started from the beginning of October 1605 to print handwritten *avise* in his printing press.

---

[4] For Augsburg scribes ("Zeitunger") towards the end of the sixteenth century compare Mathilde Auguste Hedwig Fitzler, *Die Entstehung der sogenannten Fuggerzeitungen in der Wiener Nationalbibliothek* (Baden bei Wien, 1937). About scribes in Nuremberg compare Lore Sporhan-Krempel, *Nürnberg als Nachrichtenzentrum zwischen 1400 und 1700* (Nürnberg, 1968).

Today, the merging of scribe and printer and hence the birth of the modern newspaper might seem like a spectacular bit of serendipity. But for Carolus this was, as he remarked dryly, solely a way of economic rationalization: he could now save the time which he would normally spend copying by hand.

From Script to Print

The step from handwritten to typographic copying of weekly *avise* means much more than a quantitative improvement in terms of output. Before, a scribe could make only a few copies of a newspaper per week—around 15–20. Acquisition of such newsletters was expensive and reserved for an exclusive circle of recipients. Thus, we cannot speak of a generally accessible public medium, but one which was limited to a small circle of well-heeled buyers. The printing of several hundred newspaper copies per week brought about a drastic decrease in unit costs and a qualitative leap forward; with a large and undefined audience now able to purchase the papers, one main characteristic of modern media had become reality: the diffusion of periodical, topical information.

From Print to Newspaper

The newly invented printed weekly newspapers were clearly differentiated from the many political press products that had been popular already in the sixteenth century: pamphlet and *Newe Zeytung*, calendar and chronicles, *Semestral-* or *Meßrelation*, for these genres lacked periodicity as well as topicality. Although pamphlets (*Flugblätter* and *Flugschriften*) were often topical, in that they concerned events of current interest, they only appeared sporadically. Insofar as they went beyond general propaganda, they were concerned with specific and exceptional or sensational occurrences. There were also annual political chronicles and the bi-annual *Meßrelationen* created by Michael von Aitzing during the 1580s in Cologne. The latter were so-called after their manner of sale and distribution, as they were initially offered for sale during fairs in spring and autumn in Leipzig, hence *Semestral-*, or *Meßralationen*.[5] *Meßrelationen* and

---

[5] On recent research see Ulrich Rosseaux, "Die Entstehung der Messrelationen. Zur Entwicklung eines frühneuzeitlichen Nachrichtenmediums aus der Zeitgeschichtsschreibung des 16. Jahrhunderts," in *Historisches Jahrbuch,* 124 (2004), pp. 97–123. The bibliography was compiled by the Bremen scholar Klaus Bender, *RELATIONES HISTORICAE: Ein Bestandsverzeichnis der deutschen Messrelationen von 1583 bis 1648* (Berlin and New York, 1994).

annual chronicles offered retrospective summaries of past global events and thus belong to the genre of the political annual. The same is true for the so called *Rorschacher Monatsschrift*, a political monthly chronicle written by a certain Dilbaum from Augsburg and printed in St. Gallen on the Bodensee.[6] These long-term, annual, bi-annual or monthly appearing periodicals were based—like the later printed newspapers—on regular handwritten newsletters. However, they gave only retrospective summaries, lacking the freshness that might derive from a constant stream of news coming through the weekly post system. This fresh topicality was inaugurated by Carolus, who printed according to the rhythm of the weekly arriving *Ordinari-Post* and hence offered the latest breaking news.

The effort required for producing the older type of printed monthly or yearly summary was actually greater than for the weekly newspaper. Whereas the former demanded selective and judicious editorial work, the latter simply involved publishing the newsletters unchanged—as Carolus notes, "without any effort of one's own / and not otherwise / we get them here already written."[7] This simple method of reproduction was used well into the seventeenth century and beyond, and it is responsible for the typical appearance of the early newspaper: four (later also eight) small-sized pages with a number of paragraphs usually preceded by place and date of the correspondence. The order of paragraphs does not follow any editorial design but reflects the sequence in which the correspondence arrives between the dates of printing. There are no comments on the news. Many of the oldest newspapers had neither title nor headline; for the most part they appear completely anonymous without printer name or place of publication. The bare appearance of early newspapers represents and documents their origin: they differ from the handwritten *avise* only in being printed. Both contain nearly exclusively dry political, diplomatic, and military reports from the whole known world. Non-political news is included only from time to time, and sensational reports are rare.

Early periodically printed newspapers are hence the medium par excellence for quality news in seventeenth-century Germany. Information about sensational and miraculous occurrences remained the province of the often illustrated pamphlet literature and the non-periodical *Newen Zeytung*. The unadorned appearance of early printed newspapers reminds us that their producers needed no particular professional qualification or academic education, since the business consisted of reproducing the newsletters using the printing press.

Postmasters or local printers were able to produce the newsletters as a secondary occupation and without additional payroll costs—no specialization was required.

---

[6] The otherwise commendable desription of Gerda Barth, *ANNUS CHRISTI 1597—die erste deutschsprachige Zeitung* (Rorschach, 1976) misconceives the periodical's genre affiliation.

[7] Cited from Weber, "Unterthenige Supplication Johann Caroli / Buchtruckers," p. 259.

The learned community thus did not participate actively in the creation of printed newspapers until the last decades of the seventeenth century. It is true that educated civil servants, officers, or private persons often acted as correspondents and also used the newsletters themselves early on. But the production of the medium itself stayed in the hands of sub- or non-academic service sector.

One important condition for the new genre's triumph was thus its simple production process. In addition, there was a historical condition. Carolus' idea came in a time when demand for political information rose dramatically. European politics in the beginning of the seventeenth century was highly worthy of people's attention. Indeed, after the outbreak of the Thirty Years' War in 1618, keeping up to date with current political and military events could be a matter of life or death. Although the newspaper was not an outcome of the War, it owes its swift expansion and early success to this European catastrophe.[8]

In the first 15 years after their invention in Strasbourg, *Ordinari*... newspapers emerged in at least 15 cities. Most of these foundations occurred in the key years between 1618 and 1620. After the second Defenestration of Prague the Bohemian Estates declared war; the tense political situation in the German Reich generated a desire for the latest information.

By the middle of the century the number of newspaper enterprises had risen to around two dozen; before the beginning of the war-induced depression at the end of the 1630s, there were up to 30 German language papers appearing at the same time within the Holy Roman Empire, Switzerland, Denmark, and the Baltic Sea region.

From the standpoint of Europe as a whole, the German-language newspaper situation was the most varied, due to the political fragmentation of the Empire. Over time all territorial states and many smaller cities in the area had their own paper. Newspapers from Strasbourg, Wolfenbüttel, Frankfurt, and Berlin, all established before 1617, were the oldest in the Europe. Between 1605 and 1700, at one time or another, there existed some 200 newspaper enterprises in around 80 places of publication within the German-speaking area.[9] The news supplied

---

[8] See Johannes Weber, "Der große Krieg und die frühe Zeitung. Gestalt und Entwicklung der deutschen Nachrichtenpresse in der ersten Hälfte des 17. Jahrhunderts," in Holger Böning, Arnulf Kutsch and Rudolf Stöber (eds), *Jahrbuch für Kommunikationsgeschichte* 1 (1999), pp. 23–61.

[9] The statistic is based on the Bremen microfilm archive of about 60,000 issues of German seventeenth-century newspapers of which originals are dispersed in libraries and archives across Europe. The collection is systematically captured and documented in: *Die deutschen Zeitungen des 17. Jahrhunderts. Ein Bestandsverzeichnis mit historischen und bibliographischen Angaben Vol. 1 (text) and Vol. 2 (figures)* ed. Else Bogel and Elger Blühm (Bremen, 1971), vol. 1 (text), vol. 2 (figures). Volume 3 (supplement) ed. Elger Blühm,

by these papers was geographically inclusive and comprehensive. As the number of reports available for inclusion increased, production rhythms increased proportionally, so that by the 1630s, more and more newspapers appeared two or three times per week instead of once—one reason why the medium itself became a familiar everyday object. The first real daily newspaper—with six editions per week—was published in 1650 in Leipzig.[10]

Press and Public

The effects of the printing press in making political communication available to a broader segment of society than ever before is strongly suggested by the circulation figures for these papers. The postal newspaper of Frankfurt reached a circulation of 450 already in the 1620s, whereas the *Wöchentliche Zeitung auß mehrerley örther*—its equivalent from Hamburg—possibly produced as many as 1,500 copies. Average production for newspapers in this time was between 250 and 400 copies of each number.[11] Considerable quantities of these copies reached not just single persons but were passed on to successive readers afterwards. Indeed, in widening the reach of political information, newspapers from the middle of the seventeenth century were certainly preeminent among all printed publications. Their audience obviously transcended the group of those who dealt with political news professionally—men of letters, city councilors, civil servants, and military officers. The majority of readers probably belonged to the urban middle class, which was traditionally interested in accompanying its diet of religious literature with some readings on history and politics. Even considering the favorable conditions, it is remarkable how fast this new medium transcended the circle of those who were politically involved and educated.

The newspapers' success among the middle class is all the more remarkable considering their unadorned presentation. It was easy and cheap for the entrepreneur

---

Brigitte Kolster, Helga Levis (München, 1985). About the recently added inventory of ca. 2,000 newspapers see Johannes Weber, "Neue Funde aus der Frühgeschichte des deutschen Zeitungswesens," in *Archiv für Geschichte des Buchwesens* 39 (1993), pp. 321–60.

[10] The oldest daily newspaper of the world was identified 40 years ago by Else (Bogel) Hauff, an employee of the "Deutsche Presseforschung" in Bremen; see Else Hauff, "Die Einkommenden Zeitungen von 1650: Ein Beitrag zur Geschichte der Tageszeitung," in *Gazette* (Leiden, 1963), pp. 227–35 (re-published in Kutsch and Weber (eds), *350 Jahre Tageszeitung: Forschung und Dokumente*, pp. 151–61.)

[11] See Martin Welke, "Russland in der deutschen Publizistik des 17. Jahrhunderts," in *Historische Veröffentlichungen des Osteuropainstituts an der Freien Universität Berlin. Forschungen zur osteuropäischen Geschichte* (Wiesbaden, 1976), vol. 23, p. 158.

to print the news material in the same way as it arrived at his house. But this meant for readers that they had to synthesize and interpret a pile of heterogeneous, unsorted, and uncommented news by their own resources. Additionally, news was mainly about large-scale international developments in politics. In contrast, local news which would have been of immediate importance to readers' daily lives was missing completely. One could thus imagine that the less educated portion of the audience would have viewed the early papers with a mixture of incomprehension and disinterest and soon stopped buying them altogether.

But the opposite was apparently true: newspapers prospered and were read everywhere with enthusiasm—not only by political specialists. We must therefore assume that people at the time were far less demanding than modern readers when it came to the supply of reading matter. With secular reading matter in short supply, they probably were not so worried about gaining a precise understanding of meaning and context, remaining satisfied to learn anything about new and foreign events. The newspaper provided an inexpensive connection to the wide world as well as the world's great leaders and actors, however confusing the conflicts and disputes may have seemed to the reader. Fascination for topical and distant news seems to have compensated possible deficits in understanding.

Press and Politics

Notwithstanding the ease of creating these types of newspapers and the presumed satisfaction of the audience, the new genre could not have developed the way it did without tolerant authorities. Yet such tolerance was by no means automatic. The general principle was to keep subjects away from politics, which was reserved to courts, city councils, and civil servants. Politics is understood here to mean both political action and the current information necessary to pursue this. When this information had been transmitted mostly through handwritten political correspondence, high prices had been a guarantee for social and political exclusiveness. The emergence of printed newspapers removed this guarantee. Nonetheless, governments tolerated them in general, although censorship, criminal proceedings against printers, and temporary bans of publications were part of the seventeenth-century history of newspapers.[12]

But why did governments tolerate a medium which was incompatible with the political principles of absolutist rule? The reason has to do with the immediate benefit that governments enjoyed because of the existence of newspapers. Many

---

[12] Johannes Weber, "Kontrollmechanismen im deutschen Zeitungswesen des 17. Jahrhunderts: Ein kleiner Beitrag zur Geschichte der Zensur," in Holger Böning, Arnulf Kutsch and Rudolf Stöber (eds), *Jahrbuch für Kommunikationsgeschichte* (Stuttgart, 2005), vol. 6.

newspaper entrepreneurs tried to thwart bothersome competitors by acquiring government licenses that conceded local monopolies on printing newspapers. These licenses came at a price; and aside from the money poured into government coffers, printers under license were bound to political loyalty.[13] Foreign as well as local newspapers were economically and politically beneficial. In an empire full of small kingdoms, magistrates and courtly officials were often forced into financial parsimony. Printed newspapers which could be obtained cheaply from many places meant a welcome savings compared to expensive written correspondence. Kaspar Stieler, an early newspaper researcher, remarked in 1695 that printed gazettes were of neutral origin and thus more objective than correspondence from paid courtly flunkeys. For all these reasons, governments could imagine that the advantages of tolerating printed newspapers outweighed any ideological considerations. Moreover, the unadorned and yet cryptic appearance of newspapers, and their uncommented contents, could suggest that uneducated people would understand merely what happened at the surface, whereas only the educated elite would comprehend the deeper meanings. At the time, the educated elite, far from constituting a likely source of opposition to the authorities, formed one of the mainstays of absolutist governments, in contrast to the clergy and the nobility. Printed newspapers could thus be allowed or at least tolerated despite virtually violating a sort of secular version of the *disciplina arcani*. Finally, one must keep in mind that these papers not only lacked editorial comment but also regional and local coverage. They accordingly omitted that part of reality which seemed to be of most concern. Local news, presumably, would have been more likely to lead to political discussion, possibly resulting in a local, reasoning, discussing, and maybe even oppositional public.

We have established that newspapers encountered an extraordinary demand and were tolerated by governments in general. It is thus not surprising that they also did not shock the learned guardians of the political Weltanschauung. Only very late, in the 70s of the century, did some commentators start to warn against what was by then a long-established genre. But they were not able to assert themselves against the learned apologists of the new medium since they seemed anachronistic in the face of the pervasiveness of newspapers.

On the side of tolerance, pedagogues like Jan Comensky (Johann Amos Comenius) in Bohemia, Christian Weise at the Beamtengymnasium Zittau, and Daniel Hartnack of the Gymnasium Altona[14] used and recommended newspapers

---

[13] See for this problem Elger Blühm, "Deutscher Fürstenstaat und Presse im 17. Jahrhundert," *Hof, Staat und Gesellschaft in der Literatur des 17. Jahrhundert* (Amsterdam, 1982), pp. 287–313.
[14] See Johannes Weber, "Daniel Hartnack—ein gelehrter Streithahn und Avisenschreiber am Ende des 17. Jahrhunderts. Zum Beginn politisch kommentierender Zeitungspresse," in

for educational purposes in the realms of the historical, the political, the geographical and the linguistic. Less influential were early warnings about danger from the extension of publically available information to more groups in society. Towards the end of the century Kaspar Stieler favored including every social level in the reading of newspapers; and in his view even women and ordinary citizens, even artisans and peasants could learn useful lessons from them.[15]

Stieler may be considered in some respects a forerunner of the Enlightenment, but in an important aspect he was not. In his view, scribes should be prohibited from commenting on the news: "Because one does not read the newspaper in order to get educated and trained in analyzing the issues, but in order to know what happens here and there."[16] Thus, the newspaper should remain a medium exclusively for news as it had been throughout the seventeenth century. Commentary and reasoning were to be suppressed—namely, those practices which publicly stimulate the formation of opinions or even pre-form them and which are accordingly part of the political Enlightenment.

Needless to say, due to censorship and the defense of privilege, German newspapers did not develop into politicizing, opinion-forming organs before the French Revolution. Instead, the development of supra-regional "politically-reasoning publics" from the end of the seventeenth century took place outside the medium of the newspaper, in the context of a different periodical press genre whose origins can be traced back to the 1670s: the historical–political journal.[17] This early form of a political magazine usually appeared monthly and its domain was the discussion of past political events. In this genre we find early examples of what in following centuries and in the course of social change would become the middle-class oppositional domain: namely, public discourse about the state and politics. Early newspapers had no immediate share in this development. But it is hard to overestimate their indirect role in the history of education and culture.[18]

Although newspapers remained within the (so to say) service industries of traditional, absolutist governments, the new genre nevertheless transmitted topical, political news about world affairs for a moderate price to a fast growing, socially

---

Gutenberg–Jahrbuch (Mainz, 1993), pp. 140–58.

[15] Kaspar Stieler, *Zeitungs Lust und Nutz* (Hamburg, 1695), p. 102.

[16] Ibid., p. 26.

[17] For the history of origins of the early political newspapers and the relations to the newspaper system see Johannes Weber, *Götter=Both Mercurius: Die Urgeschichte der politischen Zeitschrift in Deutschland* (Bremen, 1994).

[18] Jürgen Habermas, *Strukturwandel der Öffentlichkeit: Untersuchungen zu einer Kategorie der burgerlichen Gesellschaft* (Neuwied, Berlin, 1962); English trans. by Thomas Burger and Frederick Lawrence: *The Structural Transformation of the Public Sphere: An Inquiry into a Category of Bourgeois Society* (Cambridge, Mass., 1989).

unspecific audience because of its printed format. This phenomenon has immense historical, cultural and educational consequences, because only such precise, regular and topical information had the potential to advance the widespread formation of political opinions. Of course, the societal impact of this new medium was probably much larger than might be judged by the political content alone. Indeed, the very nature of the periodical medium itself may be even more effective, in eroding the legitimacy and the image of pre-bourgeois rule, than the single news report. Marshall McLuhan's 1964 remark that "the medium is the message"[19] fits the early periodical newspaper quite well. In the sixteenth century, the non-periodical press, including *Newe Zeitungen* and numerous pamphlets, transmitted only sensational, extraordinary political events. Actors thus appeared as glamorous and special, corresponding to claims of rule by divine right. Tedious, austere political processes, in contrast, had been completely hidden from subjects. The emergence of topical, periodical newspapers means in some way a quantum leap. For the first time, politics is presented as a laborious everyday business, in slow motion and small chunks, in reports occurring at least every seven days. International reporting leads at the same time to a leveling in individual perception of the familiar and the foreign. The quarrels of the powerful of all countries—whether Christian or Muslim—appear in the same light and in a very worldly dimension. Political business appears as an ever-repeating process. But this sphere becomes now accessible for the ordinary intellect and critical eye of contemporary subjects. Here we are in terms of mentality and perception of politics on the cusp of the Enlightenment.

Why did the representatives of seventeenth-century governments fail to suppress periodical, political newspapers? One can hardly imagine that they lacked foresight or intelligence. The periodical press seems to be one of those phenomena whose adolescence cannot be predicted at birth. The expression to "not see the forest for the trees" seems fitting. Anyway, since the latter half of the seventeenth century newspapers were for quite a considerable audience the most important worldly reading material and a familiar item of everyday life. The large-scale dimension of the subtle effect that such a phenomenon causes becomes usually only apparent after the impact becomes visible and the corresponding changes have emerged. In our case it is the secularization of the political in the minds of the subjects, a constituent, accordingly, of middle-class enlightenment and political modernity.

Summing up, we must say that the early newspaper is the medium of contemporaneity par excellence.

---

[19] Marshall McLuhan, *Understanding Media* (Cambridge, Mass., 1964)

PART 2
Time, Motion and Structure in Early Modern Communications

CHAPTER 4

The Birth of Maria de' Medici (26 April 1575): Hearsay, Correspondence, and Historiographical Errors

Alessio Assonitis

On 26 April 1575, Francesco de' Medici drafted an audacious letter intended for Maximilian II von Habsburg.[1] Carried away either by physicians' hasty speculations or simply by the law of numerical odds, the Grand Duke announced the birth of his first male heir after five daughters even before his wife and the Emperor's sister, the Grand Duchess Johanna von Habsburg, had actually delivered her child. "I wanted immediately to convey to you this news," he declared, "since I am quite sure that Your Majesty will be pleased, as I am rejoicing with you, for the new acquisition that you made, especially since Her Highness [Johanna von Habsburg] and her son are in good health."[2] As we shall examine shortly, this draft—which is included in the volumes of the *Minute* of Grand Duke Francesco's correspondence in the archive of the Medici Grand Dukes (*Mediceo del Principato*)—was never written out as a letter and sent. From this document, however, we can deduce some of the sender's motives.

Francesco was well aware that news of the birth of a male heir would have at least defused the tensions that had been building at the Imperial court for quite some time. Maximilian's plans to claim his rights over Tuscany were frustrated once Cosimo I obtained the title of Grand Duke in 1570.[3] In June of that same year, Francesco's father voiced his formal protests to Pius V regarding the Emperor's menacing scheme[4] after having attempted himself some months before to clarify in writing directly to Maximilian the circumstances that led to

---

[1] All documents in this article, unless otherwise stated, are unpublished and have been transcribed and translated by the author.

[2] ASF, *Mediceo del Principato* 59, fol. 47 recto (26 April 1575): "Ho voluto darle subito questa nuova rendendomi sicuro che la M.tà V. ne sentirà piacere si come ancora io mene allegro con lei per l'acquisto che ella ne ha fatto, massime che S. Alt.za et il figlio per la Dio gratia si trovano con intera salute."

[3] Stefano Tabacchi, "Giovanna d'Austria" in *Dizionario biografico degli italiani*, 55 (Rome, 2000), p. 490; Furio Diaz, *Il Granducato di Toscana* (Turin: UTET, 1987), 184–91.

[4] ASF, *Mediceo del Principato* 321, f. 4 r and v (4 June 1570).

his elevation.[5] Venetian *avvisi*, issued shortly after Cosimo's letter, first confirmed the Emperor's approval of this new title,[6] and shortly after underscored his perplexities, particularly in regard to the new political order that was going to ensue.[7] During the months that followed, Maximilian, along with other Italian ruling families such as the Este and Savoy, pressured Pius V to annul Cosimo's title.[8] The Grand Duke tried to gather support from King Philip II of Spain who also resented this newly formed Florence–Rome entente.[9] Towards the end of 1570, Maximilian began gradually to tolerate Cosimo's elevation.[10] Full recognition of this title, however, occurred five years later (2 November 1575) when Maximilian invested Cosimo's son Francesco with the title of Grand Duke, almost an act of defiance with regard to the one bestowed by Pius V.

Another matter was threatening the bond between the Medici and the Habsburgs. Maximilian strongly disapproved of Cosimo's marriage to Camilla Martelli in March of 1570. As a result of this union, in fact, the Grand Duke's second wife supplanted the Emperor's sister, Johanna, as the most important female at court. If this were not enough, a discontented Johanna kept Maximilian informed of the relationship that Francesco continued to have with the Venetian Bianca Cappello.[11] Not long after her triumphant entry into Florence in December 1565, Johanna began to realize that her authority was severely frustrated by the conspicuous presence of Bianca. Once the euphoria of her *entrata* died down, Johanna embarked on the arduous task of producing a Medici male heir. Without exaggeration, her Florentine period was marked by a constant state of pregnancy: a state, ironically, that would ultimately be the cause of her death on 11 April 1578.[12]

---

   5   ASF, *Mediceo del Principato* 321, fol. 2 recto (8 November 1569).
   6   ASF, *Mediceo del Principato* 3080, fol. 663 recto (24 January 1569).
   7   ASF, *Mediceo del Principato* 3080, fol. 496 recto (21 January 1570).
   8   ASF, *Mediceo del Principato* 3596, folio not numbered (22 March 1570); folio not numbered (6 April 1570); folio not numbered (10 April 1570); folio not numbered (17 April 1570); folio not numbered (27 April 1570); ASF, *Mediceo del Principato* 3080, fol. 723 recto (15 April 1570); fol. 737 (29 April 1570).
   9   ASF, *Mediceo del Principato* 321, fol. 5 recto (17 April 1570); fol. 8 recto (8 May 1570). On the crisis with Spain, see: Diaz, *Il Granducato di Toscana*, p. 189.
   10 ASF, *Mediceo del Principato* 3080, fol. 777 recto (22 July 1570); ASF, *Mediceo del Principato* 3596, folio not numbered (18 August 1570); ASF, *Mediceo del Principato* 3080, fol. 847 recto (28 October 1570); ASF, *Mediceo del Principato* 321, fol. 13 recto (10 December 1570).
   11 Maria Fubini Leuzzi, "Straniere a corte. Dagli epistolari di Giovanna d'Austria e Bianca Cappello," in Gabriella Zarri, ed., *Per lettera. La scrittura epistolare femminile tra archivio e tipografia (secoli XV–XVII)*, (Rome: Viella, 1999), pp. 413–40.
   12 Much has been written on Johanna's death by various Medici historians. See Tabacchi, "Giovanna de' Medici," pp. 489–92. Especially noteworthy are the descriptions of her agony

After almost a decade of attempts during which Johanna gave birth to Eleonora (1567–1611), Romola (November 1568–December 1568), Anna (1569–84), Isabella (1571–72), and Lucrezia (1572–74), a Medici boy seemed never to arrive. Such frantic expectations escalated after the birth of Isabella (born in September 1571),[13] while Johanna was pregnant with her fifth child Lucrezia.[14] The copious correspondence in the *Mediceo del Principato* underscores how her relationship with her father-in-law became quasi-paternal after years of silent and diplomatic mutual loathing.[15] Cosimo proved to be especially sympathetic to Johanna's male infertility. After the birth of Lucrezia in November 1572, Johanna began receiving consolation gifts (for having given birth to a girl), healing relics, and absurd *ricette*—written medical advice—intended to "stimulate" male birth. Johanna also made a pilgrimage to Loreto in spring of 1573 to fulfill a secret vow (presumably related to Cosimo's recovery from a serious illness) and pray for the arrival of male heir. When news about her sixth pregnancy broke in late 1574, a network of epistolary solidarity directed at Francesco was triggered. Wilhelm V Wittelsbach, announcing the imminent birth of his fourth child (the future Empress Anna Maria, born in November 1574), exhorted God to fulfill Francesco's vow by bestowing upon his House a male heir.[16] His brother Ernst of Bavaria, then living in Rome, expressed a similar wish during the final weeks of Johanna's pregnancy, paying little heed to the Grand Duke's proverbial superstition.[17]

Francesco's draft announcing his male heir never became a letter. As we shall see shortly, the process was interrupted by the course of the events. This document is included in corpus of *Minute* of the *Mediceo del Principato*: namely, in the collection of drafts that the Grand Duke dictated to a scribe or, in rare cases, wrote himself. These drafts were then usually written out as letters: the original was sent out and a copy was entered by the secretariat in a volume of *Registri*. Sometimes, the contents of a draft were partially or even radically

---

included in a folder entitled "*F. 39 / 2—Misc. Med.*" in ASF, *Mediceo del Principato* 5927/A.

[13] ASF, *Mediceo del Principato*, 1177, fol. 598 recto; ASF, *Mediceo del Principato* 5925, fol. 282 recto, ASF, *Mediceo del Principato* 5925, fol. 311 recto. ASF, *Mediceo del Principato* 5296, fol. 166 recto.

[14] ASF, *Mediceo del Principato* 241, fos. 36 recto.

[15] ASF, *Mediceo del Principato* 5926, fol. 133 recto.

[16] ASF, *Mediceo del Principato* 4281, fol. 94 recto (24 November 1574): "Mia moglie sta d'hora in hora in procinto di partorire. Iddio N.S.re facia sua volontà, qual Divina M.tà prego di core, che doni a V. Ecc.ia un bel herede. Alla qual li Bacio la mano, et li desidero ogni suo desiderato voto."

[17] ASF, *Mediceo del Principato* 4281, fol. 105 recto (8 April 1575): "A V. Alt.za et alla Ser.ma mia Zia [Johanna], et figliole bascio le mani pregandoli ogni felicità, et un figliolo maschio."

changed in the final letter. Furthermore, it is not uncommon that drafts fail to blossom into fully-fledged epistles. It is rare, however, for a draft to be written in anticipation of an event, as in the above mentioned example. This is confirmed by two factors. Space was left blank, and never filled in, after the words "in questo giorno, a hore …" ("on this day, at the hour …"), intended for the exact hour of the child's birth. Most importantly, the words "Fù femina" ("It was a female") were later added on the upper left margin of the page.

On 26 April 1575, the day of the composition of this draft, Maria di Francesco de' Medici—future Queen of France—was born. On that very day an official statement reporting this event was issued by Francesco's Secretariat to Alessandro de' Medici (Archbishop of Florence and future Leo XI), then living in Rome.[18] Francesco himself immediately wrote to other Cardinals in Rome announcing Maria's birth and providing updates on Johanna's health. A letter to Cardinal Zaccaria Delfino, written on the same day as Maria's birth,[19] received the prelate's prompt response three days later: "I share Your Highness's happiness for the daughter that was born, since from that very womb which continues to generate females, with the help of God, one can wait for the day when it will generate males."[20] A similar consolatory tone was employed by Cardinal Ferdinando de' Medici. Francesco admitted to his brother how daughters can solve many diplomatic situations.[21] Ferdinando in turn replied that though a boy was much overdue, the arrival of a girl should not be seen as

---

[18]   ASF, *Mediceo del Principato* 3480, fol. 266 recto (26 April 1575): "Questo giorno la Ser.ma Gran Duchessa a hore diciassette in circa ci ha partorito una bella figliolina della quale darete parte a S. B.ne in nome nostro."

[19]   ASF, *Mediceo del Principato* 244, fol. 90 recto (26 April 1575): "Poco ricerca le lettere di V.S. Ill.ma de 8 et 22; se non che io la ringratii come fò delli avvisi che gli è piaciuto di darmi, li quali sono stati letti da me di buona voglia. Quando la S.V. Ill.ma haveva comodità di farlo ricevere io per molto favore che la mi dia parte di quanto le verrà a notitia, allegrandomi con lei, d'una figliolina che mi è nata questo giorno della Ser.ma mia consorte. Da Fiorenza." Francesco also wrote a letter to Cardinal Marcantonio Colonna about a week later. ASF, *Mediceo del Principato* 244, fol. 96 recto (2 May 1575): "L'amorevolezza della Ecc. V. mi mostra verso le mie Galere ancorché non mi sia nuova, mi è stata nondimeno gratissima et le ne rendo molte gratie, si come le rendo a Dio d'una nuova figliolina che la Gran Duchessa mia ha dato in luce della quale so che l'Ecc. V. harà piacere per essere l'una et l'altra con salute."

[20]   ASF, *Mediceo del Principato* 3741, folio not numbered (29 April 1575): "M'allegro con V.A. della figliola natale, poiché da quel seno che continuano ad uscire le femine, aspettar si può, che habbiano con l'agiuto de Dio, ad uscire anco de maschi."

[21]   ASF, *Mediceo del Principato* 5088, fol. 166 recto (26 April 1575): "Hoggi sule 17 hore la S.V.I. ha hauto una bella nipotina data in luce dalla Ser.ma Gran Duchessa, et perché molte volte le femmine accomodano gran cose nelli stati a me è stata molto cara sapendo doppo tante femmine d'avere de' maschi con la gratia di Dio."

such a disappointment after all. Perhaps Francesco's brother had already begun to savor the serious possibility of becoming Grand Duke given Francesco's difficulty in producing a male heir. Most importantly, however, at the end of this reply written three days after Maria's birth, Ferdinando recounted an odd incident: two couriers had arrived in Rome that very night shouting the news that the newborn was a prince and not a princess.[22] This was hardly an isolated episode. The spurious news of the newborn son had reached far and many. Within days of Maria's birth letters from Borgo San Sepolcro and Ancona arrived at court complimenting Francesco and thanking God for the newborn male.[23] Francesco Gaetani, writing in Volterra, recounted that upon hearing news of the new Cosimo from a courier sent from Florence the entire city celebrated with fireworks and gunshots.[24] Monte Valenti, then Governor of Perugia, wrote a long periphrastic letter on the Medicean *gens* (6 May 1575) which would now be perpetuated thanks to this newborn male. Surprisingly, almost two weeks since Maria's birth, Monte Valenti in Perugia was still unaware of the true gender of the child.[25] The news of a male heir arrived almost immediately to Urbino.

---

[22] ASF, *Mediceo del Principato* 5089, fol. 97 verso, lett. no. 44 (29 April 1575): "Più caro mi saria stato un figliuolo maschio, pur ancor la femina non mi spiace per il respetto che Vostra Altezza prudentemente considera. Io mi allegro con lei dell'acquisto, et della salute di Sua Altezza della quale possiamo ben sperare de maschi ancora. Qui sù le tre hore di notte comparsono due corrieri mossisi dalla Storta sù l'arrivo del Sordo, i quali dando voce di maschio, roppono il sonno a tutta Roma, et al Vaticano principalmente, per speranza di guadagno, che è stata stimata una cosa malfatta, et di fastidio et scandolo."

[23] ASF, *Mediceo del Principato* 672, fol. 86 recto (27 April 1575); fol. 47 recto (30 April 1575).

[24] ASF, *Mediceo del Principato* 672, fol 102 recto (27 April 1575): "In questo punto a ore 3 di notte è venuto la felicissima e grande nuova del felicissimo parto di sua Altezza S.ma per corriere suto spedito qui a Monsignor R.mo di Volterra e che l'onnipotente e ghrande Iddio ci à concesso il tanto desiderato nostro nuovo e unico signore e rinovato il gran Cosimo che subito in fortezza n'abiamo fatta aleghrezza con fuochi e ghazara di artiglierie ringhraziando il ghrande e magnio Iddio di tanta segnialata grazia concessa al felicissimo stato di V.S. al che tutta la cipta al si n'affatto aleghrezza; e monsignore E.mo domatina dirà la messa delo Spirito Santo ringhraziando il ghrande Iddio primo principio di ugni nostro bene e che e' piaccia preservarà lungho tempo V.S. al suo unico figliuolo."

[25] ASF, *Mediceo del Principato* 673, fol. 106 recto (6 May 1575): "Non è bisogno Ser. mo Sig.re ch'io me fatichi in demonstrare a V. Alt.za quanta allegrezza et iubilio io habbi sentito del felicissimo parto della Sereniss.a sua consorte, poiché non solo quelli che sono nati servitori della Ill.ma sua casa come io ma tutta l'Italia e il Mondo insieme ne deve far festa e sentirne contento senza fine, perche questi doni che vengono puramente dalla man d'Idio rendono chiaro testimonio che si come i fatt et l'attioni de gloriosi Antecessori suoi et di lei Med.ma hanno sempre congiunto con la potentia et grandezza loro un vero Zelo di somma giustitia et di pura fede, così la divina bontà che de' suoi diletti tiene particolar protettione ha

Francesco Maria II della Rovere wrote separately to Francesco[26] and Johanna (27 May 1575), rejoicing about the "male son, that Our Lord has granted to Your Highness."[27] He too had heard of this from "a courier that passed by here today." Just a few days later (2 May 1575), as soon as the rectified news arrived to Urbino, Francesco Maria II expressed his regrets to the Grand Duke for having fallen for the "burla del maschio" ("the prank of the male").[28]

Given that Francesco never sent a letter claiming the birth of a son, it is probable that rumors of this event became mysteriously widespread in Florence and couriers carried it with them to foreign courts. This is partly confirmed by the sixteenth-century Florentine diarist Bastiano Arditi ("Rumor that it was a boy spread all around the city…")[29] and by Alessandro de' Medici himself in a letter to Francesco dated 30 April 1575.[30] The then Archbishop of Florence explained

---

voluto ch'ella veda quest'una maggiori contentezze che possi havere vita sua, della quale non solo V.A. ma tutta la Christianità se ne rallegra per vedere de si serena stirpe perpetuasse la successione, et io benché fra i minimi ser.ri suoi, ma però de i primi in devotione et obbligo verso la persona et casa sua, tutto ripieno di consolatione vengo fra gl'infiniti che faranno questo ufficio a segnificarli l'allegrezza tanto grande che basto ad esprimerla che ho sentita del Bambino natoli, al quale et a V.A. prego longa et felice vita."

[26] ASF, *Mediceo del Principato* 4051, fol. 154 recto (27 April 1575): "Da un corriero che è passato hoggi di qua, m'è stata data la felice nuova che porta, del figliuol maschio che N.S. Dio è piaciuto di concedere a V.A., con intiera salute dela Ser.ma Gran Duchessa sua, il che, havendo io inteso con infinito piacere et consolatione mia, conforme al molto desiderio che tengo sempre d'ogno prospero successo suo, non ho voluto tardare a rallegrarmene con V.A. e pregandone ogni sorte di contento. "

[27] ASF, *Mediceo del Principato* 5923, fol. 180 recto (27 April 1575): "La buona nuova ch'io ho havuta hoggi da un corriero passato di qua, del figliuol maschio che N.S. Dio è stato servito che V.A. partorisca con entiera salute, mi è di tal maniera piaciuta, per il continuo desiderio che tengo d'ogni felice successo suo, ch'io non ho voluto tardare punto ad allegrarmene seco, et con espressa persona appresentarle l'infinito piacere et consolatione che ne sento. Mando dunque a posta il Conte Cesare Odasio, il quale, fatta e havrà riverenza a V.A. compitamente satisferà a questo ossequio ch'io gli ho ordinato, rallegrandosi ben di cuore con lei di questo felice parto suo."

[28] ASF, *Ducato di Urbino*, Classe Prima, 236, fol. 173 recto (2 May 1575): "Mi dispiace che l'Ecc.za V. habbia havuto la burla del Maschio si come hebbi io ancora che pur mi trovavo presente."

[29] Bastiano Arditi, *Diario di Firenze (1574–1579)*, Roberto Cantagalli, ed. (Florence: INR, 1970), p. 42: "Addì 26 aprile, in martedì a ore 16 sonate, l'anno 1575 partorì una bambina la Duchessa, donna del duca don Francesco. Maria, che è la quinta figliola che detta Granduchessa ha partorita, ché 2 se n'e' morte e 3 vi ha di presente. Levossi la voce che era maschio e anche e' romore per tutta la città e la plebe che non facesino, secondo il costume loro, l'opere senza discorso e metessino a sacco le robe de bottegai…."

[30] ASF, *Mediceo del Principato* 3292, fol. 402 recto (30 April 1575): "Con l'occasione di dar hoggi conto al Papa della Serenissima Gran Duchessa mia signora, mi domandò

that Pius V had demanded explanations regarding the precise circumstances of this gender confusion given that this had originated in Florence. Alessandro clarified to the Pope that this incident was caused by the "the imagination of two couriers," the same ones described in Ferdinando's letter to Francesco (29 April 1575). This explanation seemed to have appeased Pius V.

Inevitably, rumors of the newborn prince reached also the Imperial Court.[31] The Florentine ambassador Giovan Battista Concino recounted to Francesco— exactly a month after Maria's birth—his meeting with Maximilian (22 May 1575) in which the diplomat had to set things straight. With some degree of embarrassment, he confirmed to the Emperor that the child was a girl and his sister Johanna had made a full recovery. Maximilian's reply embodied sore disappointment: "Thus, it's a female after all ... my sister surely has had many of them...."[32] The man that had fathered ten sons once again saw his hopes of putting the Habsburg foot in the door of Tuscany vanish.

Whatever mix-up took place, it was resolved—at least on a local scale—within a matter of days. From the number of prompt replies congratulating the Grand

---

strettamente Sua Santità d'onde era proceduta quella equivocazione da maschio a femina, volendo saper l'origine dell'errore, col mostrarmi, come ella haveva aviso di Fiorenza, che nella città s'era preso in principio nel modo medesimo. Io le raccontai il fatto come era veramente passato, eccome n'era stata cagione l'immaginatione di due corrieri, che stavano fermi già parecchi giorni alla porta della storta, nata loro dal vedere uno staffiere di Vostra Altezza, che veniva correndo a questa volta, dal quale essi dubitavano di non esser pervenuti con la nuova, et ne rimase Sua Beneditione quieta."

[31] Francesco sent an official note to Concino that put an end to further equivocations four days after Maria's birth. ASF, *Mediceo del Principato* 4337, folio not numbered (30 April 1575): "Alli 26 a hore circa 17 partorì la Ser.ma Gran Duchessa nostra consorte una vivace et bella Figliolina la qual vi è stata molto cara trovandosi massime con salute l'una et l'altra di loro. Datene parte a lor M.tà che ne sentiranno piacere con refrescar loro la nostra incompatibile devotione."

[32] ASF, *Mediceo del Principato* 4333, fol. 94 recto (26 May 1575): "Andai all'audienza alli 22, sicome scrissi et arrivato che fui da S. M.tà Ces.a cominciai a dirle, ch'io conoscevo bene che portandole nuova di femina non meriterei le calze et perciò havere potuto astenermi d'esserle molesto con il pigliar udienza per di fatto aviso, tuttavia che pensavo che non le dovessi essere se non grato l'intender la buona saluta della madre e della fig.la, tenendo io comandamento da V.A. di conplire a questo ufficio, haverei dubitato di mancare troppo a lasciarla sicome sarebbe parso a lei stessa fare grande fallo, se essendole quel servitore devoto, che l'è et reputando tutto quello che tiene come propria di S. M.tà Ces.a non le facessi conto d'ogni minimo accidente che occorra in quella Casa. Dunque è femina disse l'imperatore mia sorella deve essere già parecche, et affè, che mi dispiace solamente per il desiderio c'havea, che fusse maschio. Le reprentai all'hora la consolatione di V.A. essere di confermarsi con la volontà di Dio, et che la bambina fussi vivace et d'aria d'havere riuscir bella, ma che però di parere che la miglior ricetta per farli maschi."

Duke on the birth of a male heir, we can trace the speed with which the couriers disseminated the rumor that they picked up in Florence. Letters from Volterra, Borgo San Sepolcro, and Urbino were written the day after Johanna's delivery of the baby (27 April 1575); replies to Francesco from Rome and Ancona were sent off on 30 April. Whether this rumor originated at court or was ignited among the Florentine populace by circumstances yet to be clarified, Francesco and his secretariat sent letters announcing Maria's birth that same day or shortly after.

There is a rather notable aftermath to this complicated story. It seems as if Maria de' Medici's birth was destined to be plagued with confusion. The documents presented here irrefutably demonstrate that the daughter of Francesco and Johanna of Austria and wife of Henri IV de Bourbon was born on 26 April 1575. An impressive number of scholarly publications, however, still claim that she was born exactly two years before (26 April 1573). Placing Maria's date two years back is simply impossible from a strict physiological point of view. Maria's sister Lucrezia was born on 7 November 1572. It is therefore impossible that Johanna would bear another child a little more than five months later. If this were not enough, around the time of Maria's supposed birth Johanna was traveling extensively in the Marche where she made a pilgrimage to Loreto. Her letters to Florence and Urbino were written almost daily.[33] This egregious error occurs all throughout the catalog for the 2005 Pitti Palace exhibition, suitably entitled: *Maria de' Medici (1573–1642): una principessa fiorentina sul trono di Francia*.[34] Francesco Solinas begins his essay on Maria's Florentine years by stating her birth date and astrological sign ("Princess Maria was born in Florence on 26 April 1573 under the zodiac sign of the Taurus"[35]) and, further on, her age at the time when she left for France ("…from Livorno, on October 17th [1600],

---

[33] ASF, *Mediceo del Principato* 5094, fols. 4 recto (13 April 1573); fol. 5 recto (27 April 1573); fol. 152 recto (29 April 1573). ASF, *Mediceo del Principato* 5926, fols. 143 recto (21 April 1573); 144 recto (21 April 1573); fol. 145 recto (23 April 1573); fol. 146 recto (24 April 1573); fol. 147 recto (27 April 1573); fol. 163 recto (1 May 1573).

[34] Caterina Caneva and Francesco Solinas, eds, *Maria de' Medici (1573–1642): una principessa fiorentina sul trono di Francia* (Livorno: Sillabe, 2005).

[35] Francesco Solinas, "La corte di Toscana e la giovinezza di Maria" in *Maria de' Medici (1573–1642)*, p. 26: "La principessa Maria nasceva a Firenze il 26 aprile 1573, sotto il segno del Toro. Sua madre, l'arciduchessa Giovanna d' Austria (1547–1578) era figlia dell'arciduca Ferdinando, imperatore del Sacro romano impero dal 1558 al 1564, e di Anna, principessa ereditaria di Boemia e di Ungheria (1503–1547). Il padre, don Francesco de' Medici, principe colto e intellettuale raffinato, era il primogenito del duca Cosimo I (1519–1574) e di donna Eleonora di Toledo, marchesa di Villafranca (1522–1563), figlia e sorella dei viceré di Napoli e nipote del potentissimo Duca d'Alba."

the twenty-seven-year-old Maria de' Medici left for France on Tuscan galleys.")[36] This very same error also appears in Caterina Caneva's essay *Il ritorno di Maria*,[37] in Riccardo Spinelli's *Feste e cerimonie tenutesi a Firenze per le "Felicissime Nozze:" nuovi documenti*,[38] and in the chronology compiled by Elena Cattarini Léger.[39] The 1573 date is also pervasively used in the 2003 conference papers *Le siècle de Marie de' Médicis*, edited by Francesco Solinas and Françoise Graziani.[40] Aside from Solinas's essay on Maria's portrait by Pietro Facchetti, the incorrect date is also included in Miles Chappell's study on Maria's artistic education and appears in a Medici family tree included in Bernard Barbiche's paper.[41] Her birth date was mistaken by other scholars and biographers, including M. Capefigue, Philippe Delorme, and Michel Carmona.[42] Françoise Kermina confused not just the year but also the month (26 August 1573).[43] The birth date of the Queen of France was reported incorrectly (as 1574 and as 1576!) in early seventeenth-century sources, and in some instances, in publications appearing during her own

---

[36] Solinas, Francesco, "La corte di Toscana e la giovinezza di Maria" in *Maria de' Medici (1573–1642)*, p. 35: "Da Livorno, il 17 ottobre [1600], la ventisettene Maria de' Medici partiva per la Francia a bordo delle galere di Toscana ...."

[37] Caterina Caneva, "Il ritorno di Maria" in *Maria de' Medici (1573–1642)*, pp. 21–2: "Ma si è ritenuto opportuno ampliare la parte fiorentina, alla quale infatti sono dedicate due sezioni: la prima vuole essere un compendio, un microcosmo delle arti fiorentine dei decenni in cui Maria viveva a Palazzo Pitti, vale a dire dalla nascita (1573) alle nozze (1600)."

[38] Riccardo Spinelli, "Feste e cerimonie tenutesi a Firenze per le 'Felicissime Nozze': nuovi documenti", p. 130: "Maria, non giovanissima—per i tempi (nata nel 1573, aveva allora ventisette anni)—, divenne sovrana anche grazie ad una dote molto ingente, corrisposta dal granduca al re ...."

[39] Elena Cattarini Léger, "Cronologia dei principali avvenimenti storici e artistici del periodo 1534–1643," p. 362: "*1573: 26 Aprile, Nascita di Maria de' Medici a Firenze*."

[40] Francesco Solinas and Françoise Graziani, eds, *Le «siècle» de Marie de Médicis : actes du Séminaire de la Chaire rhetorique et société en Europe (XVIe–XVIIe siècles) du Collège de France*, Alessandria: Edizioni dell'Orso, 2003.

[41] Francesco Solinas, "Il Ritratto di Maria de' Medici giovane di Pietro Facchetti (1535–1613) nella Galleria del principe Lancellotti," p. 3; Miles Chappell, "The Artistic Education of Maria de' Medici," p. 20; Bernard Barbiche, "Marie de Médicis, reine régnant et le Saint-Siège, agent ou outage de la Réforme catholique?," p. 50.

[42] M. Capefigue (Jean Baptiste Honoré Raymond), *Marie de Médicis* (Paris: Amyot, 1861), p. 2, fn. 2 (1573); Philippe Delorme, *Marie de Médicis* (Paris: Pygmalion, 1998), p. 11 (26 April 1573); Michel Carmona, *Marie de Médicis* (Paris, Fayard, 1981), pp. 7, 582 (26 August 1573).

[43] Françoise Kermina, *Marie de Médicis. Reine, régente et rebelle* (Paris: Perrin, 1979), p. 14 (26 August 1573).

lifetime.⁴⁴ Even the 1966 *Inventario Sommario* of the *Medicea del Principato*— the most authoritative index to this archival corpus—indicates that she was born in 1573.⁴⁵

What is, then, the origin of this error? Gaetano Pieraccini, author of the three-volume work *La stirpe dei Medici di Cafaggiolo*, admits that Maria's birth date is "different according to different historians" and hesitantly proposes 26 April 1575.⁴⁶ He does indicate, however, that the eighteenth-century historian Jacopo Riguccio Galluzzi insisted that Grand Duke's daughter was born in 1573. In truth, the author of the *Istoria del Granducato di Toscana* came up with two dates: the correct one, partly concealed in the discussion of the death of Francesco in 1587,⁴⁷ and an utterly incorrect one (26 August 1573) included in the description of the events that led to her marriage with the King of France.⁴⁸ Giuseppe Maria Mecatti in his 1755 *Storia cronologica della città di Firenze* proposed a date which is a combination of the two: 26 August 1575.⁴⁹ Oddly, Pieraccini and other modern scholars dismissed Bastiano Arditi's chronicle of Florence from 1574 to 1579 in which Maria's birth date and the confusion of

---

⁴⁴ Jean-Baptiste de Matthieu, *Eloge historial de Marie de Médicis* ... (Paris: G. Loyson, 1626), p. 6; Mathieu de Morgues, *Les deux faces de la vie et de la mort de Marie de Médicis* ... (Antwerp: Plantin, 1643), p. 35.

⁴⁵ *Archivio Medicea del Principato: Inventario sommario* (Rome, Ministero dell'Interno—Pubblicazioni degli Archivi di Stato, 1966), pp. 251–2.

⁴⁶ Gaetano Pieraccini, *La stirpe de' Medici di Cafaggiolo: saggio di ricerche sulla trasmissione ereditaria dei caratteri biologici* (Florence: Nardini, 1986), II, p. 263: "La Maria di Francesco e Giovanna d'Austria rimase orfana a quattordici anni: era nata il 26 aprile 1575 ..."; see also, footnote "a": "La data della nascita della Maria è diversa per diversi storici. Il Galluzzi da il 1573. Noi diamo quella del 26 aprile 1575 anche in base alle notizie riferite in una lettera del cardinal Ferdinando Medici, nella filza 5089, c. 44 del Mediceo del Principato. Vedi anche Miscellanea Medicea filza 994 e Mediceo del Principato 5088, c. 166."

⁴⁷ Iacopo Riguccio Galluzzi, *Istoria del Granducato di Toscana sotto il governo della casa Medici* (Florence; Gaetano Cambiagi stampatore granducale, 1781), vol. II, p. 427: [1587] "Era il G. Duca Francesco in età di quarantasette anni allorché fu rapito dalla morte avendone regnati dieci sotto la direzione del padre e tredici dopo di esso. Non lasciò altri figli che Donna Maria, la quale è nata il 26 aprile 1575, si trovava allora in età di dodici anni."

⁴⁸ Galluzzi, *Istoria*, III, pp. 164–5: [1599] "Maria de Medici nata da G. Duca Francesco e dalla G. Duchessa Giovanna d'Austria il ventisei Agosto 1573 era allora in età di venticinque anni; dotata di singulari bellezze ed ornata di tutte quelle qualità di spirito che poteva inspirargli ..."

⁴⁹ Giuseppe Maria Mecatti, *Storia cronologica della città di Firenze* ... (Napoli; Stamperia Simoniana, 1755), p. 758: [1575] "E così egli [Francesco de' Medici] potette rallegrarsi co' suoi sudditi per avere la Granduchessa Giovanna d'Austria sua moglie con gran contento di tutti i suoi parziali, partorita il dì 26 Agosto una figliuola, alla quale fu posto il nome Maria."

the male heir are reported correctly.⁵⁰ However, the document that should have ended once and for all this centuries-long confusion has been widely ignored by current biographers of Maria de' Medici and scholars of French and/or Italian history. Ronald Millen and Robert Wolf, in their 1989 book on Peter Paul Rubens' *Maria de' Medici Cycle* (Louvre, 1621–24) published Maria's baptism records from the Duomo archives in Florence which clearly stated that Maria was baptized the day after her birth.⁵¹

As we have seen, the trajectory of the news of the birth of the future Queen of France took unexpected turns and underwent several permutations: from the curious *minuta* written by Francesco but never sent to its intended recipient; to the uncontrolled hearsay that propagated throughout the courts of Italy and Europe (which triggered a number of congratulatory letters from Medici affiliates that, in turn, were answered with corrigenda from Francesco and his secretariat); to the historical inaccuracy that, some centuries later, continued to contaminate important scholarly publications on Maria de' Medici. The archival

---

⁵⁰ Arditi, *Diario di Firenze e di altre parti della cristianità (1574–1579)*, p. 42: "Addì 26 aprile, in martedì a ore 16 sonate, l'anno 1575 partorì una bambina la Duchessa, donna del duca don Francesco. Maria, che è la quinta figliola che detta Granduchessa ha partorita, ché 2 se n'e' morte e 3 vi ha di presente. Levossi la voce che era maschio e anche e' romore per tutta la città e la plebe che non facesino, secondo il costume loro, l'opere senza discorso e metesino a sacco le robe de bottegai ..."

⁵¹ Ronald Millen and Robert Wolf, *Heroic Deeds and Mystic Figures. A new reading of Rubens' Life of Maria de' Medici* (Princeton, N.J.: Princeton University Press, 1989), pp. 30–31: "By her own statement and her father's, and on the evidence of her archive birth records as well as her horoscope known to us in manuscript, Maria was born at midday, not in darkest night. It should be noted here that our Florentine manuscript sources arguably give as 1575 not the 1573 one still often finds, and since the month was April, the discrepancy cannot even be connected with calendar reckoning more florentino; should anyone need more convincing, in April and May of 1573 Maria's mother made a pilgrimage to Loreto 'to fulfill a vow' and certainly to pray for a male child, a journey she could not have undertaken in exactly the days when, erroneously, Maria is said to have been born." See also footnote 1, pp. 31–2: "As still in Thuillier–Foucart" p. 12 (with Batiffol as source) Saward and Heiden, an error that may go back to Galluzzi. If Maria was in fact born in 1573, by 1600 she would have been a candidate for the nunnery rather than a royal bed. Archives of the Duomo of Florence register: 'Battezzati: Femmine dal 1571 al 1577'; *fol. 71v* Aprile 1575, martedì 27. Maria del Ser.mo Granduca di Toscana Fran.co di Cosimo de Medici et della Ser.ma Gio. a d'Austria, N[ata], h[ore] 16 [= 12 noon], P[opolo] S. Romolo Com[ari] il R.mo Mons. r Nunzio Carlo Cicada et la Ill.a Sig.ra Leonora de Toledo de Medici.' The Godmother, Leonora de Toledo, was the wife of Francesco's brother Pietro and would die in the next year in mysterious circumstances much romanced in nineteenth-century literature. Note that Thuillier–Foucart has Maria as the last of Francesco's children by Johanna. Not so, a son, Filippo, was born in 1577 but lived only a few years."

documentation unearthed from the corpus of correspondence in the *Mediceo del Principato* not only resolves this misunderstanding but also paves the way towards a reconstruction of the events that surrounded the birth of Francesco's sixth child which occurred in a period of political turmoil and concern over dynastic continuity. More importantly, however, these letters shed light on the vast network of information—those avenues by which both rumors and official news traveled—as well as on the speed of news circulation, and on the agents responsible for its circulation.

CHAPTER 5

Making It Present

Brendan Dooley

If ever there were a demonstration of the early modern potentate's need for a sense of geographical situatedness, such was Grand Duke Cosimo I's map room in the Palazzo Vecchio in Florence. Lining the walls were 14 maps depicting Europe, Asia and America, along with eleven depicting Africa, all drawn by by Ignazio Danti and Stefano Buonsignori between 1563 and 1580, on the doors of the same number of large wooden armoirs holding some of Cosimo's most valuable possessions. Describing the room, the Grand Duke's master of public works Giorgio Vasari insisted particularly on the accuracy of the renditions, drawn to precise scales and using the most reliable measurements.[1] Commissioned by a prince with vast ambitions and, for a time, even kingly pretensions, the room set the standard for similar decoration schemes in other princely environments around Europe—in the ducal palace in Mantua, in the Vatican palaces in Rome. Perhaps the increasingly broad scale of operations in which princes were now involved demanded a new spatial sense, due to the movement of ships, goods and men from one end of the known world to the other. The Grand Duke's geography project was only an element in a much larger information-gathering operation

---

[1] "Sua Eccellenzia con l'ordine del Vasari, sul secondo piano delle stanze del suo palazzo ducale, ha di nuovo murato a posta et aggiunto alla guardaroba una sala assai grande, et intorno a quella ha accomodatadi armari ... per riporvi dentro le più importanti cose e di pregio e di bellezza che abbi sua eccellenza; questi ha nelle porte di detti armarii spartito dentro gli ornamenti di quegli cinquantasette quadri ... dentro a' quali sono con grandissima diligenzia fatte in sul legname uso di minii dipinte a olio le tavole di Tolomeo misurate perfettamente tutte e ricorrette secondo gli autori nuovi e con le scale giuste delle navigazioni, con somma diligenzia fatte le scale loro da misurare, et i gradi dove sono in quelle, e' nomi antichi emoderni." Giorgio Vasari, *Le vite dei più eccellenti pittori, scultori e architettori* (Florence, Giunti, 1568), vol. 2 pt. 3, pp. 250–51. Concerning the works and their conception, see Mark Rosen, "The Cosmos in the Palace: The Palazzo Vecchio Guardaroba and the Culture of Cartography in Early Modern Florence, 1563–1589," Ph.D dissertation (UC Berkeley, 2004); Mark S. Rosen, "All the Things of Heaven and Earth Together: the original programme for the Guardaroba of the Palazzo Vecchio, Florence," *Actas = Proceedings = Comptes-rendus / XIX Congreso Internacional de Historia de la Cartografía = 19th International Conference on the History of Cartography = XIX Congrès International d'Histoire de la Cartographie : Madrid 1–6, VII, 2001*, Victoria Arias Roca et al., eds (Madrid, 2002); in general, Francesca Fiorani, *The Marvel of Maps* (New Haven, 2005).

that, continued and developed by Cosimo's heirs, reached far and wide. And if the Medici correspondence network could scarcely compete in scale with that of Philip II described in this volume by Cristina Beltran, nonetheless the basic intention was the same. Information was the stock in trade of the early modern prince; precise information about places, people and events marked the difference between the success and failure of a strategy or an operation. The movement of paper throughout a vast network of correspondence generated the first efforts to create systematic diplomatic archives. Accordingly, the Medici archive, preserved almost in its entirety, is one of the most comprehensive (and impressive) repositories regarding early modern information and communication practices.

My purpose in this chapter is to demonstrate, using some recently elaborated methods, moments of contemporaneity in the Medici court, chiefly centering on the figure of Don Giovanni de' Medici, the natural son of Cosimo I. Why Don Giovanni? He was in some ways a typical example of an early modern princely informer, and his career and his information practices provide a point of departure for a discussion of contemporaneity within an early modern court. He was on the scene in the Eighty Years War between the Spanish and the Dutch and in numerous other conflicts around Europe; and his dispatches were read and discussed at court. Indeed, his main goal as a communicator was to bring the realities of these conflicts to the notice of his older brothers the grand dukes (and his neices and nephews), with a view to giving them what was necessary for major decisions, backing up his demands for financial support and reminding them of his ripeness for promotion.

But before examining the documents regarding Don Giovanni, let us consider the Medici network more generally. Between the late sixteenth and early seventeenth centuries, a time when the Grand Duchy was affirming its role among more powerful European neighbors as a mid-sized territorial state, diplomatic connections continued to develop with every Italian and European power. In addition to strictly diplomatic correspondence there were letters to and from a battery of ducal secretaries, including letters from informers, semipermanent as well as ad hoc, petitioners of every variety, and local officials holding posts of every description. The emergence of the Medici bureaucracy and its communication network has been described in precise detail by Alessandra Contini as a particularly significant episode in the emergence of state institutions. Closely connected with the diplomatic correspondence, but constituting a separate body of documents, is a rich collection of handwritten newsletters, dating from the origins of the Medici Grand Duchy in the 1530s to its end in 1737. Places of origin of the newsletters range from the "Levant," that is Constantinople, to Flanders, Holland, Hamburg, Poland, France, Britain and so forth. Written anonymously and according to widely varying criteria (although always in the same standardized form), these were often included in official dispatches from the Medici representatives abroad, but not necessarily. How they arrived at court in Florence is rarely perfectly clear, except that they reflected once again the dynasty's tremendous thirst for information and attempts to procure the best possible, at whatever cost.

The story of Don Giovanni sheds some light on the production and diffusion of this and other kinds of information. For the purpose of this discussion we will not delve too deeply into Giovanni's collateral interests, from philosophy to comedy writing to military architecture. We focus on his activity as a soldier in the service of the Tuscan court, on campaign for the Habsburg dynasty, before he finally joined the forces of the Venetian Republic in the Friulian wars, on the opposite side.[2] He acted as a communicator in two key episodes, which, together, reveal much about the problems of producing and diffusing military information: namely, the voyage and eventual failure of the Spanish Armada in 1587–88, and the siege of Ostend from 1602.

Don Giovanni in Flanders

Thus, in September 1587, we find Giovanni and his small retinue presenting themselves to Alessandro Farnese, governor of Flanders and commander of the Catholic forces.[3] Alessandro, and Giovanni by extension, was about to be involved in the great enterprise of Philip II; the Army of Flanders, some 30,000 strong, was to be ferried across the English Channel under cover of the armada being fitted out now in Portugal under Admiral Don Alvaro de Bazán, Marquis of Santa Cruz. Further conquests in Flanders would thus have to be

---

[2] In general, Gaetano Pieraccini, *La stirpe de' Medici di Cafaggiolo*, second edn, 3 vols (Florence, 1947), vol. 1, pp. 222ff; G. Sommi Picenardi, "Don Giovanni de' Medici, governatore dell'esercito veneto in Friuli," *Nuovo archivio veneto*, n.s. 7, 25 (1907), pp. 104–42; 26 (1907), pp. 94–136. Concerning Giovanni de' Medici's cultural interests, Domenica Landolfi, "Don Giovanni de' Medici, principe intendente in vari scienze," *Studi seicenteschi* 29 (1988): 125–62. The biography of Don Giovanni written by his secretary Cosimo Baroncelli is still fundamental, and it exists in numerous copies in Florence, among which, Archivio di Stato, Miscellanea Medicea, filza 833bis, insert no. 20; Biblioteca Nazionale Centrale, Codici Capponi, no. cccxiii, fols 180–212. See the fine edition by Marina Macchio (Florence, 2009).

[3] In general, Leon van der Essen, *Alexandre Farnèse, prince de Parme, gouverneur général des Pays-Bas (1545–1592)*, vol. 5 (1585–92) (Brussels, 1937); B. De Groof, *Alexander Farnese and the origins of modern Belgium*, Leuven, 1995; Geoffrey Parker, *The Army of Flanders and the Spanish Road* revised ed. (Cambridge, 1990); Idem, *The Dutch Revolt*, revised ed. (Harmondsworth, 2002). For the more theoretical aspects, Martin van Gelderen, *The Political Thought of the Dutch Revolt, 1555–1590* (Cambridge, 1992).

postponed while acquiring ships, cannon and munitions. The going was rough for the Italian contingents, as Giovanni reports to Grand Duke Ferdinand I in December: "Meanwhile this new group of Italians is being miserably destroyed, dying of exhaustion, so that there are few left."[4] Soon Giovanni himself falls seriously ill, and so he suspends his reporting for nearly three months. In order for Alessandro, Giovanni, and the Army of Flanders to play their planned role, much depended upon obtaining an accurate assessment of English defense capabilities, and especially, divining the movements of Sir Francis Drake, appointed as vice-admiral of the English fleet under Charles Lord Howard of Effingham. Grand Duke Ferdinand I was particularly concerned to maintain good relations with Spain, inasmuch as he was about to be awarded the Toison de Oro (possibly in return for a sizeable contribution to the Spanish war chests)—as well as the long overdue official royal investiture papers of the dukedom of Siena.[5] In attempting to keep the court of Ferdinand I informed as accurately as possible Giovanni discovered the disadvantages of his own relatively minor position, when he was unable to find out what transpired when Alessandro was locked away in counsel with a certain Doctor Ruggieri, putative representative of Elizabeth I: "This doctor is esteemed by the English; deformed he is in appearance, and so he is wicked by nature, besides being a perverse heretic and son of a friar who left the Church under Henry VIII and was eventually burned."[6] Was Alessandro sounding out Ruggieri concerning a possible peace?

By March, Armada preparations were in a lull due to the death of Don Alvaro the previous month and the assumption of command by Alonso Pérez de Guzmán, the duke of Medina Sidonia. Handwritten newsletters available in the Florentine

---

[4] Florence, Archivio di Stato, Archivio Mediceo del Principato [hereafter MdP], filza 5151, f. 271, dated 16 December 1587: "Fra tanto questa nuova gente italiana si va distruggendo miseramente morendosi di stento in modo che son ridotti a pochi. [...]"

[5] In regard to the latter affair, MdP, 4919, f. 97, letter from Giovanni Vincenzo Vitelli to Ferdinand I dated 6 Feb. 1588. "[...] La resolutione che fu presa di despacciar quel corriere espresso che partì alle VI del passato trovo ogni dì megliore per l'occassione di ricever di costà le scritture autentiche pertinenti alle due investiture del Stato di Siena in persona del Granduca Cosimo et del Granduca Francesco poichè fin hora da questi ministri reali non sentiamo che se sieno trovati i lor registri originali per deligenza che usino, sebenne danno ferma speranza che si trovaranno et dicono haver trovato solo certe copie ..."

[6] MdP, filza 5151. f. 93, dated 9 April 1588, where Giovanni de' Medici informs about a certain Ruggieri, who is acting as a deputy of Elizabeth I in Antwerp: "È tornato il S.r duca [di Parma, Alessandro Farnese] [...] per due giorni continui dato audienza secreta solo al dottore Ruggieri deputato della regina [Elizabeth I] senza che si sia penetrato di ciò cosa alcuna, come che sene discorra diversamente. È stimato questo dottore dagli Inghilesi; come gl'è deforme d'aspetto, così di natura pessimo, oltre all'essere eretico perverso et figlio d'un frate che al tempo di Enrico [Henry VIII] sfratatosi et ammogliatosi, fu poi alla fine abruciato."

court differed greatly in kind and value. On 19 March 1588, one of them reported that 100 Spaniards had landed in England and taken over a port near the border with Scotland.[7] The newsletter writer claimed the landing had occurred at a place called "Baldras." Whether or not the place intended was in fact Berwick-upon-Tweed or some other place makes little difference, since as far as we know the story was a pure invention. By May, reports had identified the actual armada and its port of departure, but expressed a good deal of uncertainty: "The first flight will be in the port of Corignia [La Coruña] in Galitia near the cape of Finis di Terre; nothing else is known for certain except that it can only be directed to England."[8]

Don Giovanni provided his own eyewitness accounts in contrast with these, to help the Grand Duke assess the realities of the European situation. He knew very early about the difficulties that were emerging behind the scenes, and he tried to convey this knowledge as effectively as possible. "A courier from Spain arrived three days ago," he reported on 13 May: "who brought news, so they say, that the armada was ready to set out." The king, said the news, "was unhappy with the Signor Duke [Alessandro Farnese], who during all these past months was still unprepared" for the supposed rendezvous of the Army of Flanders with the naval invasion force. Yet the king's own logistical contribution, the news went on, appeared to be limited to "the religious side," of imploring divine assistance. In Giovanni's reports, it was clear that Alessandro was still under orders from the king to conclude a peace with the English representatives, although this move was a pure formality conceded on request by Alessandro.[9]

When did the Armada actually set sail? Don Giovanni, Alessandro Farnese, and the Florentine court needed to know, and there was no accurate information either about the departure from Lisbon on 30 May or the arrival in Corunna on the 19 June, where it would remain for nearly a month. At the end of June, Giovanni's entourage approached a certain Captain Morosini, who actually came away from the main fleet to land a small skiff in friendly territory: "Rumor has it that the Spanish Armada has been many days under way in this direction, and Capt. Morosini says so from first hand."[10] Alvise Morosini's putative mission was to recruit pilots for the Armada's approach to the shoreline for the rendezvous with the Army of Flanders. But even Morosini proved to be an equivocal source, because of the political issues in play, especially regarding Philip II's possible skepticism regarding Alessandro's commitment to the Armada plan.

---

[7] MdP, filza 3085, f. 621.
[8] MdP, filza 4851, f. 97, dated 11 May 1588.
[9] MdP, filza 5151, f. 117, dated 13 May 1588.
[10] MdP 5151 f. 137, Giovanni to Ferdinando I, 30 June 1588.

He [Morosini] also returned to Dunkirk to go and meet it [the fleet] again, so they say, in order to bring pilots to it and prepare its arrival, but those who see things more clearly say in order to motivate the duke of Medina Sidonia, who has orders only to go as far as Calais, to get him to pass by Dunkirk and those places which will afford more convenience to the duke of Parma in the enterprise ...[11]

In this case, one wonders, where did Morosini's information go, besides from the English Channel to Antwerp (where this letter was written) to Grand Duke Ferdinand I in Florence? We still do not know.

The fleet was still in Corunna when Alessandro Farnese began to worry about the approach to Dunkirk. Don Giovanni sent detailed reports back to Florence, based on what he heard from Captain Morosini; and the message he had to convey was anything but clear. A major problem for Philip II's enterprise was the Dutch blockade at the mouth of the river Scheldt, preventing the Antwerp troop flotilla from proceeding to the sea. Alessandro accordingly ordered a new canal to be dug so the flotilla could reach Dunkirk for the rendezvous with the Armada. Once the troop barges got as far as Dunkirk, according to Alessandro, the next move was nearly impossible; they could not proceed alone to join the fleet—rather, the fleet would have to come as close as possible to the shore to protect them. Yet apart from the dangers of English and Dutch shipping, the channel before Dunkirk was treacherous due to the irregular coastline and the sandy shoals. Morosini recruited local pilots and planned to bring them to the fleet, where no one had the required expertise. The pilots disagreed "concerning the security of the channel for conducting the armada."[12] Giovanni discounted "rumors" that Medina Sidonia planned to keep the fleet out of danger at Calais, or that he had given up hope after the "persecutions" by Francis Drake. In mid-July, the Armada was still nowhere to be seen. Commented Giovanni: "we are still sitting in Bruges with nothing to do, waiting for the Armada."[13]

---

[11] MdP 5151 f. 137, Giovanni to Ferdinando I, 30 June 1588.

[12] MdP, filza 5151, f. 141, dated 2 July 1588, Giovanni to Ferdinando I, 2 July 1588: "Quel capitano Morosino che pochi giorni sono torno dall'armata di Spagna essendosi di nuovo imbarcato per quella volta a doncherche et facendo il legno acqua tornato in dietro dovrà essersi rimesso in cammino per conducere i piloti al duca di Medina, i quali in fatto non convengono intorno alla sicurtà del canale per condurci l'armata, per eserci alcuni banchi come essi chiamano, pericolosi dell'intoppo, et pure vorrebbe in ogni maniera il sig. Duca di P che la vi si conducessi; intanto vanno cicalamenti intorno che la sia ferma nel porto di Cascai o che la sia voltasi ad assicurare il ritorno della flotta dalla persecutioni del Drachges, et altre simili cicalate; io ho hauto in mano una relazione del n.o de vascelli et de cavalieri che comandano o vengano venturieri, et la mando a V.A. accio che la possa vederla se bene io credo che l'hara vista a quest'hora."

[13] MdP, filza 5151, f. 157, 15 July 1588, Giovanni to Ferdinando I, "Già è mezzo luglio et noi aspettando l'armata siamo ancora in Bruges in otio."

On 5 August, with the Armada veering towards the Straits of Dover, Giovanni gave the grand duke his assessment of the situation, explaining the reasons why he was sympathetic with Alessandro's apparently over-cautious behavior. "As I see it," he began, "the matter is as follows." Clearly, the tiny troop rafts were incapable of withstanding even the slightest storm—much less, a direct hit from Francis Drake's guns. Therefore, the Armada would have to veer shoreward to shield them as they crossed over to England. Yet the obstacles preventing the Armada from approaching the shore to offer protection were impossible to ignore:

> Even if the channel was almost entirely of a ship's depth [quasi tutto porto], as some say it is, how could the fleet navigate securely after having passed the straits between Calais and Dover, where at every step there are those sand hills or shoals that they call "banks," on which it seems almost impossible that such a great armada with so many vessels should not run aground.[14]

Yet each side attempted to defend its own position, even at the cost of botching the whole enterprise—Medina Sidonia protecting his fleet, and Alessandro his army. At the same time, noted Giovanni, Philip II refused to change the basic plan. "The king persists in his usual resolution to undertake the enterprise, apparently constrained by his reputation."

When the Armada entered the channel before Dunkirk Giovanni made sure the Grand Duke was among the first to know—almost as soon as Alessandro Farnese. "On the occasion of a courier coming to Italy in the company of a certain gentleman of the Pigni family I informed Your Highness that the Armada had finally arrived and had entered into the channel and that on the 6th of this month a Spaniard here was sent in a fast coach to His Highness [Duke Alessandro Farnese] to tell him of this arrival." The rapid succession of events soon challenged Giovanni's ability to convey the realities of the naval battle. On the morning of 12 August, Giovanni received more reports concerning a possible victory by the fleet. The same evening these reports were contradicted. Giovanni recounted the famous chase along the coastline, with Francis Drake in hot pursuit, and eventually toward the outer shores of the Orkneys, and a route that would take the scattered remnants down past the windward side of Ireland:

> Today a rumor circulated that the armada had recovered strength and defeated the enemy, nonetheless this evening it was verified to the contrary, since news arrived that it is sailing in fact toward the north (on a westerly wind) or that it is

---

[14] MdP, filza 5151, f. 151, 5 August 1588, Giovanni to Ferdinand I.

about to land in Scotland or return to Spain after having circled the whole island of England, always pursued by Drake, who remains behind it without fighting.[15]

On the 18th, Don Giovanni was already explaining why Alessandro had refused to move his defenseless rafts with the army on them to the rendez-vous with the fleet as long as the latter was in peril. "According to the view of the experts, there was great danger that we would all be drowned by the enemy before we crossed," especially because "the English were in such complete control of the seas, and had vessels so agile that they were able to navigate between the huge [ships] of the Catholic Armada," so that "they could undo us, who were on certain unarmed low-lying rafts."[16] Farnese in his view needed a victory to offset the popular rumors about his reponsibility for the loss of the Armada, although this was solely due to the misfortunes of the Duke of Medina Sidonia.[17]

While Don Giovanni attempted to put the Grand Duke squarely in the theater of action, as it were, making him fully aware of the gravity of the situation, conflicting versions of the story continued to circulate. A Roman newsletter dated 13 August arrived in the Florentine court, still reporting on storms that had scattered the fleet on its way out of Lisbon and destroyed eleven vessels back in June. The Spanish Ambassador, it noted, had informed Pope Sixtus V of the event, adding that the remnants of the fleet had retired to La Coruña to regroup and wait for better weather. The pope was seen to "be greatly afflicted and sad" about this news, which was only mitigated by the Ambassador's reassurance that the fleet would soon resume its course.[18] As late as the 3 September, a newsletter from Antwerp told an entirely different story. The Spanish had won a major battle against the English, it said, and had actually landed on one of the Orkney Islands, called Hylandia—possibly a corruption of the word "Highlands," which is not an island, although there is an Orkney island called Hoy. "According to highly reliable sources," it went on, "the men were given provisions and other

---

[15] MdP, filza 5151, f. 162, 12 August 1588: "Et se bene oggi si spargò voci che l'armata nostra ripreso vigore habbia rotto il nimico, tuttavia stasera si verifica che no, venendo avviso che la naviga adirittura per Nort (che è Tramontana) o per fermarsi sopra la Scotia o per tornarsene in Spagna, dopo havere girato tutta l'isola d'Inghilterra, havendo sempre il Drac dietro che senza combattere senon da lontano la seguita. È ben vero che il sig. duca di Parma ha di nuovo fatto imbarcare parte della gente a Niport osia per haverla in ordine se per sorte l'armata tornassi, o pure voglia intanto assalire Ostendn, come alcuni discorrano, per la via di mare, affondando delle navi in quel porto per tor loro il soccorso."

[16] MdP, filza 5151, f. 166, dated 18 August 1588.

[17] MdP, filza 5151, f. 166, dated 18 August 1588.

[18] MdP, filza 3085, f. 663, dated 13 August 1588.

refreshments; and when word reached the king [James VI of Scotland] some say he decreed the death penalty for anyone who gave them anything." Hoping to regain the advantage, the newsletter continued, Francis Drake and Effingham consulted with Queen Elizabeth. Eager for another engagement, they had already set sail with 180 ships.[19] A newsletter from Lyons dated the 6 September brought the story to a close: Drake was a prisoner and peace had been declared: "The Spanish Armada has landed in Scotland in the province of Heslanda, although previous news was that it was already returned to Spain; and they say it will winter in that ocean, and that the English had been more badly damaged than was previously reported; and many say that Drake the Englishman has been taken."[20]

News from Ostend

Giovanni's cautious attempts to convey the complexities of the situation could be contrasted with the less successful efforts of Camillo Guidi, secretary of the grand ducal legation in Madrid. "News concerning the Armada is as uncertain as that concerning every other thing," he wrote on the 31 August, "and apparently they only speak truthfully who say they do not know the truth." His sentiments were well-founded. On the twentieth of August he had written about a Spanish victory, basing himself on a report by Bernardo de Mendoza, Spanish ambassador to France, which had even appeard in print. On the 27 August he forwarded a report that the fleet had passed Calais and Drake was nowhere to be found. Then from two couriers he received a new newsletter from Mendoza toning down the triumphalism of the earlier newsletter. Finally he managed to view a letter from the Prince of Ascoli containing the truth about the defeat. "To counter this information it is said that they [the Spanish court] caused more favorable news to be published immediately" although such accounts were "more desired than believed."[21]

---

[19] MdP, filza 3085, f. 669.

[20] MdP, filza 4851, f. 101, dated 6 September 1588: "Avisano [...] che l'armata di Spagna ha tolto porto in Scotia nella provintia di Heslanda dove si pensava che fosse già ritornata in Spagna; et si doveva invernare in quel mare, et che Inglesi havevano nauto più danno che non era stato scritto, et voglano molti che il Drac [Francis Drake] Inglese sia preso, et che vi sia seguito disordine nella armata del duca di Parma, mentre si doveva mettersi in ordine per andar a congiongersi in quella di Spagna, la quale per quello danno, la lasciarano in pace la regina d'Inghilterra et forse in tanto succederà la pace che ella di nuovo ricerca dal duca di Parma; a lui ha mandato un primo suo barone per tal effetto con molti presenti. [...]"

[21] MdP, filza 4919, f. 465, dated 31 August, 1588: "Vanno tanto segrete et incerte come ogni altra cosa, le notizie di questa armata, che pare che nessuno si possa promettere di dirne

Giovanni's information-gathering methods improved remarkably over the years, and some fifteen years after the defeat of the Spanish Armada, the siege of Ostend presented him with new challenges as a military informer. Ostend, the last Dutch outpost in Flanders during the Eighty Years War, lay on the coast between Bruges and Veurne. Archduke Albert of Austria, co-sovereign of the Low Countries, sought to regain this important strategic stronghold, a precious asset in the effort to defend the Flanders operation against Dutch shipping. Over 60,000 Spaniards died in the siege, which lasted from 5 July 1601 to 20 September 1604; and the destruction was a major factor in determining the conclusion of the so-called twelve-year truce between the belligerents, beginning in 1609.[22] In the last year of the siege Giovanni arrived with his own contingent of Italian soldiers to join the forces of Archduke Albert, headquartered in Brussels. To avoid any doubts about his status as a Medici prince, he appointed some of the best lodgings in Antwerp—an aspect which did not go unnoticed by a local newsletter writer, whose newsletters made their way to the Florentine court.[23] To keep the Medici informed about his situation (and, as always, to remind them about his money problems), Giovanni produced frequent and detailed reports of his own.

Once again, communication was rendered difficult by the presence of conflicting information—a common problem as the newsletter business more

---

la verità se non chi dica di non ne saper verità. ... Prima si disse della vittoria per la parte nostra così favorevole et fortunata come io scrissi con l'ordinario per lettera di XX. Et fu questa voce fondata su una relazione di Don Bernardo de Mendozza, il quale non solo ne scrisse, ma ne mandò alcune stampe che sopra ciò haveva fatto imprimere. Poi si pubblicò che l'armata nostra haveva pacificamente passato il Canale, et preso porto a Cales con havere veduto Drach [Francis Drake], et l'almirante inglese senz'alcun motivo loro, non che contrasto. Et questo presupposto con la verità degli altri scritti da me a V.A. per lettera di XXVII et in particolare di quello ^oro in Francia^ diede luogo a quelle considerazioni che in essa scrivevo. Ultimamente per due corrieri ci sono due avvisi uno del medesimo Don Bernardo dove si va moderando et limitando. L'altro del Principe d' Ascoli, del quale sendovi assai male nuove, se ne sono vedute copie difficilmente, et quelle poche con poco gusto di questo Cons.re di Guerra il quale si dice che per sopirle habbiano immediatamente fatto pubblicare più prosperi avvisi della sconfitta di Drach, et dell'armata inglese, che sono più desiderati, che creduti per molte ragioni, ch'io reputo superfluo numerare a V.A. ben informata d'ogni successo. Ben ho voluto mandarle le copie de detti avvisi acciò vegga come qua si dicono et variano le cose."

[22] Anna E.C. Simoni, *The Ostend Story: Early tales of the great siege and the mediating role of Henrick van Haestens*, Bibliotheca Bibliographica Neerlandica, vol. 38 ('t Goy-Houten, 2003), p. 10.

[23] MdP, filza 4256, f. 153, extract of a letter dated 16 August by Antonio Sivori: "Sig. Don Juan de Medici è arrivato a Brusselles, et si aspetta per momento qua, havendo qui preso la casa guarnita molto bene, come a cavaliere tale appartiene. ..."

and more began to take root. Just a few months before his arrival Giovanni had to report possible false alarms regarding the death of Elizabeth I, assessing the veracity of the news by the interruption of commerce that was likely to ensue. "Two Italian gentlemen came here who had been in London for recreation and left that city on 26 March ... They thought to leave before the death occurred because otherwise all the ports would be closed."[24] And Giovanni and his entourage found the city of Brussels to be a hotbed of rumor even after the siege of Ostend, if we are to take at face value comments by Giovanni's squire Cosimo Baroncelli in a letter to ducal secretary Curzio Picchena regarding the death of Pope Clement VIII: "Now the newsletters begin to be pleasant and a good pasttime, and if Your Lordship could send us some, we would be very grateful, because here the pope's death is believed to be certain, although there is no confirmation from down there; we are totally in the dark regarding the possible candidates, and the newsletters discuss all of them, giving us material for making so many castles in the air."[25] As usual, Giovanni utilized a mixture of written and oral sources, for instance when he had to convey the controversial appointment by Philip II of the aging Agustin Majia as field marshal in Flanders. "Besides the newsletters that arrived from Spain last week, as I advised Your Highness in my last message," wrote Giovanni in a letter dated 28 January 1605, "four days ago the squire of the Count of Soria came with letters of the eighth of this month, with certain news that the king had appointed don Agustin Mejia as his field marshal in these lands; and since I have not had letters from [the ambassador] monsignor Tarugi for a long time, I take this information along with what the merchants here say according to a friend from Brussels, who knows it from a good source."[26]

---

[24] MdP, filza 5155, f. 412, dated 3 April 1603, Giovanni de' Medici to Ferdinando I: "Essendo arrivati due gentilhuomini italiani, i quali essendo stati in Londra per loro spasso, partirno di quella città a 26 di Marzo. [...] Parve loro ben fatto non aspettare la morte perchè si sarebbono serrati tutti i porti. [...]"

[25] MdP, filza 5157, f. 72, 25 March 1605, Baroncelli to Picchena: "Adesso veramente cominciano le gazette ad essere piacevoli, e di badalucco, e se V.S. potrà mandarcene, cene farà sommo piacere, perchè tenendo qua per fermo la morte del papa [Clemente VIII], se bene di costà non ne habbiamo sicurezza, siamo al buio in tutto e per tutto de' soggetti papabili, e che sono in predicamento; e le gazzette discorrono sopra tutti, e danno materia a noi altri di far sei castellucci hor che nell'ozio non habbiamo altra faccenda, e piaccia a Dio che succeda al passato pontefice, un buon pastore come ciascheduno deve desiderare.

[26] MdP, filza 5157, f. 12, 28 January 1605, Giovanni de' Medici: "Oltre a gli avvisi venuti di Spagna la settimana passata, come con la mia ultima avvisai a V.A., è comparso anco quattro giorni sono il maiordomo del Conte di Sora, et ha portato lettere, degli 8 del presente, con avviso certo, che il re haveva dichiarato don Agostin Messia [Agustin Mejia] maestro di campo generale di questi paesi; et io non havendo lettere da Mons. [ambasciatore]

Description of the progress of the siege itself was rendered all the more challenging by the new technology involved. Giovanni attempted to describe a contraption devised by the Roman engineer Pompeo Targone, incorporating a moving turret and several cannons for breaking a wall:

> It is built on boats that at high tide will be pushed toward the channel. It has the form of a barrel, and the diameter where the soldiers will stay is 37 feet, and between the said space and its bulwark will be 35 feet, all full of padding that will resist cannon fire; the other part facing the sea is not so full, but is made of wood, and on it will be placed six cannons that will fire toward any approaching boats, but a few days will pass before the whole thing is put together.[27]

In fact, when Don Giovanni sent his first drawing of the contraption to Ferdinand I, the latter responded that he had difficulty understanding what Don Giovanni was intending to convey.[28] As it happened, Giovanni was not the only one, at home and on the field, with premonitions about the machine's probable ineffectiveness in action.[29]

Tarugi da un gran pezzo in qua, sento questo avviso oltre a quello, che dicono qui i mercanti, da amico di Brusselles, che lo sa da buona parte, e mi scrive, che la provisione di questo carico, nella persona del sopradetto don Agostino haveva, non solo alterato notabilmente l'animo di S. A. ma di tutta la corte ancora e della soldatesca, e molto più della nazione spagnola, per essere questo buon cavaliero grave di età e malsano, iltre a qualche altra taccherella, che gli danno gli spagnoli; soggiunge meco l'amico di Brusselles, che don Luigi di Velasco renunzierà il carico della cavalleria, o almeno se non rinunzierà, non uscirà quest'anno in campagna per sfuggire il comando di don Agostino, e se ne starà appresso a S. A. e che il marchese [Ambrogio] Spinola ha ha scritto qua al Segretario Manzizidro che non tornerà altrimenti in questi paesi sendo fieramente disgustato della corte di Spagna." Concerning Giovanni's dealinigs with newsletter writers there are even unpaid bills in Florence, Archivio di Stato, Pupilli, filza 767.

[27] MdP, filza 5155, f. 499r, 3 July 1603: "È fabbricata sopra barche che, a alta marea si spigneranno alla volta del canale. Ha forma di tino, e il diametro dove ha da stare la soldatesca resta trentasette piedi, e fra lo spazio predetto e la sua contrascarpa sarà trentacinque piedi, tutto ripieno di salcicce che reggierà alla botta del cannone; l'altra parte che guarda verso il mare non è così ripiena, ma è di legniame, e vi sarà sopra sei pezzi di cannone che tirreranno alle barche che volessin venire, ma prima che sia messa insieme ci andrà ancora qualche giorno."

[28] MdP, filza 5153, ins. 2, f. 69r, 10 January 1603, Ferdinando to Giovanni: "Quanto a quella machina del Ponte del [Pompeo] Targone non vi bisognava punto meno che mandarne il duplicato, perchè quel primo disegno si durava una gran fatica a capirlo."

[29] MdP, filza 5155, f. 532r, 28 August 1603, Giovanni to Ferdinando: "Poi si metterà la macchina, la quale è finita, e accomodata di tutto punto con sei pezzi di cannone sopra, i quali si maneggiano con un invenzione trovata dal Targone che in vece di rinculare gli fa

Indeed, Giovanni neither attempted nor commissioned a visual rendition of the siege machines. For him, far more important from a strategic standpoint was the lay of the land and the placement of the fortifications, outworks, and attack works. These he found difficult enough to draw in the middle of a battle, even when he was able to use local surveyors to take accurate measurements. With time, characteristics could change, so every drawing was a work in progress. He apologized for some inaccuracies: "Let Your Highness not be surprised by some small errors, such that in the previous drawing a mezzaluna toward the old city was missing, and some other little things, because the great number of things there are to see, and having to make them out with the danger of the musket or the cannon ever present, are the reasons why at first sight one does not identify any more than one would were one doing this purely for curiosity or as an exercise, and not by necessity and obligation."[30] At the risk of freezing in time a changing reality, Giovanni included an actual scale model of the siege, made according to his instructions by his draftsman Gabriello Ughi. Marshland was carefully distinguished from dry land by color coding. The various outworks were indicated, along with the trenches and fortifications of the besiegers. Military units were shown as raised squares on the flat field surrounding the walls, and the concentration of Catholic forces on the southwest side showed where the principal attackers were still hoping to make a breach. Roughly one meter square, and constructed of various materials including wood and plaster, the model now hangs on the wall in the Director's office of the Museum of S. Marco, inventory no. 713. It stands as a fitting tribute to an age when warfare was an aesthetic as well as a political matter. And of an age when a disastrous retreat, especially by the enemy, had a beauty quite apart from the military

---

girare; ma io dubito che di questa havrà più difficultà a muoversi e a condursi al luogo dove egli la vuol fermare per essere grande e pesante, e forse bisognerà che aspetti alla nuova luna per havere le maree più grosse che la possino alzare; e quanto all'artiglieria che vi è sopra parmi esser certo che a i primi tiri habbia a guastare e spezzare il bilico dove è accomodata, e oltre a ciò il fummo habbia a far tal danno a i soldati che vi saranno sopra che havranno poca piazza che non habbia a servire a niente."

[30] MdP, filza 5157, f. 196, about the 19 August 1604: "Venderdì passato che fumo a 16 [del mese] S. A. [Archduke Albrecht von Habsburg] andò la mattina molto per tempo a Ostendn, et io fui a servirlo, et havendo con tal occasione riconosciuto meglio le ritirate dell'inimico, e fattole riconoscere da Gabbriello [Ughi] che vi restò un giorno dopo me, habbiamo finalmente veduto che stanno conforme a questo schizzo che mando a V.A. con questa, nè si meravigli del poco errore che era nell'altro disegno mancandovi una mezzaluna di verso la villa vecchia, et alcune altre cosette, perchè la tanta quantità di cose che vi sono da vedere, et l'havere a riconoscerle con l'offesa tanto vicina del moschetto, et del cannone, sono cagione che così alla prima non si accerta tanto più che facendosi tutto questo per curiosità, et per imparare, et non per necessità, et obbligo, cagione che non si fa con tanta esquisitezza nella prima occhiata."

considerations: "Arriving at the platform with His Highness, from the highest point we saw the enemy's retreat," that is, from Ostend, "a thing well worth seeing, as it was carried out with such elegance and regularity that it seemed to be painted."[31]

Gaining accurate information was nearly as difficult for Giovanni, who was in the midst of the fray, as it was for his half-brother the grand duke, sitting in Florence—simply because no one could be in every corner of the battlefield at once.[32] "Matters here, as far as I can see, are conveyed with ... passion and partiality," he noted; yet "it seems reasonable that Your Highness should know the truth about every detail." He committed himself to communicating only what he was able to verify: "I assure you that what I write I have seen myself or have received on report from disinterested persons whom I trust." His narrative strategy, in order to confirm the veracity of his accounts, was to delve into the most minute details: "Your Highness should not be amazed if I bore you with so many particulars."

A Newsletter is Born

To ensure a constant supply of material to communicate to the grand duke, Don Giovanni organized friends and acquaintances, including the field marshal Lodovico Melzi, into a veritable news bureau for producing the newsletters of Antwerp that now appear in the volumes of his correpondence in the big round unmistakable hand of his faithful amenuensis, Cosimo Baroncelli.[33] Melzi himself had the advantage of being involved in the daily operations on the field, where planned operations were actually being carried out, so details such as the following came from a first-hand source: "They write from Ostend that the gentleman Melzi with his troop of Italians has very luckily taken the ravelin of the gate, and with the loss of few of his men."[34] Giovanni explained the pattern

---

[31] MdP, filza 5157, f. 120r, 27 May 1604, Giovanni to Ferdinando: "Arrivato così con S. A. alla piattaforma dalla sommità di essa si vedde la ritirata fatta dall'inimico, la quale certo è cosa degna di esser vista essendo fatta con tanta pulitezza, et tanto ben finita che par dipinta."

[32] MdP, filza 5157, f. 243r, dated 14 September 1604.

[33] MdP, filza 5157, f. 99r, dated 23 April 1604: "Le nuove di Ostende le vedrà V.A. nell'aggiunto foglio che è cavato da più lettere che il Cav. Melzi et altri amici mi scrivono di là continovamente; nè più di questo saprei dirle cosa alcuna poi che non si ragiona d'altro che di quest' espugnazione, la quale va veramente a buon cammino."

[34] MdP, filza 4256, f. 268r, 23 April 1604: "Scrivono da Ostende che il cav. Melzi con il suo Terzo d'Italiani si è impatronito del revellino della porta, molto felicemente, e con

of composition of the Antwerp newsletter thus: "Your Highness will find the news about Ostend in the accompanying sheet, which is compiled from various letters that Cav. Melzi and other friends are constantly writing to me." And so the news continued throughout 1604.

In his own dispatches to the Medici court, Don Giovanni simply paraphrased the newsletter he sent accompanying his own letter. Just one example, where the wording is almost identical:

Antwerp Newsletter:	Don Giovanni dispatch:
The enemy, taking the opportunity of a fair that was being held in Arlon, in the country of Luxemburg, sent about 40 footsoldiers and horse dressed as peasants, and well armed underneath, who took the portal; and in an instant there appeared four hundred horse who entered and sacked whatever there was, and took as prisoners about thirty of the principal townsmen in the city and it was, so they say, the greatest booty ever taken in these parts.[35]	As far as the news of these parts are concerned, I can only tell you that the enemy taking the opportunity of a fair that was being held in Arlon, in the country of Luxemburg, sent about 50 soldiers dressed as peasants, with good arms underneath, to take the portal of the town; and with four hundred horse entered and sacked everything, and besides taking the greatest booty ever taken in these parts, took as prisoners as about thirty of the principal townsmen who will pay the ransom for themselves and everyone else who remained.[36]

---

perdita di pochi de suoi e adesso restan solo gli spagnoli a arrivare alla contrascarpe; i quali hanno molta difficoltà per essere più vicini alla marea come anco perché il loro cammino è imboccato da due fianche da quali il nemico gli tartassa bravamente et in due tiri ne ammazò diciotto interamente e molti ne ferirno."

[35] MdP, filza 4256, dated 18 November 1604: "Il nemico presa il tempo d'una fiera che si faceva in Arlon nel paese di Luzemburgh mandò circa 40 fra a piedi et a cavallo vestiti da villani e bon armati sotto i quali presero la porta e in un istante comparsero quattrocento cavalli che entrorno dentro e sacheggiorno e svaligiorno, quanto vi era, e presero prigioni circa a 30 dei principali borgesi della vialla et è stato dicono il maggior bottino che già mai si sia fatto in questa parte."

[36] MdP, filz. 5157, f. 279r: 18 November 1604: "Quanto a nuove di queste parti posso sol dirle come, il nemico preso il tempo di una fiera che si faceva in Arlon nel paese di Luzenburghi mandò cinquanta soldati vestiti da villano con buon arme sotto a pigliar la porta della villa e con 400 cavalli entrò poi dentro e svaligiò e sacheggiò ogni cosa e hanno fatto un de maggior bottini e de più ricchi che si sia fatto da un tempo in qua in questi paesi, et oltre alla preda delle robbe migliori che erano in quella villa hanno condotto prigioni una trentina di quei borgesi principali che pagheranno la ranzone per loro e tutti gli altri che sono restati."

Occasionally, Giovanni utilized the newsletter to convey the tiniest details, while reserving his dispatch for more general remarks, as in the following example concerning operations to breach the ramparts by artillery and digging tools:

Antwerp Newsletter:
The two pieces [cannon] passed [through] the terreplein of the ravelin because they were very close and because in the past days there was much thinning due to the axe, so that the enemy not able to stay on the defensive shelter in the said ravelin. After a long time of striking and after a reasonable opening had been made, by means of this the shelter was uncovered, with buckets and hand weapons; it had been built of double [stone] slabs and full of earth, but did not resist the cannon, so that when it was pretty well beaten down many openings were made whereby it was seen that even inside the enemy could remain protected from cannons, with his musket firing.[37]

Don Giovanni Dispatch:
The tip of the shelter on the petit epaulement is being opened with the pick so that by means of two pieces, that have been placed above the rampart of the same petit epaulement, another shelter with [stone] slabs that is inside the first shelter can be uncovered.[38]

Other Antwerp newsletters in Baroncelli's hand included last-minute handwritten corrections by Don Giovanni himself, which were also reported in the dispatch (although, as we see below, leaving certain equivocations to be resolved by the reader):

---

[37] MdP, filza 4256, f. 266r, Ostend, 19 April 1604: "Le due pezze passavano il terrapieno del revellino per esser molto vicino et perché i giorni innanzi si era assotigliato assai con la zappa, onde che l'inimico non potendo stare alla difesa si ritirò dentro alla ritirata che haveva fatto dentro a esso revellino. Dopo che si fu battuto per buono spazio et fatto ragionevole apertura si cominciò mediante essa a scoprire la ritirata, la quale essendo di tavoloni doppii e ripieni di terra con cestini et ferrittoie non resisteva al cannone tal che battuta là al quanto se gli fece molte aperture mediante le quali si conobbe che ne anche quivi l'innimico poteva stare alla difesa rispetto al cannone et col calore della moschetteria."

[38] MdP, filza 5157, f. 96r, 16 April 1604: "La punta della ritirata del petit poldro si va aprendo con la zappa per poter con dua pezze che hanno messo sopra il rampato del medesimo petit poldro scoprire un altra ritirata di tavole che è dentro la prima ritirata."

Antwerp Newsletter:
On the 27th the Archduke and the Infanta of Brussels left for Ghent, where the Infanta will remain, and from whence the Archduke will advance leisurely toward Sluis or perhaps toward Ostend, on the suspicion that the enemies may be intending to relieve that town, since they have landed on the Island of Cadzand, and in order to oppose them and prevent their design all the garrisons have been gathered from the forts at ~~Mastrich~~, Rommond, ~~Strale~~, Gheller and ~~Venlò~~, in all some 5,000 soldiers, and with these and 12,000 peasants and with the heavy cavalry perhaps something good could be done.[39]

Don Giovanni Dispatch:
I had a lackey from Brussels with news that the Archduke, having heard about the landing of the enemies in Flanders on the island of Cadzand, was moving on the following day with the Most Serene Infanta to Ghent, where the Infanta will remain; and His Highness will then proceed either to Ostend or to Sluis, where it will be seen that the enemies will turn ... To oppose the enemies all the men who were in the forts at Erental [Herentals] Mastrich Gheller Strale e Venelò, have been removed, which must be about 5000 infantry and with these and with 12,000 peasants and with the heavy cavalry of the country and also the light cavalry, which could be up to 1000 horse, it will be attempted to impede the designs of the enemies.[40]

Giovanni's newsletter was not the only one that the Grand Duke received from Flanders; but it was certainly the one with the most detailed political analysis. The following is a comparison between the two newsletters. On the right is the one received from Giovanni's entourage.

---

[39] MdP, filza 4256, c. 270, dated 28 April 1604: "Il giorno de 27 partì l'Arciduca e l'Infanta di Bruselles per la volta di Gantes dove si fermerà l'infanta e l'arciduca agevolmente si avanzerà verso l'Inclusa o forse verso Ostende per dubbio che il nemico non vadia a soccorrere quella piazza essendo sbarcato nell'Isola di Cassante e per opporsegli e impedirgli il suo disegno si son cavati tutti i presidii che erano nelle guarnigioni di ~~Mastrich~~, Rommond, ~~Strale~~, ~~Gheller~~ e ~~Venlò~~, che saranno in tutto circa a 5m soldati, e con questi e con 12m paisani e con la cavalleria d'huomini d'arme, si potrebbe forse far qualcosa di buono."

[40] MdP, filza 5157 c. 100, dated 28 April, 1604: "Hebbi un lacchè di Brusselles con nuova che l'Arciduca inteso lo sbarco del nimico in Fiandra nell'Isola di Cassante [Cadzand] si moveva il giorno appresso con la Ser.ma Infanta per la volta di Gantes, dove si fermerà l'Infanta; e S. A. si trasferirà, o a Ostendn o all'Inclusa [Sluis], dove si vedrà che il nemico si volti [...] Per opporsi al nemico si è cavato tutta la gente che era ne" presidi di Erental [Herentals], che in tutto saranno circa a 5m fanti e con questi e con 12m villani e con la cavalleria degli huomini d'arme del paese e con la leggiera che ci è che arriverà vicino a mille cavalli si vedrà di impedire i disegni del nemico."

Newsletter from Antwerp (unknown): Archduke Albert returned with the Most Serene Infanta from the devotion of the Madonna as written, to distribute his men in the garrisons, where he will soon return to Brussels; and Count Maurice has send a certain number of cavalry in the lands of Gueldria and Chempon, whereas His Excellency does not wish to divide the rest of his men, nor depart from Esclusa until he has fortified that city…the Connestable of Castile is still in Arras awaiting the resolution; and the Most Christian [king Henry IV] will put the [customs] duty of 30 percent just as the protection of the Dutch estates, to whom His Majesty insisted that the merchandise of these Dutch should not go from France to Spain under a French name.[41]

Newsletter from Antwerp (Giovanni de' Medici group): The Archduke and the Signora Infanta are still in Ghent to allow time for the apartments of in Brussels, where Their Highnesses live, to be made larger and accomodated to their tastes and the orders they have given. The Connestable is still in Arras, where it is said that the king is keeping him a prisoner for having agreed in the conditions of the peace with England to certain conditions that harm the reputation of the king, from whose court the following formal phrase has issued: that the Connestable has concluded an infamous peace that cannot last.[42]

In this case Giovanni's group attempts to assess the deeper reasons for the archducal couple's prolonged absence from Antwerp, connected with Albert's well-known love of luxury, contrasted with the more flattering conclusions of the other newsletter, which supposes religious reasons. In addition, Giovanni's group informs concerning the legal problems of the Connestable of Castile, due to mishandling of the accords with Holland; whereas the other newsletter merely makes ambiguous reference to his stay in Arras.

---

[41] MdP, filza 4256, f. 312r, Anversa, 22 October 1604: "L'arciduca Alberto tornato con la ser.ma infanta della devotione della madama scritta attende a distribuire le sue genti per le guarnigioni dovendo di breve ritornare Bruselles et il co. Mauritio ha mandato certo n.ro di cav.ria nelli paesi di Gheldria et Chempon, non volendo però S. Ecc.za dividere il restante delle sue genti ne meno partire della Sclusa finchè non habbia a suo modo fortificata quella piazza ... Il contestabile di Castilia si trova tuttavia in Aras aspettando la risolutione et farà il X.pmo circa il datio dessi 30 per cento come della protezione delli stati olandesi alla cui m.ta faceva istanza, che le mercantie dessi olandesi non vadono di Francia in Spagna sotto nome francese."

[42] MdP, filza 5157, f. 273r, 22 October 1604, avviso from Antwerp: "L'arciduca [Albrecht von Habsburg] e Sig.ra Infanta [Isabel Clara Eugenia de Austria] si trattengono ancora in Gantes [Ghent] per dar tempo che gl'apartamenti del palazzo di Bruselles dove habitano loro AA.zze sieno ampliati e raccomodati secondo il gusto loro, e l'ordine che hanno dato. Il Contestabile [Juan Fernández de Velasco y Tovar] è ancora in Araz [Arras] dove dicono che il re [Philip III] lo facci ritener prigione per haver accordato nelle condizioni della pace d'Inghilterra alcuni capitoli che danno poca reputazione al suo re, dalla cui corte viene scritte le sossequenti formali parole: Il conte Stabile ha concluso una pace infame, e da non poter durare."

Normally, newsletters became merchandise almost as soon as they left the pen of the writer. Did Don Giovanni in fact dictate the contents of the newsletters taken down in Baroncelli's hand, basing himself on what the members of the news bureau were whispering in his ear? Indeed, was Giovanni in effect the author of these newsletters? If so, he would not be the only princely ghostwriter personally involved in the early information media, supposing we believe, for instance, that Louis XIII actually authored some stories published later in the Gazette de Paris.[43] However, if our hypothesis is correct, Giovanni would have been the only Italian of his rank to be involved in the newsletter business. How many copies were made of the Antwerp newsletter? Did it make its way directly into the world of printed news? No other copies besides the Medici manuscripts so far have surfaced; but this research has only just begun. There is no telling what Melzi and his associates might have done with the material they helped to produce. We must imagine that Don Giovanni was no more able to seal the precincts of his secretariat than were the many ambassadors to foreign courts, which elsewhere gave rise to a lively cottage industry merchandising diplomatic dispatches and reports and the newsletters based on them.

To trace the newsletters that are based on the Antwerp copies found in Florence the next step would be to fill in the blanks in the following figure:

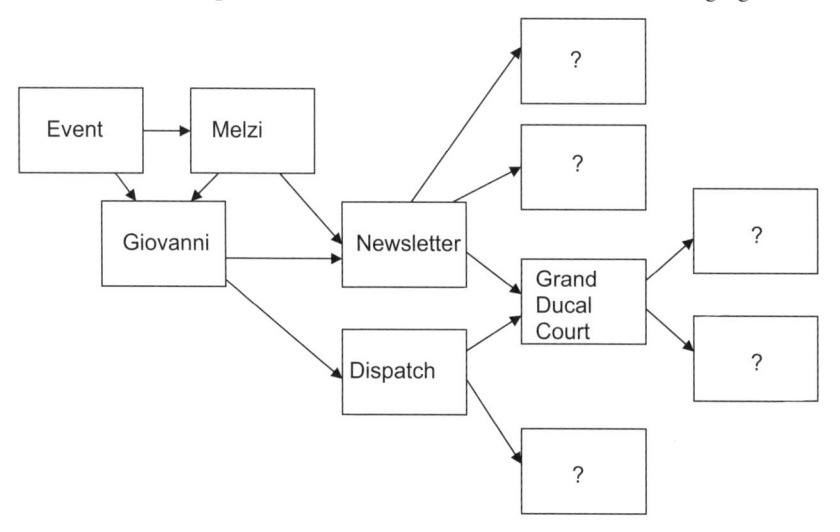

Figure 5.1   Tracing back Antwerp newspaper copies found in Florence

---

[43] Howard M. Solomon, *Public Welfare, Science and Propaganda in Seventeenth-Century France: the Innovations of Théophraste Renaudot* (Princeton: Princeton University Press, 1972), p. 149.

What can be said with some certainty is that the newsletter, and the accompanying briefings by Giovanni, achieved at least part of the desired effect: they impressed Giovanni's half-brother Grand Duke Ferdinando. The Grand Duke responded by encouraging further communications, with a promise to continue his financial support: "I received ... what you prudently remarked ... about the siege, and I was pleased to hear about everything." Indeed, "Your Excellency can go reconnoitering that country and telling me what happens, and I will do everything I can for your welfare."[44] However, over the long run, Giovanni's activities were not enough to gain him the desired promotion within Florence, and family interests dictated prudence regarding any fortune-seeking within the hierarchies of Spain and France. With these two powers the Medici remained perilously aligned, so that a job in either place would be interpreted as a slight upon the other. Giovanni's eventual turn to the Venetian Republic, where he extended his career to a generalship of the forces in Friuli, need not detain us here.

Did Giovanni succeed, by the activites we have described, in making the members of the Florentine court present in the theater of action, to share with them the same present, contemporaneously? In view of the simplicity of the methods at hand (informers, pen, paper, couriers) and given the distance and the complexity of the operations to be described, the challenge was formidable. However, if contemporaneity of any sort was possible between individuals so far apart, enabling reflections concerning shared interests and common behavior, then we must imagine that some sort existed in this case. To test the extent to which the information gathered by Giovanni helped to create a community beyond the court and its dependents, we would need far more knowledge regarding the diffusion of the newsletters themselves and their eventual spread into the world of print. This aspect we promise to explore in another installment.

---

[44] MdP, filza, 5155 f. 25r: "Potrà Vostra Eccellenza andare scoprendo paese di man in mano, et ragguagliarmi di quello che passi, che molto volentieri m'impiegherò sempre per ogni suo benefitio, et honore; ho di poi ricevuto questa settimana l'altra sua de 23 del passato con il disegno de salsiccioni comciati per riempire il fosso; et quanto prudentemente ella ne discorre sopra essi, et sopra quell'assedio; che tutto m'è piaciuto sentire."

CHAPTER 6

Contemporaneity in 1672–1679: the Paris *Gazette*, the *London Gazette*, and the *Teutsche Kriegs–Kurier* (1672–1679)

Sonja Schultheiß-Heinz

Introduction

The news market in seventeenth-century Europe was characterized by great variety, as German, English, French, Dutch, and Spanish newspapers circulated, presenting a vast number of news items concerning political, military, and dynastic events. Particularly, war times increased news production and led not only to the founding of new authorized periodicals but also to the publication of many unauthorized pamphlets and other printed items. The period roughly corresponding to the Dutch War from 1672 to 1679 is no exception. A conflict which originally began as a bilateral war between Holland and France developed quickly into a European war involving the Emperor, various estates of the Holy Roman Empire, Spain, Lorraine, Sweden, Denmark, and England, the latter having initiated a naval war against Holland in 1672.[1] For delving into the issue of the contemporaneity of news, the articles of three European journals shall be compared with one another— newspapers published in countries that were directly and indirectly involved in this war and other conflicts of the time. These newspapers are the *Teutsche Kriegs–Kurier* based in Nuremberg, the *Gazette* in Paris and the *London Gazette* of London.[2] So that the news contents and connotations are duly placed into historical context we shall first undertake a brief survey of the rise and development of the three. Next, by way of content analysis the general topics of the three papers shall be presented in order to consider similarities and differences regarding their reporting. Finally,

---

[1] Max Braubach, *Vom Westfälischen Frieden bis zur Französischen Revolution* (Handbuch der deutschen Geschichte 10), 9th edn (Stuttgart, 1988), pp. 48–59.
[2] *Teutscher Kriegs–Kurier / Aus dem [!] Käyserlichen und Frantzösischen Feld=Lägern* (Nuremberg, 1673–98); *Gazette* and *Nouvelles Ordinaires: Recueil des toutes les Gazettes, Nouvelles Ordinaires & Extraordinaires & autres Relations* [...], (Paris 1631–1792); *The London Gazette* [at the beginning: *The Oxford Gazette*], *The appointed organ for all announcements of the Executive* (London, 1665–1867).

we elucidate in detail the question of contemporaneity in light of the events surrounding the Fürstenberg Affair in 1674.

Survey of the Three Journals: *Gazette, London Gazette,* and *Teutscher Kriegs-Kurier*

Although all three newspapers were founded during the seventeenth century, their emergence, development, and existence were marked by highly divergent conditions and parameters.

The *Gazette* was established in 1631 in Paris and was, from its foundation, a semi-official organ of the royal government. Brought into being with the active assistance of Cardinal Richelieu it embarked upon "a career in the service of the monarchy"[3] and maintained the monopoly bestowed upon it by the monarchy nearly until the Revolution in 1789.[4] It was founded by the royal physician and court historiographer Théophraste Renaudot; and in the period from 1672 through 1679 that interests us, was published by François and Eusèbe Renaudot.[5] On into the eighteenth century the *Gazette* remained the property of the Renaudot family who had owned their own print shop since 1643.[6] The journal could be purchased in Parisian bookshops or borrowed for reading for a slight fee at a stand at the Pont Neuf.[7]

---

[3] François Bluche, *Dictionnaire du Grand Siècle* (Paris, 1990), p. 647.

[4] Jean Sgard (ed.), *Dictionnaire des Journaux 1600–1789* (2 vols, Paris, 1991), vol. 1, pp. 443–9; Eugène Hatin, *Histoire de la Presse en France: Histoire politique et littéraire de la presse en France avec une introduction historique sur les origines du journal et la bibliographie générale des journaux depuis leur origine*, 2nd edn (8 vols, Genf, 1967), vol. 1, pp. 61–192; Jeremy Popkin, "L'histoire de la presse anciénne: bilan et perspectives," in H. Duranton, C. Labrosse and P. Rétat (eds), *Les Gazettes Européennes de langue française (XVIIe–XVIIIe siècles)*, (Saint-Etienne, 1992), pp. 299–311, especially pp. 302–305.

[5] *Archives biographiques français, Fusions dans un ordre alphabétique unique de 180 de plus importans ouvrages de référence biographiques français publiés du 17e au 20e siècle* (Microfiche), S. Bradley (ed.), (London, Paris and New York, 1988), no. 884, pp. 3–6, 81–5, 86–8; Sgard, *Dictionnaire des Journaux*, vol. I, pp. 446–7; Jean Sgard, *Dictionnaire des Journalistes (1600–1789)* (Grenoble, 1976), p. 312; *Nouvelle Biographie Générale depuis les temps les plus reculés jusqu'à 1850–1860*, ..., M.M. Firmin Didot Freres (ed.), (46 vols, Kopenhagen, 1962–69), vol. 41, pp. 994–9; Bluche, *Dictionnaire*, pp. 1322–3.

[6] Sgard, *Dictionnaire des Journaux*, vol. I, p. 445.

[7] Roger Chartier, "Pamphlets et Gazettes," in R. Chartier and H.J. Martin (eds), *Histoire de l'édition française. Le livre conquérant du Moyen Âge au milieu du XVIIe siècle* (4 vols, Paris, 1982–86), vol. 1, pp. 405–25, especially p. 418.

All newsprint in France was subject to the royal government until the Revolution of 1789. Every new newspaper required the grant of royal privilege and was subjected to continuous state control by the censorship commission, which is, the "Maître de la Librairie" and its individual channels such as the "Lieutenants de police."[8] Additionally, the Departments of War, Marine, and External Affairs[9] undertook a pre-censoring which primarily extended to the diplomatic and foreign policy items in the *Gazette*. The central figure in these matters at the time of Louis XIV was Jean-Baptiste Colbert who was responsible not only for financial, economic, transportation, colonial, and building policy but for cultural policy as well. Through the establishment of academies he promoted art, literature, and science, and purposely created a cultural machinery geared in every way for the glorification of the crown.[10] The media forms of magazine and newspaper were part of this machinery as well, and especially the *Gazette*, which had held a unique position from the very beginning.

---

[8] Daniel Roche, "La censure," in H.-J. Martin and R. Chartier (eds), *Histoire de l'édition française. Le livre triomphant 1660–1830* (4 vols, Paris, 1982–86), vol. 2, pp. 76–83; Daniel Roche, "La police du livre," in H.-J. Martin/R. Chartier (eds), *Histoire de l'édition française. Le livre triomphant 1660–1830* (4 vols, Paris, 1982–86), vol. 2, pp. 84–91; Henri-Jean Martin, "La direction des lettres," in H.-J. Martin and R. Chartier (eds), *Histoire de l'édition française. Le livre triomphant 1660–1830*, pp. 65–75, especially pp. 65–6; Henri-Jean Martin, *Livre Pouvoirs et Société a Paris au XVIIe Siècle* (Histoire et Civilisations du Livre 3), (2 vols, Genf, 1969), vol. 1, pp. 440–71, and vol. 2, pp. 678–98; Ernest Lavisse, *Louis XIV. Histoire d'un Grand Règne 1643–1715*, second ed. (Paris, 1996), pp. 241–7, 272–80; Robert Mandrou, *Staatsräson und Vernunft 1649–1775* (Propyläen Geschichte Europas 3), 2nd ed (Frankfurt am Main, 1981), pp. 52–4; Joseph Klaits, *Printed Propaganda under Louis XIV. Absolute Monarchy and Public Opinion* (Princeton, 1976); H.D. MacPherson, *Censorship under Louis XIV. (1661–1715)* (New York, 1929).

[9] Sgard, *Dictionnaire des Journaux*, vol. I, p. 448; Klaits, *Printed Propaganda under Louis XIV*, p. 40.

[10] Martin, "La direction," pp. 65–6; Jürgen Voss, "Mäzenatentum und Ansätze systematischer Kulturpolitik im Frankreich Ludwigs XIV," in A. Buck, G. Kauffmann, B.L. Spahr and C. Wiedemann (eds), *Europäische Hofkultur im 16. und 17. Jahrhundert. Vorträge und Referate gehalten anläßlich des Kongresses des Wolfenbütteler Arbeitskreises für Renaissanceforschung und des Internationalen Arbeitskreises für Barockliteratur in der Herzog August Bibliothek Wolfenbüttel vom 4. bis 8. September 1679* (Wolfenbütteler Arbeiten zur Barockforschung 9) (3 vols, Hamburg, 1981), vol. 2, pp. 123–32; Etienne François, "Der Hof Ludwigs XIV," in A. Buck, G. Kauffmann, B.L. Spahr, C. Wiedemann (eds), *Europäische Hofkultur im 16. und 17. Jahrhundert*, vol. 3, pp. 725–33; Klaus Malettke, *Jean-Baptiste Colbert. Aufstieg im Dienste des Königs* (Persönlichkeit und Geschichte 99/100) (Zürich, Frankfurt, 1977); Werner Faulstich, *Medien zwischen Herrschaft und Revolte. Die Medienkultur der frühen Neuzeit (1400–1700)* (Die Geschichte der Medien 3) (Göttingen, 1998), p. 193; Peter Burke, *The Fabrication of Louis XIV* (New Haven, 1994), p. 185.

Théophraste Renaudot's *Gazette* had been protected by royal privilege since the day it was established, allowing it to overshadow the competing paper *Nouvelles Ordinaires de divers endroits* by Louis Vendosme and Jean Martin,[11] since the privilege included both a monopoly for printing and reprinting, as well as for dissemination of all news in the kingdom into the eighteenth century.[12] Reprints were established in various French provinces and more than 30 cities, including Lyon, Avignon, Rouen, and Toulouse.[13] The *Gazette*'s news and printing monopoly was further reinforced by the previous establishment of the "Bureau d'Adresse et de recontre" in 1631. The "Bureau" which was originally formed as an information and referral office for job-seekers and those suffering from illness quickly developed into the place to go for announcements of all kinds: "... a centre of information and publicity, a sort of employment agency and commission ... "[14] and became " ... little by little a meeting place for novelists, similar to an academy."[15] Out of this there emerged in 1633 the first advertizing sheet in France, the *Feuille du Bureau d'adresse*,[16] which was sold from the beginning both separately and as a supplement to the *Gazette*.[17]

The *Gazette* remained in octavo format until 1805 and consisted of the two regularly-appearing papers, the *Gazette* and the *Nouvelles Ordinaires* with the occasional supplement, *Extraordinaires*.[18] Published weekly and most often on

---

[11] Sgard, *Dictionnaire des Journaux*, vol. II, pp. 967–70; Howard M. Solomon, *Public Welfare, Science and Propaganda in Seventeenth Century France. The Innovations of Théophraste Renaudot* (Princeton, New Jersey, 1972), p. 114.

[12] Sgard, *Dictionnaire des Journaux*, vol. I, p. 446; Solomon, *Public Welfare*, pp. 114, 117.

[13] Sgard, *Dictionnaire des Journaux*, vol. I, pp. 445–6; Gilles Feyel, *La "Gazette" en Province a travers ses réimpressions 1631–1752. Une recherche analytique de la diffusion d'un ancien periodique dans toute la France [...]* (Amsterdam, 1982).

[14] Eugène Hatin, *Bibliographie historique et critique de la presse périodique française ou catalogue systématique et raisonné de tous les écrits périodiques de quelque valeur publiés ou ayant circulé en France depuis l'origine du journal jusqu'à nos jours, [...]. Précédé d'un essai historique et statistique sur la naissance et les progrès de la presse périodique dans les deux mondes*, 2nd edn (Hildesheim, 1965), p. LXII; Sgard, *Dictionnaire des Journaux*, vol. I, pp. 238–40; Hatin, *Histoire de la Presse*, vol. 2, pp. 56–100; Egon Koßmann, *Aus den Anfängen des Anzeigenwesens, in Zeitungswissenschaft*, 13 (1938), pp. 200–207, especially p. 203.

[15] Hatin, *Bibliographie*, p. 3.

[16] Hatin, *Bibliographie*, p. LXII; Sgard, *Dictionnaire des Journaux*, vol. I, pp. 416–22.

[17] Koßmann, "Aus den Anfängen," p. 204; G. Gilles de la Tourette, *Théophraste Renaudot d'apres des Documents inédits* (Paris, 1884), pp. 55–6.

[18] Sgard, *Dictionnaire des Journaux*, vol. I, pp. 443–5; Hatin, *Bibliographie*, pp. 10–11.

Saturday, the *Gazette* and the *Nouvelles Ordinaires* filled between 12 and 16 pages, amounting to an annual total of about 600 to 800 pages.[19]

The contents of the *Gazette* were significantly affected by the authors, who were not only members of the Renaudot family but also members of aristocratic, clerical, political, and literary circles, and traditionally displayed a strong inclination towards official policy.[20] Statements from envoys, officers, and correspondents, as well as information from journals in Brussels, Amsterdam, and other cities were included in the *Gazette*. For example, the poets, dramatists, and court historiographers Jean Racine and Nicolas Boileau Despreaux were formative contributors to the *Extraordinaires*[21] while the French ambassador to Constantinople from 1677 to 1685, Gabriel-Joseph de Lavergne, Comte de Guilleragues,[22] was responsible for various news items in the *Gazette*. Against this backdrop it becomes very clear that the news in the *Gazette* was official royal news, and the paper was a "vehicle for planted stories."[23]

The English *London Gazette* was also an organ for a royal government. It was founded in 1665 in Oxford, relocated shortly thereafter to London, and was the only officially authorized newspaper in the kingdom of England during the time from 1672 to 1679.[24] The *London Gazette* was not only printed with royal permission, it was at the same time "the appointed organ for all announcements of the executive."[25]

Decisive for the control held over the English news press and thus over the *London Gazette* were the actions of Roger L'Estrange as "Surveyor of Press"

---

[19] Sgard, *Dictionnaire des Journaux*, vol. I, p. 444; Sonja Schultheiß-Heinz, *Politik in der europäischen Publizistik. Eine historische Inhaltsanalyse von Zeitungen des 17. Jahrhunderts* (Beiträge zur Kommunikationsgeschichte 16) (Stuttgart, 2004), p. 66.

[20] Éric Walter, "Les auteurs et le champ littéraire," in H.-J. Martin and R. Chartier (eds), *Histoire de l'édition française. Le livre triomphant 1660–1830* (4 vols, Paris, 1982–86), vol. 2, pp. 383–99, especially pp. 383–7.

[21] Burke, *Fabrication*, p. 76; Martin, La direction, p. 71; Bluche, *Dictionnaire*, pp. 1293–6, especially p. 1293.

[22] Sgard, *Dictionnaire des Journalistes*, p. 187; Bluche, *Dictionnaire*, p. 696.

[23] Klaits, *Printed Propaganda under Louis XIV*, p. 59.

[24] Peter Fraser, *The Intelligence of the Secretaries of State and their monopoly of Licensed News 1660–1688* (Cambridge, 1956), pp. 1, 36; Jürgen Enkemann, *Journalismus und Literatur. Zum Verhältnis von Zeitungswesen, Literatur und Entwicklung bürgerlicher Öffentlichkeit in England im 17. und 18. Jahrhundert* (Medien in Forschung + Unterricht Serie A Bd. 11) (Tübingen, 1983), p. 62.

[25] Hartmut Walravens (ed.), *Internationale Zeitungsbestände in Deutschen Bibliotheken. Ein Verzeichnis von 18.000 Zeitungen, Amtsblättern und zeitungsähnlichen Periodika mit Besitznachweisen und geographischem Regis*ter, 2nd edn (München, New Providence, London, Paris, 1993), pp. 333–4; Enkemann, *Journalismus und Literatur*, p. 62.

as well as the state news monopoly under the supervision of the Secretaries of State.[26] The Secretaries of State who also controlled the Post Office[27] scrutinized every form of news transfer, procural and print. Reports from envoys, residents, and spies, as well as the news in foreign newspapers were the foundation for the contents of the *London Gazette*.[28] Fraser characterized the office of the secretary of state as a "commercial news agency"[29] and emphasized the secretaries' enormous influence on news management in England, for all articles printed in the *London Gazette* were checked by them and thus constituted official domestic and foreign news. Upon the initiative of the office of the Secretary of State the *London Gazette* was translated word for word into French starting in November 1666 and appeared under the title *Gazette de Londres* up until 1705 in order to exert a deliberate influence on the continental readership through the dissemination of controlled reporting.[30]

The bi-weekly *London Gazette* was published as a single sheet printed front and back in folio format, amounting to between 206 and 210 pages per annum.[31] Although a political news-sheet in its origin, each edition had its own, often lengthy, advertising section at the end.[32]

Thomas Newcomb the Elder was the publisher, printer, and owner of the *London Gazette* during the 1670s.[33] A member of the Stationers Company

---

[26] Fraser, *The Intelligence*, p. 1; Florence M. Greir Evans, *The Principal Secretary of State. A Survey of the Office from 1558 to 1680* (Publications of the University of Manchester: Historical Series 43), (Manchester, London and New York, 1923), pp. 265–6; George Kitchin, *Sir Roger l'Estrange. A Contribution to the History of the Press in the Seventeenth Century* (London, 1913). See also David Ogg, *England in the Reign of Charles II*, 2nd edn (Oxford, New York, 1984), pp. 514–16, and John Miller, "Public Opinion in Charles II's England," in *History*, 80 (1995), pp. 359–81.

[27] Evans, *The Principal Secretary*, pp. 278–97; Fraser, *The Intelligence*, p. 3, and pp. 20–21. See also Joseph George Muddiman, *The Kings Journalist 1659–1689. Studies in the Reign of Charles II*, 2nd edn (New York, 1971), p. 173, and J.C. Hemmeon, *The History of the British Post Office* (Harvard Economic Studies 7), (Cambridge, 1912), p. 27.

[28] Fraser, *The Intelligence*, pp. 3, 52.

[29] Fraser, *The Intelligence*, p. 1.

[30] Fraser, *The Intelligence*, p. 51, and Sgard, *Dictionnaire des Journaux*, vol. I, pp. 470–71.

[31] Schultheiß-Heinz, *Politik*, p. 66.

[32] J.B. Williams, *A History of English Journalism to the Foundation of the Gazette* (New York, Bombay, Calcutta, 1908), p. 198; R.B. Walker, "Advertising in London Newspapers 1650–1750," in *Business History*, 15 (1973), pp. 112–30, especially p. 113, and Muddiman, *The Kings Journalist*, p. 179.

[33] *British Biographical Archive, A one-alphabet cumulation of 310 of the most important English-language biographical reference works originally published between 1601 and 1929* (Microfiche), L. Baillie, P. Sieveking (eds), (München, New York, London and Paris, 1984),

and deputy Guild Master, member of the London City Council and printing wholesaler, Newcomb was one of the few and privileged printers in London.[34] He commanded a proportionately large print shop and in addition was named royal printer in 1675 which granted him an official commission for printing all Bibles, royal statutes, and proclamations.[35] The *London Gazette* could be obtained directly from Newcomb's shop or read in the numerous English coffee shops, clubs, and reading circles.[36]

Over the time frame from 1672 until 1679 several Secretaries of State were responsible for the contents of the *London Gazette*, including Sir Henry Coventry and Sir Joseph Williams.[37] Undersecretaries of State Robert Yard and James Vernon served as official authors in the 1670s and 1680s.[38] Their responsibilities encompassed procuring and compiling news items as well as excerpting from, copying, translating, and at times compiling foreign newsletters and letters received from envoys, spies, and agents.[39]

In contrast to the French and English gazettes the German newspaper was not a government organ. The *Teutsche Kriegs-Kurier* was established in September 1673 in the imperial free city of Nuremberg and was like many other journals in the Holy Roman Empire a private initiative.[40] The *Kurier* was launched by Wolf Eberhard Felsecker, a printer and publisher from the city of Bamberg who later became an honorary member of the Nuremberg Council.[41]

---

no. 812, p. 234; Henry R. Plomer et al., "A Dictionary of the Printers and Booksellers Who Were at Work in England, Scotland and Ireland from 1668–1725," in *Dictionaries of the Printers and Booksellers Who Were at Work in England, Scotland and Ireland 1557–1775* (Reprinted in Compact Form in one volume), 2nd edn (Ilkley Yorkshire, 1977), pp. 136–7.

[34] Karl Tilman Winkler, *Handwerk und Markt. Druckerhandwerk, Vertriebswesen und Tagesschrifttum in London 1695–1750* (Stuttgart, 1993), pp. 56–7, 382.

[35] British Biographical Archive, no. 812, p. 231.

[36] Bob Harris, *Politics and the Rise of the Press. Britain and France, 1620–1800* (Historical Connections), (London, New York, 1996), p. 64; Karl Tilman Winkler, *Wörterkrieg. Politische Debattenkultur in England 1689–1750* (Stuttgart, 1998), pp. 813–41.

[37] Evans, *The Principal Secretary*, p. 351.

[38] Phyllis M. Handover, *A History of "The London Gazette" 1665–1965* (London, 1965), pp. 19, 21.

[39] Fraser, *The Intelligence*, pp. 2, 59, and Ch. III, V; see also Evans, *The Principal Secretary*, p. 217.

[40] Else Bogel/Elger Blühm, *Die deutschen Zeitungen des 17. Jahrhunderts. Ein Bestandsverzeichnis mit historischen und bibliographischen Angaben* (Studien zur Publizistik: Bremer Reihe, Deutsche Presseforschung 17), (2 vols, Bremen, 1971), vol. I, pp. 213–22.

[41] Walter Zimmermann, *Entwicklungsgeschichte des Nürnberger "Friedens—und Kriegskuriers" ("Nürnberger Kurier") von seinen ersten Anfängen bis zum Übergang an den "Fränkischen Kurier" 1663–1865. Ein Beitrag zur Geschichte des deutschen Zeitungswesens* (Nürnberg, 1930), pp. 39–46, 62.

Felsecker earned a name primarily as the publisher of a novel which was released in Nuremberg in 1668, *Simplizius Simplizissimus* by Hans Jakob Christoffel von Grimmelshausen.[42] After Felsecker had published a series of calendars, prayer books and songbooks, and occasional astrological and theological works the Nuremberg Council unexpectedly granted him the right in 1673 to print the *Teutsche Kriegs–Kurier*.[43] Thus, the *Kurier* appears to be the first newspaper to be allowed and to be printed periodically in Nuremberg, as the Nuremberg Council had thus far maintained a cautious policy towards news and newspapers, refusing to permit any.[44] In 1675, Felsecker was granted the imperial privilege for his news-sheet which was extended repeatedly and included a prohibition for reprinting.[45] Thus, Felsecker was, according to the Holy Roman Empire's censorship laws, the recipient of official permission for printing.

The *Teutsche Kriegs–Kurier* was published as a bi-weekly quarto normally consisting of eight pages, thus amounting to around 800 pages per year. Additionally, there were numerous political pamphlets which were announced at the end of the *Teutsche Kriegs–Kurier* and eventually led to further newspaper editions.[46] The journal was available for purchase "bey Felseckern im Rathauß–Gäßlein."[47] As its title states, the *Teutsche Kriegs–Kurier* was fashioned from its inception to report about political happenings, most especially the war-related events of the time. Yet it is difficult to determine its authors as was frequently the case with German newspapers in the seventeenth century. Only rarely did newsprint include references to the author's identity. Fear of censorship authorities probably played a decisive role in this matter, more so than the scanty recognition bestowed by society upon compilers of newspapers. When the *Teutsche Kriegs–Kurier* was launched in 1673 it seems that Felsecker compiled the newspaper himself from other written newspapers and letters, according to the complaints of Felsecker's competitors as published by Zimmermann.[48] In addition, he obtained his information from other printed newspapers, for example

---

[42] Josef Benzing, *Die Buchdrucker des 16. und 17. Jahrhunderts im Deutschen Sprachgebiet* (Beiträge zum Buch—und Bibliothekswesen 12), 2nd edn (Wiesbaden, 1982), p. 367.

[43] Zimmermann, *Entwicklungsgeschichte*, pp. 52–6.

[44] Bogel/Blühm, *Die deutschen Zeitungen*, vol. I, pp. 213–22, especially p. 221; Lore Sporhan-Krempel, *Nürnberg als Nachrichtenzentrum zwischen 1400 und 1700* (Nürnberger Forschungen 10) (Nürnberg, 1968), pp. 67–76.

[45] *Teutscher Kriegs–Kurier* 20/30 December 1675, no. CV, fol. [Nnnnn iiij v].

[46] Bogel/Blühm, *Die deutschen Zeitungen*, vol. I, pp. 220–21; Schultheiß–Heinz, *Politik*, p. 66.

[47] *Teutscher Kriegs–Kurier* 30 December/9 January 1679, no. III, fol. [C iiij v].

[48] Zimmermann, *Entwicklungsgeschichte*, pp. 55–6.

from papers in Frankfurt, Leipzig, and Vienna, from Nuremberg's *Post*, and from salespeople and wartime couriers.[49] In any case, it was the owner and publisher Felsecker who was responsible for the newspaper's contents as is demonstrated by various censorship measures directed against him by the city of Nuremberg.[50] Most particularly, the sometimes difficult relationship between the Protestant free city and the Catholic Emperor led to such censorship measures. This relationship to the Emperor also had consequences for the contents of the *Teutsche Kriegs-Kurier*. It was necessary for Felsecker to be considerate of imperial politics in his newspaper. Despite these limitations Felsecker still had more possibilities in terms of reporting than did the authors of the French and English journals whose authorities subjected them to a very different level of control.

Comparison of News Subjects

The three newspapers cover an abundance of diverse news items printed within relatively little space, commenting—often in full flow, and with a trans-European scope—about the movements and positioning of troops, deaths, the travels of diplomats, marriages, battles, the weather, and quartering arrangements. There is no demonstrable outline for the contents, and formal structures such as the names of locations or marginalia in the *Teutsche Kriegs-Kurier* are of some help for reading comprehension but none at all for structuring the contents; as they normally merely provide a brief summary of the news item. Dividing a newspaper into sections such as politics, finance, culture, sports, local interest, and advertisements is a product of the twentieth century and has nothing to do with the news subjects of the seventeenth century. In order to study the numerous news items, content analysis was employed to draw up thematic divisions which in turn assist in comparing the overriding fields and themes of the three newspapers.[51] A total of six overriding fields emerged for the time span from 1672 to 1679 based upon a differentiated categorical system.[52] These six areas include:

---

[49] Friedrich Kapp/Johann Goldfriedrich, *Geschichte des deutschen Buchhandels*, 2nd edn (5 vols, Leipzig, 1970), vol. 2, pp. 45–6; Schultheiß-Heinz, *Politik*, pp. 67–8.

[50] Arnd Müller, "Zensurpolitik der Reichsstadt Nürnberg. Von der Einführung der Buchdruckerkunst bis zum Ende der Reichsstadtzeit," in *Mitteilungen des Vereins für Geschichte der Stadt Nürnberg*, 49 (1959), pp. 66–169, especially pp. 141–3; Zimmermann, *Entwicklungsgeschichte*, pp. 46–68.

[51] Schultheiß-Heinz, *Politik*, pp. 75–94.

[52] Schultheiß-Heinz, *Politik*, p. 81.

- war and conflicts
- domestic politics
- economics and trade
- the royal courts and legations
- sensational news items
- advertisements.

The bulk of reporting in all three newspapers is concerned with the area of wars and conflicts with 70 to 78 percent of all articles describing military operations and diplomatic activities related to the various European conflicts.[53] News in the three journals is especially dominated by the Dutch War from 1672–79, the Third Anglo-Dutch War from 1672–74, the Messina Revolt of 1674–78, and various conflicts between the European states and the Ottoman Empire in Poland, Russia, and the Mediterranean area.[54] The Dutch War had the highest percentage of coverage with 50 to 70 percent of total reporting whereas articles concerning the other wars averaged between 1 and 14 percent of coverage. It is remarkable that all three newspapers write about the same subjects although the conflicts appear at first glance to be very different and not all European states were equally involved. The question arises, for example, why the *London Gazette* covers the Messina Revolt although England was neither financially nor militarily involved. The most obvious reason for common coverage probably stems from the fact that there was a common European interest in these conflicts as they reflect the political rivalry between the houses of Habsburg and Bourbon. This rivalry, dating back to the fifteenth century, dominated European politics including diverse wars, assorted participants in and locations of wars, and manifests itself as well in the three journals' reporting. The Messina Revolt as such represented a transfer of the French–Habsburg conflict from Imperial to Italian ground.[55]

That the three newspapers concentrated on similar subjects is also demonstrable in the second area, that of domestic politics, an area accounting on average for 4 to 8 percent of all reported items.[56] In this subject area, the three journals report mostly on changes in the European governments such the new governor in the Netherlands in 1672, the choice of a Polish king in 1674, or the Exclusion Crisis which broke out in England in 1678 and 1679 and the denominational clashes it entailed. In light of the Dutch and the Third

---

[53] Schultheiß-Heinz, *Politik*, pp. 94–6.
[54] Schultheiß-Heinz, *Politik*, pp. 99–115, 122–50.
[55] Heinz Duchhardt, *Krieg und Frieden im Zeitalter Ludwigs XIV* (Historisches Seminar 4), (Düsseldorf, 1987), p. 19.
[56] Schultheiß-Heinz, *Politik*, pp. 169–76.

Anglo-Dutch Wars the selection of William of Orange as new governor of the Netherlands is of particular interest. Especially the *London Gazette* assigns a great deal of attention to these events covering not only the discussion surrounding the re-introduction of the governorship and the eventual acknowledgment of William III in July 1672 but also the violent disturbances surrounding the event culminating in the murder of retired councilman Johan de Witt on 20 August 1672.[57] The *London Gazette* passes on the report written and printed in Holland about this murder, which opened with an expression of sympathy such as is rare, particularly for newspapers: "I tremble when I take my Pen into my hand and acquaint you with the sad spectacle we have seen here ...."[58] Similar to the coverage in the *London Gazette* the French journal also describes the murder as a "massacre full of horrors."[59]

The close connection between foreign and domestic politics is clearly discernible here as changes in government frequently brought direct consequences for the political situation of the day. For example, the election of Prince William of Orange as the new Governor and Commander in Chief of the Netherlands led to a modified constellation as William entered into new alliances with several European countries in the Dutch War and, as opposed to past strategy, launched a military offensive against France.[60]

Comparable foreign policy repercussions followed the selection of a king in Poland 1674. A number of European contenders were candidates for the Polish throne including Duke Charles V of Lorraine, the future Duke John William of Newburg, the Prince de Condé, Prince Charles Emil of Brandenburg, and the Polish Grand Marshal John Sobieski.[61] Such a list of aspirants including

---

[57] For the acknowledgement of William III as governor and admiral, see *London Gazette* 11–15 July 1672, no. 694, [col. 3]. About the disturbances, see *London Gazette* 20–24 June 1672, no. 688, [col. 3], and *London Gazette* 1–4 July 1672, no. 691, [col. 2]. See also Ivo Schöffer, "Die Republik der Vereinigten Niederlande von 1648 bis 1795," in Th. Schieder and F. Wagner (eds), *Handbuch der Europäischen Geschichte. Europa im Zeitalter des Absolutismus und der Aufklärung* (7 vols, Stuttgart, 1968–87), vol. 4, pp. 634–58, especially p. 649; Lavisse, *Louis XIV*, p. 642; Arie Th. van Deursen, "Wilhelm (III.) von Oranien. Der Generalstatthalter der Niederlande (1672–1702)," in H. Duchhardt (ed.), *Der Herrscher in der Doppelpflicht. Europäische Fürsten und ihre beiden Throne* (Veröffentlichungen des Instituts für Europäische Geschichte Mainz, Abteilung Universalgeschichte Beiheft 43) (Mainz, 1997), pp. 141–64.

[58] *London Gazette* 15–19 August 1672, no. 704, [col. 4].

[59] *Gazette* 3 September 1672, no. 104, pp. 891–3.

[60] Braubach, *Vom Westfälischen Frieden*, pp. 50–51.

[61] Hans Roos, "Polen von 1668 bis 1795," in Th. Schieder and F. Wagner (eds), *Handbuch der Europäischen Geschichte. Europa im Zeitalter des Absolutismus und der Aufklärung* (7 vols, Stuttgart, 1968–87), vol. 4, pp. 690–752, especially pp. 704–707.

their dynastic and denominational ties is itself ample proof of the significance of this election for Europe. Hence the announcement in the *London Gazette* in March 1674 as reported from Warsaw: "Ambassadors are ... coming hither, from most of the Princes of Europe, to be present during the time of the Election."[62] Two aspects are of particular concern in this royal election: first, the question of to what extent the new Polish king is for or against continuing the Turkish wars; and secondly, whether the new king will be oriented more towards the Habsburgs or the Bourbons. All three journals consider these aspects in their reporting; however, the *Gazette* demonstrates the most vivid interest. Following a series of reports commenting on the chances of each individual aspirant, the diverse forms of influence on the part of the Habsburgs, the Polish nobility, and the papacy, the *Gazette* at last recorded in May 1674 that the election had been decided for the Grand Marshal Sobieski: "We have also had news from Poland that the Grand Marshall Sobieski was elected king."[63] Of the three journals, the Parisian *Gazette* most clearly records that this election was also a foreign policy scuffle between Austria and France—one that the House of Habsburg lost with the election of the Francophile Sobieski: "The House of Austria receives a foreign humiliation on this occasion: it shows that the great expectations that relied on the election of Prince Charles de Lorraine have been turned down.[64] Similarly, the *London Gazette* and the *Teutsche Kriegs-Kurier* describe the assorted candidates, yet devote much less attention to the episode than the French publication.

Similar reporting, albeit filling a much lower percentage of newsprint, can be ascertained for the third area of economics and trade, which contents accounted for an average of 2 to 3 percent.[65] The reports mainly contain announcements of European ships, frequently with detailed information regarding the import and export of goods, thus having at least an indirect influence on the stock markets. They also reported on trade agreements, on natural phenomena and the financial consequences thereof, and on epidemics. Hence, for example, all three journals informed extensively about the plague which was rampant in Vienna and Prague in 1679 which cost many lives and thus posed a direct threat to European trade.[66]

Differences in the three journals' reporting are discernible to some extent in the fourth area which deals with the royal court and legations and which amounts to highly divergent portions of coverage, namely between 10 and 23

---

[62] *London Gazette* 16–19 March 1674, no. 869, [col. 1].
[63] *Nouvelles Ordinaires* 16 June 1674, no. 68, p. 535.
[64] *Nouvelles Ordinaires* 16 June 1674, no. 68, p. 536.
[65] Schultheiß-Heinz, *Politik*, pp. 151–4.
[66] Schultheiß-Heinz, *Politik*, pp. 152–3.

percent.[67] In general, the three papers are very similar in their informing about festivities, receptions, and banquets, or about the arrivals and departures of the various envoys to the European courts. They record the individual events as well as the conflicts and uncertainties regarding appropriate ceremonials which often came in tow and which symbolically reflect the political situations of the day. In the coverage of diplomats the permanent Imperial Diet in Regensburg plays a special role as it became a European stage upon which war was fought with diplomatic means. Not only were all of Europe's diplomats present there, they also used the Imperial Diet as a place for discussion, intrigue, and espionage. One example for the similar coverage of court-related news items concerns the Munich Residence fire in April 1674. According to the German newspaper in its edition from 6–16 April:

> Eight days ago, on 23 March/2 April, Monday evening at ten o'clock the beautiful and great and widely famous Munich Residence more than half burned down because a burning candle was neglected. In addition to the shock a lot of hurtful damage has been done....[68]

The English and the French *Gazette* also comment on this occurrence including listing the date of the fire in a very similar way. Further, both of these papers devote more attention to the financial losses resulting from the fire than does the German *Kurier*:

> That on the 9 instant between 10 and 11 a clock at night, a Fire happened in the Electors [of Bavaria] palace, by what accident not known, which burnt with so much violence, that in a short time it consumed great part of the said Palace and particularly, the Apartment of the Electoress, and of the Princess's her Daughters, and therein all the rich Furniture and Moveables, valued to have been worth several Millions.[69]

And in the *Nouvelles Ordinaires* from 16 April 1674, we read:

> On the ninth of this month the fire began at eleven hours of the evening in the palace of our Elector [of Bavaria] because of the carelessness of a woman, and it took with such violence that the beautiful domicile was half consumed before anyone could begin to arrest the progress of the flames. Indeed, the greatest

---

[67] Schultheiß-Heinz, *Politik*, p. 155.
[68] *Teutscher Kriegs–Kurier* 6/16 April 1674, no. XXXI, fol. [Hh v].
[69] *London Gazette* 16–20 April 1674, no. 878, [col. 3], *London Gazette* 20–23 April 1674, no. 879, [col. 1], and *London Gazette* 23–27 April 1674, no. 880, [col. 2 and 3].

part of the ornaments and wealth of the palace, which had rendered it no less considerable than its magnificent structure, were enveloped, as well as various persons of both sexes: our Electress was just barely saved, accompanied by her ladies, almost all in dishabillée.[70]

One relatively major difference in the three journals' reporting on the royal courts is demonstrably evident in the French news items regarding the court of Versailles. The *Gazette* reports quantitatively in great detail about life at the French court and also concentrates emphatically upon the person of Louis XIV, draping reports concerning him in a decidedly religious and glorifying style. A typical example is the traditional Maundy Thursday ceremony in which the King and Queen washed the feet of 13 indigents as was reported in detail in the *Gazette* late in March of 1674:

> On the 22nd, the King, after having heard ... a sermon ... and the absolution made by the Cardinal of Boüillon, Grand Almoner of France, performed the Cermony of the Supper, washing the feet of 13 paupers, serving each of them an equal number of dishes, the first brought by Monsignor the Dauphin, and Monsieur. Next, His Majesty assisted at the High Mass sung by the Musicians, then at the Procession of the Holy Sacrament, where there were also the Queen, Monsignor the Dauphin, and Monsieur and Madame.[71]

With the fifth subject area, that of sensational events (1–2 percent), a new aspect of reporting can be recorded as this news area also deals with local items.[72] However, this local bent is found almost exclusively in the *Teutsche Kriegs–Kurier* such as when it describes the sentencing of a thief named Johann Georg Perger in Nuremberg.[73] Normally, though, local news items were rarely published in the newspapers of the seventeenth century, in order to avoid possible matters of local dispute together with the censorship such matters might entail.[74] Instead, it is characteristic that all three newspapers reported about catastrophes, miracles, monstrosities, and celestial phenomena such as comets.

---

[70] *Nouvelles Ordinaires* 5 May 1674, no. 50, p. 388.
[71] *Gazette* 24 March 1674, no. 34, p. 264.
[72] Schultheiß-Heinz, *Politik*, p. 165.
[73] *Teutscher Kriegs–Kurier* 12–22 October 1677, no. LXXXV, fol. [Qqqq iiij v].
[74] Johannes Weber, "Die Novellen sind eine Eröffnung des Buchs der gantzen Welt: Entstehung und Entwicklung der Zeitung im 17. Jahrhundert," in K. Beyrer and M. Dallmeier (eds), *Als die Post noch Zeitung machte. Eine Pressegeschichte* (Frankfurt am Main, Gießen, 1994), pp. 15–25, especially p. 23.

Matters of local interest find their place after all in the sixth and last area, in advertising (1–7 percent).[75] Especially the *London Gazette* includes a relatively large percentage of advertising. Numerous brief announcements deal with such subjects as missing people, dogs and horses, and inform about newly published books and maps, about new business ventures, and the current markets and auctions in and near London. These reports are, however, only typical of the *London Gazette*; the German *Kriegs-Kurier* and the French *Gazette* publish only a few announcements concerning the political books and pamphlets of the time.

In sum, let us state that the various subject areas and the individual topics already demonstrate, in their own right, how similar news reporting was in the three journals. They focus their attention primarily upon political events in Western Europe and particularly upon the wars fought there at the time. This similarity in reporting is an important prerequisite for contemporaneity.

The Fürstenberg Affair 1674

In order to examine contemporaneity in terms of parallels in newsprint's time and content it is useful to compare the precise dates and contents of the three journals, specifically in their coverage of the scandal involving William of Fürstenberg in 1674. This affair has been well-researched and documented and offers for comparison chronological timetables and events that are well known, thus enabling a comparison of the news reports in terms of their differences, selection, and intent.

In 1673 during the Dutch War and the Third Anglo-Dutch War a peace congress was summoned in the imperial free city of Cologne. The congress was supposed to lead to peace between the Netherlands and France as well as to create a general peace as by then numerous European states were involved in the war. While the congress convened a significant number of European ambassadors were present in Cologne, directly and indirectly offering the newspapers a wealth of news material. Accordingly, all three of the journals took note of the diverse diplomat-related activities and wrote of the negotiations' progress and difficulties. During this time a great political scandal arose when on 14 February 1674 the officer and envoy William of Fürstenberg was abducted from the free and neutral imperial city of Cologne and taken to Vienna.[76] As an envoy of the

---

[75] Schultheiß-Heinz, *Politik*, pp. 165–9.

[76] Markus Baumanns, "Die Sache trug sich zu Cöllen den 14. des Hornung in der Statt also zu. Die Gefangennahme Wilhelms von Fürstenberg auf dem Kölner Kongreß 1674 im Spiegel zeitgenössischer Chroniken und Gazetten," in *Geschichte in Köln*, 31 (1992), pp. 51–76, especially pp. 55–7.

archbishop of Cologne, William of Fürstenberg represented French interests and he hoped to arrange for an alliance between Cologne and France. His political activities and Francophile leaning made him very unpopular at the imperial court in Vienna as well as at many Holy Roman Empire courts, since the war by then involved the Holy Roman Empire, where anti-French sentiments were particularly strong due to French rampages in the Rhine area.

Just prior to 10 February 1674, Bongart, who had once served in Cologne's military, made the first attempt against Fürstenberg, and failed. Bongart had stood waiting for Fürstenberg before the Cologne Theatre, threatening him with a pistol.[77] The second attack, shortly thereafter, was more successful: in the afternoon hours of 14 February, Fürstenberg was on his way from his mistress, the Duchess of La Marck, to the Archbishop of Cologne's residence in the convent of St. Pantaleon. In the center of Cologne Fürstenberg's coach was attacked by imperial troops who overpowered his escorts after a brief scuffle. Afterwards Fürstenberg was taken, in his coach, to a meeting place outside of the gates of Cologne where further imperial troops were waiting for him. From there Fürstenberg was taken first to Bonn and a few days thereafter to Vienna. In Vienna Fürstenberg was held as a prisoner until the end of the Dutch War in 1679.

Coverage in the three newspapers is marked by varying points of emphasis and connotations, as follows.

The German newspaper reports very briefly about the first attack on Fürstenberg by Bongart and refrains from all form of commentary.[78] When Fürstenberg was abducted on 14 February the *Kurier* reported it nine days later.[79] This report describes in detail the route taken by Fürstenberg and his escorts and the scene of the abduction, noting that the soldiers involved belonged to the troops of the Duke of Grana. However, the *Kurier* does not devote a single word to the imperial troops that were waiting for Fürstenberg outside of Cologne's city gates. Rather, the journal emphasizes the abduction's legal aspect, claiming that Fürstenberg had been abducted not in his capacity as a diplomat but as a French officer. Further, it argues that the motive for the kidnapping could be found in the abduction of the Imperial Count Strozzi which had occurred a few days previously. The *Kurier* goes on to describe the general agitation in the city of Cologne and reports that French party supporters wanted to storm the lodgings of the Imperial Minister Lisola. Finally, the paper mentions possible consequences of this abduction such as the premature dissolution of the peace conference and the imminent departure of the legations in the event that

---

[77] Max Braubach, *Wilhelm von Fürstenberg (1629–1704) und die französische Politik im Zeitalter Ludwigs XIV.* (Bonner Historische Forschungen 36), (Bonn, 1972), p. 285.

[78] *Teutscher Kriegs-Kurier* 30 January–9 February 1674, no. XII, fol. M [iiij v].

[79] *Teutscher Kriegs-Kurier* 13–23 February 1674, no. XVI, fols Q [i–ii v].

Fürstenberg was not released. Two editions later it reported on the presence of diplomats sent from Cologne and Sweden to the Emperor and about the direct threat posed by the French military to Cologne.[80]

Another view is presented by the French *Gazette* with the first article being published ten days after the abduction. The *Gazette* begins its coverage with the first threat to Fürstenberg through Bongart and emphasizes the grave danger in which Fürstenberg stood.[81] Then, the journal describes the abduction, recording the route that Fürstenberg took and particularly highlighting the staunch resistance of his escorts with special emphasis upon the soldiers' belonging to the imperial regiment of Grana. In contrast to the *Kurier* the *Gazette* explains that additional imperial troops were waiting outside Cologne to take Fürstenberg to Bonn in his coach. Describing the events surrounding the abduction is merely one aspect of the French coverage; there were also comments on the case's international law aspects. The *Gazette* reports vigorously that the kidnapping was a terrible surprise amounting to a violent break with international law as the envoy Fürstenberg should have had diplomatic immunity. At the same time it points out that supposedly all the European legations would lodge a complaint over this imperial act in the free and neutral imperial city of Cologne. It suspects that the abduction was the brainchild of the Imperial Minister Francis Paul Baron of Lisola who was known for his anti-French stance.[82] Against this backdrop the *Gazette* spotlights the just position of the French king in the Dutch War. A report from March 1674 stresses that this incident is not only damaging to the Empire's reputation, it forces the King of France to continue a war

> ... so prejudicial to the reputation of the Emperor ...; to show the just reason that obliges the said Majesty to wreak vengeance by arms, for the injury that was done to what is the most sacred in the Law of Nations, and to force his Enemies, by war, to a peace that they attempt to delay by such intolerable means.[83].

Coverage in the *London Gazette* is of a different nature, although it too, as with the French *Gazette*, was published ten days after the kidnapping.[84] The English journal employs more information and detail than the other two papers in its description of the route taken by Fürstenberg and his escorts in Cologne. Like the French journal it notes the resistance of Fürstenberg's escorts and also identifies the soldiers as imperial troops. Here, too, we encounter the report that

---

[80] *Teutscher Kriegs–Kurier* 20 February–2 March 1674, no. XVIII, fols S [i–ii r].
[81] *Gazette* 24 February 1674, no. 24, pp. 187–8.
[82] *Gazette* 3 March 1674, no. 26, p. 199.
[83] *Gazette* 31 March 1674, no. 36, pp. 275–6.
[84] *London Gazette* 12–16 February 1674, no. 860, [col. 4].

soldiers waiting before Cologne's gates were supposed to take Fürstenberg first to Bonn and then to Vienna. In the last section of the first article this paper concluded by commenting on Cologne as a neutral city and Congress site, the imperial orders behind the abduction, the French diplomats' complaints, and the first inquiries and activities of the magistrate in Cologne. In the following editions the *London Gazette* refers to the approaching end of peace negotiations between France and the Netherlands and of the bloodshed likely to follow.[85] It is typical of the *London Gazette* that all information is delivered without the slightest commentary. This is also true of the account of the first attack by Captain Bongart.[86]

As can be seen in the above newspaper texts, in the abduction case there exists some correspondence both in chronological and in textual terms. Similar dates and basic information are apparent. Dissimilarities in coverage are to be found in the details and, above all, in the evaluation of the event, as is clearly the case with the French *Gazette* and the German *Kurier*. This most likely results from the specific selection of news items. After all, it is known fact that French, Swedish, English, Dutch, and Imperial diplomats resided in Cologne and often sent daily dispatches to their governments reporting the latest developments.[87] Hence, the French government was well-informed and so also was the *Gazette*. Further, Fürstenberg maintained close contact with the French Court and wrote regularly to the king, informing him of the political situation in Cologne. In January 1674, Fürstenberg informed the French king about rumors concerning a possible plot against himself.[88] For this reason he wanted to leave the city of Cologne and the Holy Roman Empire and take up residence in France.[89] The first, unsuccessful plot against him was already common knowledge before 10 February.[90] And on 14 February, more rumors were audible, claiming that the abduction was to take place on that very day. Accordingly, Fürstenberg appealed for help to the French legation in Cologne which, however, in refusing, set stock in his status as an emissary.[91] We thus discover that in the various European royal houses and in Cologne, Fürstenberg was known to be in danger due to his pro-French political bent. Also, the Imperial reaction to the abduction was revealed to the assorted royal courts. The early uncertainty as to whether the empire

---

[85] *London Gazette* 26 February–2 March 1674, no. 864, [col. 2]; *London Gazette* 2–5 March 1674, no. 865, [col. 2], and *London Gazette* 5–9 March 1674, no. 866, [col. 3].
[86] *London Gazette* 2–5 February 1674, no. 857, [col. 4].
[87] Baumanns, *Die Sache trug sich zu Cöllen*, pp. 55, 67.
[88] Baumanns, *Die Sache trug sich zu Cöllen*, p. 62.
[89] Braubach, *Wilhelm von Fürstenberg*, pp. 284–5.
[90] Braubach, *Wilhelm von Fürstenberg*, p. 285.
[91] Baumanns, *Die Sache trug sich zu Cöllen*, p. 62.

had commissioned the deed was soon resolved. One day after the abduction, on 15 February, the Duke of Grana, who held a position in the service of the emperor, published a much-copied memorandum in which he declared that the abduction had taken place upon the emperor's orders because Fürstenberg's activities had been contrary both to the general peace and to his duties as the emperor's subject.[92] Late in February and early in March the emperor had two additional letters published in which he further justified his actions against Fürstenberg.[93] These letters, as well, were sent to the various European courts. Lisola, the Imperial Minister, however, must be considered to be one of their "intellectual creators."[94]

When the French *Gazette*'s report is considered in this light one must conclude that the abduction could not have been so very much of a surprise, even though several articles deny this repeatedly. In fact, the steady flow of French statements about the violation of neutrality and breach of international law serve ultimately to legitimize the war's continuation. The abduction of Fürstenberg offered Louis XIV the opportunity to cease negotiations for peace, an intention that France had harbored for weeks.[95] The *Gazette*, accordingly, publishes selectively in this matter, in favor of the French king and contrary to Imperial policy.

Upon closer evaluation of the German newspaper, similarly selective reporting comes to light, albeit with a different aim. From the very beginning the *Teutsche Kriegs–Kurier* emphasizes that Fürstenberg was not an envoy but rather merely a French officer. Additionally, Fürstenberg is portrayed as an imperial subject whose political activities were directed against the emperor. In this way the German paper makes it clear that the abduction was not a breach of international law or violation of neutrality but rather the legitimate act of an emperor towards one of his subjects. In keeping with this imperial stance the *Kurier* published Grana's memorandum from 15 February.[96] Also, following the publishing of the emperor's letters late in February in the *Kriegs–Kurier* the same arguments surface as were employed by the emperor:

> The causes of the abduction of Prince William of Fürstenberg ... are kept secret but it has been discovered that he 1: Is a vassal and heir to the emperor, 2: Has tempted Cologne to dangerous treaties, 3: Talked badly about the Majesty during mealtimes and other get-togethers, 4: Is a French officer and did not respect the

---

[92] Baumanns, *Die Sache trug sich zu Cöllen*, p. 67; Braubach, *Wilhelm von Fürstenberg*, p. 287.
[93] Baumanns, *Die Sache trug sich zu Cöllen*, pp. 68–70.
[94] Braubach, *Wilhelm von Fürstenberg*, p. 288.
[95] Baumanns, *Die Sache trug sich zu Cöllen*, p. 75.
[96] *Teutscher Kriegs–Kurier* 9–19 March 1674, no. XXIII, fols Z [ii–iii r].

warning of the emperor, 5: Carried out dangerous attacks against the Majesty and the empire, 6: Did not request safe guards like other delegates but did insist on opposing the respect due to the Majesty. These are supposed to be the primary reasons for his imprisonment ...[97]

Let us remember in this light that the *Kurier* justified and legitimized imperial politics in all of its articles. This is most likely not merely the result of overall emperor-oriented reporting standards but is also to be understood foremost in light of the French devastation of imperial lands and of resulting anti-French sentiments.

Finally, let us consider the mostly commentary-free articles of the *London Gazette*. As has been mentioned, the English newspaper reports on this event in great detail, aided by direct observers on site, including the later Secretary of State Joseph Williamson who, at that time, was an envoy dispatched to Cologne.[98] The English journal reports on both Swedish and French activities and complaints as well as covering the Empire's justifications. Of particular interest in this context is the article in which the *London Gazette* publishes the Imperial viewpoint in a literal translation:

> In the interim, to justifie this proceeding the Imperialist publish, That the said Prince of Fürstenberg owed all he had to the Emperors favor; That he is a vassal of the Emperor, because of several Lordships which he possesses in the Archdutchy of Austria; That he is actually inrolled in the Register of the Nobles of Austria; That he is a natural born subject of the Emperor; and, That he was not Ambassador or Plenipotentiary duly constituted; allowed this, his offence is, That he hath taken command in Foreign service, and that he hath disobeyed the Emperors commands, recalling all his subjects out of Foreign services.[99]

With this publication the likewise well-informed *London Gazette* mirrors the changes taking place in English foreign policy as England was abandoning its French alliance partner at this time, choosing instead to make peace with the Netherlands.

---

[97] *Teutscher Kriegs–Kurier* 13–23 March 1674, no. XXIV, fols Aa [i–ii r].
[98] Baumanns, *Die Sache trug sich zu Cöllen*, p. 55.
[99] *London Gazette* 12–16 March 1674, no. 868, [col. 2].

Conclusion

Despite their different political and publishing paradigms the three journals reflect a similar interest in the same political events of the time. Though they inform their readers at first glance in a very similar way as regards time and content there remain substantial differences in their coverage as demonstrated through their comments regarding the Fürstenberg affair. These dissimilarities are above all a product of the intentions of those responsible for the papers. Particularly the publishers of the French *Gazette* and in part also those of the *Kriegs–Kurier* and the *London Gazette* used the newspaper as an organ for legitimizing their governments' policies.

CHAPTER 7

"The Blowing of the Messiah's Trumpet": Reports about Sabbatai Sevi and Jewish Unrest in 1665–67

Ingrid Maier and Daniel C. Waugh[1]

Introduction

A definitive treatment of the spread of news in seventeenth-century Europe is still a project for future generations of scholars. The challenges are both practical and conceptual. By practical we mean in particular the still pressing need to identify and make accessible the sources of the news and analyze their interrelationships. While there is reasonably good bibliographic control over early newspapers (to the extent that we now know at least where to find the majority of the extant copies and know what some of the major gaps are), we are less well served for published separates.[2] Our knowledge of manuscript sources for the news and

---

[1] The authors presented this paper at the 2007 conference in Bremen, "Places of News: The Creation of International News Networks in Early Modern Times," although it incorporates ideas from their contribution entitled "Did 'Contemporaneity' Emerge in Early Modern Russia?," presented at the 2006 Bremen conference "Time and Space on the Way to Modernity."

[2] As examples, the collection of the Deutsche Presseforschung in Bremen contains copies of most of the extant German newspapers for the seventeenth century, although there are huge gaps in the runs of many of them which presumably will never be filled. The project of the Koninklijke Bibliotheek in The Hague to digitize historical Dutch newspapers will certainly make it somewhat easier for us to work with them, although there will still be many collections outside the Netherlands that will not be covered. On the continuing importance of separates even in the era of the first newspapers, see, for example, Mario Infelise, "The war, the news and the curious. Military gazettes in Italy," in Brendan Dooley and Sabrina A. Baron (eds), *The Politics of Information in Early Modern Europe* (London; New York, 2001), pp. 216–36, and Jutta Schumann, "Das politisch-militärische Flugblatt in der zweiten Hälfte des 17. Jahrhunderts als Nachrichtenmedium und Propagandamittel," in Wolfgang Harms and Michael Schilling (eds), *Das illustrierte Flugblatt in der Kultur der Frühen Neuzeit. Wolfenbüttler Arbeitsgespräch 1997* (= Mikrokosmos: Beiträge zur Literaturwissenschaft und Bedeutungsforschung, vol. 50) (Frankfurt am Main, 1998), pp. 226–58. Holger Böning, *Welteroberung durch ein neues Publikum. Die deutsche Presse und der Weg zur Aufklärung. Hamburg und Altona als Beispiel* (= Presse und Geschichte—Neue Beiträge, vol. 5)

their interrelationship between them and published news is still distressingly limited.[3] So also, with some noted exceptions, is the study of readership.

Some of the most important advances in the analysis of the spread of news adhere to what we might loosely call the "paradigm of modernization."[4] That is the focus in the first instance is on the great invention of the seventeenth century, the appearance of the first regularly published newspapers, and the way in which the spread of the news through this medium paved the way for the emergence of the "modern world," whatever exactly one might mean by that concept. Certainly a developing sense of contemporaneity amongst those who partook of the media revolution is part of this story. The danger of this conceptual framework though is that it may exclude a serious examination of the many ways news spread through means other than via published newspapers and may limit the exploration of the cultural world of readers to those aspects of world view which somehow incorporate "the modern." Thus, secular world views eclipse religious ones, rationality trumps superstition, the European-wide replaces the parochial. One certainly should bear in mind Sabrina Baron's assertion that "there is no evidence that print carried more influence on the formation of public opinion than did manuscript," and Henry Ettinghausen's cautionary: "Far from there being a single or uniform awareness of current affairs or a single collective imagination, nascent public opinion varied from the substantial, if not almost total ignorance of more or less remote and illiterate peasants to the highly sophisticated awareness of the well-connected and well-informed."[5] Of course insofar as one might attempt to emphasize the continuing prevalence of the "non-modern" in societies where the newspaper began to spread, one

---

([Bremen], 2002), pp. 136–44, admits their undoubted importance but claims it is as yet impossible to say much on the subject since they are so little studied (see esp. p. 136 n. 387).

[3] The presentations at the Bremen conference in 2007 by Mario Infelise, "The Manuscript of News," and by Alessio Assonitis exploring a specific example from the Medici Archive project, while focusing on the period prior to the appearance of printed newspapers, both illustrate how essential it is to analyze the manuscript sources and networks of correspondents.

[4] Apart from the title of the present volume (and the emphasis of the conference from which it derives), one can find examples of this approach in the important and meticulously researched books by Böning. *Welteroberung durch ein neues Publikum*, and Wolfgang Behringer, *Im Zeichen des Merkur: Reichspost und Kommunikationsrevolution in der Frühen Neuzeit* (= Veröffentlichungen des Max-Planck-Instituts für Geschichte, vol. 189) (Göttingen, 2003).

[5] Sabrina A. Baron, "The guises of dissemination in early seventeenth-century England: News in manuscript and print," where she is criticizing Joad Raymond; and Henry Ettinghausen, "Politics and the press in Spain," both in Dooley and Baron (eds), *The Politics of Information in Early Modern Europe*, pp. 41 and 204 respectively.

immediately confronts the practical challenge of locating source material. How far can we ascertain the knowledge or world view of peasants or ordinary burghers? We cannot even begin to solve that problem in this chapter. What we can offer is a specific example to illustrate how the modernizing paradigm may need to be reconsidered before it will be possible to write a sufficiently broadly based history of news in seventeenth-century Europe.

The broad and interrelated questions which underlie our study include:

- What is the relationship between manuscript and printed news sources?
- What is the relationship between newspapers and separates (pamphlets and broadsides)?
- What role was played by oral transmission of news?
- Is it possible that certain networks of correspondents were more influential and even efficient in spreading news than were the distribution mechanisms for published newspapers and broadsides?
- Does the evidence of interest in news need to be expanded to include sources which of themselves do not contain news reports?
- Can and should we attempt to draw boundaries between fact and fiction? And the corollary: Do different rules operate about the production and dissemination of news, depending on whether it is objective and rational, or fantastic and seemingly irrational?
- Finally, to what degree is there regional variation in the spread of the news in Europe?

Sabbatai Sevi

Our subject is news concerning Jewish unrest in the Middle East and North Africa and in particular the rise and fall of the false messiah Sabbatai Sevi of Smyrna and his prophet Nathan Ashkenazi of Gaza, Palestine.[6] On 31 May 1665, a rabbi Sabbatai Sevi who had already acquired a reputation for unorthodox conduct proclaimed himself the new messiah in Gaza. The spread of messianic fever was due largely to his self-appointed prophet, a charismatic young rabbi Nathan Ashkenazi, who reinterpreted kabbalistic sources to proclaim the need for repentance in anticipation of the imminent coming of the new Kingdom on Earth. The earliest news reports about a movement among the Jews paid less

---

[6] For the history of the Sabbatean movement we rely on Gershom Scholem, *Sabbatai Sevi. The Mystical Messiah 1626–1676* (Princeton, 1973). Note that there are many variant transcriptions for Sabbatai's name (among the more common, Shabbatai Zevi); we follow that adopted for the translation of Scholem's book.

attention to Sabbatai and Nathan than to fantastic rumors about the movement of the Lost Tribes of Israel and their capture of the Muslim Holy Cities. Only during late autumn 1665 did the focus shift to Sabbatai. Sabbatai left Palestine and traveled via Aleppo to Smyrna, where in December prophetic frenzy developed.

He then left for Constantinople where, it was believed, he would confront the Sultan and bring an end to Ottoman rule. When he arrived in the Dardanelles in January the Turkish authorities promptly arrested him. Nonetheless, the Sabbatean movement grew and peaked during winter 1666. By late summer, the Turkish authorities had had enough. They summoned Sabbatai to Adrianople where the Sultan was in residence and presented him with an ultimatum: apostatize (convert to Islam) or die. Sabbatai chose life. Despite this news, Sabbatean belief did not entirely die, but its later history is not our subject here.

During the height of interest in Sabbatai, news about real or imagined events spread remarkably widely and rapidly in the Mediterranean world, the Middle East, and Europe.[7] As our title suggests—the reference being to the prophecy in Isaiah about the coming Day of Judgment—the news media indeed trumpeted the news of the messiah. It stimulated imaginations in both Jewish and Christian communities in Europe. That said, perhaps it is an exaggeration to claim, as some believe, that this is the first instance of media hype analogous to what we find on a daily basis in our own time. Indirect evidence about the extent of the movement is to be found in the publishing history of the devotional manual Nathan of Gaza had compiled. Initially it spread in manuscript form, then appeared in print in Constantinople, Amsterdam, Frankfurt, Mantua, and Prague.[8] Even if we did not have the confirmation provided by pamphlet and newspaper reports, the popularity of this manual is testimony to the rapidity with which news of the Sabbatean movement spread.

Until the appearance of Gershom Scholem's massive study of Sabbatai in the 1950s, serious analysis of the movement was a non-topic for most Jewish scholars. Even in Sabbatai's own time, there were many Jewish skeptics about his claims. The denouement of the affair was quite simply embarrassing for Jews. Scholem's study draws upon an impressive array of sources including ones in Hebrew which we cannot access. He mined unpublished letters, for instance those in the contemporary collection of Sabbatean news assembled by the Christian theologian Johann Hottinger in Zürich. Scholem also studied the published pamphlet literature but knew little of the extent to which the regularly

---

[7] As Scholem notes, p. 549, it even reached the English colonies in America, where Increase Mather in Boston was inspired to preach several sermons referring to the movement of the Jews, if not to their new messiah.

[8] See Scholem's list of editions, pp. 936–9.

published newspapers reported on Sabbatai.[9] A great deal more evidence has come to light since. As Ingrid Maier has shown, there is much to learn about the textual filiation and printing history of the pamphlets.[10] While some Jewish scholars had doubted that the Sabbatean movement was much in evidence in Poland, that view can no longer be defended.[11] The movement also attracted considerable interest in Moscow.[12] Although we now have a more balanced picture than did Scholem of the array of news sources, most collections of manuscript newsletters in European libraries await study.

Correspondence Networks between the Middle East and Europe

Our information about correspondence networks is often distressingly vague. News circulating within or coming out of the Middle East was transmitted in the first instance in manuscript form. Correspondence was being exchanged

---

[9] See Jetteke van Wijk, "The Rise and Fall of Shabbatai Zevi as Reflected in Contemporary Press Reports," *Studia Rosenthaliana*, 33/1 (1999): 7–27, based on her unpublished dissertation, which includes as an appendix a transcription of all the articles from the *Oprechte Haerlemse Courant* concerning Sabbatai. Earlier, transcriptions of selected articles about Sabbatai from that newspaper are in Jaap Meijer, *Soo wort men van dromen wacker. Nederlandse bijdrage tot de geschiedenis van Sabbatai Tswi—drie eeuwen na diens optreden 1666–1966* (Haarlem, 1967); Daniel Clarke Waugh, "Seventeenth-Century Muscovite Pamphlets with Turkish Themes: Toward a Study of Muscovite Literary Culture in its European Setting," Unpublished Ph.D. Dissertation (Harvard University, 1972), Appendix 2, pp. 490–509.

[10] Ingrid Maier and Wouter Pilger, "Polnische Fabelzeitung über Sabbatai Zwi übersetzt für den russischen Zaren (1666)," *Zeitschrift für slavische Philologie*, 62/1 (2003): 1–39; Ingrid Maier, "Acht anonyme deutsche und polnische 'Sabetha Sebi'-Drucke aus dem Jahre 1666. Auf der Spur nach dem Drucker," in *Gutenberg-Jahrbuch 2008*, pp. 141–60; Ingrid Maier and Winfried Schumacher, "Ein Medien-Hype im 17. Jahrhundert? Fünf illustrierte Drucke aus dem Jahre 1666 über die angebliche Hinrichtung von Sabbatai Zwi" *Quaerendo*, 39/2 (2009): 133–67. Since these articles provide exhaustive bibliographic references, they obviate the necessity to repeat here all the long seventeenth-century titles, library locations and shelf marks.

[11] See Maier and Pilger, "Polnische Fabelzeitung," which includes references to the various earlier publications concerning Polish sources on Sabbatai.

[12] First discussed and published in modernized transcription in Daniel Clarke Waugh, "News of the False Messiah: Reports on Shabbetai Zevi in Ukraine and Muscovy," *Jewish Social Studies*, 41/3–4 (1979): 301–322; since supplemented by Maier and Pilger, "Polnische Fabelzeitung." *Vesti-Kuranty 1656g, 1660–1662, 1664–1670 gg.*, 2 vols, ed. V.G. Dem'ianov et al. (Moscow, 2008–2009), contains all the Russian translations and their sources. For an overview of the Sabbatai material, see Ingrid Maier's introduction to vol. 2, sections 3.5.1 and 3.5.2.

among Jewish community leaders scattered in cities such as Gaza, Jerusalem, Cairo, Alexandria, Aleppo, Smyrna, and Constantinople, and even as far away as Baghdad and Yemen. Once the prophet Nathan decided to publicize the new messiah a flood of Sabbatean propaganda spread from Gaza. Yet it is difficult to probe beneath such expressions as "a stream of letters," "a bag full of letters," or where only one is preserved be sure that a given mail contained some 30 of them.[13] To a considerable degree, we rely upon indirect evidence if we are to believe Scholem when he states: "Every mail brought dozens of letters, and every recipient of such a letter could report a detail that was not in the news received by his neighbor. The extant collections of letters faithfully reflect the composite nature of this mosaic of news."[14]

The information from the Middle East arrived in Europe through various channels, in Hebrew (and vernaculars) intended for the Jewish communities and in European languages transmitted by Christian traders, diplomats, and others. Ships bearing messengers and letters would take about a month to reach Livorno from Alexandria or Alexandretta. Smyrna, a major seaport visited by European traders, was a collecting point for news from Constantinople as well as an important center of the Sabbatean movement. Ships from Smyrna might make it to Venice but many went to Livorno or Marseilles. From Smyrna to Livorno also took about a month. In contrast, news from Tunis might reach Livorno in about two weeks. Alternative routes for news were overland through the Balkans—Belgrade, Buda, and on to Vienna—or north to Ukraine and Poland. On all these routes local communities received letters and listened to the tales told by their bearers. The news was broadcast from the pulpit in almost every synagogue and was the subject of intense discussion.

For example, we know that Greek merchants created quite a stir at the market in L'viv (L'vov, Lemberg), in February 1666 with the news they brought from Constantinople, an event later reported in the *Oprechte Haerlemse Courant*.[15] Even after Sabbatai's arrest a Jewish delegation from L'viv set out to visit him in August and returned with a glowing report of their impressions.[16] Ironically they might have felt differently had they known about his apostasy which had occurred while they were returning home in September. A good deal of the Sabbatean propaganda seems to have spread during 1665 and 1666 by virtue of such personal contact.

---

[13] Scholem, pp. 259, 362, 418 n. 193.

[14] Scholem, p. 470.

[15] *Oprechte Haerlemse Dingsdaegse Courant*, no. 10, 9 March 1666, fol. 1v, datelined 14 February. All copies of the Haarlem newspaper quoted in this article are kept at Museum Enschedé, Haarlem; the Royal Library in The Hague has microfilms.

[16] Scholem, pp. 599–601.

Individual Collectors of Sabbatean News

We can document how certain individuals consciously collected and disseminated news about Sabbatai. Even if these are narrow examples of highly educated individuals with distinct religious interests, they are amongst our consumers of the seventeenth-century news. One is the theologian, church historian, and specialist in Semitic languages, Johann Hottinger in Zürich, who is well known for his news collection in which Sabbatean materials occupy a prominent place. His collection, much referred to, still must be mined for what it may tell us about seventeenth-century news networks and what he personally may have believed about the Sabbatean movement. Among the letters Hottinger collected was at least one written by the chiliast Protestant Petrus Serrarius in Amsterdam. Serrarius wanted to believe Sabbatai was the new messiah since this then supported his own eschatological views[17] but there seems little reason to think that he was fabricating the letters he received from his network of correspondents and sent on to like-minded chiliasts. Serrarius had close connections with the important Jewish community in Amsterdam and thus was able to obtain immediately the latest news and rumors from the Middle East.

One of the most important individual collectors of Sabbatean material was Jacob Sasportas, a controversial conservative rabbi and kabbalist, who fled the plague in London in late 1665 and took up residence in Hamburg.[18] Hamburg, like Amsterdam, was one of the most important centers for dissemination of news. In the reports about the messiah Sasportas may have hoped to find support for his own kabbalistic beliefs. However, with one brief lapse, he never was convinced of the messiah's *bona fides*. For the most part Sasportas collected the information in order to discredit the movement. He frequently expressed to his wide circle of correspondents frustration at not being able to learn the truth. Since much of what he received was generated by Sabbatean supporters he consciously censored material and, with posterity in mind, re-wrote his diary in order for it to present a consistent picture of his anti-Sabbataian credentials.

---

[17] About Petrus Serrarius and his interest in the Sabbatean movement see Ernestine G.E. van der Wall, *De mystieke chiliast Petrus Serrarius (1600–1669) en zijn wereld* (Leiden, 1987), esp. Ch. 10.

[18] Scholem makes extensive use of Sasportas's correspondence, primarily from the now standard edition of it in Hebrew, *Sisath Nobel Sevi*, ed. Is. Tishby (Jerusalem, 1954), which we have not consulted. For a brief summary of Sasportas's career, see Scholem, pp. 566–9.

"Fake" Pamphlets?

The earliest accounts of Jewish unrest which came to the attention of Serrarius and Sasportas concerned the armies of the Ten Tribes of Israel, some of which even were believed to have taken Mecca. As Scholem acknowledges, such reports might have been fabricated by European Christians and then spread to the Middle East, but he argues such rumors and expectations were already to be found there in the Jewish communities.[19] An external, Christian stimulus was not necessary to fuel the eschatological expectations of the Jews. However, quite apart from the obvious legendary aspects of the stories, we might distrust the indications in the pamphlets that they are based on letters sent from specific locations in the Middle East.

One example is a broadside entitled *Wahre historische Erzählung* which contains a report about the Ten Tribes and siege of Mecca datelined Smyrna, 3 May 1665.[20] The earliest extant version of the text was printed most probably in early August by the established newspaper publisher in Breslau, Gottfried Jonisch. A later edition printed at the end of November changed the dateline to 3 October, probably in order to give the appearance that the news was fresh.[21] We also have a condensed Russian translation based on what must have been a third version of the German text delivered by a Hamburg merchant to the Diplomatic Chancery in Moscow on 15 January 1666.[22]

The pamphlet includes some of the widely known fictions about Islam and prophecies about the fall of the Ottoman Empire. One legend tells how a lodestone was used to suspend Mohammed's coffin in the air, this ostensible miracle intended to deceive gullible Muslims. Not the least of the inaccuracies in this legend is the fact that Muhammad's tomb is located in Medina and not in Mecca. Nonetheless, our pamphlet relates how during the siege of Mecca a stray cannon shot hit the tomb, the coffin fell, and this signaled the imminent demise of the Ottoman Empire. The pamphlet also contains seemingly realistic details about Ottoman armies, and a section describing improbable battle standards with slogans and images on them. Those descriptions later migrated from this text into others which combined the news about the Jewish armies with

---

[19] Scholem, p. 332.

[20] *Wahre Historische erzehlung/ welcher gestalt Die grosse und fürnehme Stadt Mecha Belägert/ eingenommen und geplündert...*, n.p., n.d. [copy in the library of Wrocław Cathedral, XV.68.Qu]. On the history of this edition see Maier and Schumacher, "Ein Medien-Hype."

[21] This edition is known in a single copy, Uniwersytet Mikołaja Kopiernika [Toruń], Biblioteka Główna, Pol.7.II.3634.

[22] Text in Waugh, "News of the False Messiah," pp. 310–311, and in *Vesti-Kuranty*, vol. 1, text no. 32, pp. 147–9.

information about Sabbatai and his prophet. There is nothing in this text which we should necessarily believe would have originated in the Middle East. It could all be a European fabrication.

Yet even the sober *Oprechte Haerlemse Courant* in a report from Vienna dated 6 January 1666 related how on 30 December a courier arrived in 18 days from the Habsburg ambassador in Constantinople bringing letters to the Imperial Court.[23] The account goes on: "In them was definite information that the Jews and Arabs have despoiled the Grave of Mohammed at Mecca, and have seized many places. As a result, the Turkish Court offered to turn over to them Alexandria, Tunis and other places, but they demand the whole Holy Land." In addition to appearing in the Haarlem paper this report from Vienna was sent in a letter to Italy.[24] There is no way to know whether this bit of fantastic news originated in communities of the Middle East or might not instead have been stimulated by circulation there of the rumors sparked by the European pamphlets.

A second example of the spread of tales about the Ten Tribes involves Serrarius who provided the letters published in English chiliast pamphlets in the autumn of 1665. Scholem believes that these letters originated in Jewish communities. At least one of them is quite plausibly attributed to Raphael Supino, a distinguished Rabbinic scholar from Livorno who visited London. One of the more widely reproduced texts which passed through Serrarius' hands purports to be a letter from Salé in Morocco.[25] Its tale about mysterious Hebrew-speaking armies is so intermixed with chiliastic propaganda as to cast doubt on Scholem's assertion that "the letter does seem to have been sent from Morocco."[26] In one of the letter's more interesting incarnations, it is the centerpiece of a pamphlet introduced by what surely is a fiction based on tales about the Flying Dutchman.[27] Very likely its London printer fabricated the introduction in order to recycle the Salé letter, which had already appeared in print. We would emphasize here that the Salé letter, fantastic as its content may appear to us, seems to have been viewed as

---

[23] *Oprechte Haerlemse Saterdaegse Courant*, no. 4, 23 January 1666, fol. 1v.

[24] Scholem, pp. 247–8, esp. n. 31.

[25] *The Last Letters, To the London-Merchants and Faithful Ministers concerning The further Proceedings of the Conversion and Restauration of the Jews* ... (London, 1665) [Wing L489, available through Early English Books Online], pp. 4–6. The presumed source is *Translaet uyt een Brief van Sale in Barbaryen, In Dato den 6 Augusti 1665, aengaende den wonderlijcken en machtigen aentocht de 10 Stammen Israels, onder haren nieuwen Messias*, n.p., n.d. [copy in Bibliotheca Rosenthaliana], which is reproduced as Ill. 2 in Adri K. Offenberg, "Uit de Bibliotheca Rosenthaliana," *Studia Rosenthaliana*, 29/1 (1995): 91–9.

[26] Scholem, p. 342.

[27] *A New Letter from Aberdeen in Scotland, Sent to a Person of Quality. Wherein Is a more full Account of the Proceedings of the Jewes, Than hath been hitherto Published*. By R.R. (London, 1665) [Wing R63, available through Early English Books Online]; Scholem, pp. 348–9.

credible by Serrarius who certainly wanted to believe its content. This was very real and important news for him. And he was a man well aware of and taking pains to be informed of what was going on in the wider world.

Our third example involves broadsides and pamphlets devoted to the rise and fall of the false messiah. Some of them vividly illustrate the supposed miracles and tortures inflicted on him. A careful examination of the engravings reveals how the printed images served as the basis for the creation of new plates.[28] Since one of the editions has a specific indication that the pamphlet was "first published in Augsburg" Scholem somewhat incautiously attributed a number of related Sabbatean prints to Augsburg as well. At least one version probably was printed at the bishopric in Konstanz, a whole group of related texts were undoubtedly printed by the newspaper publisher David Friedrich Rhete in Danzig.[29] Rhete's press had an array of fonts and catered to several linguistic communities. In all, he published at least eight Sabbatean pamphlets including separate German and Polish editions and in one case a dual-language German/Polish edition. It is the only example known to date where it is certain that a single printer produced two editions of the same Sabbatean book.

The Rhete editions are of particular interest in connection with the spread of Sabbatean news in Poland and even to Muscovy. At least three of them were obtained by a Ukrainian Orthodox Christian cleric Ioannikii Galatowski (Galiatovs'kyi), most probably when he was resident in the Western Ukrainian city of L'viv, at that time part of the Polish-Lithuanian state.[30] Galatowski would then return to Kiev (now under Muscovite suzerainty) and use them as sources when he published there a massive anti-Jewish polemic in Ukrainian and separately in Polish.[31]

The Jewish communities in Poland and Ukraine were caught up in the Sabbatean fervor.[32] They paraded in the streets carrying images of the messiah

---

[28] See Maier and Schumacher, "Ein Medien-Hype."

[29] Maier, "Acht anonyme deutsche und polnische 'Sabetha Sebi'-Drucke."

[30] Waugh, "News of the False Messiah," pp. 301–305; Maier and Pilger, "Polnische Fabelzeitung über Sabbatai Zwi," pp. 3–8. Rhete's editions cited by Galatowski are: *Wunderlicher Anfang und Schmählicher Außgang des Jüdischen Königes Sabetha Sebi ... / Dziwny Początek á strasny Koniec ták nazwanego Zydowskiego Krola Sabetha Sebi*; *Opisanie Nowego Krola Zydowskiego Sabetha Sebi Ktorego Początek, Starość, Osoba, Uczynki, Przystawstwo y cuda ... W Rouku* [sic! = Roku] *1666. drukowano; Obszerna Continuatia, w ktorey się znajduje Dalszy progress, Tego co się w Orientalskich Krajach ... Drukowano w Roku 1666*. For details see Maier, "Acht anonyme deutsche polnische 'Sabetha Sebi'-Drucke."

[31] The Polish edition is Ioaniciusz Galatowski, *Messiasz prawdziwy Iezus Chrystus Syn Boży* ... (Kiev, 1672), a copy of which is available on line at http://pbc.biaman.pl/Content/424/messiasz_prawdziwy.pdf, accessed 11 March 2008.

[32] Scholem, pp. 591–602.

and his prophet.[33] These demonstrations provoked Christian attacks on the Jews. In an effort to maintain public order, the Polish king issued a decree in May 1666 forbidding the Jews to carry Sabbatai's picture. In it he noted: "They ... are spreading, as plain and indubitable truth, a false report from foreign lands, about some messiah, and they prove this to the simple-minded by printed pamphlets and pictures."[34] Thus the king ordered that all printed pictures, pamphlets, and broadsheets about the messiah be destroyed.

Of course this evidence leaves us with unanswered questions concerning what imprints might no longer be extant and where the Rhete imprints would fit. After all, certain of them could hardly have been used as Sabbatean propaganda. Moreover, the king's decrees should not mislead us into thinking that the printed word and image were necessarily the most important means for stimulating Sabbatean enthusiasm in Poland. The massacres of the Jews during the Khmelnits'kyi uprising in 1648 had prepared the way psychologically for the appearance of a messiah who might lead the remaining Jews to the Promised Land.

Sabbatai in Moscow

Copies of David Rhete's *Dantziger Ordinari Zeitung* and at least three of his Sabbatean pamphlets were processed in Moscow by the translators in the Diplomatic Chancery.[35] Such foreign pamphlets and newspapers were classified

---

[33] We cannot be certain what these images were. The more "realistic" portraits of Sabbatai and Nathan include those in the engravings of Thomas Coenen's book on the movement published in 1669 and reproduced in Scholem, frontispiece and facing p. ix. The perhaps realistic depiction of Nathan, published as *Warhaffte Abbildung dess Newen Jüdischen Propheten Nathan*, n.p., 1665, also exists in a manuscript copy, as do the upper part of the figure shown in *Warhafftige Abbildung Josuae Helcams*, n.p., n.d. [Niedersächsisches Staatsarchiv Wolfenbüttel, 1 Alt 22—Nr. 227]. This file also contains some manuscript newsletters about Shabbetai. As Ingrid Maier has shown, two of the known Shabbetai images—etchings in folio made by the famous etcher Jan Bensheimer—were printed 1666 in Danzig by D.F. Rhete, as illustrations (folding plates) of anonymous pamphlets about Sabbatai and Nathan. For details about location and reproductions of those "portraits" see Maier, "Acht anonyme deutsche und polnische 'Sabetha Sebi'-Drucke," illustrations no. 13 and 14.

[34] Quoted by Scholem, p. 597.

[35] The best overview of the Muscovite acquisition and translation of foreign news is Ingrid Maier's introduction to *Vesti-Kuranty 1656 g., 1660–1662 gg., 1664–1670 gg.*, vol. 2. See also S.M. Shamin, "Dostavka i obrabotka v Posol'skom prikaze inostrannykh gazet v tsarstvovanie Fedora Alekseevicha," in *Issledovaniia po istochnikovedeniiu istorii Rossii (do 1917 g.)* (Moscow, 2003), pp. 121–34. Shamin is the most productive scholar in Russia

as state secrets in Muscovy. Their translations normally did not circulate beyond the immediate entourage of the Tsar who would listen to the news read aloud while his boyars listened in the antechamber. We assume his personal interest to a considerable degree dictated what was selected for translation. Fortuitously the Muscovite government had just established regular postal communication with Riga specifically to ensure biweekly delivery of news.[36] Between mid-January and mid-July an impressive two dozen items in the Muscovite *kuranty*—the translations prepared from foreign news sources— contained information about the Jewish unrest. These items included longish texts such as the account about the siege of Mecca and the Rhete pamphlets. Other items were at most a sentence or two. The source for several of the reports was the *Oprechte Haerlemse Courant*.

Since one of our topics here is reader response we need to ask why this apparently unusual interest in the story about Sabbatai in Moscow. The most likely explanation is that the news coincided with a religious upheaval and eschatological expectations involving a schism in the Russian church.[37] We know that Tsar Aleksei Mikhailovich was extremely devout and took an active role in church affairs. Another explanation may be the longstanding concerns of Muscovite foreign policy about anything that might affect neighboring Poland or the Ottoman Empire. Finally, in a city where there was no significant Jewish community there was a scandal brewing in which a Jewish-born doctor, Daniel von Gaden, was accused of proselytizing for Judaism even though he had converted to Protestantism years earlier on his arrival in Moscow.[38]

---

currently working on the Muscovite news translations; he has a forthcoming book on the subject, where the focus will be the last third of the seventeenth century. The present authors are preparing a more general overview of Muscovite acquisition of news.

[36] For a new assessment of Muscovite news communication with Europe, see Daniel C. Waugh and Ingrid Maier, "How Well Was Muscovy Connected with the World?" in *Imperienvergleich. Beispiele und Ansätze aus osteuropäischer Perspektive. Festschrift für Andreas Kappeler*, eds G. Hausmann and A. Rustemeyer (Wiesbaden, 2009): 17–38. The article includes information on the postal service and calculations of transit times for news reports.

[37] This idea, suggested in Waugh, "News of the False Messiah," has been documented best by T.A. Oparina, "Chislo 1666 v russkoi knizhnosti serediny—tret'ei chetverti XVII v," in *Chelovek mezhdu Tsarstvom i Imperiei. Sbornik materialov mezhdunarodnoi konferentsii* (Moscow, 2003), pp. 287–317.

[38] On this incident involving Daniel von Gaden in 1665, see Sabine Dumschat, *Ausländische Mediziner im Moskauer Russland* (= Quellen und Studien zur Geschichte des östlichen Europa, vol. 67) (Stuttgart, 2006), pp. 536–8. Perhaps to avoid further unpleasantness, von Gaden and his wife converted to Orthodox Christianity in 1667.

Newspaper Coverage of Sabbatai

So far we have been focusing on the pamphlets and broadsides. What about the newspapers? Our example here is the well-preserved *Oprechte Haerlemse Courant*. This material can be supplemented by evidence from England and despite the fragmentary preservation from the German-language press. While the German papers followed the story, it is apparent that they reported it in less detail than did the Haarlem paper.[39] Even among Dutch papers (the Amsterdam ones are unfortunately not so well preserved) the Haarlem *Courant* may in fact have been unique for the extent of its coverage.

The earliest of the European published accounts mentioning Sabbatai Sevi appeared both on the verso of the 14 July 1665 edition of the *Haeghsche Post-Tydingen* and as a separate broadside.[40] The focus of this piece is a chiliast message rather than the Jewish news *per se*. But this was an isolated early example of a newspaper account mentioning the messiah. The flood of reporting about Sabbatai was yet ahead.

Abraham Casteleyn's *Oprechte Haerlemse Courant* had a deserved reputation for its international coverage. Like most of the contemporary newspapers it generally stuck to reporting the facts which makes its emphasis on the story of Jewish unrest the more striking. Between late 1665 and early 1667 the Haarlem newspaper published some 39 articles in which there is information directly relating to the Jewish events.[41] Some are feature stories, in one case occupying nearly a quarter of the space in that issue of the paper. Understandably, the only ongoing news which consistently received more attention was the Anglo-Dutch naval war. The reportage on Sabbatai peaked in March 1666 when some 11 articles contained information on the Jewish events. Standards of objective reporting were relaxed. There is even evidence of trying to anticipate reader expectations: the paper might note the arrival of news from the Middle East and

---

[39] We have not systematically examined all German papers. Note, however, that the important Hamburg *Wochentliche Zeitung*, which seems to be complete for this period, included a good many short news items about Sabbatai and related Jewish affairs (each of the three weekly issues has a different title): *Ordinari Diengstags Zeitung* [= *ODZ*], no. 43 (1665), fol. [1v]; *ODZ*, no. 47 (1665), fol. [2r]; *Appendix der Wochentlichen Zeitung* [= *AWZ*], no. 49 (1665), fol. [2v]; *ODZ*, no. 49 (1665), fol. [2r]; *Wochentliche Donnerstags Zeitung* [= *WDZ*], no. 50 (1665), fol. [2v]; *ODZ*, no. 4 (1666), fol. [2r]; *ODZ*, no. 8 (1666), fol. [1r]; *WDZ*, no. 14 (1666), fol. [2v]; *WDZ*, no. 15 (1666), fol. [2r]. The Hamburg paper is no. Z9 in the standard bibliography of the early German press: Else Bogel and Elger Blühm, *Die deutschen Zeitungen des 17. Jahrhunderts: ein Bestandsverzeichnis mit historischen und bibliographischen Angaben*, 3 vols (Bremen, 1971–85).

[40] Van Wijk, p. 17.
[41] Van Wijk, p. 22.

then specify that it contained no new information about the Jewish events.[42] The editorial position of the paper was hardly pro-Jewish; it welcomed news of the apostasy.

Although there is no way to quantify the impact the newspaper coverage undoubtedly contributed to the growth of excitement about the messiah in Europe. This same reportage also provides evidence about the significant impact from receipt of the latest news through the post in manuscript newsletters. We know that skeptics such as Sasportas who first heard the rumors about the Jewish unrest from manuscript propaganda or possibly the printed broadsides demanded confirmation from more reliable sources. The newspapers were considered to be such a source. Yet it is clear that much of what the Haarlem paper published about Sabbatai and Jewish unrest was not accurate since rumor and misinformation were endemic in some of the paper's sources.

The nearly intact runs of the Haarlem paper allow us to calculate transit times for news. We often can determine how long it took a Sabbatean story to reach Europe, appear in print, and then be spread to distant subscribers. The most frequent datelines are Constantinople, Smyrna, or the intermediary transit point Livorno. Once the news had arrived in the latter city it predictably would reach Haarlem in 22 to 25 days. A story datelined Smyrna, 16 January 1666, was printed in Haarlem on 16 March and arrived in Moscow nearly 50 days after that.[43] In other words 108 days elapsed between its origin and its translation into Russian. In another example, probably more typical, Smyrna news of 1 April appeared in the Haarlem paper on 18 May and probably arrived in Moscow 25 June, some 86 days after the original report had been sent from Anatolia.[44] The pamphlets published by David Rhete in Danzig presumably arrived much more quickly in Moscow, even if their contents might have been equally dated. Possibly the Muscovite diplomatic files will eventually reveal evidence that other Sabbatean news arrived via the more direct route from Constantinople through Ukraine.

---

[42] *Oprechte Haerlemse Saterdaegse Courant*, no. 13, 27 March 1666, fol. 1r, datelined Aleppo 29 December: "Dese brieven melden van de Joodtse Saecke niet."

[43] The text is published in Waugh, "News of the False Messiah," p. 312; *Vesti-Kuranty*, vol. 1, text no. 38, p. 164. The source is *Oprechte Haerlemse Dingdaegse Courant*, no. 11, 16 March 1666, received and translated in Moscow on 23 April (3 May, New Style).

[44] The text is published in Waugh, 'News of the False Messiah', pp. 315–16; *Vesti-Kuranty*, vol. 1, text no. 48, p. 185. The source is *Oprechte Haerlemse Dingsdaegse Courant*, no. 20, 18 May 1666, most likely received and translated on 15 June (25 June, New Style).

The Appeal of Sabbatean News to Europeans

It is easy to appreciate the complex responses of Jewish communities to the Sabbatean news. What about the interest among Christians? This was still an age when religious belief and practice were central to most individuals' world views. Only a very small percentage of Europeans had what we might term a secular and rational outlook.[45] Most of those who might learn the news from reading printed newspapers or brochures and manuscript correspondence or from oral communication surely would pay attention to stories which might have cosmic importance for their lives. Thus the interest cannot have been limited to small groups such as the chiliasts who had a definite focus on an imminent Final Judgment or the Tsar in a Moscow where public ritual and private belief affirmed that the Russians adhered to the one true faith and their capital was the heavenly Jerusalem.[46] Surely for most consumers of the news, it was precisely the seemingly irrational and fabulous aspects of the Sabbatai story which provided its appeal.[47]

---

[45] For an introduction to some of the ways in which older views regarding modernizing secularism are being reassessed, see the review article by Caroline Ford, "Religion and Popular Culture in Modern Europe," *Journal of Modern History*, 65 (1993): 152–75. A good example of mid-seventeenth-century religious devotion which seemed to know no class or educational boundaries is the pilgrimages to Hornhausen in Saxony, where it was believed that Divine dispensation worked through healing waters of a local spring. Testimonials by elite visitors and long lists of cures were reported in pamphlets, for example, *Gründlicher unnd Warhaffter Bericht/ von dem Wundersamen Heilbrunnen/ so newlicher Zeit auß sonderbahrer Göttlicher Gnade/ in dem Stifft Halberstadt bey einem Dorff Hornhausen genant* ..., n.p., n.d. [copy in Dresden, SLUB, Hist.urb.Germ. 723,56]; *Weiterer Bericht Von dem wundersamen Heyl-Brunnen/ Welcher von einem Knaben/ als derselbe am fünfften Martii auß der Schuel gegangen/ zuerst erfunden worden* ..., n.p., 1646 [copy in Herzog August Bibliothek Wolfenbüttel, Mx 85(2)]. Both accounts about the miraculous watering hole were translated in Moscow (see *Vesti-Kuranty 1645–1646, 1648 gg.* [Moscow, 1980], pp. 133–42).

[46] On Muscovy as the new Israel or new Jerusalem, see Daniel B. Rowland, "Moscow—the Third Rome or the New Israel?" *The Russian Review*, 55/4 (1996): 591–614. See also Oparina, "Chislo 1666 v russkoi knizhnosti" for a detailed account of how, oddly enough, the western calendar reckoning of 1666 as the apocalyptic year found resonance in Russia even amongst the Old Believers. She places the interest in Sabbatai in this eschatological context. Note that Scholem, pp. 94–102, emphasizes the need to separate the Jewish responses from those of the Christian chiliasts, and he is skeptical about any wider resonance of the Sabbatai news amongst Christians.

[47] See the comments of Böning, *Welteroberung durch ein neues Publikum*, pp. 45–46, 105, 132–5, on the limited degree to which wondrous events were reported in regular newspapers. Wonder tales certainly figured in the selection of foreign news translated in Moscow. See S.M. Shamin, "Chudesa v kurantakh vremen pravleniia Fedora Alekseevicha (1676–82 g.)," *Drevniaia Rus'. Voprosy medievistiki*, no. 4 (2001): 99–110, and his "'Skazanie o dvukh startsakh': K voprusu o bytovanii evropeiskogo eskhatologicheskogo prorochestva

The Christian and Jewish communities shared millenarian concerns, at the same time that for both communities the appeal of the news played into deeply ingrained biases about how misguided adherents of the other faith were. Thus one can easily understand how reportage about Sabbatai became anti-Semitic propaganda and Jewish demonstrations were often confronted by Christian, anti-Jewish satire, and even violence.

Apart from considerations of belief, there is another explanation for the phenomenon of Sabbatean news. Given the importance of Jewish merchants, commerce was bound to be affected by Jewish unrest.[48] Contemporary sources emphasize that in key cities commerce came to a halt as Jews stopped working, spent their time in penitential devotions, and in many cases packed their bags and set out to meet their messiah. The impact of Sabbateanism on commerce must have concerned the readership we imagine for a sensible newspaper such as the *Haerlemse Courant*. Thus the focus on this particular news is of a kind with reportage which in the normal order of things might include lading lists from newly arrived East Indiamen.[49] Jewish unrest was suddenly real and not a matter of rumor, irrespective of one's personal beliefs about the Final Judgment.

Conclusion

As we have demonstrated here, the example of the "Messiah's Trumpet" in 1665–67 opens a great many fruitful lines of inquiry if we wish eventually to develop a full understanding about the spread of news in the seventeenth century. We do not pretend that it was a typical news story; how far one may safely generalize from it is a good question. Some of the distinctive features of the Jewish correspondence networks and the impact of religious fervor might not be found in other communities or be expected to extend to other kinds of news stories. At very least though we might wonder whether in our study of the news we should separate fact from fiction, print from manuscript, or newspaper from broadside in order to consider only those aspects of the story which by a priori assumption embody modernity.

---

v Rossii," *Vestnik tserkovnoi istorii*, 10 (2008): 221–48. For a thoughtful examination of how the perception of "wonders" in Europe changed over time, see Lorraine Daston and Katharine Park, *Wonders and the Order of Nature, 1150–1750* (New York; Cambridge, Mass., 1998).

[48] On this point see van Wijk, pp. 24–5.

[49] For an example of such a list and its translation in Muscovy, see Ingrid Maier and Wouter Pilger, "VOC–Ladinglijst vertaald voor de Russische tsaar (1667)," in Wim Honselaar et al. (eds), *Die het kleine eert, is het grote weerd. Festschrift voor Adrie A. Barentsen* (= Pegasus Oost-Europese Studies, vol. 1) (Amsterdam 2003), pp. 191–213.

PART 3
Inter-European Spaces and Moments

CHAPTER 8

Handwritten Newsletters as Interregional Information Sources in Central and Southeastern Europe

Zsuzsa Barbarics-Hermanik

"The *Neuenzeitungen* are the lords' and potentates' helm, so that they can successfully lead and govern their states."[1]

This quotation from Georg Wintermonat's *Zehnjähriger Historischer Relation* printed in 1609 emphasizes how important it was for politicians to have up-to-date information in their decision-making. According to Wintermonat this "Turkish" proverb shows that the Ottomans definitely recognized the "usefulness of the knowledge of news." Moreover, he stressed that the Ottomans who were "otherwise barbarian peoples," "knew better what was going on in Christendom than [the Christians] did in relation to them."[2] As printing with Ottoman-Turkish letters was forbidden in the Ottoman Empire until the first half of the eighteenth century news was written down and multiplied by hand.[3] Therefore this proverb draws the attention directly to the close connection between ink and politics in early modern times. Wintermonat identified the two main subjects of the early modern communication system as well: a specific medium as a place of memory and as a distributor of information on the one hand, and on the other, a specific group of recipients. With particular regard to Central- and South-Eastern Europe, these "newsletters," and the "lords and potentates," and their relations are the main focus of this chapter.

---

[1] Georg Wintermonat, "Von Nutzen und Erspiesslichkeit der neuen Historien, 1609," in Elger Blühm and Rolf Engelsing (eds), *Die Zeitung. Deutsche Urteile und Dokumente von den Anfängen bis zur Gegenwart* (Bremen, 1997), p. 22. The German word *Neuenzeitungen* means both the news themselves and newsletters or newspapers as a form the media. *Kluge. Etymologisches Wörterbuch der deutschen Sprache*, 23. erweiterte Auflage (Berlin and New York, 1999), p. 206.

[2] Wintermonat, "Von Nutzen und Erspiesslichkeit der neuen Historien, 1609."

[3] Gábor Ágoston, "Információszerzés és kémkedés az Oszmán Birodalomban a 15–17. században," in Tivadar Petercsák and Mátyás Berecz (eds), *Információáramlás a magyar és a török végvári rendszerben* (Eger, 1999), p. 154.

In the sixteenth and seventeenth centuries conflicts dragging on between the two most powerful empires of early modern age, that is, the Habsburg and the Ottoman, determined the political development of this region. Nonetheless, to the "lords and potentates" of this area, not only the issue of the Ottoman threat and expansion mattered: of great importance were other tensions such as struggles between central powers and estates or religious conflicts. The rulers always needed the latest news "in peace as well as in wartime"[4] on a regular basis and not only from their home regions but from other parts of Europe and from the known world. It was crucial to be well informed about the actual events of the European political scene.

The infrastructure of Central- and South-Eastern Europe in the second half of the sixteenth century was considerably different from that of Western Europe. In particular, only a small part of this region was integrated into the continental postal networks. The few existing mail routes passing through the Habsburg territories were not well organized. Traveling through regions under Ottoman control was even more exhausting. Up until now, these aspects have generally reinforced the view that the region did not participate in principal networks of cultural exchange until the eighteenth century.[5] This chapter denies such theories and aims to present a well-functioning network of handwritten newsletters.

Until recent times the history of early modern media has been analyzed almost exclusively from the point of view of the history of printing,[6] which means that only one type of journalism was actually taken into consideration. New trends in research on "the communication revolution" in early modern times demonstrate that the circulation of handwritten media kept its importance even after the rise of printing and gained even more significance with the development of private and public bureaucracy.[7]

---

[4] Wintermonat, "Von Nutzen und Erspiesslichkeit der neuen Historien, 1609."

[5] For instance: Francisco Bethencourt and Florike Egmond, "Introduction," in ibid. (eds), *Correspondence and Cultural Exchange in Europe, 1400–1700*, vol. 3. (Cambridge, 2007), p. 15.

[6] For example Wolfgang Harms, "Das illustrierte Flugblatt in Verständigungsprozessen innerhalb der frühneuzeitlichen Kultur," in Wolfgang Harms and Alfred Messerli (eds), *Wahrnehmungsgeschichte und Wissendiskurs im illustrierten Flugblatt der Frühen Neuzeit (1450–1770)* (Basel, 2002), pp. 11–21; Thomas Schröder, *Die ersten Zeitungen: Textgestaltung und Nachrichtenauswahl* (Tübingen, 1995); Michael Giesecke, *Der Buchdruck in der Frühen Neuzeit. Eine historische Fallstudie über die Durchsetzung neuer Informations—und Kommunikationstechnologien* (Frankfurt am Main, 1998); Roger Chartier (ed.), *The Culture of Print. Power and the Uses of Print in Early Modern Europe* (Princeton, 1989); Craig Harline, *Pamphlets, Printing, and Political Culture in Early Dutch Republic* (Boston, 1987).

[7] Brendan Dooley, *A Social History of Skepticism. Experience and Doubt in Early Modern Culture* (Baltimore and London, 1999); Uwe Neddermeyer, *Von der Handschrift zum gedruckten Buch. Schriftlichkeit und Leseinteresse im Mittelalter und in der Frühen*

In spite of this general historiographical shift, research has still paid only slight attention to handwritten newsletters.[8] Although several studies on early modern media have pointed out that handwritten newsletters constituted the first step on the path to printed newspapers, a thorough analysis of these sources is completely missing. Apart from occasional mention of the most famous collection, the so-called *Fuggerzeitungen*,[9] such tendencies have been present since the 1920s and 1930s and still persist.[10]

Whatever textual studies were done concerning newsletters were based almost exclusively on the *Fuggerzeitungen*. Individual newsletter-texts were published,[11] but these transcriptions and their interpretations included a lot of mistakes. These studies attempted to trace the origins of the collection itself,[12] and to analyze the economic news of *Fuggerzeitungen*.[13] Such studies, however, concentrated on individual newsletter examples and never progressed to a systematic examination of the volumes.

In recent studies on the *Fuggerzeitungen* two tendencies can be observed. On the one hand, they repeat the results of the studies written in the 1920s and

---

Neuzeit. Quantitative und qualitative Aspekte (Wiesbaden, 1998); Francisco Bethencourt and Florike Egmond (eds), *Correspondence and Cultural Exchange in Europe*, vol. 3.

[8] Most of studies from the German and Italian speaking area published in the 1920s and 1940s are based on the following works: Joseph Chmel, *Die Handschriften der k. und k. Hofbibliothek in Wien*, 2 Bd. (Wien, 1840); Richard Gasshoff, *Die briefliche Zeitung des XVI. Jahrhunderts*, unpubl. Ph.D thesis (Leipzig, 1877); Georg Steinhausen, "Die Entstehung der Zeitung aus dem brieflichen Verkehr," *Archiv für Post und Telegraphie*, 23 (1895); 347–57; S. Bongi, "Le prime gazzette in Italia," *Nouva Antologia*, XI. (1869): 311–46.

[9] For instance: Karl Schottenloher, *Flugblatt und Zeitung* (Berlin, 1922), pp. 152–6; Otto Groth, *Die Zeitung. Ein System der Zeitungskunde (Journalistik)*, Bd.1. (Mannheim, Berlin and Leipzig, 1928), pp. 2–14; Adolf Dresler, *Die italienische Presse. Ein Leitfaden* (Würzburg, 1941), p. 3; ibid, *Geschichte der italienischen Presse. 1. Teil. Von den Anfängen bis 1815* (München, 1931), pp. 12–19.

[10] See Schröder, *Die ersten Zeitungen: Textgestaltung und Nachrichtenauswahl*, pp. 15–18; Jürgen Wilke, *Grundzüge der Medien—und Kommunikationsgeschichte. Von den Anfängen bis ins 20. Jahrhundert* (Köln, 2000).

[11] See Johannes Kleinpaul, *Die Fuggerzeitungen 1568-1605* (Leipzig, 1921); Viktor Klarwill, Fugger-Zeitungen. *Ungedruckte Briefe an das Haus Fugger aus den Jahren 1568–1605* (Wien, Leipzig and München, 1923).

[12] Mathilde Fitzler, *Die Entstehung der sogenannten Fuggerzeitungen in der Wiener Nationalbibliothek* (Baden bei Wien, 1937); Kleinpaul, Die Fuggerzeitungen 1568-1605; Theodor Neuhoffer, *Fuggerzeitungen aus dem Dreißigjährigem Krieg 1618–1623* (Augsburg, 1936).

[13] Kaspar Kempter, *Die wirtschaftliche Berichterstattung in den so genannten Fuggerzeitungen* (München, 1936).

1940s without any critical approach.[14] On the other hand, they concentrate on specific topics such as the arrival of the silver fleet from overseas in Spain, the expedition of Sir Francis Drake to the Caribbean Sea,[15] or the image of Poland in the *Fuggerzeitungen*.[16] A thorough analysis is completely missing to date; and this is also the case for other collections.

Although a number of studies were published concerning handwritten newsletter collections, there is no consensus regarding the nature and function of these media. The interpretation of handwritten newsletters as an independent medium remains to be undertaken. Historians considered them as an integrated part of the communication network of political elites[17] or of merchants.[18] The problem of the emergence of handwritten newsletters as an independent media is still to be solved and many questions regarding their network (for example its development and collapse, its geographical extension) are to be answered.

Two reasons for this lack of close attention to the newsletters might be suggested. First, there are evident difficulties in researching them. Only in exceptional cases are they found as separate collections in archive registers or library catalogues. Moreover, they are known by various names such as *avvisi*, *Relatio*, *Zeitung*, *Nova*, amongst others, which illustrates the ambiguity

---

[14] Michael Schilling, "Zwischen Mündlichkeit und Druck: Die Fuggerzeitungen," in Hans-Gert Roloff (ed.), *Editionsdesiderate zur Frühen Neuzeit* (Amsterdam, 1997), pp. 717–27; ibid., "Die Fuggerzeitungen," in Josef Pauser et al. (eds), *Quellenkunde der Habsburgermonarchie (16.–18. Jahrhundert). Ein exemplarisches Handbuch* (Wien and München, 2004), pp. 876–9.

[15] Renate Pieper, *Die Vermittlung einer neuen Welt. Amerika im Nachrichtennetz des Habsburgischen Imperiums 1493–1598* (Mainz, 2000), pp. 162–207; ibid., "Le corrispondenze dal Nouvo Mondo nel tardo XVI secolo sull' esempio delle 'Fuggerzeitungen,'" in Adriano Prosperi and Reinhard Wolfgang (ed.), *Il Nouvo Mondo nella coscienza italiana e tedesca del cinquecento* (Bologna, 1992), pp. 183–206.

[16] Czesława Pirożińska and Jan Pirożiński, "Berichterstattung aus und über Polen in den 'Wiener Fuggerzeitungen,'" in Walter Leitsch and Jan Pirożiński (eds), *Quellenstudien zur polnischen Geschichte aus österreichischen Sammlungen* (Vienna, 1990), pp. 83–120.

[17] Pierre Sardella, *Nouvelles et spéculations à Venise au début du XVIe sciècle* (Paris, 1948); Ágnes R. Várkonyi, "A tájékoztatás hatalma," in Tivadar Petercsák and Mátyás Berecz (eds), *Információáramlás a magyar és a török végvári rendszerben* (Eger, 1999), pp. 9–31.

[18] Margot Lindemann, *Nachrichtenübermittlung durch Kaufmannsbriefe. Brief-Zeitungen in der Korrespondenz Hildebrand Veckinshusens (1398–1428)* (München, 1978); Theodor-Gustav Werner, "Das kaufmännische Nachrichtenwesen im späten Mittelalter und in der Frühen Neuzeit und sein Einfluss auf die Entstehung der handschriftlichen Zeitung," *Scripta Mercaturae*, Heft 2 (1975), pp. 9–31; Federigo Melis, "Intensità e regolarità nella diffusione dell'informazione economica generale nel Mediterraneo e in Occidente alla fine del Medioevo," in *Mélanges en l'honneur de Fernand Braudel*, vol. 1: *Histoire économique du monde méditerranéan, 1450–1650* (Toulouse, 1973), pp. 389–424.

concerning these sources. Since they were sent to the addressees as a supplement to correspondence, they are not even mentioned in registers or catalogues. Secondly, collections of handwritten newsletters in several European countries have been examined separately and as a result of this they were defined as "unique" like the *Fuggerzeitungen*. With exception of studies on Italian *avvisi*,[19] until recent times the scholarly community did not realize that these European collections were valuable and belonged to a single type of source material. The lack of systematic analyses and comparative studies explains this failure.[20]

Collections are known of handwritten newsletters from Italy,[21] from the Iberian Peninsula,[22] from England,[23] from France,[24] and from the German principalities.[25] This material gives the impression that the network of these

---

[19] See Brendan Dooley, *A Social History of Skepticism*; Mario Infelise, *Prima dei giornali. Alle origini della pubblica informazione (secoli XVI e XVII)* (Roma and Bari, 2002).

[20] Except for works of Renate Pieper, Zsuzsa Barbarics-Hermanik and Cornell Zwierlein: Zsuzsa Barbarics and Renate Pieper, "Handwritten Newsletters as Means of Early Modern Age," in Francisco Bethencourt and Florike Egmond (eds), *Correspondence and Cultural Exchange in Europe, 1400–1700*, vol. 3. (Cambridge, 2007), pp. 53–79; Zsuzsa Barbarics, *Tinte und Politik in der Frühen Neuzeit. Handschriftliche Zeitungen als überregionale Nachrichtenquellen für die Machthaber*, unpublished Ph.D thesis (Graz, 2006); ibid., "Die Sammlungen handschriftlicher Zeitungen im Mittel- und Ostmitteleuropa in der Frühen Neuzeit," in Vaclav Bužek and Pavel Kral, eds, *Společnost v zemích habsburgské monarchie a její obraz v pramenech (1526–1740)*, Editio Universitatis Bohemiae Meridionalis, Opera Historica 11 (České Budějovice, 2006), pp. 219–44; Cornell Zwierlein in his Ph.D thesis analyzed the perception and influence of religious wars in France at the court of the count of Kurpfalz and the duke of Urbino. His comparative study deals with handwritten newsletters and diplomatic correspondence. Cornell Zwierlein, *Discorso und Lex. Die Entstehung neuer Denkrahmen und die Wahrnehmung der französischen Religionskriege in Italien und Deutschland, 1559–1598*, unpublished Ph.D thesis (München, 2003).

[21] See the collections examined by Brendan Dooley and Mario Infelise in Venice, Rome, Bologna, Florence, Modena, and Naples. Dooley, *A Social History of Skepticism*; Infelise, *Prima dei giornali*.

[22] Pieper, *Die Vermittlung einer Neuen Welt*, pp. 185–226.

[23] Frank C. Spooner and Fernand Braudel analyzed handwritten newsletters from the first half of the seventeenth century conserved in the London Public Record Office. Fernand Braudel, *The Mediterranean and the Mediterranean World in the Age of Philip II*, tr. S. Reynolds (New York, 1976), vol. 1, pt. 2, chap. 1.

[24] Frantz Funck-Brentano, *Les nouvellistes* (Paris, 1905); *De bonne main: La communication manuscrit au dix-huitième siècle*, ed. François Moureau (Paris, 1993).

[25] Johannes Kleinpaul draw attention to the existence of the collections in Berlin, Dresden, Karlsruhe, Leipzig, Marburg, München, Nürnberg, Stettin, Stuttgart, Weimar, Wolfenbüttel, Bamberg and in Augsburg. Johannes Kleinpaul, *Das Nachrichtenwesen der deutschen Fürsten im 16. und 17. Jahrhundert. Ein Beitrag zur Geschichte der Geschriebenen Zeitungen* (Leipzig, 1930), pp. 20–27.

sources was restricted to Western Europe. However, the analysis of the collections I have chosen proves that also Central- and South-Eastern Europe took part in the cultural exchange processes of the time. These collections are: the *Nádasdy-* and the *Thurzó-Zeitungen* in Budapest, the *Bullinger-Zeitungen* and the *Wickiana* in Zurich, the papers collected by the Habsburg emperors and by their librarians Hugo Blotius and Sebastian Tengnagel in Vienna, and by the estates of Styria, and the archdukes of Inner Austria in Graz. For the comparative analysis of these collections the *Fuggerzeitungen* serves as a pivotal point. Regarding these collections the following questions will be raised in this chapter:

- What is typical of the collections being compared?
- What are the characteristic features of handwritten newsletters as independent media?
- How are they related to other forms of correspondence?
- What other kinds of correspondence has their emergence to do with?
- Who were the addressees? What motivated them to collect and conserve the handwritten newsletters in their archives?
- Who were the intermediaries and avvisi–writers?

General Characteristics of the Collections

All the above mentioned collections date from the second half of the sixteenth and the first half of the seventeenth centuries. This period allows us to give an overview of the changes taking place under three generations of collectors. The territories where the collections analyzed in the present chapter came into being belonged to the Habsburgs by that time. The members of this family exercised authority over these areas either as dukes of Austria and kings of Hungary or as Holy Roman Emperors.[26]

Only the collectors living in the Habsburg residential cities of Vienna (collections of the Emperor and of the librarians Hugo Blotius and Sebastian Tengnagel) and Graz (collections of the Styrian Estates and of the Archduke of Inner Austria) or in Augsburg, also the center of the Fuggers, had the opportunity to use continental postal services.[27] Nonetheless, neither in Sárvár (*Nádasdy-Zeitungen*) and Biccse (*Thurzó-Zeitungen*) in Western- and North-Western part

---

[26] Until the official recognition of their independence in the Treaty of Westphalia (1648) Switzerland belonged under the authority of the Holy Roman Empire ruled by the Habsburgs. See Erich Zöllner, *Geschichte Österreichs* (Wien, 1990), pp. 35–40.

[27] For example, Wolfgang Behringer, *Thurn und Taxis. Die Geschichte der Post und ihrer Unternehmen* (München, 1990).

of Hungary[28] nor in Zurich (*Bullingerzeitungen* and *Wickiana*) in Switzerland[29] was it possible to transport handwritten newsletters with the help of regular mail services such as the Taxis or the Paar postal service.

In the archives and libraries handwritten newsletters were kept safe in two ways. First, separate newsletter collections were bound into volumes by the collectors or kept in the form of bundles. Secondly, in some cases they were mixed with other sources. Philipp Eduard and Oktavian Secundus Fugger, Hugo Blotius, Sebastian Tengnagel, and to some extent Heinrich Bullinger kept their newsletters bound into volumes. All these collections have been preserved in the manuscript departments of libraries,[30] while others (newsletters sent to Tamás Nádasdy and György and Szaniszló Thurzó, and a part of the newsletters of the Emperor)[31] are to be found in archives.

Within the second category we can distinguish four subgroups:

1. Handwritten newsletters were kept together with diplomatic correspondence. It was typical of the newsletters dispatched by imperial envoys or by their secretaries in Rome, Venice, and Constantinople as a supplement to their correspondence.[32]

---

[28] After 1541 the former mediaeval Kingdom of Hungary was divided into three parts: 1, The Western and North-Western regions were ruled by the Habsburgs as kings of Hungary (since 1527); 2, In the Eastern parts the principality of Transylvania emerged, which paid tribute to the Ottomans; and 3, the territories between these were under Ottoman control. For details see: Thomas Winkelbauer, *Ständefreiheit und Fürstenmacht. Länder und Untertanen des Hauses Habsburg im konfessionellen Zeitalter*, Teil 1. (Wien, 2003), pp. 5–27; Justin McCarthy, *The Ottoman Turks. An Introductory History to 1923* (London and New York, 1999), pp. 87–91.

[29] See Arthur Wyss, *Die Post in der Schweiz. Ihre Geschichte durch 2000 Jahre* (Bern and Stuttgart, 1987), pp. 43–4.

[30] ÖNB, Vienna, Handschriftensammlung: the "Fuggerzeitungen," Cod. 8949, 8959, 8966, 8966, 8975; the collections of Blotius and Tengnagel, Cod. 7319, 8838, 8871, 5911; The Bullinger collection: Zentralbibliothek Zürich, Ms. A 43, 44, 63, 65, 66, 69, Ms. J 304.

[31] MOL (Hungarian State Archive), Budapest: the Nádasdy-Zeitungen, A Magyar Kamara Archivuma, Lymbus E 211, 134cs. 19.t: the Thurzó-Zeitungen, A Magyar Kamara Archivuma, Archivum Familiae Thurzó, E 196, 8.cs. fasc. 28, 29; the collection of the Emperors: HHStA, Vienna, Reichskanzlei, Geschriebene Zeitungen, fasc. 7a, 8. 10.

[32] HHStA, Vienna, Böhm 595 W 290, Litterae et Acta Caesaria Italica, 1553–1647, Bd. 1, 2, 6, 8, 11; Böhm 108 W 57, Collectanea Historica, Bd. 1–5; Türkei, Turcica, Karton 27–9, Karton 57, 79–81, 87–8; Venedig, Berichte 1575–1610, Karton 13.

2. Handwritten newsletters were also mixed with learned and private correspondence. The classic example of this is the Bullinger collection, or at least a part of it.[33]
3. They can be found as supplements to the correspondence between the addressees, their newsletters-mediators and professional newsletter-writers. This was typical of the newsletters of the Styrian estates and of the archdukes of Inner Austria.[34] Newsletters belonging to these subgroups are kept in archives: they do not form, however, separate books.
4. In the famous collection of Johann Jakob Wick, the so-called Wickiana, handwritten newsletters were kept together with private and diplomatic correspondence, but also with printed newsletters and newspapers.[35]

These collections vary in size. The most extensive is that of the *Fuggerzeitungen* with 27 volumes. The *Wickiana* contains 24 books, although not exclusively of handwritten newsletters. The imperial collection, Blotius', or Tengnagel's, or Bullinger's material is even more impressive in size. The newsletters ordered by the Styrian estates, by the archdukes of Inner Austria, and by the Hungarian noblemen Nádasdy and Thurzó survived in a smaller number, but the inventories are still remarkable.

The Origin of Handwritten Newsletters and their Development into an Independent Medium (Hypothesis)

General Characteristics of Handwritten Newsletters

A comparison of the above mentioned eight Central- and South-Eastern European collections demonstrates that since the 1540s at the latest a general pattern existed which distinguished handwritten newsletters clearly from other media of the early modern age. Starting from this date there is testimony from handwritten newsletters sent to two members of the first *avvisi*–collector generation, to Tamás Nádasdy in Hungary and Heinrich Bullinger in Switzerland.

The newsletters start with a heading indicating the place and date of compilation which is followed by paragraphs of news. After the last news, the documents end without any further remark. Addressees were occasionally

---

[33] Staatsarchiv des Kantons Zürich, Zurich, E II 340, 342a, 350, 351, 352, 355, 363, 365, 366, 368, 369, 376, 377, 378, 380, 441, 442a, 442b, 453, 455.

[34] Steiermärkisches Landesarchiv, Graz, Laa. Antiquum IV. Sch. 98, 99.

[35] Zentralbibliothek Zürich, Zurich, Ms. F. 19, 34.

mentioned on the reverse of the last page for example "Il s. Tomas Nadasdino,"[36] "Al Molto mag.co et ecc.te S.or il s.or Dottor Vgo Blotio Bibliothecario della M.ta Ces.mi,"[37] "dem wolgebornen Graven Herrn Georgio Thurzo von Bettlehemsdorff zu Arva,"[38] or "Den wolgebornen, edlen, vnd Gestrengen, Herren, Herren N. ainer Loblichen Lanndtschafft In Steyr verordneten, meinen Gnädigen Herren. Grätz."[39]

Newsletters were collected generation after generation up to the 1780s–90s. In the course of this period the form of this medium did not change considerably,[40] just a few modifications took place:

1. Sixteenth-century handwritten newsletters contained one, two, four or six news-paragraphs and they were written on one or two sheets of paper. From the first half of the seventeenth century the number of news-paragraphs and pages increased: on the average eight to ten sections dedicated to the news three or five pages were needed. Writing and compiling handwritten newsletters became more and more professional as regards the composition, the language, or the syntax.[41]
2. In the mid-seventeenth century the size of the newsletters started to vary, from that time on both small- and large-format documents can be found.
3. Until the first half of the seventeenth century they were written predominantly in Italian and German, occasionally in Latin, Spanish, and French.[42] From later periods there are no Latin pieces, whereas the number

---

[36] MOL, Budapest, A Magyar Kamara Archívuma, Lymbus E II 211, 134. cs. 19t. fol. 5v.

[37] ÖNB, Vienna, Handschriftensammlung, Cod. 5911, fol. 22v.

[38] MOL, Budapest, E II 196, A Magyar Kamara Archívuma, Archivum Familiae Thurzó, 8. cs. 28. fasc., 27r.

[39] Steiermärkisches Landesarchiv, Graz, LaaA. Antiquum IV. Schuber 98, 120v.

[40] See documents preserved in the Hungarian State Archive, in the Manuscript Department of the Zentralbibliothek in Zurich and in the Österreichische Nationalbibliothek in Vienna, or in the Steiermärkisches Landesarchiv in Graz. Brendan Dooley observed the same phenomenon concerning the *avvisi* in the Italian archives: Dooley, *A Social History of Skepticism*, p. 11. For the German territories see: Joseph Mančal, "Zu Augsburger Zeitungen vom Ende des 17. bis zur Mitte des 19. Jahrhunderts: Abendzeitung, Postzeitung und Intelligenzettel," in Helmut Gier und Johannes Janota (eds), *Ausgburger Buchdruck und Verlagswesen. Von den Anfängen bis zur Gegenwart* (Wiesbaden, 1997), pp. 683–733; Ulrich Blindow, *Berliner geschriebene Zeitungen des 18. Jahrhunderts* (Berlin and Würzburg, 1939).

[41] See Barbarics, *Tinte und Politik*, pp. 46–52.

[42] Especially the Fugger and the imperial collections contain newsletters in French and Spanish. The few newsletters in Latin, otherwise small in number, are more typical of the collections of Tamás Nádasdy, Heinrich Bullinger and Hans Jakob Wick. More detailed see: Barbarics, *Tinte und Politik*, pp. 50–51.

of Spanish, French, and English newsletters increased. The great variety of languages we meet in eighteenth-century handwritten newsletters sheds light upon the constantly growing geographical extension of this information network.
4. Until the 1580s handwritten newsletters were distributed twice a month afterwards every week.

Nevertheless, there is one characteristic of this type of source that did not change across the centuries: anonymity remained its main attribute. This feature distinguished them definitely from other forms of correspondence. Contrary to business, diplomatic, and learned letters of the early modern ages handwritten newsletters lacked all kinds of salutation as well as the author's signature. The newsletter writers took advantage of this anonymity in two ways: on one hand they could avoid the control and censorship of lay and ecclesiastical authorities; on the other, after copying the same newsletters could be sent to different addressees.

As a result of this practice identical texts appear in different collections—a fact which stands as a clear evidence of the statement that printing was not the only means by which the reproduction of texts was possible.[43] The reception of same texts, contents, and patterns was a general characteristic of the communication praxis of the *res publica literaria*: the concept of the humanistic *copia*[44] must have been adapted to the network of handwritten newsletters.

Development of Handwritten Newsletters into an Independent Medium

The emergence of handwritten newsletters was directly related to the development of the correspondence of business and diplomatic figures as well as of intellectuals and humanists. After these forms of correspondence had already been crystallized and their networks had been completely established in fifteenth-century Italy some new processes started. First, personal notes and remarks were separated from "pure" news and the latter were normally placed at the end of the letter. Then news was organized into a separate column under headings such as *Nova, Novissima, Avvisi, Zeitung* or *Relatio*. Soon after they were written on a separate sheet of paper which was then enclosed with the

---

[43] The role of printing was emphasized by Johannes Burkhardt, *Das Reformationsjahrhundert. Deutsche Geschichte zwischen Medienrevolution und Institutionenbildung 1517–1617* (Stuttgart, 2002), pp. 19–21.

[44] For more detail see: Andrea Schütte, "Die humanistische Copia," in Jürgen Fohrmann (ed.), *Gelehrte Kommunikation. Wissenschaft und Medium zwischen dem 16. und 20. Jahrhundert* (Wien, Köln and Weimar, 2005), pp. 100–107.

letter.[45] This division took place in Italy towards the end of the fourteenth century,[46] and in the Southern part of the Holy Roman Empire not before the second half of the fifteenth.[47]

Several examples in the collections of Tamás Nádasdy, Heinrich Bullinger, and Johann Jakob Wick illustrate the second and third phase of this development. It is apparent, however, that in the studied region older practices were still in use in the second half of the sixteenth century. Stephan Mathesy, Nádasdy's agent in Mantua, then in Brussels and Vienna, used both practices in the 1560s. In a letter dated from Vienna on 6 August 1561 the news was represented at the end of the document under the heading *Sumario di diversi avisi* (Summary of Diverse *Avisi*),[48] yet on 17 August 1561 Mathesy enclosed a newsletter with the heading *Avvisi* written on a sheet of paper separate from the correspondence he sent to Nádasdy.[49] At the end of these developments newsletters were produced, multiplied, dispatched and distributed on regular basis as independent media.

There is still debate, however, about which form of correspondence this development is based on. Historical research emphasizes the decisive role of merchant letters.[50] But to what extent was this practice influenced by the correspondence of intellectuals? This question has not been raised at all until now. It is also possible that two parallel lines of development had begun in the later Middle Ages which came together in the first half of the sixteenth century and became intertwined, henceforward developing together. Therefore, I would not say that the system of handwritten newsletters emerged only within the mercantile environment. Humanist intellectuals made their contributions to the emergence of this independent medium as well. Besides the above mentioned concept of the humanistic *copia*, humanist "writing practices" were of great importance. Especially the production of excerpts marked this new type of source.

The sources for the material in handwritten newsletters were various kinds of correspondence. Newsletter-writers summarized the contents of the original

---

[45] To this process see also: Grasshoff, *Die briefliche Zeitung*, pp. 58–9; Otto Groth, *Die Zeitung. Ein System der Zeitungskunde (Journalistik)*, (Mannheim, Berlin and Leipzig, 1928), Bd. 1, pp. 6–7.
[46] Dresler, *Geschichte der italienischen Presse*, p. 12.
[47] Lore Sporhan-Krempel, *Nürnberg als Nachrichtenzentrum zwischen 1400 und 1700* (Nürnberg, 1968), p. 16.
[48] MOL, Budapest, E II 185, A Magyar Kamara Archívuma, Archivum Familiae Nádasdy, Schachtel 19, 29r.
[49] MOL, Budapest, E II 185, A Magyar Kamara Archívuma, Archivum Familiae Nádasdy, Schachtel 19, 30r.
[50] Werner, *Das kaufmännische Nachrichtenwesen*, pp. 23–4; Infelise, *Prima dei giornali*, pp. 3–4.

letters or made excerpts of them. Then these parts were put together by writing them simply one after the other without any further concept. In this way a new document was created from the fragments of earlier constructions. This technique may be called syncretism or hybridization.[51] These ways of compiling corresponded with the two types of handwritten newsletters and newsletter-writers. Syncretism was typical of professional newsletter-writers and it meant that information from different written and oral sources—which originally had nothing to do with each other—was used to compile a completely new source of information, the handwritten newsletter. Then a number of copies were made and distributed like "commodities" regularly to subscribers. All of the above mentioned collectors in Central- and South-Eastern Europe were in contact with professional newsletter-writer. This is an important point of my research.

Hybridism characterized the work of non-professional newsletter-writers who distributed their newsletters in most cases without remuneration. These people, such as Heinrich Bullinger and Johann Jakob Wick, commonly used only one single correspondence while compiling their newsletters. The result was a mixture of the original source and final product. The Fuggers, Hugo Blotius, and the estates of Styria also received handwritten newsletter of this type.

Corresponding to these two ways of compiling, two kinds of headings can be identified. In case of syncretism the heading contains only place and date of production, for example: "*Di Venetia li 3. augusto 1576*"[52] or "*Auß Rom von 7. Augustj Ao. 93.*"[53] Newsletters compiled with the technique of hybridism include a quotation of the original source(s) in their headings besides the date and place of the composition, for example: "From the camp before Hatwan on 2 May, year [15]94,"[54] "By letters from Constantinople on 6 October 1558,"[55] or "Further writings about these deaths from Venice the 7th of January 1586."[56]

In these two ways of composing newsletters the central ideas of Renaissance reception, that is, the ideas of "filter" and "creative reception" can be discerned.[57]

---

[51] Peter Burke used these terms to describe the reception of the Renaissance and new forms of Italian culture. Peter Burke, *The European Renaissance. Centres and Peripheries* (Oxford, 1998), p. 7.

[52] Zeitungssammlung von Hugo Blotius, ÖNB, Handschriftensammlung, Vienna, Cod. 5915, fol. 17r.

[53] Fuggerzeitungen, ÖNB, Handschriftensammlung, Vienna, Cod. 8966, fol. 335r.

[54] Zeitungssammlung der steirischen Landstände, Steiermärkisches Landesarchiv Graz, Laa. Antiquum IV. Sch. 98, fol. 223v.

[55] Nádasdy-Zeitungen, MOL, Budapest, E II 211, A Magyar Kamara Archívuma, Lymbus, 134 cs. 19t. 43r.

[56] Wickiana, Zentralbibliothek Zürich, Handschriftensammlung, Ms. F. 34. fol. 25r.

[57] Burke, *The European Renaissance*, p. 8.

In this way newsletter writers of the sixteenth and seventeenth centuries "combined, adapted, transposed," thus producing "something at the same time composite and original."[58]

Addressees, Mediators and Writers of Handwritten Newsletters

The addressees My research on the addressees of handwritten newsletters in the second half of the sixteenth and in the first half of the seventeenth century focuses on the collectors from Central- and South-Eastern Europe. By that time the daily life and politics of this region were determined by the ideas and events of the Counter Reformation and by the expansion of the Ottoman Empire.

Among the addressees there were Catholic monarchs (the Habsburg emperors or the Archdukes of Inner Austria), merchants (Philipp Eduard and Oktavian Secundus Fugger), intellectuals (the Dutch humanist librarians, Hugo Blotius and Sebastian Tengnagel), Protestant reformers and canons (Heinrich Bullinger and Hans Jakob Wick), and the members of the political elite (the Styrian estates or the leaders of the Hungarian estates, Tamás Nádasdy, György, and Szaniszló Thurzó).

These collectors did not belong only to one "professional group" and did not participate in one communication network only. Tamás Nádasdy and György Thurzó, for instance, were successful politicians and military leaders but also experienced merchants, diplomats, and well-educated intellectuals. Nádasdy exchanged letters with leading European humanists regularly such as Erasmus.[59] György Thurzó was in contact with the kings of England and Denmark, with the princes of Bavaria and Liechtenstein, and with the elector of Saxony.[60]

Most of the collectors were connected to each other by family ties or by common political, religious, and economic interests. Sometime they got to know each other during their studies. Philipp Eduard and Oktavian Secundus Fugger were relatives of the Thurzó family[61] and were in contact with the Emperor Rudolf II. They played an important role in financing the Habsburg

---

[58] Ibid., p. 7.
[59] Nádasdy did not only collect handwritten newsletters and printed materials, but established his own printing press in Sárvár. Zsuzsa Barbarics, "Die Bedeutung der handgeschriebenen Zeitungen in der Epoche Ferdinands I. am Beispiel der so genannten 'Nádasdy-Zeitungen,'" in Martina Fuchs et al. (eds), *Kaiser Ferdinand I. Ein mitteleuropäischer Herrscher* (Münster, 2005), pp. 179–205; Concerning all collectors in general see: Barbarics, *Tinte und Politik*, pp. 53–135.
[60] Ilia Bálint, "A Thurzó-család levéltára," *Levéltári Közlemények*, 10 (1932): 41.
[61] Götz Freiherr von Pölnitz, *Die Fugger* (Frankfurt am Main, 1959), p. 155.

campaigns against the Ottomans in the 1580s and 1590s.[62] At the end of the 1550s and the beginning of the 1560s representatives of the Styrian estates studied in Padua just like some members of the Fugger family (Philipp Eduard Fugger or his cousin Alexander Secundus Fugger)[63] and Hugo Blotius.[64] Owing to the Counter Reformation György Thurzó got in closer contact with the Styrian estates.[65] Johann Jakob Wick was one of Bullinger's collaborators, then his successor.[66] Hugo Blotius and Sebastian Tengnagel—both from the Netherlands—were in the service of the Emperors Maximilian II and Rudolf II. Before that employment Tengnagel had worked as an assistant for Blotius[67] who himself was in touch with the Hungarian estates and with the Archduke of Inner Austria, Charles II, by reason of the Ottoman expansion.[68]

All the addressees were educated according to the humanist tradition, thus becoming representatives and distributors of humanist ideas and values. They made study trips to Dutch, German, and especially to Italian universities. Besides the *studia humanitatis* they became skilled in the communication practices of the *res publica literaria*, so they obviously came in contact with handwritten newsletters.

The most important places of knowledge transfer were Rome, Bologna, and especially the University of Padua. Tamás Nádasdy, Hugo Blotius, Philipp Eduard, and Oktavian Secundus Fugger, the representatives of the Styrian estates,

---

[62] Fitzler, *Die Entstehung*, p. 40.

[63] In his diary Philipp Eduard Fugger mentioned the names of Styrian noblemen "*Christophorus Barones in Herberstein*" and "*Georgius Andreas,*" "*Sigismund Fredericq*" as his student-colleages in Padua. ÖNB, Handschriftensammlung, Vienna, Cod. 7447, fol. 55. Further see: Beatrix Bastl, *Das Tagebuch des Philipp Eduard Fugger (1560–1569) als Quelle zur Fuggergeschichte* (Tübingen, 1987), p. 48; Gábor Almási, "Két magyarországi humanista a császári udvar szolgálatában: Dudith András (1533–1589) és Zsámboky János (1531–1584)," *Századok,* 139 (2005) 4, p. 896.

[64] Ferdinand Mencsik, "A Páduában tanuló Blotz Hugó levelezése erdélyi és magyarországi barátaival," *Erdélyi Múzeum*, 27 (1910): 22–3.

[65] Ilia, "A Thurzó-család levéltára," p. 7.

[66] Matthias Senn, *Die Wickiana. Johann Jakob Wicks Nachrichtensammlung aus dem 16. Jahrhundert* (Zürich, 1975), pp. 7–9.; Franz Mauelshagen, *Wicks Wunderbücher. Entstehung–Überlieferung–Rezeption*, unpubl. Ph.D thesis (Zürich, 2000), p. 112.

[67] Josef Benz, "Die Wiener Hofbibliothek," in Josef Pauser et al. (eds), *Quellenkunde der Habsburgermonarchie (16.–18. Jahrhundert). Ein exemplarisches Handbuch* (Wien and München, 2004), pp. 49–51.

[68] Johanna von Ernuszt, "Die ungarischen Beziehungen des Hugo Blotius. Beiträge zur Geschichte des Humanismus in den Donauländern aus dem Briefwechsel eines Wiener Humanisten im XVI. Jahrhundert," *Jahrbuch des Graf Klebensberg Kuno Instituts für ungarische Geschichtsforschung in Wien* 10 (1940): 7–53; Joseph Chmel, *Die Handschriften der k. und k. Hofbibliothek in Wien im Interesse der Geschichte, besonders der österreichischen*, vol. 2 (Vienna, 1840), p. 221.

the members of the Thurzó family, and the chancellors and vice-chancellors of the Habsburg emperors, Ferdinand I, Maximilian II, and Rudolf II (the actual addressees of the handwritten newsletters sent to the imperial court) studied in these cities. Bullinger, Tengnagel, and Wick preferred the German universities of Cologne, Tübingen, Marburg, and Leipzig.[69] The Habsburg emperors, like the other addressees of handwritten newsletters, were educated in a humanist spirit and they looked upon themselves as members of the *res publica literaria*.[70]

In respect to religion, the addressees formed two groups: First, Heinrich Bullinger, Johann Jakob Wick, Tamás Nádasdy, György and Szaniszló Thurzó, Hugo Blotius, the Styrian estates (and the chancellors and vice-chancellors of the Habsburg Emperors) belonged to the Protestant "majority." Secondly, the Habsburg Emperors, the Archdukes of Inner Austria, Sebastian Tengnagel, and the Fugger brothers were Catholics. All of them were involved in the religious struggles of that time; indeed, due to the religious differences some of the addressees were actually political enemies. The Catholic Archdukes Charles II and Ferdinand II of Inner Austria were in permanent conflict with the Protestant Styrian estates,[71] just as the Protestant Hungarian estates were in conflict with the Catholic Habsburg emperors[72] and Heinrich Bullinger conflicted with Ferdinand I. In the last case the Protestant reformer could hardly tolerate that during the time of the Counter Reformation the emperor supported Catholics in Switzerland.[73] At the imperial court Blotius had quarrels with the Catholic leading officials.[74]

These religious conflicts were indirectly connected with the question of the Ottoman threat in Central- and South-Eastern Europe. The above mentioned addressees were all involved in the organization of defense against the Ottoman Empire although not in the same way. The Habsburg Emperors, the Archdukes of Inner Austria, the Styrian estates, and the leaders of the Hungarian estates, Tamás Nádasdy and György and Szaniszló Thurzó had a lot to do with the Ottoman threat in practice so they were often forced to make religious compromises. Philipp Eduard and Oktavian Secundus Fugger provided the Habsburgs with financial support to fight the Ottomans in Hungary. Hugo Blotius was involved in the war at an abstract,

---

[69] More detailed see: Barbarics, *Tinte und Politik*, pp. 53–135.

[70] Gábor Almási, "A császári udvar és a respublica litteraria a 16. század második felében," *Aetas*, 20 (2005) 3, pp. 15–17.

[71] Wolfgang Sittig, *Landstände und Landesfürstentum. Eine Krisenzeit als Anstoß für die Entwicklung der steirischen landständischen Verwaltung* (Graz, 1982).

[72] Paula Sutter-Fichtner, *Ferdinand I. Wider Not und Glaubensspaltung* (Graz, Wien and Köln, 1986), pp. 86–146.

[73] *Geschichte des Kantons Zürich*, Bd. 2. (Zürich, 1996), pp. 185–204.

[74] Howard Louthan, *The Quest for Compromise: Peacemakers in Counter-Reformation Vienna* (New York, 1997), pp. 58–9.

theoretical level. For him "the library was an intellectual arsenal where one could learn the ways and tactics of the enemy. He was "the humanist quartermaster of an army of scholars formed to fight against the Ottomans."[75] Sebastian Tengnagel followed this tradition and became one of the first "orientalists" at the imperial court.[76] Heinrich Bullinger was of another opinion: he considered the Habsburg emperors responsible for the expansion of the Ottoman Empire and identified them with the "real enemy."[77] Thus, he supported the Hungarian Protestants in their struggles against the Habsburgs and the Ottomans.[78]

A permanent flow of the latest news was essential for every political decision. Having an overview of international politics helped the addressees to interpret their own position in a wider context and to recognize the parallel developments in the region, in Central- and South-Eastern Europe and in the known world. Handwritten newsletters made these parallel developments visible and the addressees were surely aware of that.

The close connection between ink and politics gave inspiration to the actors of the political and intellectual scene to collect handwritten newsletters. It must be noted that they ordered the first newsletters when:

- they came to power (took up a profession, began a political career, or made an important step along their career path) or when;
- they intended to regain their lost political power.

On 9 December 1531 Heinrich Bullinger was appointed as the successor of Zwingli,[79] the first handwritten newsletters (compiled by hybridism like "An die Herren Kriegs lutt zu Wien nuwe Zittung vß Hungern Ao. 32"[80]) were sent to him a few months later in 1532. An example of syncretism is the first avviso sent to Tamás Nádasdy on 14 January 1543 from Rome[81] shortly after he had been appointed general of Transdanubia (late 1542), responsible for the defense

---

[75]   Louthan, *The Quest for Compromise*, p. 75.
[76]   Claudia Römer, "An Ottoman Copyist Working for Sebastian Tengnagel, Librarian at the Vienna Hofbibliothek, 1608–1636," *Archív Orientální*, 66 (1998): 331–50.
[77]   Michael Baumann, "Heinrich Bullinger und das weltlich Schwert," *AOG-Mitteilungsblatt*, 4 (2004), p. 32.
[78]   *Bullinger Henrik levele a magyarországi egyházakhoz és lelkipásztorokhoz 1551*, transl. by Barna Nagy (Budapest, 1967).
[79]   For his appointment see: Hans Ulrich Bächtold, "Bullinger, Heinrich," *Historisches Lexikon der Schweiz*, Bd. 2. (Basel, 2003), p. 825.
[80]   Staatsarchiv des Kantons Zürich, E II 350, fol. 313. Further examples from 1532: Staatsarchiv des Kantons Zürich, E II 350, 311–12, 313–14.
[81]   MOL, Budapest, A Magyar Kamara Archivuma, Lymbus, E 211, 134. cs. 19t. fol. 1r.–v.

of Habsburg Hungary against the Ottoman campaigns.[82] In 1558 Ferdinand I was elected emperor, and the first handwritten newsletter in the collection of the Habsburg rulers is from 1559.[83] After he had finished his studies at Italian universities Philipp Eduard Fugger went to Antwerp where he got all the skills a merchant needed at that time. His master was Hans Georg Ött who ran the Fugger factor there. The first volume of the *Fuggerzeitungen* is from the year Philipp Eduard arrived in Antwerp—1568.[84]

The first handwritten *avvisi* in Blotius' collection are dated from 1573. In 1571 he became the tutor of János Liszthi and Johann Wilhelm Schwendi, both of whom were then studying in Padua. In 1573 the three began a trip in Italy that lasted until November 1574.[85] During this trip several handwritten newsletters were sent to Schwendi which were collected by Blotius.[86] Blotius arrived in Vienna at the end of 1574; the negotiations concerning his appointment as court librarian started somewhat later. By that time the handwritten newsletters were already addressed directly to him.[87] György Thurzó had been one of the most important representatives of the Hungarian estates[88] since 1586—exactly at that moment he started collecting handwritten newsletters.[89]

Finally, as a result of the political steps taken by Archduke Charles II in 1582 aiming to block the Reformation in Styria, the Styrian estates lost their political influence over the Inner Austrian administration and thus their control over printing and the postal service.[90] Due to this loss of power the estates were forced to start collecting handwritten newsletters.

---

[82] Géza Pálffy, "Nádasdy Tamás, a Dunántúl főkapitánya (1542–1546 és 1548–1552)," in *Nádasdy Tamás (1498–1562). Tudományos emlékülés: Sárvár, 1998. szeptember 10–11.* (Sárvár, 1999), p. 34.

[83] The first handwritten newsletter was compiled by hybridism: "*Schreiben auß Messina, vom 5. Decembris 59.*" ÖNB, Handschriftensammlung, Vienna, Zeitungsprotokolle der Reichskanzlei, Cod. 9102, fol. 993v.–94r.

[84] ÖNB, Handschriftensammlung, Vienna, Cod. 8949.

[85] Louthan, *The Quest for Compromise*, pp. 57–9; Mencsik, "Blotz Hugó levelezése a magyarokkal," p. 205.

[86] For instance: ÖNB, Handschriftensammlung, Vienna, Cod. 8838, 5915, 5911.

[87] Ernuszt, "Die ungarischen Beziehungen," p. 16.

[88] Tünde Lengyel, "Thurzó György nádor biccsei udvara," in Nóra G. Etényi, and Ildikó Horn, eds, *Idővel paloták ... Magyar udvari kultúra a 16–17. században* (Budapest, 2005), pp. 128–9.

[89] MOL, Budapest, Magyar Kamara Archívuma, Lymbus, E 211. 134. cs. 120t.

[90] More detailed see: Winkelbauer, *Ständefreiheit und Fürstenmacht*, pp. 46–8; Friedrich Kelbitsch, "Die Residenzstadt Graz als Heimat des steirischen Buchdruckes. Ein Überblick über die Zeit der steirischen Frühdrucker (1559–1619)," *Publikationen des Steiermärkischen Landesmusem und der Stiermärchischen Landesbibliothek*, vol. 3: *Innerösterreich 1564–1619* (Graz, 1967), pp. 298–305.

The mediators Like the addressees, the mediators of handwritten newsletters were also of various social and religious origins. Most of them received a humanist education, too. Regarding their relations to the collectors two groups can be identified:

- friends or companions of the addressees;
- in service of the above.

The social status of the friends was almost the same as that of the collectors. This was a mutual relationship; both parties sent free handwritten newsletters as supplements to their correspondence. During his stay in Antwerp (1568–72) Philipp Eduard Fugger was in regular contact with his former student-colleagues in Italian cities who sent him handwritten newsletters regularly.[91] Later, the 1570s and 1580s cardinal Granvelle forwarded handwritten *avvisi* (copies or originals) from Rome to his friend Philipp Eduard Fugger in Augsburg.[92]

Numerous Protestant priests and humanist intellectuals in Switzerland sent handwritten newsletters to Heinrich Bullinger—for instance, Theodore Beza, Calvin's successor in Geneva, Rudolf Gwalter, and Wolfgang Haller, priests in Zurich, or Johann Fabricius Montanus and Tobias Egli Iconius, Protestant churchmen in Chur. Beza specialized in newsletters from France; in Bullingers' collection, however, they can be found in German (for example "Zytung avß Marsilia den 28. marty 1573" or "Newe Zytung von Rochelle 1572"[93]). Johann Fabricius Montanus and Tobias Egli from Chur sent Bullinger some French newsletters in German, too. Most probably these newsletters, which were passed on to Bullinger by Beza, Montanus, and Egli, were translated in Switzerland, because they were all written in Swiss German.

Montanus and Egli were mediators in that they did not write handwritten newsletters themselves but copied or forwarded originals to Bullinger. The addressee of a newsletter compiled on 24 June 1562 in Lyon was Fabricius Montanus: "D. Joani Fabritio Curium ecclesiae fideli ministro domine suo. Chur."[94] Then, he transmitted this original to Bullinger. A newsletter which had been sent to the French envoy in Graubünden[95] fell into Egli's hands—Bullinger remarked on the copy: "Tobias Egli mans."[96]

---

[91] Bastl, *Das Tagebuch*, pp. 318–19. Examples are to find in: ÖNB, Vienna, Handschriftensammlung, Cod. 8949.
[92] Fitzler, *Die Entstehung*, pp. 19–20.
[93] Zentralbibliothek Zürich, Ms. F 63/1, fol. 57r.–58r., 58v.
[94] Zentralbibliothek Zürich, Ms. a. 43, fol. 204.
[95] *Vß Parys den 12 tag Novembris 1567*. Staatsarchiv des Kantons Zürich, E II 378, 1797r.
[96] Staatsarchiv des Kantons Zürich, E II 378, 1797v.

Egli (whose humanist name was Iconius) ordered some handwritten *avvisi* from Italy too. In the 1570s Scipio Lentulus, a protestant preacher in Chiavenna, received them from professional Venetian *avvisi*–writers, he sent them to Chur, and then Egli forwarded these Italian originals to Bullinger. On the reverse of *avvisi*[97] sent on 8 October 1573 from Chiavenna to Chur there are two remarks: first from Scipio Lentulus *"Clarissimo D. Tobia Iconio Ecclesia Curiensis,"* the second from Egli "D.H. Bullingero."[98] When Tobias Egli fell ill in the second half of 1574, the *avvisi* were addressed directly to Bullinger.[99] Nevertheless, this relation was not one-sided: Bullinger also sent handwritten newsletters to Egli[100] and the relationship between Bullinger and Johann Jakob Wick functioned in a similar way.[101]

In the second group of mediators there were:

- representatives of the above mentioned addresses who ran diplomatic and business affairs in foreign countries;
- agents residing in commercial and political centers;
- persons in service of other authorities who sold information.

The imperial envoys in Rome, Venice, and Constantinople as well as the factors of the Fugger brothers in important European centers belonged to the first category. The example of the Fugger factors in Venice, Antwerp, and Cologne illustrates how the system of handwritten newsletters actually functioned. In the 1570s David Ott was working in Venice where he got in touch with two professional *avvisi* writers. His sons continued to maintain these contacts: as the *avvisi* writers got their loan from the Ott family, the increase of their salary was a subject of negotiation after David Ott's death in 1579.[102] In 1588 Oktavian Secundus Fugger wrote to Jeremias and Christoph Ott the following: "You will know how to deal with the writers so that the weekly course will happen just as before also for this,"[103] which proves that the Otts forwarded *avvisi* to Augsburg every week. A decade before the newsletters were sent every second week. The

---

[97] *Antverpia 30. Augusti 1573, Spira p.o Septembris 1573, Lugduno 3. Septembris 1573, Roma 12. Septembris 1573, Venetys 25. September 1573*. Staatsarchiv des Kantons Zürich, E II 355, 286r.–286a.
[98] Staatsarchiv des Kantons Zürich, E II 355, 286av.
[99] For example Staatsarchiv des Kantons Zürich, E II 365, 388v., 390r.
[100] For example Staatsarchiv des Kantons Zürich, E II 342a, 615r. 623v. 628r.–v., 632r. 633r. 634r.
[101] For example Wickiana, Zentralbibliothek, Zürich, Ms F 19, 190r., 238v.
[102] Fitzler, *Die Entstehung*, pp. 18–19.
[103] Kempter, *Die wirtschaftliche Berichterstattung*, p. 3.

avvisi which the Fuggers received from Venice were both originals and copies, sent either separately or attached to the usual business correspondence.

Hans Georg Ött, the Fugger factor in Antwerp cooperated with Hans Adelgais and Hans Fritz who was a factor in Cologne. In the Netherlands Ött was in contact with newsletter writers: he sent original newsletters to Cologne which were copied there and these copies were forwarded to Augsburg. On 12 April 1578, for instance, Hans Adelgais wrote to Philipp Eduard Fugger: "As we wanted to close this letter we received a letter from Hannß Georgen Ötten from Antorff including ... a newsletter ... Did not have time to copy the same newsletters."[104] Adelgais and Fritz not only copied the handwritten newsletters coming from Antwerp, they translated them, too. Hans Adelgais wrote on 11 December 1578 to Philipp Eduard and Oktavian Secundus Fugger: "The newsletters that are sent to me ... I have to translate them from Dutch to German."[105] Most probably the Ötts translated the Italian handwritten newsletters as well—on occasion we can find German versions of Italian originals in the Fugger collection. Newsletters from Constantinople and from other cities of the Ottoman Empire also appear among the *Fuggerzeitungen*.[106] Similar to the previous cases they were translated and transmitted by the Fugger factor residing in Constantinople.[107]

During the 1570s the imperial envoys in Venice, Balthasar, and Veit von Dornberg sent handwritten *avvisi* to Vienna. These pieces were in Italian and came from different *avvisi* writers since neither the handwriting nor the structure of the language or the watermarks on the *dispacci* and on the *avvisi* attached to them were the same. Before 1580 newsletters were sent every second week, then at weekly intervals. The envoys themselves received forwarded handwritten newsletters as well. In 1573 István Kenderessy, who was active as a Habsburg and Ottoman double agent in the Balkans,[108] sent to Venice copies of *avvisi* originally compiled in Zara and Corfu attached to his account from Ragusa.[109] Veit von Dornberg forwarded them to the imperial court.

Bernardino Rossi was the imperial envoy's secretary in Venice (1586–1604). In his *dispacci* Rossi occasionally mentioned news from the *avvisi* as his source of information. The imperial diplomats in Rome—Conte Prospero D'Arco and

---

[104] Fitzler, *Die Entstehung*, pp. 34–5.
[105] Ibid., p. 28.
[106] See for example the volume of the year 1586: ÖNB, Handschriftensammlung, Vienna, Cod. 8959.
[107] To the Fugger representative in Constantinople see: Ferenc Szakály, *Mezőváros és reformáció. Tanulmányok a korai magyar polgárosodás kérdéséhez* (Budapest, 1995), p. 87.
[108] To the activities of Kenderessy see: Žontar, *Obceščevalna služba*, p. 192.
[109] *Di Zara il 2 julio Ao. 73. Per lettere di Corfu*. HHStA, Venedig, Berichte, Karton 13, 68r.–69r.

Francisco Strossi in the 1570s and Giovanni Battista Berniero in the 1580s—used the information of handwritten newsletters in a similar way. Rossi as well as the imperial envoys in Rome forwarded also originals and copies of handwritten *avvisi* to the imperial court.

During the 1570s and 1580s the imperial envoys of Constantinople were in contact with professional and non-professional newsletter writers. Although not so often, they sent newsletters to the imperial court as supplements to their accounts. Between November 1593 and 1610 the Habsburgs did not have representatives in Constantinople. Nevertheless, handwritten newsletters were still sent to the imperial court in Prague. Until the 1590s the handwritten newsletters were written in German, then in Italian, too. Italian pieces were composed by syncretism ("Di Constantinopoli li 13 Giogno 1593"[110]). On the cover of an *avviso* compiled on 22 February 1604 in Constantinople[111] we can find the following remark: "Avisi del Dragomano Ces.o in Const.li."[112] This remark can be read in two ways. It is possible that the dragoman, therefore, the interpreter of the Ottoman sultan, was the addressee of handwritten *avvisi*, and he forwarded them to a person who was in contact with the Habsburg imperial court. Alternatively, the dragoman himself could have been the writer of this *avviso*. There is no available personal data about the mediators working in the Ottoman capital between 1593 and 1610; nonetheless, handwritten newsletters were sent to Prague in this period as well. It seems that there were good connections between newsletter writers who wrote *avvisi* for Venetian merchants as a heading of the following newsletter shows: "Yet another *aviso* from Constantinople from the 20 July for a noble Venetian merchant."[113]

Some of the above mentioned collectors appointed private agents who acted similarly to the merchant houses and the representatives of states. These agents worked in European political and commercial centers in the service of Tamás Nádasdy, György and Szaniszló Thurzó, Heinrich Bullinger, or of the Styrian estates.

Bullinger had two agents in Switzerland: Scipio Lentulus in Chiavenna in the Southern part of the land close to Italy and Hans Liner in St. Gallen in the North in the neighborhood of the German principalities. The location determined their activities. In the 1570s Lentulus ordered and forwarded handwritten Italian *avvisi* from Venice, Hans Liner was in contact with newsletter-writers in

---

[110] HHStA, Türkei I. Turcica, 1593 V–VI, Karton 80, fol. 111r.–v.
[111] *Di Constantinopoli di 22 Febraro 1604.* HHStA, Türkei I. Turcica, 1603–1604, Karton 87, fol. 115r.
[112] HHStA, Türkei I. Turcica, 1603–1604, Karton 87, fol. 115v.
[113] HHStA, Türkei I. Turcica, 1593 VII–1598, Karton 81, fol. 70v.–71r.

Nuremberg and Augsburg. Between 1565 and 1575 he sent originals as well as copies of handwritten German newsletters to Zurich.[114]

From 1582 two agents of the Styrian estates are known. The Counter-Reformation in Styria forced Kaspar Hirsch, the former secretary of the estates, to leave the land. From his exile in Eßlingen he transmitted information and handwritten newsletters to the Styrian estates. Hirsch ordered handwritten newsletters in Nürnberg and sent them in packages to a second agent, Matthäus Paller, who lived in Augsburg. Then Paller forwarded them to Graz.[115] Paller also passed on handwritten newsletters that the Styrian estates ordered from professional newsletter writers in Augsburg.[116]

Stephan Mathesy was Nádasdy's agent in Mantua, Brussels and Vienna. Georg Irmkher lived in Prague and worked for György Thurzós. The handwritten newsletters he sent to Biccse were written in German.[117]

The mediators of the third category were primarily chancellors and secretaries who sold information as a sideline. Sometimes they forwarded copies of handwritten newsletters which arrived in the chancery or they compiled some new pieces by hybridism. The chancellors of the elector of Kurpfalz provided Bullinger and the Styrian estates with handwritten newsletters;[118] the administrators in the service of the prince of Württemberg, as well as the dragomans of the Ottoman sultans, sent such documents to the Habsburg Emperor;[119] and the secretaries of the Emperors' chancery sent *avvisi* to the *Fugger*, to *Blotius* and *Bullinger*.[120] The salary of these mediators was 100 fl. per year on average.

This information at the chanceries was normally to be kept secret. A decree issued by Maximilian II on 12 November 1570 forbade forwarding the newsletters

---

[114] For example *Auss Augsburg vom 27. Decembris 1566*. Staatsarchiv des Kantons Zürich, E II 350, fol. 175r.–176r.

[115] Matthäus Paller to the Styrian estates on 3 August 1583. Steiermärkisches Landesarchiv Graz, Laa. Antiquum IV. Sch. 98, 51r.–v.

[116] For detail see: Barbarics, *Tinte und Politik*, pp. 163–6.

[117] MOL, Budapest, E II 196, A Magyar Kamara Archívuma, Archivum Familiae Thurzó, 8. cs. 28. fasc., 29.fasc. More detail see: Barbarics, *Tinte und Politik*, pp. 167–9.

[118] For example StA des Kantons Zürich, E II 355, 284r.–v.; Stmk. LaA, Graz, Laa. Antiquum IV. Sch. 98, 26r.–v.

[119] For example HHStA, Vienna, Reichskanzlei, Geschriebene Zeitungen, fasc. 7a, 802v.; Türkei I, Turcica, 1603–1604, Karton 87, fol. 115r.–v; 595 W 290, Bd. 11, fol. 57r.–v.

[120] For example ÖNB, Handschriftensammlung, Vienna, Cod. 8951, fol. 142r.; 8966, fol. 267r. 419r.–420r.

received by the chancery. The prohibition was repeated several times.[121] This fact shows that authorities had a mutual relation to handwritten newsletters.

The newsletter writers Many collectors and mediators acted as newsletter writers as well and thus formed a group of non-professional newsletter writers. In this regard we have already referred in this chapter several times to the activities of Heinrich Bullinger, Johann Jakob Wick, and of the employees of other authorities. During the 1560s Philipp Eduard Fugger and his mentor in Antwerp, Hans Georg Ött also wrote handwritten newsletters, using the method of hybridism.[122] After the beginning of the 1570s the role of professional newsletter writers increased. Those who were in contact with the collectors in Central- and South-Eastern Europe concentrated mainly in two cities: Venice and Augsburg.

In Venice two famous *avvisi*-writers, Hieronimo Acconzaicco and Pompeo Roma, worked among others for the Fugger brothers. There they were directly in contact with the Fugger factors who forwarded their *avvisi* weekly to Augsburg and paid their salary. The account book of Philipp Eduard and Oktavian Secundus Fugger shows for the years 1585–86 a salary of fl. 113.48.4: "that is how much was paid in Venice to two writers of 85 and 86 years if the men wrote the weekly newspaper."[123] In Venice there worked at the same time two further professional newsletter-writers, Michaelo Ciliano and Nicolo Lucangelo. They were directly in contact with, for example, Hugo Blotius.[124] In their correspondence with Blotius they always complained about missing salary payments.[125] Scipio Lentulus, Bullinger's agent in Chiavenna, was actually in contact with one of these four newsletter-writers too.

In Augsburg there worked Marx Hörwart, Jeremias Krasser, and Jeremias Schiffle at the same time as professional newsletter-writers. To their customers belonged the Styrian estates, the archdukes of Inner Austria, Philipp Eduard, and Oktavian Secundus Fugger.

The analysis of the Central- and South-Eastern European collections suggests that in the late sixteenth and the beginning of the seventeenth centuries the personages we have mentioned were joined by professional newsletter-writers in other Western and Central-European cities and in South-Eastern Europe as well. To identify them by name will be one of the tasks of my further research activities.

---

[121] Lothar Gross, *Die Geschichte der Reichskanzlei von 1559 bis 1806* (Wien, 1933), p. 155.
[122] For more detail see: Barbarics, *Tinte und Politik*, pp. 53–135.
[123] Fitzler, *Die Entstehung*, pp. 17–18.
[124] They are also mentioned namely in Blotius' address book: ÖNB, Handschriftensammlung, Vienna, Cod. 9690, fol. 23v.
[125] For example Edith Rühl, *Die nachgelassenen Zeitungssammlungen*, PhD Diss. (Vienna: 1958), pp. 53–60.

Conclusion

This comparative study of eight Central- and South-Eastern European collections has shown that handwritten newsletters were an important means of cultural transfer originating in Italy. At some points the present analysis rejects the results of former studies which ignored the role of Central- and South-Eastern Europe in these networks of cultural exchange. The Nádasdy and Bullinger collections formed an integrated part of the handwritten newsletters network since the 1530s and 1540s.

A new approach to this topic sheds light upon the nature and function of the medium and its role in cultural transfer systems. Concerning the emergence and development of handwritten newsletters into an independent medium we can state with certainty that it was not only confined to merchants: humanist intellectuals contributed a lot to its development. The ways of compiling handwritten newsletters, the form of syncretism and hybridism, correspond with the two groups of newsletter writers described in the paper—namely, professional and non-professional. In the development and functioning of the systems of handwritten newsletters the concept of the humanist *copia* played a decisive role. Humanist education and tradition encouraged powerful authorities to start collecting these information sources. The collectors became important actors in the network as they supported mediators and newsletter writers.

Usually the collectors participated in different networks of correspondence at the same time. Still, they ordered handwritten newsletters too. The advantage of this source was that these handwritten newsletters offered an overview of political and military developments taking place simultaneously in different regions of Europe and of the known world on a regular basis. The newsletters helped them to interpret their own position in a wider political–geographical context. In that sense the handwritten newsletters were an important helm of the lords and potentates so that they could successfully lead and govern their states. They also encourage historians to reassess the meaning of the notions of secrecy and *arcana imperii* in early modern times.

CHAPTER 9

Between the French *Gazette* and Dutch French Language Newspapers

Charles-Henri Depezay

Introduction

In the second half of the seventeenth century a double market of information emerged in France, due to activity by the French government and by the Renaudot Family. Two different kinds of *gazettes* coexisted within this market. On the one hand, there was the official *gazette*, which supposedly enjoyed a monopoly on news, and which should have stood as a sort of *gazette* of record.[1] The other kind of *gazette* was produced in Holland but tolerated on French territory. The existence of this complex media system was not due merely to the tacit cooperation of the government. Nor could it be explained by the political context. In fact, it was due to a powerful European demand.[2] The popularity of the French language among the European courts, along with the intrinsic power of Louis XIV's France together determined the impetus given to Francophone *gazettes* from the 1650s onwards.[3] Almost continuous warfare by Louis XIV between 1688 and 1714 required people to seek information regarding ongoing political events. More than ever before, readers were able to compare the information they read in the two different types of *gazettes*. Seeing both sides in political and symbolic matters, as well as in the military operations, readers could gain a fairly accurate impression of what was going on.

Obviously, all readers did not share the same views or have the same expectations. Likewise, we may assume that that they were socially and culturally heterogeneous. However, regarding readers' backgrounds and reading habits, historical documentation is scarce and our knowledge is very limited. I propose to get around this problem by focusing on the content of the texts. For this quantitative and stylistic comparison of the editorial content of the *Gazette*

---

[1] Here as elsewhere in this book, *gazette* is defined as a political paper; it is generally written and edited by a single person, the "*gazetier*."
[2] Gilles Feyel, *L'Annonce et la nouvelle, la presse d'information en France sous l'Ancien Régime (1630–1788)* (Oxford: Voltaire Foundation, 2000), p. 1387.
[3] Ferdinand Brunot, *Le Français en France et hors de France au XVIIe siècle*, Tome V de *l'Histoire de la langue française des origines à nos jours* (Paris: Armand Colin, 1966), p. 171.

of France and Dutch *gazettes*, I have chosen two Dutch *gazettes*: the *Gazette d'Amsterdam* and the *Gazette de Leyde*. My study will hopefully suggest a wide range of hypotheses about the social and cultural milieu of the *gazettes*' readers. It may also cast some light on the intellectual and political as well as financial elites of the time, to the extent that they were readers of the *gazettes*.

Of course, the existence of an intricate system of information implies the existence of debates among a readership whose social and cultural boundaries are still unclear. We therefore also propose to examine the potential influence that such a readership may have had on power. More generally, we will then study the birth and the rise of the public, that is, the birth of a group of individuals whose personal opinions, values, and representations were not connected with the exercise of power.[4] Indeed, the publication of representations of such a public was all the more uncertain due to political and economic dependence on the information or media market. Now, although the media market enabled the state to control the rising public of readers and more generally the whole community, nonetheless the influence of the state at the time was incomplete. For one thing, the monarchy tolerated the spread of information in the *gazettes*; indeed, one might say that rather than opposing political debates, the monarchy preferred to show its own representations, especially in the *Gazette* of France. Furthermore, public spaces such as *cafés*, gardens, or even letters, that is to say, places and objects where information was generally exchanged and pooled and topics were debated, could not be controlled. Thus, if we recall the context of the wars of the time and if we also keep in mind that the last years of Louis XIV's reign were particularly warlike we can say that in France there existed what we may call an *opinion cantonnée*, that is, a limited, respectful, and yet attentive readership.[5] The novelty of this situation is best appreciated if we consider that previously the community had always been kept away from political information and only a privileged few and the Prince could be directly informed on political matters.

In the first part of what follows, I will demonstrate that the Dutch *gazettes* and the *Gazette* of France complmented each other. Next I will refer to the years 1688–89 and the year 1702—these are the years of the War of the League of Augsburg and the Spanish Succession War—and I will demonstrate that the paradoxical relationship between the Dutch *gazettes* and the *Gazette* of France led the reporters of the two *gazettes* to conflicting views on battle reports and

---

[4] Jürgen Habermas, *L'Espace public. Archéologie de la publicité comme dimension constitutive de la société bourgeoise*, trans. Marc B. de Launay (Paris: Payot, 1978), p. 322.

[5] Jean-Pierre Vittu, "'Le peuple est fort curieux de nouvelles:' l'information périodique dans la France des années 1690," *Studies on Voltaire*, 320 (1994): 105–44.

on political matters leading to wars; we will have to explain these and other discrepancies between the two types of *gazettes*.[6]

The Complementary Relationship between the Dutch *Gazettes* and the *Gazette* of France

Although the Dutch *gazettes* were banned in France, they were nonetheless well-known. Consider the evidence from a sonnet written in 1666 by French poet François Colletet, clearly showing the activity around the shop of the *Quai des Grands Augustins* in Paris—a place where people could buy and read a wide range of *gazettes* including those from Holland and Anvers.[7]

The war of Holland gave such an impetus to the sales of Dutch *gazettes* that Eusèbe Renaudot, the grandson of Théophraste, founder of the French *gazette*, put pressure on the State in order to have the French borders closed to foreign publications. Whatever sort of nuisance the Dutch *gazettes* represented to Eusèbe Renaudot, the state considered that such commerce with Holland was worth encouraging—also because any border closing would damage the French minister Louvois, who received an income for such trade. In March

---

[6] The War of the League of Augsburg—also known in Great Britain as "King William's War"—started in October, 1688. Most of the German princes, the emperor, the kings of Spain and Sweden rebelled against the king of France's policy of meetings, and so they allied against the Crown of France. In June, 1688, Louis XIV foisted the cardinal of Fürstenberg, a supporter of France, on the archbishopric of Cologne. Thus, he plunged the nation into war. William of Orange, who had come to be known as William III of England after James II had fled the country, teamed up against France. The war ended in 1697 with a confirmation of the status quo. The War of Succession to the Spainish Throne was led by France and Austria and took place right after the death of the last of the Habsburg kings, Charles II. Austria defended the rights of Archduke Charles, who was emperor Leopold's second-born son and the descendant of the Spanish Infantas. France supported Philippe d'Anjou, the grandson of Louis XIV, whose rights were in a certain way similar to his Austrian rival's. Charles II's testament, which was made known to the public in November 1700, did not allow the sharing of the Spanish heritage and designated Philippe as the new sovereign. As most of the European states anxiously expected a union of the French and Spanish kingdoms under the rule of a single Bourbon sovereign, the states sided with the emperor in 1702 and declared war on France. The 1713 and 1714 treaties of Utrecht and Rastadt maintained Philippe on the throne of Spain, but they divided the Spanish monarchy. Moreover, Philippe's hopes to become the king of France ended with the treaties.

[7] François Colletet, "Tracas de Paris," in Antoine Raffé (ed.) (Paris, 1666), quoted by Ferdinand Brunot, p. 269.

1672, Louvois in fact became the sole owner of the duty on foreign letters.[8] More importantly, the French government itself had changed its policy on the spreading of news. The change had taken place over a number of years. Until September 1671, that is, until the death of Hughes de Lionne, the minister of foreign affairs, the Crown had a tough policy concerning the *gazettes*. Yet, as a result there was no significant decrease in publication. After the Dutch War, the French government thus changed its policy. A ban on the sale and reading of the Dutch *gazettes* now appeared to be impractical. The best thing therefore was to request the *gazetiers* themselves to rectify information when necessary. Another solution was to threaten the Dutch *gazetiers* with closing the borders. Such a threat could be imagined to have some effect, since France was an important customer. We still do not have precise information on the dynamics of the situation. However, the French authorities knew they could not prevent all the Dutch periodicals from entering France; closing the borders would not work, indeed, would produce opposite effects because making the *gazettes* harder to get would automatically increase demand. Worse than that, there would be an increasing demand for *libelles*, which were far more subversive than the *gazettes*. Indeed, the *libelles* were more radically opposed to the royal order than any of the "institutionalized" periodicals including Dutch *gazettes*. The relationship between the Crown of France and the *gazettes* of Holland can then be summed up as follows: complex and including impracticable threats that were yet reliable enough to put effective pressure on the Dutch *gazetiers*.[9]

Consequently, the Dutch *gazetiers* occasionally showed how cooperative they could be with France and other countries. For example, the *Gazette d'Amsterdam*, when it launched a new, biweekly newspaper on 18 November 1688, asked French officials for an informal agreement or at least toleration allowing sale of newspapers in France. Claude Jordan, the chief editor of the *gazette*, was well-known to the French government as a writer of articles in the 1679 *Gazette de Leyde*. He attempted to distinguish himself from writers who wrote injurious and anonymous *libelles*. Jordan's policy is best exemplified in an article dated "*La Haye*," published in an issue dated 24 February 1689:

> The men of the Estates ordered to be burned by the hangman all the books and engravings that have appeared for some time wherein the honor and glory of various powers find themselves shocked, either with respect to the friends or the enemies of this state; their Exalted Excellencies have forbidden, on rigorous

---

[8] Gilles Feyel, *L'Annonce et la nouvelle, la presse d'information en France sous l'Ancien Régime (1630–1788)*, pp. 505–506.

[9] Pierre Rétat, "Les gazetiers de Hollande et les Puissances politiques: une difficile collaboration," XVIIIe siècle, 25 (1993): 319–35.

punishments, that there should appear in future anything on which the author and the printer should not be indicated.[10]

In the above excerpt we do not know which countries are meant by "various powers" but they could well be France, England—led by James II—and the papal states. These three areas were at that time, according to the *libelles*, the official enemies of Protestantism.

The Dutch *gazettes* were clearly seeking official recognition by the European governments as quality papers following a neutral policy. But that was not the Dutch *gazetiers*' sole aim. They also wanted to meet readers' demand for detailed accounts. Since the supply was shaped by the demand, the policy of the *gazette* was necessarily ambiguous and variable. The *gazetiers* consequently took the risk of choosing hot topics that concerned some state's political matters, occasionally daring to add commentary on those subjects. As they wrote and published, the *gazetiers* had to take three agents into account: the reader; the state, and themselves, as holders of personal views.

The Dutch *gazetiers* were very competitive, and they did what they could to lure readers into their market. They made their *gazettes* attractive to the eye in order to induce the prospective customer to read the articles often and take out a subscription. They particularly sought subscriptions as they made better deals this way than by selling unit price *gazettes*. Yet prices were such that generally prospective readers would have been wealthy. For a 12-month subscription to the *Gazette* of France, a Parisian had to pay around 20 *livres* in 1689–90. A subscription to a Dutch *gazette* was even more expensive because of the transportation cost. In 1714, an annual subscription to the *Gazette d'Amsterdam* cost a Parisian 78 *livres*.[11] Consequently, the mere fact of reading a Dutch *gazette* launched the reader into the social elite. The social significance and indeed the allure of these papers was further enhanced by their falling outside the realm of officially sanctioned publications. Due to group readings, group subscriptions, and lending of the *gazettes* we estimate that for a few hundred Dutch *gazettes* sold in France, there would have been from three to four times that many readers. We will now undertake a study of the editorial content of the *gazettes* to determine what might have been the social characteristics of these three hundred presumed readers.[12]

---

[10] *Nouveau journal universel où l'on voit tout ce qui se passe de considérable dans toutes les cours de l'Europe* (Gazette d'Amsterdam), 24 February 1689.

[11] Gilles Feyel, *La Presse en France des origines à 1944. Histoire politique et matérielle* (Paris: Ellipses, 1999), p. 20.

[12] Vittu, "'Le peuple est fort curieux de nouvelles:' l'information périodique dans la France des années 1690."

Claude Jordan and Jean Tronchin Dubreuil together founded the *Gazette d'Amsterdam* in November 1688 and both wrote for it. Both belonged to the Walloon Reformed Church. Jordan, a Huguenot, had fled persecution in France, whereas Tronchin Dubreuil came from Geneva.[13] Jean-Alexandre de La Font founded the *Gazette of Leyde* in 1677 and first called it *Traduction libre des gazettes flamandes et autres*. La Font's background was slightly similar to Jordan's.[14]

The religious affiliation of Jordan and Tronchin Dubreuil is evident in the *Gazette d'Amsterdam* through the frequent allusions to biblical characters and the Old Testament. Consider an article dated 17 March 1689 from Paris, where the *gazette* mentions the Earl of Tyrconnell. Tyrconnell as governor of Ireland had remained faithful to James II and rebelled against William of Orange and Orange's supporters. The *gazette* directed attention to that event in the following way: "Zimri, the fifth king of Israel, burned himself on purpose in the Palace of the Tirzah; but the Count of Tyrconnell contents himself by permitting others to suffer such deaths, without taking part himself."[15] Clearly enough, the writers of the *Gazette d'Amsterdam* draw on the comparison with Zimri to convey their own feelings regarding a deed they perceived as barbarous. But one may assume that the readers would have shared the same feelings. In this context, the *gazetiers* targeted the *Gazette d'Amsterdam* at readers who were Huguenot, mainly Protestant, supporters of the Stathouder William of Orange, who was the protector of Protestantism in Europe.

In the *Gazette de Leyde* of 1702 there are no similar examples. We can explain this by a change in the political stakes that had occurred in the interval between the War of the League of Augsburg and that of the succession to the Spanish throne.

Meticulously truthful and accurate, the Dutch *gazetiers* informed the reader about their modes of writing and frequently called upon the reader to observe the quality of their papers. This concern confirms the *gazetiers'* self-image as representing the centers around which the information that was gradually shaping history would always turn. The periodicals, on this view, would then be theatres where all historical events would occur. The metaphor of the center is moreover reinforced by the use the *gazetiers* make of the personal pronouns "I" and "we."[16] The Dutch *gazetiers* may thus be considered to have adopted an attitude more characteristic of contemporary education; indeed, the notion of "public" frequently found in their writing is a clear sign. In a note on the last page

---

[13] Jean Sgard (ed.), *Dictionnaire des journalistes (1600–1789)* (Grenoble, 1976), pp. 529–30.

[14] *Dictionnaire des journalistes (1600–1789)*, pp. 554–5.

[15] *Gazette d'Amsterdam*, 17 March 1689.

[16] Pierre Rétat and Jean Sgard (eds), *Presse et histoire au XVIIIe siècle: l'année 1734* (Paris: Editions du CNRS, 1978), p. 57.

of the issue of 20 January 1689, Claude Jordan claimed he was looking for a new correspondent in France. There he reminded readers about the conditions under which he wrote—that is to say, the obligation to publish moderate information that was respectful of authorities and of important persons; then he detailed his requirements: a prospective writer would have to produce information that brought "satisfaction" and that was "useful" to the "public."[17] The linking of these three terms shows particularly well that the term "public" at the time of the Dutch *gazetiers* was a value common to the writer and to the reader. Indeed, the term possessed far greater weight than its simply having been uttered by the writer; in effect, any text evoking the public automatically spoke in the name of the public.[18] So the Dutch *gazetiers*, while identifying themselves to a specific public, could decide on what was supposed to be useful to the public and what was not.

This image of the public, its needs, and its expectations, formed a quite accurate representation of the social world of the readers targeted by the Huguenot *gazetiers*. And indeed, the *gazetiers* may have achieved their goals since the image supposedly fit the reality. Among the relevant news and information that might stand as an indication of the social level of the readers of Dutch *gazettes* were the advertisements for unusual auctions like that of the earl of Orléans' jewels published in the issue of 23 March 1702 in the *Gazette de Leyde*.[19] There was also, perhaps more seriously, the publication of the lists of French officers killed or wounded after military battles.[20] Such news, of course, spoke first to families at the French Court but they also were of interest to the other European courts because of the intrinsic allure of news from Versailles.

Among the readership of Dutch *gazettes* were also merchants, whose business was largely affected by relationships between the European countries at the geopolitical level. International conflicts determined changes in trade routes to avoid loss and damage to goods. The Dutch *gazettes* demonstrated their awareness of these interests, especially in respect to seaborne trade, the key occupation of all the United Provinces and the Atlantic coast.

The *Gazette* of France was forced to react to what we have so far described as a relationship of intimacy and almost friendliness between some competitive periodicals and the readers.

The *Fronde* and the outburst of pamphlets against Mazarin and Anne of Austria led the *Gazette* to change its policy in 1652 and distinguish itself from

---

[17] *Gazette d'Amsterdam*, 20 January 1689.
[18] Hélène Merlin, *Public et littérature en France au XVIIe siècle* (Paris: Les Belles Lettres, 1994), p. 46.
[19] *Nouvelles extraordinaires de divers endroits* (*Gazette de Leyde*), 23 March 1702.
[20] *Gazette d'Amsterdam*, 5 September 1689.

the politically engaged *libelles*, which were always written with passion.[21] In 1702, Eusèbe Renaudot, recently promoted secretary of the minister of war and publisher of the *Gazette* from 1677, addressed a long letter to Chamillart giving his opinion on journalism. Renaudot thought it detrimental to the *Gazette* to be "frivolous, idle." To him, the *Gazette* must adopt a "serious" voice that should make the paper similar to a royal institution led by an academician.[22] With many other foreign correspondents all over Europe, some of them even belonging to the *ministère des Affaires Etrangères* (Foreign Office), Eusèbe Renaudot thus turned the *gazette* into a diplomatic paper with a very simple style similar to the style of official letters. Not surprisingly, the voice of the periodical was never in the first person. The third person was preferred, thus privileging the piece of news rather than the voice of the *gazetier*. Information thus presented would appear to reflect transparent, unquestionable truth.[23] We may then say that Renaudot's periodical by contrast to the Dutch *gazettes* did not respond to the public's demand but rather initiated a demand. The Dutch *gazettes* referred to the public in order to evoke common interests. The relatively few times when the *Gazette* did mention the public were to highlight the public's manipulation by the enemies of France as at the time of William of Orange's expedition in England, in Scotland, and in Ireland. So the *Gazette* of France did not adopt the same conceptual approach as the Dutch *gazettes*'. Renaudot's periodical was above all a space where power was represented.[24] Therefore it was very much concerned with the description of the important ceremonies that marked the sovereigns' lives. The information given by the *Gazette* was much more repetitive than it was original; for instance, I could not find, for the years under examination, any "news in brief."

Louis XIV settled permanently in Versailles in 1672. Authority could then no longer be represented since the King of France would not enter the provinces anymore. But the monarchy could still rely on the *Gazette* to offer its subjects an insight into the royal power. The redactor of the *Gazette* had to be restrained and accurate in order to target as many persons as possible. Perhaps because of this, the circulation of the *Gazette* was extraordinary for those times: the Paris edition amounted to 1,200 to 2,000 copies; whereas the provincial re-editions increased the total number of copies to between 3,400 and 8,800. However, this official periodical offered the Court and the various administrative offices a wealth of

---

[21] Stéphane Haffemayer, *Presse périodique et développement de l'information dans la France du milieu du XVIIe siècle: la Gazette et ses lecteurs dauphinois de 1647 à 1663* (Grenoble II, 1998), p. 598.

[22] Service historique des armées, AI 1604, pièce 145, Lettre de Renaudot à Chamillart, 21 septembre 1702.

[23] *Presse et histoire au XVIIIe siècle: l'année 1734*, p. 58.

[24] Habermas, pp. 17–37.

free press offices.[25] We may conclude that the *Gazette* focused on a readership of provincial elites and the agents of the monarchy. But the letters of young Pierre Bayle demonstrate that the *Gazette* was also read by the Huguenot Diaspora as a means to fill in the gaps of the information of the Dutch *gazettes*.[26]

So, it seems that the *Gazette* of France and the Dutch *gazettes* complemented each other, in their relations with their readers as well as in their editorial contents. On the one hand, the private *gazettes* presented the reader with "news in brief" and practical information. On the other hand, the royal institution for which the *Gazette* stood took part in the political and cultural centralization of the country. What they shared in common was merely their concern with being meticulously truthful and accurate, "to speak the truth." Even if we cannot use the term competition from a purely economic point of view we can however claim that they were politically competitive. The redactors' personalities themselves were politically opposed. The context of the European wars increased the natural state of competition already existing with the *Gazette* of France obviously describing in the accounts of the battles the French armies as more powerful than the enemy and the Dutch *gazettes*, on the contrary, giving details that made the armies of the allies out to be the most powerful.

Comparing the Coverage of War

More generally, the *gazettes* tended to complement each other's geostrategy. This idea is best exemplified by looking quantitatively at the relative amount of attention given to particular areas. If we consider the month of April 1689 we note that around 3 percent of the total amount of news in the *Gazette* was concerned with the military battles on the Rhine, whereas around 15 percent of the news in Jordan's periodical concerned that same subject including the Netherlands. Such a discrepancy between the two *gazettes* is explained by the fact that the allies resisted the French troops in that area from the spring of 1689 onwards. By contrast, the *Gazette* of France laid particular stress on Regensburg since it was precisely here that factions were observed between the allies, due to the Diet of Regensburg. Renaudot focused on the news from Vienna and on the suspension of any hopes of peace between the Imperial armies and the Ottomans.

---

[25] François Moureau, *De bonne main. La communication manuscrite au XVIIIe siècle* (Paris: Universitas, 1993), p. 9.

[26] Antony McKenna, "La lecture contradictoire des gazettes par le jeune Pierre Bayle" in Henri Duranton, Claude Labrosse and Pierre Rétat (eds) *Les Gazettes européennes de langue française: XVIIe–XVIIIe siècles* (St-Etienne: Publications de l'Université de St-Etienne, 1992), p. 173.

When we examine the month of September 1702 we note that 25 percent of the news published in the *Gazette* of France and the *Gazette de Leyde* was concerned with Northern Italy, the area where decisive battles were taking place. Since the French were soon in trouble on the Rhine Renaudot did not dwell on the subject and instead turned attention to the situation in Poland and the Great Northern War. In that context there was expectation of a future French involvement in the diplomatic and political maneuvers of the Charles XII of Sweden, Louis XIV's ally.

According to Grotius's doctrine, a just war is where the power declaring war proves that the war in question is undoubtedly just and absolutely necessary before undertaking it. In 1688–89, the *Gazette d'Amsterdam*, applying Grotius's doctrine, tried to demonstrate that the King of France was the aggressor. To do so, Jordan pointed to the "Politique des Réunions" that Louis XIV had pursued in the 1680s to "rejoin" to France the areas on the left bank of the Rhine. But Jordan also seemed to imply that the death of the Palatine elector Charles in 1685 had contributed considerably to reinforcing Louis XIV's claims on the Palatinate. Jordan thus implied that the Elector had not died from natural causes: "The Count de Castel is being sought, as well as a physician of Charles, the late Elector Palatine, on the suspicion that there is something extraordinary in the death of this prince, and that these men may know something about it."[27]

Jordan did not pronounce the word "assassination" but it is obvious that the hypothesis of assassination could explain the elector's death. Indeed, who more than Louis XIV could have benefited from the murder? It is true that Charles' death rekindled Louis XIV's policy of aggrandizement. This indirect accusation was in fact in keeping with the rumored immorality of the king of France, in a time when many pamphlets circulated regarding the king's ambiguous personality.[28] Jordan also often denounced the systematic destruction of the Palatinate by the French army, whereas the *Gazette* of France's writers hade depicted the event as a victory due to superior strategy, but nothing out of the ordinary, in spite of the violence of the allied troops toward the inhabitants of the occupied country.

However, the *Gazette d'Amsterdam* showed respect for the French army. This was not the case for all the armies since the *Gazette d'Amsterdam* could sometimes be disdainful towards some of the allies of the United Provinces, such as Spain. So, Jordan noticed the French troops' achievements or the French soldiers' bravery. That form of respect also mirrored the fear that the allies felt when faced with the French armies. But there is no sign of such a respect in the 1702 *Gazette de Leyde*; on the contrary, La Font showed himself to be very

---

[27] *Gazette d'Amsterdam*, 2 December 1688.
[28] Peter Burke, *Louis XIV, Les Stratégies de la gloire*, trans. Paul Chemla (Paris: Seuil, 1995), p. 138.

scornful and indeed sarcastic. On many occasions the *Gazette de Leyde* referred to the incident of the Maréchal of Villeroy, captured during a battle of the allies in Cremona. La Font painted Villeroy in an unflattering light, for instance, when in a 2 March report, he described Villeroy's failed attempts to corrupt his jailer:

> Villeroy omitted nothing, on the route from Cremona to Castiglione, in his attempt to gain release from [the jailer] and to escape with him to a safe place, offering him 6000 golden Louis for the purpose, and a respectable position in the French army. But [the jailer] responded that he would not committ such treachery against the emperor for three times that much money, even though the king of France should make him Marshall of France in place of Villeroy, adding that generally all the imperial officers and soldiers were too faithful to their sovereign to do such a despicable deed.[29]

In other words, the Imperials (*Impériaux*) would rather go to war for the sake of their sovereign than for money, so their feelings seem nobler than those of Villeroy. La Font's account was in fact very much in keeping with the idea that no ally would ever have any concourse with the enemy, would ever compromise. The *Gazette de Leyde* thus appears much more opposed to the French monarchy in 1702 than the *Gazette d'Amsterdam* had been in 1688–89. However, this difference between the two *gazettes* can be interpreted differently. Perhaps the French market represented a greater part in the sales figures of Jordan's *gazette* than was the case for La Font in his periodical. The *Gazette d'Amsterdam*'s writers might thus be more inclined than the writers of the *Gazette de Leyde* to take seriously any pressure put on the Dutch *gazettes* by the French government. Unfortunately, we do not possess any account books. But this difference in the editorial contents of the *gazettes* may also be justified by the progressive political radicalization among Huguenots that had occurred between 1688–89 and 1702, which had occurred because of the quasi-permanent state of war in Europe in the period.

As we have seen, the press war involved attacks on the political institutions of the belligerents; moreover, these attacks became more and more explicit. Although Claude Jordan directed implicit criticism to Louis XIV's foreign policy, he was nonetheless respectful of the royal authority, and he interpreted Louis's persecutions of the Protestants as having occurred only because the King had been very badly advised. His claims are reminiscent of the rhetoric in the era's popular and noble revolts, whose leaders questioned not the royal authority but rather the agents' influence. Jordan preferred to attack the "papists" who threatened both the French and the British monarchies. In this context, it seemed natural that the

---

[29] *Gazette de Leyde*, 2 March 1702.

Gazette d'Amsterdam would follow and support William of Orange's expedition to England. William, it claimed, quoting him, would be the one who would rescue liberty and Protestantism from papist and tyrannical influences.

The *Gazette* of France too dwelt on the political matters of England, but it claimed that William of Orange's expedition was in fact a war of religion against the English Catholics. When faced with the sudden decline of James II's power Renaudot seemed to resign himself to William's victory. However, he highlighted William's illegitimacy and claimed that William's Parliament was convened illegitimately. The grievances of the English nation were listed by the Lords and the Commons in order to make James II's abdication official. After that event on 12 March 1689 the *Gazette* stated the pre-eminence of the royal power over the parliaments. There thus appeared to be two conflicting views of the monarchy. One view, mainly supported by the Protestants, tended to demystify the institution, questioning the miraculous power received by the kings of France and England during the coronation ceremony. In the *Gazette*, this view in the following report is attributed to William of Orange:

> The 7th of this month, the Prince of Orange dined with Mylord Newport. That day, according to the custom, he had to perform the ceremony of touching the sick and washing the feet of many paupers, as all the legitimate kings have always done. But he declared that he believed these ceremonies were not devoid of superstition; and he only gave orders for alms to be destributed among the poor according to the custom.[30]

The *Gazette*, however, supported the sacred essence of monarchy, whereas the *Gazette d'Amsterdam* agreed with William's decision: "The king did not touch for scrofula, nor did he wash feet according to the custom; but instead he gave great charities that comforted the poor even more."[31] Here, Jordan's position foreshadows the intellectual maneuver of the 1721 *Lettres Persanes* in which Montesquieu, using a Persian character, ironically defined the king of France as a "great magician."[32]

Both of the periodicals commented upon the decisive events occurring in England—decisive also because of England's deep involvement in the War of the League of Augsburg. While doing this the *gazetiers* also revealed their preferred political model: divine right kingship in the case of Renaudot, and in that of Jordan, limited monarchy and a cameral system capable of representing the

---

[30] *Gazette de France*, 12 March 1689.
[31] See *Gazette d'Amsterdam*, 5 February 1689.
[32] Charles de Secondat, baron de la Brède et de Montesquieu, *Les Lettres persanes* (Amsterdam, 1721), Lettre XXIV.

nation. Indeed, whereas Jordan simply posited a counter-model for the structure of power, La Font was much more aggressive in 1702 when attacking the absolute monarchy of Louis XIV. To be sure, the French monarchy was far weaker in 1702 than it had been 13 years earlier. La Font accordingly listed the more or less official grievances concerning absolutism. In fact, the measures undertaken by the monarchy at war were deeply questioned in this period; and not only did La Font list the objections to them, but he also cruelly described the difficulties encountered by Philip V, Louis XIV's grandson, recently crowned as king of Spain. La Font's *Gazette de Leyde* tended to oppose the system of absolute monarchy and the dynasty of the Bourbons and so it openly attacked the personality of Louis XIV and his heirs. The physical and psychological decline of the king and the lack of bravery and dynamism of the Duke of Bourgogne were detailed. The *Gazette* of France seemingly wished to react against the collapse of the image of the royal family and so it made favorable descriptions of the Bourbons. But as France and Spain were in trouble in every field Eusèbe Renaudot himself questioned the cameral system in the end. He then tried to show that the Polish Diet defended private interests only and therefore did not defend the community. He also thought that a representative government could have a power as arbitrary as that of a monarch, passing laws harmful to liberty. The repression of the Jacobites by the English parliament exemplified that idea.[33]

Conclusion

To conclude, it seems that the *Gazette* of France and the *Gazette d'Amsterdam* targeted a pro-French monarchy readership or at least a readership that was respectful of the monarchy's power and reputation. Renaudot's periodical contributed to centralization when it described to the French provincial elites the ceremonies that occurred in Versailles and made them aware of what was at stake for the monarchy. Jordan's *gazette* seemingly targeted a Parisian, European readership, appealing to the political elite and to the French social elite and to the Huguenot Diaspora. The *Gazette de Leyde* however targeted mostly a European readership. It did not support any religion in particular, but it was basically opposed to the French monarchy and its symbols. But La Font could probably not have done without the French market and in fact his periodical was well-known in France—consider how many copies of the *Gazette de Leyde* were available at the Parisian libraries. We may then suppose that La Font's attacks against Louis XIV and against the French king's reign influenced or at least

---

[33] *Gazette de France*, 30 July 1689.

intrigued some Parisian groups. Why were they intrigued? They were intrigued because of the collective need to be informed. With the increase in the number of *gazettes* readers could compare the quality of information received and debate about what they read. The virtual debate created by the contrasting accounts of the european wars in the different *gazettes* probably contributed to create a public debate in eighteenth-century France and Europe.

CHAPTER 10

Antwerp and Brussels as Inter-European Spaces in News Exchange

Paul Arblaster

"Wat nieus hebt ghy vernomen in de stat?"[1] (What newes have you heard in the Citty?)
"Que dizen de nuevo en està villa?"[2] (What newes do men report in this towne?)

Introduction

To understand the legal/institutional regimes and the social and economic conditions under which in early-modern Europe news were circulated internationally, printed or transcribed, and disseminated further, the researcher has to focus and refocus on international, national, provincial, and local contexts, from emerging patterns of global commerce and communication down to the level of the printer's shop, the newswriter's desk, the scholar's study, and the tavern, barbershop, or coffee house. The most important intermediate level for early-modern communication is the city.

In newsletters and newspapers reports were attributed not to a named agency or reporter but were generally datelined "from Venice," "from Rome," "from Paris," and so forth. Working in the field of translation studies, Anthony Pym has found that the places that intercultural mediators "moved between were not nations, not cultures, not languages, but cities, mostly the largest cities of the day, the cities most open to intercultural comings, goings and mixings."[3] Early-modern disseminators of news seem to have functioned in pretty much the same terms.

The "comings, goings and mixings" that led to the sharing and dissemination of news were of various types. In a proclamation of 1609 the Archdukes Albert

---

[1] Marten Le Mayre, *The Dutch Schoole-master* (London, 1606; facsimile reprint Scolar Press, 1974), sig. F4r.
[2] William Stepney, *The Spanish Schoole-master* (London, 1591; facsimile reprint Scolar Press, 1971), p. 109.
[3] Anthony Pym, "The Problem of Sovereignty in Regimes of European Literature Transfer," <http://www.tinet.org/~apym/on–line/intercultures/sovereignty.html>, consulted 13 September 2007; first published in *New Comparison* 15 (1993), pp. 137–46.

and Isabella, Habsburg rulers of the Low Countries, listed barges, taverns, and banquets as places where undesirable debates were taking place.[4] Pamphlets and phrasebooks regularly set discussion of news at tavern tables and occasionally in other places where the paths of travelers might meet. Those who came, went, and mixed included place-seekers and place-holders in royal and noble households and in chambers, courts, and councils; merchants, factors, and exchange brokers; litigants and lawyers; scholars and students, and those for whom foreign travel was a finishing school in itself; medical men (including mountebanks), and those who traveled "to take the waters" or "for a change of air;" soldiers on the march and their commanders and camp–followers; pilgrims, clergymen on visitation or at convocation, religious refugees; other fugitives from justice or debt, and refugees from war, plague, and famine; besides the couriers, postmen, carters, bargemen, seamen, gypsies, hawkers, itinerant artisans, performers, tramps, and so on, for whom "coming and going" was a way of life or a daily job.

Any town with a garrison, a famous shrine or living saint, a reputable school, a law-court, a fashionable spa, even a curious monument (or multiple combinations of the above) would be a place of mixing and the exchange of national and international news; all the more so if in the shorter term it became a military headquarters, or the scene of rioting or public controversy, or was chosen to host a royal visit, a meeting of the estates, a synod, or a treaty negotiation. All such towns could be both markets for newsletters and newspapers and sources for the news that they provided, but in the early and middle decades of the seventeenth century only two types of city became significant locales for the regular production of newswriting and/or newspapers: major centers of commercial exchange and seats of political decision-making; in short, ports and courts.

My purpose here is to consider the role of two such cities, the port city Antwerp and the court city Brussels, as "inter-European spaces." Each was in its own way an important node in the interlocking communications networks of seventeenth-century Europe although both decreased in importance as the century progressed. Both can be found datelined in foreign newsletters and newspapers as direct sources of reporting although seldom appearing with the regular weekly basis of such cities as Rome, Venice, Vienna, Frankfurt, and Amsterdam. They were both among the four cities in the Habsburg Netherlands in which news was regularly printed in the middle decades of the seventeenth century. In this regard Antwerp was the most important: it was where the first newspaper in the Habsburg Netherlands was published from 1620 onwards and

---

[4] Proclamation issued Brussels, 13 July 1609, *Byde Eertzhertogen* (Brussels: Ruter Velpius, 1609). Single sheet.

where two more newspapers were founded once the first failed in the 1630s.[5] Brussels was an entirely different case: newspaper publication began relatively late, in 1649, and the only newspaper printed there in the course of the seventeenth century came close to being an official gazette with its owner and editor granted a legal monopoly on news printing that for one reason and another was never actually enforced.[6] The other two newspaper cities, also sources of occasional reports in the foreign press, were Ghent and Bruges: respectively the provincial seat of government for the county of Flanders and the *entrepôt* for the ports of the Flemish coast. These ports—Ostend, Nieuwpoort, Dunkirk—were also occasional sources of international news but neither they nor Ghent and Bruges can compare to Antwerp and Brussels in importance.

Brussels

Brussels was the center of royal government in the Netherlands. In the sixteenth century Charles V had frequently held court in Brussels and in 1556, the year that Charles V's formal act of abdication took place there, the city could briefly boast of being home to seven crowned heads at once (including Mulay Hassan, former king of Tunis). After Philip II's departure in 1559, apart from an interlude of autonomy under the Archdukes Albert and Isabella (1598–1621), the king was represented in the person of a governor general whose main residence was the ducal palace. The households of the high nobility (knights of the Golden Fleece, grandees of Spain) and of the Spanish ambassador and the papal nuncio were themselves miniature courts. Other satellite courts in the first decades of the seventeenth century were those of the Prince–Bishop of Liège (throughout this period a Bavarian Wittelsbach), the Duke of Neuburg, and the Count of Emden, all of whom spent a great deal of time in Brussels. The Brussels court itself even more so than most was a cosmopolitan institution, reflecting the international reach of the Habsburg dynasty, with many Spaniards, Italians, and Germans, as well as Netherlanders, Luxemburgers, and Burgundians, a scattering of English, Irish, Scottish, and French exiles, and even the occasional Hungarian or Pole. In the words of one of James I's emissaries, the city was "verie populous, of all nations that are Catholick and civill, full of brave soldjers and men active for

---

[5] Paul Arblaster, "Policy and Publishing in the Habsburg Netherlands, 1585–1690," in Brendan Dooley and Sabrina Baron (eds) *The Politics of Information in Early Modern Europe* (London and New York, 2001), pp. 185–6.
[6] Arblaster, "Policy and Publishing," pp. 188–91.

command, full of verie hansome women, and the best fashioned that can be, full of religious orders and houses."[7]

The minster St Gudula's was the most important church in Brussels. Although there was a separate court chapel, times of general celebration and mourning brought city, court, and councils together in processions and ceremonies centered on St Gudula's as did an annual eucharistic procession.[8] There were other parish churches and numerous monasteries, convents, chapels, shrines, and hermitages in and around the city, increasing in number throughout the reign of the Archdukes Albert and Isabella (1598–1621) and during the widowed Isabella's governor-generalship (1621–33).

Brussels was also home to the three main governing councils of the Habsburg Netherlands: the Council of State composed of the great nobility of the country which advised on matters of policy; the Privy Council where jurists decided legal and administrative matters; and the Council of Finance which managed the royal domains and oversaw the whole operation of paying for the government, a business carried out through Chambers of Accounts one of which was also situated in Brussels. At a provincial level, the Sovereign Council of Brabant, the supreme law court for Brabant, Limburg, and Overmaas, sat in Brussels, and the sates of Brabant held their sessions and maintained their permanent delegation there. Finally, there was the government of the city itself, elected according to a system of power-sharing between patrician lineages and craft guilds, with its own clerks, pensionaries, and officers.[9] Of these various institutions, the court, the Council of State, the Privy Council, and the Council of Brabant all in various ways, at various times, took an active interest in the press, particularly in seeking to suppress or promote specific stories.[10] While petitioners and place-seekers thronged for access to the court, the councils drew litigants and lawyers from throughout the "Burgundian" domains and beyond. The Emperor Charles IV's Golden Bull of 1349 granted Brabanders the privilege of only being sued within the duchy, a cause of resort of litigants to Brussels from the neighboring principalities of the Empire.

---

[7] Sir George Chaworth's diary of his embassy to Brussels in 1621, in Alfred John Kempe (ed.), *The Loseley Manuscripts* (London, 1836), p. 456.

[8] Margit Thøfner, *A Common Art: Urban Ceremonial in Antwerp and Brussels during and after the Dutch Revolt* (Zwolle, 2007), esp. pp. 255–64.

[9] *Costuymen ende Rechten der Stadt Brussel* (Brussels, Jan Mommaert, 1657).

[10] Paul Arblaster "Dat de boecken vrij sullen wesen. Private Profit, Public Utility and Secrets of State in the Seventeenth-Century Habsburg Netherlands," in *News and Politics in Early Modern Europe (1500–1800)*, edited by Joop W. Koopmans (Leuven, Paris and Dudley MA, 2005), pp. 79–95.

Because of the court and councils much French was spoken in Brussels although the language of the civic and ecclesiastical institutions was still Dutch, the daily tongue of the natives of the city.[11] The steep hill crowned by the court and its park provided a clear geographical boundary between the French-speaking "Burgundian" elite of the upper city and the civic and provincial elites of the lower city—men such as Philip Numan (*d.* 1617), secretary to the city council who wrote in praise of Dutch as a literary language.[12] The combination in Brussels of royal councils and diplomatic representations in a city which was otherwise no more than an important provincial center, and the language difference between Dutch-speaking Brussels and the French of the national institutions, augmented by Spanish and Italian at court, gave the public life of the city a slightly schizophrenic character.

As the location of the court, the councils, provincial institutions, law courts, and a local city government, Brussels was above all a place of political power. It did have some minor importance in trade and industry. Its international reputation was for the trades which relied heavily on the court and the nobility, particularly luxury textile products such as damask, lace and above all tapestries although several other luxury manufactures were established in the course of the early seventeenth century including coaches, gilt leather, crystal, soap, delftware, and the refining of sugar.[13]

In terms of communications Brussels lay at one of the most important international crossroads in Western Europe where the ancient road from Cologne to Calais crossed an overland route from Paris to Antwerp (and ultimately Holland). Thanks to a canal completed in 1561 Brussels was also linked to the Rupel, a tributary of the Scheldt, and so by water to Antwerp. There were daily passenger barges between Antwerp and Brussels, their timetables published in seventeenth-century almanacs. Brussels was a center of particular importance for the transmission of news along international networks because it was where the Tassis family, hereditary imperial postmasters, had established their headquarters. But the Tassis family did not make it their main residence by chance: besides its importance as a crossroads Brussels was a significant source of news in its own right and a city with a high demand for information. Its

---

[11] Paul de Ridder, "De Publicatieboeken van de stad Brussel en het taalgebruik in de 'princelycke hoofdstadt van't Nederlandt' (1635–1793)," *Eigen Schoon en De Brabander* 80 (1997), pp. 123–68.

[12] Prefaced to Richard Verstegan, *Neder-duytsche epigrammen* (Mechelen: Henry Jaye, 1617).

[13] R. de Peuter, "Industrial Development and De-Industrialization in Pre-Modern Towns: Brussels from the Sixteenth to the Eighteenth Century. A Provisional Survey," in H. van der Wee (ed.), *The Rise and Decline of Urban Industries* (Leuven, 1988), pp. 213–40.

importance in this respect was not as great as in the days of Charles V but should not be underestimated--particularly as it remained the northernmost Catholic capital in Western Europe and the nerve-center of Spanish Habsburg diplomatic and military endeavors north of the Alps and the Pyrenees.

Antwerp

The importance of Brussels as a center of culture, patronage, and luxury trades relied on its significance as the political center of the Netherlands. Antwerp on the contrary drew all its political strength from its importance in commerce and finance. Like Brussels, seventeenth-century Antwerp was a shadow of its sixteenth-century self. The city suffered a serious slump in the years 1576–88 but from 1589 the Exchange made a rapid recovery and it held its own for almost half a century before Amsterdam's dominance was fully established. This recovery, mirrored in many places in the loyal provinces, was all the more impressive given the depressing picture of devastation throughout the Habsburg Netherlands in the 1580s: war in 1581–85, pestilence 1585–89, and famine 1587–89—depopulation the inevitable result.[14] Antwerp's population was almost halved between 1580 and 1589, from around 80,000 to under 47,000; but the figure had again climbed to over 50,000 by 1600, and it continued to increase until stabilizing around 70,000 at mid-century.[15] Even with only 50,000 inhabitants, Antwerp was a populous urban center, in 1600 surpassed north of the Alps only by London, Amsterdam, Rouen and Paris.[16] But as Herman Van der Wee has stressed with regard to the economy of the Habsburg Netherlands as a whole: "It was no doubt an amazing come-back, urban as well as rural, but only a come-back none the less."[17] There was no new growth.

Far from sealing Antwerp's decline, its reconquest in 1585 was instrumental in the city's partial recovery from a downturn which had already been in progress for a decade. It created new opportunities in finance as Antwerp's Exchange became the main money market in the Spanish Monarchy's *asiento* system for payments to the Army of Flanders; and in commerce as Antwerp's merchants could again openly trade with the Spanish Monarchy in Italy, Iberia, and, indirectly, the

---

[14] Alfons K.L. Thijs, *Van Geuzenstad tot katholiek bolwerk. Maatschappelijk beteknis van de Kerk in contrareformatorisch Antwerpen* (Turnhout, 1990), p. 38.

[15] R. Boumans, "De demografische evolutie van Antwerpen," *Statistisch Bulletin* 34 (1948), pp. 1683–93.

[16] Jan de Vries, *European Urbanization* (London, 1984), pp. 270–78.

[17] H. Van der Wee, "Industrial Dynamics and the Process of Urbanization and De-urbanization in the Low Countries," in *The Rise and Decline of Urban Industries*, p. 352.

Indies.[18] The money market was boosted by Antwerp's reintegration into the Spanish Monarchy's system of public credit but was not dependent on it, as is shown by the swift recovery after the royal bankruptcy of 1596.[19] The diaspora of Antwerp's merchants to Holland, Germany, England, and elsewhere, although diminishing the concentration of capital, reinforced an extensive network of contacts for international trade.[20] Even the war itself provided opportunities to finance military pay and provisioning, or directly supply cash, bread, arms, cloth and ancillary services to the army. This was potentially a very lucrative business, but one with a high element of risk.[21] From 1601 the military authorities dealt with a single contractor for provisions, the *proveedor general*, but he in turn relied on a wider network of financiers and suppliers in order to meet his contractual obligations; similarly, the *asentista* who handled payments to the military treasury was expected from 1585 to provide payments part in cash and part in clothes—a benefit to the Antwerp tailors as well as to cloth merchants and financiers.[22] These were not by any means all locals. English Catholic merchants such as Arthur Aynscombe and Lionel Wake sold thousands of pounds worth of cloth to the *asentista* Louis Clarisse and Wake also sold cloth "for the clothing of soldiers" directly to the government in Brussels.[23] But far more important were the Genoese and later the Portuguese. Antwerp's exchange like the court in Brussels was a place where "all nations that are Catholick and civill" might be represented--not to mention Jews and Protestants as long as they were discreet.

For a few decades after 1589 Antwerp played a central role in the trade between Dutch, English, and Northern German firms on the one side, and Iberian, Italian and South-Netherlandish on the other. In times of embargo an intricate system of camouflaged exchanges was developed, with correspondence

---

[18] E. Stols, "De triomf van de exotica of de bredere wereld in de Nederlanden van de aartshertogen," in Werner Thomas and Luc Duerloo (eds), *Albert & Isabella, 1598–1621. Essays* (Turnhout, 1998), pp. 294–5.

[19] Herman Van der Wee, *The Growth of the Antwerp Market and the European Economy* (Fourteenth—Sixteenth Centuries) (The Hague, 1963), vol. 2, pp. 276–7.

[20] Wilfrid Brulez, *De firma della Faille en de internationale handel van Vlaamse firma's in de 16e eeuw* (Brussels, 1959), pp. 452–7; Maurits Alexander Ebben, *Zilver, brood en kogels voor de koning. Kredietverlening door Portugese bankiers aan de Spaanse kroon, 1621–1665* (Leiden, 1996), pp. 130–31.

[21] Ebben, Zilver, *brood en kogels*, pp. 163–4; Jules Finot, *Inventaire sommaire des archives départementales antérieures à 1790. Nord. Archives civiles. Série B. Chambre des Comptes de Lille*, nos 2788 à 3228 (Lille, 1888), vol. 6, p. 103.

[22] Geoffrey Parker, *The Army of Flanders and the Spanish Road* (Cambridge, 1972), pp. 162–4.

[23] Roland Baetens, *De nazomer van Antwerpens welvaart* (Pro Civitate in 8 no. 45; 1976), vol. 1, p. 247; Finot, *Chambre des Comptes*, vol. 6, p. 119.

under false names and addresses in Italy or England and goods routed via Calais or Cologne.[24] Cargoes were not often transported in Antwerp bottoms nor did they always touch Antwerp's quays but there was an active *Dispositionshandel*: trade which did not pass through Antwerp but was financed and directed by the city's merchant houses.[25] Nor was Antwerp's role as an intermediary between North and South confined to trade between Christians: the Portuguese *marranos* resident in Antwerp were a link between the Sephardim of Amsterdam and Hamburg and the New Christians of Portugal and Spain.[26] The Antwerp Portuguese community as a whole, although it shrank dramatically from the 1570s onwards, still numbered between 40 and 50 households in 1648.[27]

The continuing extent of Antwerp's role as a commercial *entrepôt* as distinct from a money market should also not be underestimated. The "closing of the Scheldt" is a misleading formulation for the Dutch blockade was a financial, not a physical barrier, comprising tolls, licenses and trans-shipments, hindering trade but only prohibiting it in occasional years of embargo. The trade in silks through Antwerp was revived in the 1590s, having died out in the mid-1570s—a sign of considerable investment, given that silk was transported from Milan in armed convoys.[28] In the early seventeenth century there was a flourishing trade in furniture, paintings, books and engravings, tapestries, lace, Italian silk, English wool and unfinished cloth, local cloth (dyed and undyed), German ticking and ribbons, soap made locally from Spanish olive oil, diamonds from Goa, sugar from Brazil, tropical dyes, French wine, and Italian rice.[29]

Merchants engaged in any of the activities outlined—financial exchanges, *Dispositionshandel*, transit trade, the importation of consumer commodities, production for export, or buying for export—needed accurate and speedy information of international affairs if they were to operate with any measure of success. One of the new techniques of late sixteenth-century commerce was frequent correspondence with partners and factors, exchanging not just commercial

---

[24] Wilfrid Brulez, *De firma della Faille en de internationale handel van Vlaamse firma's in de 16e eeuw* (Brussels, 1959), pp. 243–4.

[25] Van der Wee, *The Growth of the Antwerp Market* (The Hague, 1963), vol. 2, pp. 281–2.

[26] Eddy Stols, "Aspects de la vie culturelle aux Pays-Bas espagnols à l'époque de Rubens," in *Bulletin de l'Institut Historique Belge de Rome* 48–9 (1978–79), p. 217.

[27] Ebben, *Zilver, brood en kogels*, p. 130.

[28] Brulez, *De firma della Faille*, p. 247; Karel Degryse and John Everaert, "De handel," in Genootschap voor Antwerpse Geschiedenis, in *Antwerpen in de XVIIde eeuw* (Antwerp, 1989), p. 124.

[29] E. Stols, "Handel-, geld- en bankwezen in de Zuidelijke Nederlanden," in *Nieuwe Algemene Geschiedenis der Nederlanden* (Haarlem, Antwerp, amongst others, 1980), vol. 7, pp. 131–4; Degryse and Everaert, "De handel," pp. 111–13.

information but news of anything which might affect exchange rates, the costs of commodities, the costs and risks of transport, the level of taxes, the opening of new markets or the interruption of regular patterns of trade. These are topics on which other contributors have said enough for me to pass over them quickly.

With regard to the physical carriage of messages the two cities Antwerp and Brussels together formed the hinge between Central and Atlantic Europe, Catholic and Protestant lands. There were daily services between Antwerp and Brussels and thence weekly services to Paris and along the main route to Northern Italy; there were also services to Dunkirk and thence by sea to Dover, and ultimately London, and to Lisbon, Seville, and the ports of Northern Spain.[30] From 1586 until his death in 1610, Charles de Tassis was postmaster of Antwerp. He was a younger brother of postmaster-general Jean-Baptist de Tassis, and like the postmasters Jakob Hennot in Cologne, Matthias Sultzer in Frankfurt, or Octavio Tassis in Augsburg, he treated the office as his personal fief, passing it on to his son, Maximilian, at his death.[31] A protracted legal battle with the postmaster-general ensued and from 1613 to 1614 the disputed post office was managed by a court-appointed "sequester," Jan-Baptist Roelants.[32] Only from 1615 were there again reliable regular posts in Antwerp.

Alongside the royal posts, Antwerp maintained an extensive system of merchant carriers or *coopmansboden* often operating in direct competition with the Tassis company. These carriers based at the Exchange operated under license from the city.[33] Being forbidden from "riding post," they provided a slower service but had the advantage of low overheads and adaptability: the posting stations made the Tassis service fast but were also expensive and tied it to a specific road. Carriers traveling on foot, by wagon, or by boat could change their route according to the weather, the state of the road, and other eventualities.[34]

---

[30] Even without regular correspondence, the cross-channel packets brought passengers bearing news, for example "Some who crossed on the English ship that calls here each week, report that...," report datelined Dunkirk, 19 September, in *Den Ordinarissen Postilioen* (Antwerp: Martin Binnart, 1639) no. 46 (23 September).

[31] Wolfgang Behringer, "Brussel, Centrum van het internationale postnet," trans. G. Van Cauwenberge, in *De Post van Thurn und Tassis*, ed. Luc Janssens and Marc Meurrens (Brussels, 1992), pp. 34–3; Alexander Dietz, *Frankfurter Handelsgeschichte* (Frankfurt, 1921), vol. 2, p. 78.

[32] Maarten Coppens, Piet de Gryse, James van der Linden and Leo de Clercq, *De post te Antwerpen van aanvang tot 1793* (Antwerp, 1993), pp. 67–70.

[33] P. Voeten, "Bijdrage tot de geschiedenis van het handelsleven te Antwerpen tijdens de eerste jaren van het Twaalfjarig Bestand (1609–1612)," unpublished licence thesis (Leuven, 1954), p. 48.

[34] M. Coppens and P. De Gryse, "De Antwerpse stadsboden," in *Liber alumnorum Karel Van Isacker s.j.* (Bijdragen tot de Geschiedenis, 63, 1980), p. 152.

The city claimed the customary privilege of licensing a carrier service open to paying customers to Cologne, Nuremberg, and Frankfurt. This was a source of litigation from the moment the Antwerp branch of the Tassis company was re-established in 1586. In 1587 the Privy Council decreed that the carriers were not infringing the Tassis monopoly as long as they did not ride post or deviate from their customary routes but this judgment was challenged by the Tassis family every time their own privileges were renewed.[35]

By 1609, the magistrates had also licensed carriers to Paris, London and Calais, as well as destinations within the Habsburg Netherlands. Packets to Spain could be sent to Paris by an Antwerp carrier, forwarded to Bordeaux with the Parisian carrier, and then taken from Bordeaux to Spain by Spanish carriers, competing with the Tassis family's direct but unreliable Spanish service.[36] In 1609, after the signing of the Truce, Antwerp's magistrates went on to license carriers to Dordrecht, to Emden via Groningen, to Rotterdam, to Hamburg and to Amsterdam, and after a year of legal wrangling with the Tassis company the Council of Brabant upheld their right to do so.[37] Thus vindicated, the city issued licenses for Delft, The Hague, Leiden, Haarlem, Middelburg, and Liège. On 19 March 1611 four more carriers were licensed to travel between Antwerp and Liège.[38]

By 1620, Antwerp was thus at the heart of two different international mail services carrying messages to Paris, London, and the towns of Germany, one also carrying to Holland and Zeeland, the other also to Italy, Spain, and Portugal. All post from the Northern Netherlands to Spain, England, or France passed through Antwerp as did almost all post from England to the Continent and much of that from Italy and Germany to Spain.[39] Antwerp so dominated the postal services from Germany and the Low Countries to England that in 1632 the London intelligencer John Pory wrote to a client that "touching forraine newes, we can have but very little, or none at all, ... because it is nowe a fortnight since we had any post from Andwerpe."[40] In February and March 1648 Philip IV

[35] Marc Meurrens, "De stadsboden," in *De Post van Thurn und Tassis*, ed. Janssens and Meurrens, pp. 76–81.
[36] Voeten, "Bijdrage," pp. 50–53.
[37] Coppens et al., *De post te Antwerpen*, p. 42; M. Coppens, "Hans Thieullier," in *Nationaal Biografisch Woordenboek* IX (1981), col. 750; Voeten, 'Bijdrage,' pp. 49–50.
[38] Voeten, "Bijdrage," p. 50.
[39] J.C. Overvoorde, *Geschiedenis van het postwezen in Nederland vóór 1795 met de voornaamste verbindingen met het buitenland* (Leiden, 1902), pp. 229, 250.
[40] John Pory to John Scudamore, London, 13 October 1632 o.s., in William S. Powell (ed.), *John Pory, 1572–1636. The Life and Writings of a Man of Many Parts. Letters and Other Minor Writings* (Chapel Hill, 1977), p. 306. Similarly, p. 213: "here hath come no post of Andwerp since this day fortnight, and so consequently little or no newes out of Germany," same to same, 18 February 1632 o.s.

wrote to his Governor General in the Netherlands asking him to pass on news from southern Italy as it came to Madrid faster via Brussels than via Naples.[41] This hinge function is much less obvious from a German perspective as Cologne generally functioned as a funnel or filter for the news from the Low Countries. In the German press, reports direct from Antwerp or Brussels became quite rare fairly early in the seventeenth century.

The End of Antwerp as a Center of Information

The cities of the Dutch Republic were connected to one another by frequent carrier services but for international communications they were entirely dependent on the carriers of Antwerp, Cologne, and Hamburg who each had their own post office in Amsterdam.[42] This remained so up to the middle of the century when postmaster Hendrik Jacobsz. van der Heyde erected posting stations from Holland to Hamburg and Brussels.[43] From 1660 direct routes were developed from Holland to London, Paris and Danzig, ending Dutch reliance on foreign carriers and by-passing Antwerp. Before the end of the century Amsterdam had largely assumed Antwerp's former role as Northern Europe's postal interchange.[44] It was in a sense inevitable that Amsterdam, having replaced Antwerp as a financial and commercial center, would also replace it as a center of information—as it did not only with regard to the posts but also to the book trade. However, Antwerp did not give up its position without a fight. The cooperation of the Tassis family and the Dutch postmasters to cut Antwerp's civic posts out of the carrying market precipitated Antwerp's most serious political crisis of the seventeenth century.

The crisis came to a head in 1659 and resulted in the occupation of Antwerp by royal forces and the imposition of a more absolutist civic constitution. This was an action which the semi-official newspaper of Brussels implicitly likened to the destruction of Sodom by beginning the report with a large decorated initial featuring Lot and his daughters in the foreground and Sodom in the background. A special edition dedicated to the events described the governor-general's use of force in Antwerp as the intervention of an able physician in a sick

---

[41] Henri Lonchay, Joseph Cuvelier and Joseph Lefèvre (eds), *Correspondance de la Cour d'Espagne sur les affaires des Pays-Bas au XVIIe siècle* (6 vols, Brussels, 1923–37), vol. 4, p. 39.
[42] M. Schneider and J. Hemels, *Nederlandse krant 1618–1978* (Baarn, 1979), pp. 19–20.
[43] Overvoorde, *Geschiedenis*, pp. 190, 209.
[44] Overvoorde, *Geschiedenis*, pp. 235, 251; Coppens et al., *De post te Antwerpen*, p. 104.

body politic, letting just the right amount of blood at the crisis of the disease.[45] Discontent and disorders had indeed been a recurrent problem in Antwerp for at least four years.[46] Since January 1655 the constables of the wards and the deans of the guilds had been disputing the revision of the civic constitution and the reinstitution in 1654 of the import and export duties abolished in 1648.[47] These disputes were the occasion for demonstrations, agitation, and the intimidation of customs officials. There was further friction over increases in the taxes on beer in 1655 and 1657 and over the tax exemptions claimed by royal officials.[48]

The old rivalry between the Tassis posts and the civic carriers had also gained a new dimension: since 1650 the Tassis service had been running posts to Holland, previously the preserve of the local carriers or *stadsboden*. This was perceived as an attempt by a royal monopolist to overthrow the city's established liberties. An anonymous petitioner of 1656 had warned the government that foreign agitators were stirring up trouble[49] and in the same year the magistrates warned that they would be best left to deal with the problems themselves as "an alteration, revolution and general combustion" would follow any interference from the Council of Brabant. In December 1658 the Council of Brabant, giving their verdict in the suit between the Tassis posts and the civic carriers, found that

---

[45]   *Relations Véritables*, extra edition (8 November 1659). This seems to be an allusion to Cicero's *De Officiis*, lib. I, cap. xxiv: "As to destroying and plundering cities, let me say that great care should be taken that nothing be done in reckless cruelty or wantonness. And it is a great man's duty in troublous times to single out the guilty for punishment, to spare the many, and in every turn of fortune to hold to a true and honourable course. [...] Accordingly, in encountering danger we should do as doctors do in their practice: in light cases of illness they give mild treatment; in cases of dangerous sickness they are compelled to apply hazardous and even desperate remedies." M. Tullius Cicero, *De Officiis*, trans. Walter Miller (1961), p. 83.

[46]   Karin van Honacker, *Lokaal verzet en oproer in de 17de en 18de eeuw. Collectieve acties tegen het centraal gezag in Brussel, Antwerpen en Leuven* (Standen en Landen 98; 1994), pp. 142–9, 299–300. A detailed recent treatment of this episode that came to my attention too late to use here is Birgit Houben, "Violence and Political Culture in Brabant," in *Hoge rechtspraak in de oude Nederlanden*, edited by Hugo de Schepper and René Vermeir (Maastricht, 2006), pp. 23–49.

[47]   *Reglement Provisioneel ende Additioneel aen de Ordonnantie Albertine Der Stadt van Antwerpen* (Brussels, Hubert Anthoon-Velpius, 1654); P. Voeten, "Antwerpens verzet tegen de licenten tussen 1648 en 1670," *Bijdragen tot de Geschiedenis*, 50 (1957), pp. 72–80.

[48]   *Vertoogh aen De Heeren van t'Magistraet, ende andere Leden der Stadt Antwerpen, Door Die Provosten ende Gheswoorene van Sijne Mats Munten in Brabant, Tot Bewys, Dat de selve, inghevolghe van hunne Privilegien, Concordaten ende vonnissen, niet en zijn tauxabel oft quotisabel, nopende de wijnen ende bieren gesleten wordende, soo binnen hunne huysen, als wel den Kelder vande Munte alhier* (n.p.d. [1657]).

[49]   Van Honacker, *Lokaal verzet*, p. 299.

both services were entitled to carry to Holland but only the Tassis service could do so by "post." This clashed with the guilds' interpretation of their civic liberties and when the deans of the guilds forcibly took the postbag for Holland from the Tassis postman "a public outcry and seditious impression" spread throughout the city.[50] The Governor General, the Marquis of Caracena, then marched between seven and eight thousand troops to Antwerp and occupied the city while the Council of Brabant, sitting in special session, ordered the ringleaders hanged.

Conclusion

This was not the end of the matter in the sphere of publicity. In the aftermath of the postal war in Antwerp the court printer put out the official version of the settlement of affairs: *Acten van Accommodement van de ongheregeltheden Veroorsaeckt binnen der Stadt Antwerpen, door resistentien van de dekens ende ambachten Teghens d'Executie van den Vonnisse by den Rade van Brabandt ghewesen op het stuck van de Posterye*. But this official text and the report in the Brussels gazette were not the only accounts circulated. The government's resort to force against its subjects occasioned various "pasquinades and scandalous and injurious satires" which caused the Privy Council and the Council of Brabant grave concern.[51] The worst of these, a pasquil entitled the *Litanie van Antwerpen*, listed the many lords and officials—native, foreign, and ecclesiastic—to whom the Antwerpeners bent the knee, abandoning the ancient privileges of their city. There was some truth in this: the magistrates and guilds had to gain the intercession of the Dukes of York and Gloucester, the Prince of Condé, the bishop and chapter of Antwerp and the abbots of St Bernard's and St Michael's before Caracena would agree not to impose his understanding of order on the city by martial law.[52] No fewer than three copies of the *Litanie* were brought to the attention of the Officer Fiscal of Brabant.[53] Public opinion was a major concern when there was fear of "*emotions populaires*" (the emotions of the populace). Brussels retained its position as an international postal interchange and as a newswriting center of minor importance across Europe. Meanwhile, Antwerp's dominant position in the European postal system was not surrendered without a fight and it was ended as much as a direct result of Spanish policy as by foreign competition.

---

[50] Van Honacker, *Lokaal verzet*, pp. 144–5.
[51] Brussels, Algemeen Rijksarchief, Geheime Raad Spaane Periode, 1279/170.
[52] *Acten van Accommodement* (Brussels: Hubert Anthoon Velpius, 1659), p. 22.
[53] Brussels, Algemeen Rijksarchief, Officie Fiscaal van de Raad van Brabant, liasse 632 dossier 5883: 190 no. 62.

CHAPTER 11
Offices of Intelligence and Expanding Social Spaces

Astrid Blome

"The Advantages, which such an Office as this is, will bring to the Society of Mankind, will bee altogether innumerable." (John Dury, 1647)[1]

Introduction

In 1647, John Dury (1596–1680) and Samuel Hartlib (1600–1662) made plans for an "Office of Publike Addresse," a universal center of communication and knowledge that was part of a proposal to reform state and church and constitute a new societal order.[2] The planned office had "Two Parts or Branches: the One for Bodily, the Other for Spirituall Matters."[3] The "bodily" part was an institution that dealt with the organization of practical information of everyday life, especially for the poor in order to help them find employment. The "spiritual" matters on the other hand were subject to the Office of Addresse for Communications. Based on a global correspondence network the office would serve as a central point where information was to be collected, registered, systematized, and disseminated. The conception was provided by Francis Bacon's utopian work "New Atlantis," where in Salomon's House scholars compiled, selected, and archived social and natural science findings (which were achieved by their traveling brethren), discussed and reflected upon the accumulated knowledge and gave suggestions for continued research. Bacon therefore described a perpetuum mobile of research and studies which on the one hand viewed knowledge as the sum of empirical results and experiences but on the other hand also considered it a discursive and future-

---

[1] John Dury, *A brief discovrse Concerning The Accomplishment of our Reformation: Tending to shew, That by an Office of Publike Addresse in Spirituall and Temporall Matters, the Glory of God, and the Happinesse of this Nation may be highly advanced* (London, 1647), p. 41.

[2] John Dury, "Considerations tending to the happy Accomplishment of Englands Reformation" (London, 1647), in Charles Webster (ed.), *Samuel Hartlib and the Advancement of Learning* (Cambridge, 1970), pp. 119–39.

[3] Dury, *A brief discovrse*, p. 42.

oriented process.[4] Following Bacon and others,[5] the ambition of the Office of Addresse for Communications was to achieve an encyclopedic synthesis of knowledge with a firmly secular orientation. This office would answer inquiries from interested parties and publish the most useful findings for the benefit of the state, "that they might be publikely made use of."[6] It was linked to the reform program by its ideological as well as institutional focus. Its function combined research with encyclopedic and utilitarian aspirations. The office of addresse was therefore thought of as a means of preserving but also of inspiring the creation and perfection of global knowledge resulting in practical achievements for the benefit and well-being of mankind. Its orientation furthermore regarded both past and future, so that, thus established, it was situated on a critical threshold of sensitivity towards time.

The fundamental function of the Office of Publike Addresse was to facilitate, speed up, and liberate the circulation of information and to establish new infrastructures of communication. Circulation of information, of novelties and news in early modern times was almost always limited—limited for example to the power elite, to the members of a company, to a guild, a craft, a family, a neighborhood, a particular sex. This is not surprising due to the fact that communication was mainly based on speech rather than on writing. The private or public networks sharing information existed due to personal relations or direct interaction, they were limited by space, time, situation and selection. According to Benedict Anderson and his study of 1983, *Imagined Communities*, this changed considerably with the expansion of print capitalism.[7]

Anderson's concept of figurative or imaginative communities was based on an older sociological approach which understands "reality" as a process and result of societal constructions.[8] The perception of a collective "reality," shaping opinions and forming of identities, is therefore the result of communication processes during which new information is passed on and connected to prior knowledge.[9] Accordingly, changes and enhancements of communication

---

[4] Francis Bacon, *New Atlantis. A Work Unfinished* (London, 1659), p. 16f.

[5] See below.

[6] Dury, "Considerations," p. 132.

[7] Benedict Anderson, *Imagined Communities. Reflections on the Origin and Spread of Nationalism* (London, 1983).

[8] Peter L. Berger, Thomas Luckmann, *The Social Construction of Reality. A Treatise in the Sociology of Knowledge* (Garden City, NY, 1966).

[9] "Communication" in this context is not limited to the meaning of news transmission, but is understood as process and result of a mutual giving sense by the participating communication partners. See Roland Burkart, *Kommunikationswissenschaft. Grundlagen und Problemfelder. Umrisse einer interdisziplinären Sozialwissenschaft* (fourth rev. and ext. edn

possibilities influence the preconditions of perception, shaping of opinions and identity formation. This is especially true for the enlargement of spatial visualization capacity over the previously valid borders of orientation which during the early modern period were very much set by individual experience and personal environment.[10] This enlargement then led to "imagined communities" of cities, regions, countries, or continents such as Europe. The idea of space as a symbolic order has also been rediscovered by newer historical research with a stronger emphasis on the aspects of communication theory.[11]

This contribution picks up the symposium's basic ideas and the central question for the "Emergence of Contemporaneity in European Culture" with the example of early modern Offices of Intelligence.[12] The approach was deliberately chosen on a small scale. This way, one can first of all easily point out the relationship between fundamental structural changes in the organization and circulation of information and their significance for the expansion of knowledge; secondly, one can look at possible boundary shifts of "imagined communities" with special emphasis on how those influenced daily life. The main foci of this chapter are the relationships between and consequences of some attempts to intensify information exchange from a practical daily life perspective, involving the enlargement of individual communication networks; attention will also be devoted to the effects on the historical mindset of the enlargement of social spaces.

Wien etc., 2002), pp. 20 and ff; Barbara Stollberg-Rilinger, "Symbolische Kommunikation in der Vormoderne. Begriff—Thesen—Forschungsperspektiven," *Zeitschrift für Historische Forschung*, 31 (2004): 489–528.

[10] See for example Ralf-Peter Fuchs, "Ob Zeuge wisse, was das Burggraftum Nürnberg sei? Raumkenntnisse frühneuzeitlicher Untertanen," in Achim Landwehr (ed.), *Geschichte(n) der Wirklichkeit. Beiträge zur Sozial- und Kulturgeschichte des Wissens* (Augsburg, 2002), pp. 93–114; Franz Irsigler, "Raumerfahrung und Raumkonzepte im späten Mittelalter und in der frühen Neuzeit," in Gerhard Brunn (ed.), *Region und Regionsbildung in Europa. Konzeptionen der Forschung und empirische Befunde* (Baden-Baden, 1996), pp. 163–74.

[11] See Alexander C.T. Geppert, Uffa Jensen, Jörn Weinhold, "Verräumlichung: Kommunikative Praktiken in historischer Perspektive, 1840-1930," in idem. (ed.), *Ortsgespräche: Raum und Kommunikation im 19. und 20. Jahrhundert* (Bielefeld, 2005), pp. 9–49; Marcus Sandl, "Bauernland, Fürstenstaat, Altes Reich. Grundzüge einer Poetologie politischer Räume im 18. Jahrhundert," in Cornelia Jöchner (ed.), *Politische Räume. Stadt und Land in der Frühneuzeit* (Berlin, 2003), pp. 145–65.

[12] For the history of early modern Offices of Intelligence see detailed Astrid Blome, "Vom Adressbüro zum Intelligenzblatt," *Jahrbuch für Kommunikationsgeschichte*, 8 (2006): 1–27.

Origins

The idea of the Offices of Intelligence can be traced back to the sixteenth century and is commonly attributed to Michel de Montaigne's father. He wished for a special place where all offers and inquiries related to purchasing, sales, traveling, servant and other services could be centrally recorded.[13] Montaigne considered the lack of a medium which could be used to reconcile the interests of those offering and those needing services to be a structural deficit, a communication deficit. In order to solve this problem a new public and equally accessible communication infrastructure had to be created. The first concrete plans for such an institution were outlined in London. Here Sir Arthur Gorges (1557–1625), poet, translator, and former Member of Parliament, and Sir Walter Cope (?–1614), Chancellor of the Exchequer of James I, received the exclusive right to open an Office or Register of Intelligence in 1611.[14] They aimed at achieving a consolidation of public communication lines so as to provide everyone with a means to exchange and access economically relevant news. The hope was that the circulation of such public information would result in a number of advantages: increased number of offers and takers, an expanded market, new means to regulate prices, and better protection of the individual from fraud and usury. While Gorges in his comments stressed the diverse economic advantages of such an Office, he described it as a virtual marketplace. This virtual marketplace—virtual as in Latin *virtus* (power or strength)—had the potential to become a nationwide market when established in all bigger cities.

Renaudot

At around the same time, in 1612, Théophraste Renaudot (1586–1653) began building the famous Parisian Bureau d'Adresse which opened in 1628.[15] Renaudot was a physician, general commissioner for the poor and primarily known for founding *La Gazette*, the weekly newspaper under the protection of Richelieu

---

[13] Michel de Montaigne, "D'un defaut de nos polices," in idem, *Essais. Reproduction photographique de l'édition originale de 1580 avec une introduction et des notes sur les modifications apportées ultérieurement au texte en 1582, 1587, 1588 et sur l'exemplaire de Bordeaux*, ed. Daniel Martin (2 vols, Genf and Paris, 1976), vol. 1, pp. 343–5.

[14] Arthur Gorges, *A True Transcript and Publication of His Maiesties Letters Pattent. For an Office to be erected, and called the Publicke Register for generall Commerce* [...] (London, 1611. Facsimile Amsterdam, 1974).

[15] Gilles Feyel, *L'Annonce et la nouvelle. La presse d'information en France sous l'Ancien Régime (1630–1788)* (Oxford, 2000).

and centerpiece of the *communication monarchique* (royal communication) in seventeenth century France.[16] Renaudot's economic motives were thus linked to his charitable intentions, and the Bureau d'Adresse was devoted to social welfare. Its main purpose was the communication of jobs because administrative and judicial resources charged with keeping order were as inefficient as those of public or private welfare to solve the problems of unemployment and poverty. Mainly an employment agency, the Bureau further acted as a pawn shop and also offered free medical care and legal advice. Renaudot thus wanted to fight the urgent social problems of his time: unemployment and consequent social tensions, poverty, disease, begging, and procurement criminality.[17]

The Bureau d'Adresse did not only provide help with the organization of daily chores but it was also a "place of knowledge."[18] Renaudot held regular weekly conferences in French in which scientific problems were described and subsequently discussed from the most diverse perspectives.[19] Any person could attend, regardless of education and class. The principle of involving the general public in open discussions meant that the debated themes were accessible to a larger audience and thus went beyond the limits of academic scholarship. In addition, the oral information presented in the proceedings was regularly made available as printed minutes, thus archived and further enabling a distribution of the information.[20]

The Bureau d'Adresse can be taken as the prototype of centralizing and coordinating a highly diverse information supply. The Bureau itself was a novel means of communication which registered, archived, and systematized information of the most diverse kinds and origins, and made this available to a similarly heterogeneous audience. In the course of the workflow the individual

---

[16] Stéphane Haffemayer, *L'information dans la France du XVIIe siècle. La Gazette de Renaudot de 1647 à 1663* (Paris, 2002), p. 752.

[17] Théophraste Renaudot, *Inventaire des Adresses dv Bvreav de rencontre, Ou chacun peut donner & reçevoir avis de toutes les necessitez, & comoditez de la vie societé humaine* (Paris, 1630). See Howard M. Solomon, *Public welfare, science, and propaganda in seventeenth century France. The innovations of Théophraste Renaudot* (Princeton, NJ, 1972), pp. 21–59.

[18] For some newer German research on "Knowledge" see Dirk Tänzler, Hubert Knoblauch, Hans-Georg Soeffner (ed.), *Zur Kritik der Wissensgesellschaft* (Konstanz, 2006); Richard van Dülmen, Sina Rauschenbach (ed.), *Macht des Wissens. Die Entstehung der modernen Wissensgesellschaft* (Köln, 2004); Carsten Kretschmann (ed.), *Wissenspopularisierung. Konzepte der Wissensverbreitung im Wandel* (Berlin, 2003); Claus Zittel (ed.), *Wissen und soziale Konstruktion* (Berlin, 2002); Michael Hagner (ed.), *Ansichten der Wissenschaftsgeschichte* (Frankfurt am Main, 2001).

[19] Feyel, *L'annonce et la nouvelle*, pp. 78–130; Solomon, *Public welfare*, pp. 30–99.

[20] Published as: *Première [Seconde ...] centurie des questions traitées ez [aux] du Bureau d'Adresse* [...] (Paris, 1634–55).

inquiries and offers were written down in a journal in exchange for a small fee (for the poor the service was free of charge). Anybody could offer anything, and everyone could ask for information on the respective potential seller or buyer, employer or employee, money lender or borrower. Having connected potential trading partners and so enabled their social interaction, the Bureau d'Adresse had fulfilled its task. The trading partners subsequently completed their transaction in a traditional manner.

The services of the Bureau d'Adresse were not only limited to information exchange but also laid new foundations. The Bureau provided a new infrastructure which freed each individual from dependence on personal acquaintances, relationship networks and individual communication structures. The exchange of information between a "sender" and a "receiver" was no longer limited to personal contacts. Anybody who used the services at the Bureau d'Adresse was aware of and intent on simultaneously contacting an unlimited number of anonymous communication partners. Dependence on one another in need was one of the most powerful driving forces for the establishment and the success of the early modern Offices of Intelligence.

This is also due to another invention of Renaudot which should be mentioned in this context. In 1633 he started to publish an advertiser named *Feuilles du Bureau d'Adresse*. The advertiser included four to 16 pages of registered offers and inquiries which were listed according to specific categories, for example: "Non-noble houses and inheritances of land for sale," "Houses for sale in Paris," "Offices requested for purchase," "Furniture for sale," "Furniture sought to purchase," "Mixed business matters." The entries were numbered continuously and each was furthermore identified with a short abbreviation for the journal entry. This format reproduced the Bureau's standards of registration, archiving and systematization which were applied to the selected information. The extent to which the *Feuilles du Bureau d'Adresse* were well known can no longer be assessed because there is no reliable information available. Feyel attributes autonomous significance to them, if only for introducing the activities of the Bureau to a greater public.[21] Despite this, the advertiser had an important influence on the history of the press and of communication. For the first time in history, city residents had access to a printed information medium for everyday needs, which represented an enhancement of existing communication media, enabling residents to reach a much larger group of people beyond their own personal contacts and networks.

---

[21] Feyel, *L'annonce et la nouvelle*, p. 56.

Offices of Intelligence in England

Although Renaudot's Bureau d'Adresse was closed in 1644, it became a model for several projects in the German- and English-speaking areas. According to Rogers, the dissemination of this concept can be described as a diffusion, a specific communication process which communicates a new idea within a social system, leading in turn to changes within the system. The "Innovation-Decision Process" outlined by Rogers involves a number of steps regarding the recognition and implementation of this process (knowledge, persuasion, decision, implementation, confirmation).[22] The concept of the Offices of Intelligence went through the same stages. A selected number of examples will introduce some new and significant aspects of the process.

The projects for Offices of Intelligence in England mostly followed Renaudot's example and were focused on economic advantages. While Henry Robinson (1605–64) concentrated on employment policy,[23] Henry Walker (?–1660) is credited with having introduced advertizing into the English press because of his advertisements for the Office of Entries, founded in London in 1649.[24] In 1657 Marchamont Nedham (1620–87), one of England's most famous seventeenth-century-journalists, edited a *Publick Adviser* for a few months, a journal which described itself in the subheading as "For the better Acomodation and Ease of the People, and the Universal Benefit of the Commonwealth, in point of Publick Intercourse."[25] Several other advertisers followed with headings such as *The City Mercury: or advertisements concerning trade*, *Mercurius Civicus* or *The City Mercury, published every Monday for the promotion of trade.*[26] They are proof for the acceptance of the Offices of Intelligence and for the accomplishment of newspaper advertisings for private and economic matters, especially when they began to specialize—like *Mercurius librarius, or, a catalogue of books printed and published [...] collected by, and printed for the booksellers of London* (every three

---

[22] Everett M. Rogers, *Diffusion of Innovations* (fourth edn New York and others, 1995); see Ch. 1 "Elements of Diffusion" and Ch. 5 "The Innovation-Decision Process."

[23] Henry Robinson, *The Office of Adresses and Encovnters* (London, 1650); Blome, "Vom Adressbüro zum Intelligenzblatt," p. 11.

[24] For example in *Perfect Occurrences of Every Daie iournall in Parliament [...]*, Aug. 10 to 17 (1649), pp. 1216f [= 1218f].

[25] Carolyn Nelson, Matthew Seccombe (ed.), *British Newspapers and Periodicals 1641–1700. A short-title Catalogue of Serials printed in England, Scotland, Ireland, and British America [...]* (New York, 1987), p. 516.

[26] Ibid., pp. 28f, 217f, 29.

months since 1668)[27] or the *Lloyd News* (1696–97).[28] The temporary end of this kind of advertisements came in 1695 when the Printing Act was not renewed and advertisements became part of the newspapers.

On the whole, projects for Offices of Intelligence in seventeenth-century England failed more often than they succeeded.[29] The ones that succeeded were practically oriented and focused on economic benefits. Their most important task was the transmission of information which primarily supported the economic development and the regulation of the labor market and prices. The Offices enriched the service offers in various ways, such as by providing categories to find lost and stolen property, missing children and marital partners, or by solving cases of burglaries and murder. The financial services included information about the businesses at the stock exchange, financial options, collection agencies, and even dubious investment opportunities. The Offices of Intelligence thus contributed to the extension of the communication and trade framework in the local and regional environment, enabling each individual to benefit from a much wider sphere of activity. Their achievement was the common purpose to intensify the exchange of information and communication, independent of limited media such as speech, leaflets or posters and accessible to everyone. They freed every individual, at least economically, from his or her personal network, affording new perspectives beyond the person's previous experience of the world and his or her limited social space.

Offices of Intelligence in the Old Empire

In the German-speaking countries the Parisian Bureau d'Adresse was the first inspiration for the project of an Öffentliche Fragstube (public conversation parlor) in Habsburg Vienna. In 1636 Johannes von Sumaran referred to Renaudot's Bureau when he submitted a request for a privilege to Archduke Leopold Wilhelm. Sumaran underlined the economical utility of an Office like this and he especially pointed out that it might be helpful to eliminate usury and middlemen in trade.[30] He also mentioned disciplinary intentions in combating swindlers and preventing rudeness among servants since through the Fragstube it was possible to find replacements for very little money.[31] Like Renaudot,

---

[27] Ibid., pp. 226, 24–6.
[28] Ibid., p. 144.
[29] See Blome, "Vom Adressbüro zum Intelligenzblatt," p. 13.
[30] [Karl Schrauf], "Zur Geschichte des Wiener Frag-Amtes," *Wiener Kommunal-Kalender und städtisches Jahrbuch*, 31 (1893): pp. 419–26.
[31] Ibid., p. 424.

Sumaran had in mind a public center of scholarship, a place of knowledge where foreign languages and arts could be practiced and newspapers would be read and discourses held regarding them. Everyone would be free to participate and give an opinion; and as in Paris, the collected lectures would be archived and made available for later consultation. Furthermore, this Fragstube was not only supposed to be a center of information and communication but also a place of available knowledge within the walls of academic knowledge, a public academy within the university.[32]

The above ideas were pragmatically exploited in the German language area. While Sumaran's Fragstube corresponded to the practical model of Renaudot, the ideas of Gottfried Wilhelm Leibniz and the cameralist Wilhelm von Schröder as well as mercantile economic concepts contributed to the success of the so-called "Intelligenzwesen" [intelligence service]. Leibniz' 1678 work entitled "Thoughts Concerning the Administration of the State" [Gedanken zur Staatsverwaltung], contained recommendations for useful initiatives and facilities with the primary purpose of serving the economic administration of the country but also suggestions to establish institutions which would be responsible for the collection, registration, and processing of information and knowledge. According to him, such institutions could be distributed over the whole empire and thus become an essential part of a cameralistic economic policy. Also, Leibniz' work refers to the utopian concept of Dury and Hartlib for an Office of Publike Addresse, which should have been known to him through his correspondence with members of the former Hartlib circle.[33]

Leibniz' Offices of intelligence were supposed to communicate not only figuratively but also substantively on everything there was to see, to learn, to use, to experience.[34] Like the Office of Publike Addresse, these offices would be at the same time the point of collection and the origin of an information system covering the whole of the empire, present in every town, usable by everybody, capable of generating information to be shared or possessed.

Twenty years later, when Leibniz decided upon the foundation of a learned academy in Saxony, some financing for it was to come from a so-called "house

---

[32] Sumaran's project was rejected on economic and ethical grounds, based on an opinion of the theological faculty.

[33] Leibniz became a member of the Royal Society in 1673. Among his correspondence partners were next to the secretaries Henry Oldenburg and later John Wilkins also other members of the former Hartlib circle. See Gottfried Wilhelm Leibniz, *Sämtliche Schriften und Briefe*, ed. Preussische Akademie der Wissenschaften (Series 1, 20 vols, Berlin, 1927–2006), vols 1 and 2.

[34] "To see, to learn, to use, to know"; Leibniz, "De Republica" in ibid., vol. 2, pp. 74–7, cit. p. 76.

of intelligence" built according to the English model.[35] Moreover, Leibniz assigned central policy tasks to this house of intelligence, following the example of the Parisian government, which in the 1630s had turned Renaudot's Bureau d'Adresse into a registration office for foreigners and thus into an "institution of good policy [*police*]".[36] Summarizing these tasks,[37] Leibniz described his offices as constituting a government institution with powers of control and spheres of action, "where one can find information about issues concerning internal politics, laws and health ... which moreover could be combined with the perpetual care of public welfare [perpetua cura sanitatis publicae]."[38] The ambiguous wording of the last phrase apparently referring to a possible public health policy must actually be understood figuratively as a reference to the desire to influence the common welfare through good policy. The intelligence service in Leibniz' sense thus became both a fiscal and a political instrument which stabilized the community of the subjects.

Finally, a main formative factor for the German intelligence service was the thinking of the cameralist Wilhelm von Schröder (1640–99). In his work entitled "The Princely Treasury and Exchequer" [Fürstliche Schatz- und Rentkammer][39] Schröder focused on measures to promote commerce and craftsmanship and considered the intelligence service to be a source of state funding. His concept was simple and effective. He conceived of a country-wide "general office of intelligence" or Generalintelligenzwerk with local offices,

---

[35] Gottfried Wilhelm Leibniz, "Einige Puncta die aufrichtung einer Societät der Wissenschaften betreffend," in idem, *Œuvres*, ed. Louis Alexandre Foucher de Careil (7 vols, Paris, 1867–75. Reprint, Hildesheim, New York, 1969), vol. 7, pp. 237–48, here p. 239.

[36] When the economic and social situation of Paris worsened in the late 1630s, several government regulations turned Renaudot's Bureau D'Adresse into a registration point for foreigners. Newcomers looking for jobs had to register there within 24 hours after their arrival, it was illegal to host non-registered foreigners for more than one night. Isaac de Laffemas, "Ordonnance [...] enjoignant aux hôteliers, cabaretiers et autres logeant en chambres [...]. Paris 9.12.1639" in Gérard Jubert (ed.), *Père des Journalistes et Médecin des Pauvres. Théophraste Renaudot (1586–1653)* (Paris, 2005), pp. 241f.

[37] The Academy of Sciences was supposed to be responsible for censorship, legislative issues and parts of the market surveillance, and to embody a scientific society, a statistical office as well as an Office of Intelligence all at once. The integrated Office of Intelligence was among other things responsible for book auctioning, private and public auctions, lotteries, and gambling. Leibniz, *Œuvres*, vol. 7, pp. 218–77 (Akademie von Sachsen), here pp. 249–65.

[38] Leibniz, "Einige Puncta," p. 239.

[39] Wilhelm von Schröder, "Project Eines freywilligen / ungezwungenen Intelligentz-Wercks / Zur consolation der länder / Ingrossirung der Commercien / Propagirung der manufacturen / und Vermehrung Ihro Kayserl. Majest. einkommen [...]," in idem, *Fürstliche Schatz- und Rent-Kammer/ Nebst Seinem nothwendigen Unterricht vom Goldmachen* (Leipzig, 1704), pp. 396–407.

structurally comparable to the postal services. This organizational parallel again reinforces the impression that there was a perceived need to improve existing means of communication. The importance of the early modern postal system for the optimization and intensification of the communication process and for the circulation of (political) news through the establishment of a new infrastructure is without question.[40] The services provided by the post were to be mirrored by the Intelligenzwerk, which aimed at a quantitative as well as qualitative improvement and consolidation of publicly accessible communication structures, as well as country-wide accessibility and usability of these structures.

The subsequent development in the German language area shall only be touched upon briefly. In 1689, a French migrant from Paris who knew about the Bureau d'Adresse founded the first Adreß-Haus in Berlin, which was to become a model for other German towns like Halle, Magedeburg, Halberstadt and Dresden.[41] In Berlin, the communication of employment and information would in particular improve the economic situation of French refugees, since Duke Frederick William had encouraged the immigration of Huguenots with the edict of Potsdam in 1685. In the history of the intelligence service, the Adreß-Haus in Berlin opened up a new chapter by being the first to realize the potential of the model information service as a virtual marketplace in the German language area. The impact on the living conditions of those who were able to use this concentration and availability of information was immediately obvious. The economic benefit, in fact, which had been the first concern, was verified in two ways. Not only were individual customers able to enlarge their social spaces and thus improve their personal situation by the instruments placed at their disposal. Frederick William I, King of Prussia, benefited so much from the Adreß-Haus of the Electorate of Brandenburg that he decided to transfer the profits of the Prussian intelligence service (founded in 1727) to the military orphanage of Potsdam.[42]

The 1707 establishment of the Vienna Versatz- und Fragamt (Pawn and Inquiry Office) finally turned the address office into an integral part of a top-down, cameralistic economic policy. As in other instances, the search for appropriate measures to develop the economy and to fight poverty provided the background and occasion for establishing such an office. Pawn-broking, the office's main task, was first and foremost seen as a means of controlling the credit system and thus of

---

[40] Wolfgang Behringer, *Im Zeichen des Merkur. Reichspost und Kommunikations revolution in der Frühen Neuzeit* (Göttingen, 2003).
[41] See Clara Gelpke, "Zur Geschichte des Berliner Intelligenz- und Adreßwesens", *Mitteilungen des Vereins für die Geschichte Berlins* 49 (1932): 117–25.
[42] Joachim August Christian Zarnack, *Geschichte des Königlichen Potsdamschen Militärwaisenhauses, von seiner Entstehung bis auf die jetzige Zeit [...]* (Berlin, Posen, 1824), p. 440.

preventing unfair business practices and usury. In regard to the contemporaneity of information, the printed lists of the Versatz- und Fragamt were of particular importance. Published from spring 1715 in the *Wienerisches Diarium*, Vienna's semiofficial newspaper, these lists described unredeemed objects as well as offers and enquiries by the Office of Intelligence after the latter had been separated from the pawn-broking business. Thus, the lists by the Versatzamt, regularly published in the *Wienerisches Diarium*, were already advertisers in terms of their function and became an independent publication after a few months.

Leibniz' Synthesis

While address offices in Berlin and Vienna were established on the basis of practical needs and experiences, Leibniz drafted another sketch for an office following the British and French model, which can be understood as a synthesis of the previous versions.[43] His designs were related to plans for an imperial academy and combined essential aspects of planned and yet to be realized projects for address offices. Additionally, Leibniz formulated trendsetting elements which—although not immediately realized—foreshadowed many of the intelligence papers founded later on. These were a very specific type of newspaper that, along with the political papers and magazines, became vital for the Enlightenment.[44] The starting point for Leibniz' ideas was the need for improved and reliable communication structures in order not to lose important information during transmission, a need that had been continuously emphasized from Montaigne onward. The office was supposed to arrange supply and demand as well as job offers and transportation, estate services and locations for auctions and lotteries. The economic advantage of such offerings was the main emphasis: "The one gives the other nourishment and both add to the mutual benefit."[45] Like others before him, Leibniz stressed the potential of such an institution to provide economic stimulus as well as economic regulation, by assigning to the intelligence office the above mentioned functions (which in previous projects had been more potential than actual).[46] He described the basic functions of Offices of Intelligence as those

---

[43] Gottfried Wilhelm Leibniz, "Errichtung eines Notiz-Amtes," in idem, *Œuvres*, vol. 7, pp. 358–66. The text does not carry a date, but is related to the founding efforts for the Imperial Academy of Sciences and thus should have been written around 1712/13. See ibid., pp. 298–382 ("Société impériale").

[44] See below.

[45] Leibniz, "Errichtung eines Notiz-Amtes," p. 366.

[46] The mentioned steps included, for example, controlling supervision of Jewish business activities, the financial and credit system, as well as of measures and weights.

of furnishing information markets as well as places of knowledge. In order to increase efficiency he suggested the publication of a periodical paper or *Diarium* capable of enlarging considerably the circle of recipients, even crossing the city limits. This idea of a weekly intelligence paper, previously voiced by Schröder, was supposed to facilitate the national publication of information on offer and being requested beyond the local market.[47] Leibniz' *Diarium* was not supposed to contain intelligence information but instead information about, for example, new medications, useful inventions, books, works of art and other chief attractions in all realms of science and arts—items to be kept intact for future generations through registration in the Office of Intelligence, and which otherwise would be forgotten.[48] Leibniz' thoughts are reminiscent of Dury's and Hartlib's vision of a universal registrar which would compile, register, and file existing knowledge. This gave the Offices of Address the encyclopedic function of a universal reservoir of knowledge, a task that many of the intelligence sheets founded later would claim as their agenda at least regarding contemporary knowledge.[49]

Leibniz also conceived that the Office of Address and the *Diarium* ought to have the function of knowledge reservoirs regarding government. "Whatever the authorities want to be known" should be published in the *Diarium* in order to inform everybody and at the same time to preserve such information in perpetuity. Thus, a periodical emitted by an Office of Intelligence became, for the first time, also a message platform for the authorities. Leibniz saw two functions here: as a producer of knowledge by means of publication on the one hand and, on the other hand, as a reservoir of knowledge by means of its archiving of official messages to maintain the memory of past ordinances.[50] Most of the intelligence sheets that were founded during the eighteenth and nineteenth century were indeed supposed to take over the above described function of semi-official organs of publication and archiving, irrespective of whether they were founded by private persons or by the authorities. In many territories they became the first and practically the only periodicals to publish legislative matters and thus were direct forerunners of official legislative papers. As institutions connected with policy they contributed to the internal communication of norms and were able to combat the lack of knowledge among officials and subjects about existing legislation.[51]

---

[47] Schröder, "Project Eines freywilligen / ungezwungenen Intelligentz-Wercks," p. 405.
[48] Leibniz, "Errichtung eines Notiz-Amtes," p. 362.
[49] See Wolfgang Wüst, "Sammlungsauftrag und Wissensicherung in: Intelligenzblättern. Regionale Alternativen zur großen Enzyklopädie?," *Zeitschrift des historischen Vereins für Schwaben* 95 (2002): 159–82.
[50] Leibniz, "Errichtung eines Notiz-Amtes," p. 362.
[51] See Lothar Schilling, "Policey und Druckmedien im 18. Jahrhundert. Das Intelligenzblatt als Medium policeylicher Kommunikation," in Karl Härter (ed.), *Policey*

Summary

A new age characterized by the circulation of everyday news was initiated by the Frankfurt printer Anton Heinscheidt in 1722. In January, the first issue of the *Frankfurter Frag- und Anzeigungs-Nachrichten* was published. By the mid-nineteenth century, more than 500 similar publications followed the Frankfurt paper in the German language area. These weekly advertisers or intelligence publications became the third big genre of the Enlightenment press after political newspapers and magazines. They contained not only all kinds of private and commercial advertisements but also public notifications as well as entertaining and informative articles. As the first regular publications published in a given region, they played a key role in the formation of a regional identity. They were used as instruments of economic development, as means of state communication of norms, as an official gazette, as platforms for enlightenment and popular knowledge, as disseminators and repositories of regional history.

In a preliminary report Heinscheidt explained to his readers the purpose and tasks of the first German intelligence paper:

> The current state of humanity is such that no person, from whatever class, can afford to live without others. Any person needs advice and social contact as well as help and assistance, either because of need or because of happiness. This is true for every person who wishes to live a rational life without sorrow.[52]

Heinscheidt used keywords such as assistance, rationality, bliss, need and insight which placed his intelligence paper as a practical instrument for the rational organization of human life within the spirit of Enlightenment. This thought, which was the basis of the idea of the Offices of Address, had been coined by Michel de Monaigne in the sixteenth century. The main motive of all projects was to consolidate communication, search for new and effective communication structures, and create institutions that would take over the collection, registration, and distribution of existing information which then was available for everybody.

---

und frühneuzeitliche Gesellschaft (Frankfurt am Main, 2000), pp. 413–52. Bernd Wunder, "Vom Intelligenzblatt zum Gesetzblatt: Zur Zentralisierung inner- und außeradminstrativer Normkommunikation in Deutschland (18./19. Jahrhundert)," *Jahrbuch für europäische Verwaltungsgeschichte* 9 (1997): pp. 29–82.

[52] Anton Heinscheidt, *Außführlicher und deutlicher Bericht Von einem Zu Franckfurt am Mayn aufzurichtenden Gemein-nützlichen Werck; Welches wochentlich unter nachfolgemdem Titul soll publiciret werden. Wochentliche Franckfurter Frag- und Anzeigungs-Nachrichten […]* (Frankfurt, 1721), p. [2]. Alexander Dietz, *Frankfurter Nachrichten und Intelligenz-Blatt. Festschrift zur Feier ihres zweihundertjährigen Bestehens 1722/1922* (Frankfurt, Main 1922).

Leibniz described this key function of the offices of address as the foundation of an imagined community. He used the metaphor of city and countryside, because the city concentrated people, brought them together, made it easy to find each other and to network even if the people do not live physically together in the same space.[53] The intelligence offices and papers took over such functions of a virtual marketplace of information, solely aimed at news circulation, open to everybody according to their individual needs.

The need for a virtual market of information emerged as a reaction to the immediate living conditions of the early modern society. The authors here cited, from Montaigne to Leibniz, emphasized contrasting points in their argumentation, but they were united in their view of the Offices of Address as effective instruments of economic advancement. Leibniz verbalized this thought best with the following words: "One [person] sustains the other and both add to their mutual benefit."[54] Seeing to common welfare was the function and central task of the territorial authorities and administrations. Not surprisingly, many authors supposed that the job of improving communication infrastructure ought to go to the authorities, and these ought to establish, maintain, and control the new information network to make it an effective tool of mercantilism. However, communication enhancement as an adjunct to good policy not only meant support but also control and disciplinary action in order to eliminate nuisances and solve central societal problems such as poverty and unemployment. Although these aspects were connected to the office of address idea, still, a one-dimensional interpretation of Leibniz' idea as a mere policy center would not do justice to its complexity.[55]

The basic connection between the Offices of Intelligence in the seventeenth century and the intelligence agencies of the eighteenth and nineteenth century was the belief in an inherent force for changing society. Dury and Hartlib connected utopian goals with the Office of Publike Adresse by drafting it as a universal center of information, communication and knowledge, and as an instrument for reform by state and church. The German intelligence system was more pragmatic and at first glance less ambitious. The main focus was the improvement of the economic situation of society in order to form the basis of a well-structured state. The intelligence system was endorsed by authorities and by

---

[53] Leibniz, "Errichtung eines Notiz-Amtes," p. 368.
[54] Ibid., p. 366.
[55] The individual orientation of the more than 500 German papers of intelligence dependend on many variables, especially on the publisher, who influenced the content and emphasis of a paper according to the censorial, economic, and intellectual means available to him. See Astrid Blome, "Das Intelligenzwesen in Hamburg und Altona," in Sabine Doering-Manteuffel, Josef Mančal, Wolfgang Wüst (ed.), *Pressewesen der Aufklärung. Periodische Schriften im Alten Reich* (Berlin, 2001), pp. 183–207.

Enlightenment thinkers alike as a suitable means to promote economic growth; it thus became an institution within a few decades.

From the perspective of the history of communication, the similarities between all of the above projects and the Offices of Address become most apparent. The need for basic information to secure living conditions, resulting from the practical demands of everyday life, led to the establishment of new communication structures and enhanced the quality of early modern "information management." The traditional and mainly oral ways of communication were complemented by an agency that prepared the transition from individual networks to an anonymous acquisition of individually chosen information. This initiative took on many functions that had previously been carried by personal networks, connections, financial potential, and chance.

The Offices of Intelligence and the intelligence publications laid the structural foundations for the contemporaneity of information exchange and for integrating a broad audience—in principle, unrestricted—into a common communication process. As opposed to political news, the process was not restricted to a mere transmission of information, since sender and receiver simultaneously shared an interest in recognizing a common purpose. Whoever went to an Office of Intelligence wanted either to offer or to purchase something. Whoever read an intelligence publication wanted to buy or to sell, was looking for employment or employees, or else was interested in official notifications for professional or private reasons. In order to make use of the services of an office of intelligence or of an intelligence publication, as advertiser or reader, one needed to be aware of the contemporaneity of complementing needs.

The novel organization of information exchange, the collection, registration, systematization, and the possibility of permanent and unrestricted access, established a new infrastructure of communication which was much more efficient in crossing time and space than the traditional personal networks. Every receiver was aware that they were part of a larger social context, for this was the only reason why the institution existed. An additional aspect should not be underestimated in this context. The systematization of the information brought to the Office of Intelligence, the standardized delivery via the gazettes, gave anonymity to the publically displayed needs. The anonymity of a person and his or her needs went hand in hand with the delimitation of his or her personal communication space. The Offices of Address led the individual to a higher level of perception which considerably expanded mental confines and emancipated the individual horizon of experience. The political press of the seventeenth century achieved this for the educated reader; now, the Offices of Address did the same for everybody else, by constructing a common purpose, an "imagined community" based on the principle of contemporaneity of everyday life and labor.

PART 4
New Methods and Approaches

CHAPTER 12

Narrating Contemporaneity: Text and Structure in English News

Nicholas Brownlees

Introduction

In this chapter I wish to examine the significance of textual structure in the narration of contemporaneity in seventeenth-century English news. Focusing on printed periodical news between 1620 and 1660 I shall analyze salient textual features in English corantos of the 1620s and 1630s and newsbooks of the English Civil War and Interregnum. My analysis will concentrate on news reports revolving around a monothematic story and amounting to at least 100 words. By "monothematic" I mean news stories which despite having one or more sub-themes nevertheless revolve around one central topic.

In the analysis of textual structure I shall refer in particular to the terminology and model of analysis developed by van Dijk in his seminal studies on the structure of late twentieth-century news discourse.[1] His work on the contemporary press provides a valid framework for an examination of the textual structure of hard news in seventeenth-century news texts.[2]

My analysis will focus on two key elements: first, on whether or not news reports are generally introduced by a summary consisting of headline and lead and secondly, to what extent the narration of news follows a broadly linear chronological structure. Both aspects provide the news analyst with important information as to how the seventeenth-century English news writer

---

[1] Particularly relevant works are: "Structures of news in the press," in Teun A. van Dijk (ed.), *Discourse and Communication: New Approaches to the Analysis of Mass Media Discourse and Communication* (Berlin, 1985), pp. 69–93; *News Analysis: Case Studies of International and National News in the Press* (Hillsdale, New Jersey, 1988); and *News as Discourse* (Hillsdale, New Jersey, 1988).

[2] For further studies on the structure of news reports, see Allan Bell, *The Language of News Media* (Oxford: 1991) and "The discourse structure of news stories" in Allan Bell, Peter Garrett (eds), *Approaches to Media Discourse* (Oxford, 1998), pp. 64–104; Norman Fairclough, *Media Discourse* (London: Arnold, 1995); Andreas H. Jucker, "Mass Media Communication at the Beginning of the Twenty-first Century," *Journal of Historical Pragmatics*, 4/1 (2003): 129–47; and Rick Iedema, Susan Feez and Peter White (eds), *Media Literacy* (Sydney, 1994).

considered himself in relation to the news he was reporting.[3] Did he consider himself a dispassionate chronicler of the world around him or was he instead the interpreter of contemporaneity? Did he want to act as guide or, aware his readership preferred to have their news straight without any authorial intervention whatsoever, did he simply present the news as it had unfolded in real time and leave to the reader all interpretation as to the relative significance of individual events within the narrative?

Structure of News Stories

In his analysis of hard news in the modern press van Dijk refers to two overarching theoretical categories which are respectively the semantic macrostructures and schematic superstructures of news discourse. These categories comprise various features of which two are particularly interesting for the present discussion. As regards semantic macrostructures, van Dijk says that news stories in the press do not follow a strict chronological framework. Rather than reflecting clear, linear temporal progression, hard news is characterized by flashbacks, flash-forwards, and reverse tellings. As Boyd says, "in the body of the story, perceived news value overturns temporal sequence and imposes an order completely at odds with linear narrative. It moves backwards and forwards in time, picking out different parts on each cycle or giving more detail on previously mentioned matters."[4] This non-chronological model of news reportage is the consequence of several intertwining characteristics relating to news production including: first, the high news value attached to recency which means in practice the frequent reporting of the most recent temporal event at the beginning of the news story and, secondly, the news writers' need to find an angle to the story, that is, to highlight what is considered most significant regarding the news event which as stated is likely to be the most recent in the first few lines.

The non-chronological mode of narration referred to in van Dijk's analysis of macrostructures of news reportage is further developed in his exposition of news discourse superstructures. These latter are subdivided into news schemata which include summary (consisting of headline and lead), main event, background (history, context, previous events), consequences, verbal reactions, comment, and closure. This overall form of hard news texts has no rigid order but what is

---

[3] As the world of early seventeenth-century English news writing was peopled by the male sex, my use of the third-person male pronoun extends generically to news writers as a whole at that time.

[4] Andrew Boyd, *Broadcast Journalism—Techniques of Radio and Television News* (Oxford, 2001, fifth edn), p. 213.

indispensable is the presence of the summary and it is this which most interests us in relation to the reporting of contemporaneity and time. Van Dijk says that in the summary the headline provides the first essential information about a story that is then elaborated to a lesser or greater extent in the body of the text. While the text-orienting headline is classified as part of news discourse schemata, the semantic principles of relevance (or news angle) and recency inform headline writing in that the sub-editor (the person usually responsible for headline writing in the modern press) is well aware of the importance of these news values. The close connection between news schema and semantic macrostructures is also seen in the lead. The lead often provides a non-chronological reporting of events, a characteristic that was previously mentioned as one of the semantic principles of news discourse. An example of the way the summary, consisting of headline and lead, relates to the rest of the news story is seen in the following reportage quoted by Iedema, Feez and White:

> SHOCKING RAILWAY FATALITY
> The mutilated remains of a foreign seaman named Axel Rossman, one of the crew of the ship Star of Italy, were found on the railway line at Honeysuckle Point last night.
> The discovery was made by the stationmaster, Mr Edwin Anstey, whose attention was attracted by what appeared to be a bundle of clothing on the down line immediately underneath the overhead bridge at Honeysuckle Point railway station. An examination of the body disclosed the fact that the head had been cut in two. Every bone of the body was broken, but the only abrasion on the remains was a cut on the left arm. Deceased was fully dressed, with the exception of his coat, which was found today. The police were informed, and the remains were conveyed by Senior-constable Broder to the city Morgue, where they were identified this morning by second mate of the vessel. It is presumed that Rossman was walking along the line, when he was overtaken by the Northern express as that train was approaching Newcastle. The deceased joined the "Star of Italy" at Port Pirie, and had again signed on at this port for a voyage to Honolulu. The City Coroner will hold an inquest on the body tomorrow morning.[5]

The headline is represented by "Shocking Railway Fatality" while the lead is seen in the first paragraph. The lead foregrounds the crisis event, that is, the seaman's body. Following the lead there is what Iedema, Feez and White call the lead development consisting of details regarding the background to the event as well as its causes and consequences. Furthermore, as regards the

---

[5] Iedema, Feez and White p. 94.

linear realization of the respective topics, the story as a whole does not follow a chronological structure in that throughout it jumps from past to present to future and back again.

What is interesting about the story is not only its exemplification of standard news structure but the date of its publication. The piece comes from the Australian newspaper *The Herald* and was published on 25 May 1899. The year is significant because according to Iedema, Feez and White it was only towards the end of the nineteenth century that the non-chronological text accompanied by headline and lead began to appear in news stories. They state along with other news analysts that up until then the textual organization of the news story had reflected the real time occurrence of the events.[6] The news writer had written down the events as they occurred in real time irrespective of their relevance in relation to one another. This simple narrative structure, reflecting what occurs in natural stories, just involves the narrator beginning the story with the recounting of the first chronological occurrence and progressing towards closure which is represented by the last chronological event. There is not the temporal zigzagging that is so characteristic of modern news stories.

As exemplification of the early form of news "narrative," Iedema, Feez and White quote another story from *The Herald*. The story, appearing on 9 May 1831, has neither separate headline nor lead, and follows the linear, chronological mode of narration:

> On Tuesday evening, about the hour of eight o'clock, a puncheon of rum in the bonded store at the back of the Gazette Office burst, and the intoxicating stream found its way through the drain into St. George street, the invigorating cry of "grog ahoy" was immediately raised, and pots, pans, buckets, &c were put into instant requisition for saving the precious liquid, which by this time had obtained the consistency of pea soup; some who had not the convenience of utensils stretched themselves on mother earth and lapped up the beverage, until they became incapable of rising; others were staggering off in various directions scarcely capable of maintaining their equilibrium, and even a batch of children were seen quaffing the beverage with much gusto. A bacchanalian scene ensued, and the conservators of the peace were required to put it down.[7]

---

[6] Iedema, Feez and White, pp. 94–6. I agree with Bell, *The Language of News Media*, pp. 172–3, and Iedema, Feez and White p. 136, who argue that the non-temporal organization of news reports emerged in the late nineteenth century rather than during the American Civil War as has sometimes been claimed.

[7] Iedema, Feez and White, p. 91.

Since this above narrative structure is considered typical of pre-twentieth-century hard news textual organization it will be borne in mind in the rest of the chapter for my intention is to analyze seventeenth-century news structure in regard to van Dijk's model of analysis and with the focus on two specific questions: first, does seventeenth-century periodical news always reflect the chronological narrative form and absence of the initial headline and lead as would be supposed if modern news structure only appeared at the end of the nineteenth century; secondly, what contextual considerations determined the news writer's choice of textual structure in his reporting of contemporaneity?

Corantos 1620–1641

The periodical English news pamphlets that were published between 1620–41 were generally called corantos.[8] The first extant English coranto dates back to 2 December 1620 and was published in Amsterdam. Similar to other English language corantos printed between December 1620 and the summer of 1621 this one-sheet news publication was a translation of a previously published Dutch coranto. In fact, the imprint of the earliest English coranto reads "Imprinted at Amsterdam by George Veseler, Ao. 1620. The 2 Decemember (sic). And are to be soulde by Petrus Keerius, dvvelling in the Calverstreete, in the uncertaine time."[9]

The coranto, consisting of one leaf in small folio, with two columns of news on each side, mostly contained news about the Thirty Years War—indeed, the conflagration that had started to envelop most of central Europe since the

---

[8] Although I use the term "coranto" generically to cover this form of periodical news publication between 1620–41, the publications themselves were sometimes referred to as "books" by their authors. This is especially common between 1622–24 when the general editor of the series, Thomas Gainsford, routinely used this term. See, for example, *The last newes, relating these particulars* (17 May 1623) and *More newes of the Duke of Brunswick* (22 June 1623). See Folke Dahl (Stockholm, 1953) for an invaluable bibliography of English corantos, where the author not only provides illuminating bibliographical detail as to individual numbers but also gives an insightful overview of the evolution of coranto publication as the genre progressed over the twenty-year period. For a contextually-rich account of corantos, see Joad Raymond, *The Invention of the Newspaper: English Newsbooks 1641–1649* (Oxford, 1996), pp. 87–100 and *Pamphlets and Pamphleteering in Early Modern Britain* (Cambridge, 2003), pp. 130–51. Analyses of linguistic and discourse features in coranto news are found in Nicholas Brownlees, *Corantos and Newsbooks: Language and Discourse in the first English Newspapers 1620–1641* (Pisa, 1999) and "Spoken discourse in early English newspapers," in Joad Raymond (ed.), *News Networks in Seventeenth Century Britain and Europe* (London, 2006), pp. 67–83.

[9] *The new tydings out of Italie are not yet com*, 2 December 1620.

summer of 1618 was one of the principal factors behind the publication of news in the first place. People in England as elsewhere in Europe wanted to find out how the respective Protestant and Imperial forces were faring in what appeared a struggle of historic significance and capable of affecting everyone in Europe. However, the fact that throughout the twenty-year period in which corantos were published, foreign affairs almost totally dominated the news contents was not just a reflection of the readers' interest in foreign matters but more prosaically the result of the variously structured and intermittently enforced English censorship regulations preventing the publication in periodical news publications of domestic news.[10] It was only in 1641 with the abolition of the Star Chamber and a general relaxation of other instruments of censorship that domestic news began to be reported on a continuous basis.[11]

Given the interest the first corantos of late 1620 and early 1621 created in London it is not surprising that before long London publishers recognized the market possibilities of translating and printing English versions of the Dutch corantos themselves. In fact, the first extant London-printed coranto was published on 24 September 1621. It, like other corantos published during the next 20 years, would probably have had a print run of between 250–850 copies and would have been bought by gentry, the educated elite, and merchants. However, the actual number of readers of corantos both in and outside London would have been much higher than the number of individual buyers. Apart from copies being passed from friend to friend it was not uncommon for corantos to be affixed to walls in public places or read out aloud at street corners. For example, the poet and satirist Abraham Holland, in his conclusion to *A Continu'd just Inquisition of Paper-Persecutors* (1625), expresses his anger at seeing through London "the wals Butter'd with Weekly Newes compos'd in Pauls."[12]

---

[10] See, for example, Sabrina Baron, "The Guises of Dissemination in Early Seventeenth-century England: News in Manuscript and Print" in Brendan Dooley and Sabrina Baron (eds), *The Politics of Information in Early Modern Europe* (London and New York, 2001), pp. 41–56. In contrast, McElligott emphatically disputes much of the revisionist literature on the inefficacy of seventeenth-century censorship, but in my opinion his invigorating reading of the censorship debate, and in particular of the role of the Stationers' Company, is more applicable to the 1650s rather than to earlier decades. See Jason McElligott, "'A Couple of Hundred Squabbling Small Tradesmen'? Censorship, the Stationers' Company, and the State in Early modern England," in Raymond (ed.), *News Networks in Seventeenth Century Britain and Europe* (Routledge, 2006), pp. 85–102.

[11] One of the few examples of domestic news reported in the coranto press is that of 4 September 1622. In *Count Mansfields proceedings since the last battaile* we find an account of a "fearefull storme and Tempest" that had struck the county of Devon.

[12] "Pauls" refers to St. Paul's church, a common meeting-point in London for people involved in the transmission of news. It was there that news was exchanged, or, as the contemporary critics of print news would say, idle gossip bandied about.

As with the Amsterdam-printed corantos, the London publications must have also been commercially successful for in the spring of 1622 five London publishers formed a kind of news syndicate focusing around the printing of this news genre.[13] One of the syndicate's first actions was to expand the amount of text in the coranto. In place of the broadsheet, the news was now set out in the more traditional quarto form that was characteristic of general pamphlet publication. From 1622 until 1632 when corantos were banned for six years this remained the fixed format.[14] However, when corantos were reauthorized by the crown in 1638 the format and frequency of publication were altered. The format was a little different in that unlike pre-1632 corantos those published after 1638 consisted of fewer but slightly larger quarto pages and no longer always included a contents-summarizing title-page. Instead, the first pages were now often headed by short caption-titles. As for frequency of publication, instead of coming out more or less once a week, these shorter corantos often appeared three or four times the same week and even occasionally more than once the same day.

Standard Narrative Structure in Coranto News

Although in my analysis of corantos I shall be examining news stories containing thematic continuity, much of the hard news in these publications comes in the form of brief unconnected news items. This kind of reportage ranged from one to a couple of sentences of factual information relating to foreign affairs. Typical of such snippets of news are the following lines taken from a 1626 coranto:

> From Rome, April the 11.
> We learne from Mantua, that their Duke hath dismist all his Souldiers except a few, which are to be kept in garrison.
> At Livorno ariued two gallies of Genoa, that are laden with 600 Barrells of Powder.
> On Thursday last the Pope washed the feet of twelve poore men, and attended aftrerwards on them when they were at dinner.
> The Pope a few dayes agoe was in the Castle of S.Angelo, and gave 400 Crownes to the Souldiers which are in it.

---

[13] In using the word "publisher" I realize I am being slightly anachronistic in that in the early seventeenth century the person performing the general functions of a publisher, as well as occasional editor, usually refers to himself as "printer." See, for example, *Weekely newes from Germanie, and other places of Europe* (13 December 1623).

[14] Generally speaking, between 1622 and 1624 the corantos were 24 pages long whilst after that and up until 1632 they usually came out in 16-page editions.

From Prage April 25.
From Sedan they write likewise in this manner: It is thought that the Marquis of Baden who is inquartered betwixt Metz and Zwebrug, with 2000 men, both horse and foot, is to set vpon the Palatinate. And that the Imperialists, and Bavarians are sending into the Palatinate for feare of an invasion, the Colonel Merode, and diuers other chiefe Commanders, with their forces.[15]

These news items that in their concision and factuality are similar to contemporary news agency dispatches usually consist of declarative sentences of generally quite simple syntactic structure. In reporting contemporaneity these brief dispatches occasionally offer authorial point of view regarding the portrayed event, be it positive or negative evaluation, but as regards the focus of my present research such news items lack pertinence in that they have insufficient textual length. As stated above, in my analysis of coranto reportage I shall limit my examination to more developed news stories.

An example of such a broadly-based story is presented below. It appears on the first page of a 1640 coranto immediately after the title of the publication.

Century 3.   Numb. 9.   33
            THE CVRRANTO FOR THIS
            Weeke from FRANCKFORD
From the Marquisate of Brandenburg the 12.22 of Febr.
The Swedish troops which under the command of Generall Major Axel Lillie lay from the 5. of Ian. to the 5. of Feb. in Havelberg, they forsooke the same passage and the whole country of Prignitz, and tooke likewise along with them the garrison in Rippin, and thus marched forward, pretending that they would go towards New Brandenburg, and so forwards into Pomerania, but they passed through Zedenick and marched towards Berlin and Collen on the River of Sprew, thinking to surprise both Cities, as Colonell Dewitx did last year, to which end the other day about 4. of the clocke in the evening, they arrived about 3000 strong both horse and foot together with two field pieces, neere the outworkes at Berlin, but being the day before Colonell Kracht with his Regiment of foot and 300. horsemen and Dragooners was sent from Spandaw with all speed to aid those of Berlin; the Citizens at Berlin resolved not to suffer the Swedes to come into the City, because they could pay no more the little contributions unto them, and because they knew well enough that they had not need to come through the City, but that they came onely for a sum of money ... The 11. of this month betimes

---

[15] *The Continuation of our weekely Newes from the 17 of May, to the 23 of the same* (23 May 1626).

in the morning the said General Major Axel Lillie, and Colonell Kerberger departed with their Swedes in full battaile array & marched towards Copenick, where they lie now enquartered, whether they will passe the River of Sprew, or goe into the Countrey of Tellaw, time will shew; of the next neighbouring little Cities they have demanded great summes of money. Many are of opinion that the said General Major Axel Lillie hath order to go towards great Glogaw, and to joyn with Generall Major Stolhans.[16]

In respect of its macrosyntactic and semantic organization this piece characterizes much monothematic coranto reportage. As regards the macrosyntax, the report is headed by a simple date-line but no headline and the first few lines of the report have no summarizing function whatsoever. Instead of being told, albeit in general terms, of the report's focal topic as would be the case today the reader is plunged immediately into the story itself. The story's protagonists are the "Swedish troops" and in the semantic organization of what the Swedes and their commanders do the narrator follows a chronological narrative. The story first refers to what they did in Havelberg from 5 January to 5 February, then reports their arrival on the outskirts of Berlin "the other day about 4. of the clocke in the evening," and concludes with the description of the Swedish troops leaving with their commanders on 11 February. In the narration of the Swedish army's movements there is no attempt to foreground relevance.[17]

What is interesting is determining why this default textual structure should have been adopted in coranto news. Why was it that the writers and publishers of the first periodical news in seventeenth-century England regarded this means of narration as the most appropriate for the reporting of contemporaneity? The first, most obvious answer lies in the source of the news. The above news report is a translation of a news story previously published in the *Franckford* coranto. The fact that so much of periodical English news between 1620–41 consisted of more or less literal translations of foreign news publications meant that the narrative structure of English news had a continental imprint. The conventional form of news reporting in mainland Europe (and in particular in those countries providing the main news sources for English corantos, that is, the United Provinces, Spanish Netherlands, Germany, Italy, and France) followed the simple chronological narrative structure common to chronicle writing generally with neither headline nor lead that is found in the above 1640 report. Therefore, by and large, the English coranto publishers adopted the chronological narrative

---

[16] *The Cvrranto for this Weeke from Franckford* (24 March 1640).
[17] The only part of the narrative which deviates from a strict chronological account is when the writer refers to the arrival of Colonell Kracht's troops "the day before."

structure because that was what was found in continental news publications.[18] Of course, instead of translating foreign news texts literally it would have been possible for English news publishers to adopt other forms of translation strategy including even loose adaptation but the former translation technique had undoubted commercial and editorial advantages.[19]

The primary commercial advantage in literal translation concerned its relative speed in comparison with other more complex translation strategies involving different degrees of rewriting. In the world of the press then as now speed was all. News had to be above all fresh and as little time as possible would have been given to the translation of the foreign news text. The unfolding events in the Thirty Years War would only have been newsworthy if the circumstances referred to had not been overtaken by other news.[20] Keeping the same wording and textual organization also made good editorial sense. With literal translation the publisher could tell at a glance how much space the foreign news story would take up in his own publication.

---

[18] For wide-ranging studies on news and news networks in early modern Europe, see Brendan Dooley, *The Social History of Skepticism: Experience and Doubt in Early Modern Culture* (Baltimore, 1999), Dooley and Baron (eds), and Raymond (ed.), *News Networks in Early Modern Britain and Europe*.

[19] The fact that the translation of foreign news took place in England rather than abroad is indicated in the following address by the "Printer to the Reader" in a 1623 coranto:

Gentle Readers: By this time I hope you your selues will iustifie my simplicity or innocency, that I acquaint you with nothing, but what is extracted out of true and credible Originals; that is to say, either Letters of iustifiable information, or *Corantos* published in other Countries in the same manner, as we here accustome; and these you know are either publiquely brought ouer by the Posts from *Amsterdam*, and *Antwerp*; or priuately sent to such friends and Gentlemen as do correspond with vnderstanding men in forraigne parts ...

(*Weekely newes from Germanie, and other places of Europe*, 13 December 1623).

[20] This absolute need for fresh news is lampooned in Ben Jonson's, *The Staple of News* (London, 1626). In one scene Peniboy, who is involved in the publication of one-penny corantos, goes to a news staple, where he informs the news monger, Cymbal, of the motive of the visit:

Peniboy: We come for newes, remember where you are. I pray thee let my Princesse hear some newes, Good Master Cymbal.

Cymbal: What newes would she heare? Or of what kind, Sir?

Peniboy: Any, any kind. So it be newes, the newest that thou hast ... (III.ii, 15–19).

For analyses of Jonson's satire, see Stuart Sherman, "Eyes and ears, news and plays: the argument of Ben Jonson's *Staple*," in Dooley and Baron (eds), *The Politics of Information in Early Modern Europe* London and New York, 2001), pp. 23–40; and Marcus Nevitt, "Ben Jonson and the serial publication of news" in Raymond (ed.), *News Networks in Early Modern Britain and Europe*, pp. 51–66.

However, a literal translation also had another very important advantage. Especially in the first years of English corantos it was in the publisher's interest to stress the foreign origin of the news. Since Amsterdam and Antwerp were the news centers of Northern Europe, news reports coming from there, that is, translations of these towns' corantos, acquired greater credibility than they would have possessed had the English public thought the news was the sole expression of English news publishers. Time and again we see the English publisher underlining the fact that his publication has been translated out of the Dutch or other foreign coranto. Yet, apart from straightforward references in either the title-page or at the end of the English coranto to the news being a translation or indeed the inclusion of the actual original foreign text itself in the English publication there are also addresses from the publisher to the reader in which he refers to the process of translation as a means of providing impartiality in the news coverage.[21]

For example, in a prefatory address to his readers in a 1630 coranto, the publisher writes:

> Because we intend to giue you a true relation of the affaires in Italy, as farre as we can; We doe here present vnto you, First, what is written from Turin: and then we will also represent vnto you a relation of the same things, translated out of the French Copie, printed in diuers parts of France, with License: so that you may see what both parties say for themselues.[22]

A literal translation that necessarily kept the same default narrative structure found in the source text therefore helped to guarantee the authenticity of the

---

[21] For an example of an English publisher's presumption of his readers' bilingual competence see the coranto, *A Relation of the Late Horrible Treason against the Prince of Orange* (19 February 1623), where the publisher provides not only the English translation of the Dutch text but the Dutch text itself. Instances of the coranto publishers' references to their numbers being translations include *The Copie of Newes translated out of the High Dutch* (15 October 1622); and *Relations of Newes from most parts of the world, translated out of the low Duch* [sic] Copies printed in *Holland* (28 January 1623).

[22] *Continuation of the weekely Newes* (21 April 1630). See also *The newes of forraine partes* (28 February 1623) where the editor writes that the news has "come something late to our hands, hauing beene sent first of all into Germanie, and thence to vs, in the high Dutch Tongue." Similarly in *More Newes of the Good Successe of the Duke of Brvnswicke* (29 July 1623) one finds the editorial assurance that "wee haue added no one particular in the writing, but can readily shew the effect of euery point, out of the seuerall letters of seuerall dates … And wee further affirme, that all but the last encounter of the last three daies, is already printed Newes in high Dutch."

English news[23] and the textual reference to the translation process was one of the strategies the publisher adopted to convince the reader that what was written on the page and paid for by the reader was "true and honest" news rather than something invented just to sell the pamphlet.

However, although the role played by literal translation in establishing the simple, chronological mode of news narrative in English periodical news is very significant, it would be wrong to think that this style of narration did not anyway respond to the needs and expectations of both English news writer and reader. This reportage structure suited much of the English news world of the early seventeenth century. For the news writer the essential advantage of filing a news report in which he provides no initial summary of the main event but simply offers a temporal recount of what happened is that in doing so he is distancing himself from the event itself. He is regarding himself and is regarded as a provider rather than interpreter of news. In seventeenth-century England, as indeed on mainland Europe, this suited the news writer. An obvious danger confronting him, whether in England or on mainland Europe, was the possibility of offending local authority through both the actual reporting of the news itself and the interpretation given by the writer to that news. As just the reporting of news could be controversial—the writer could stand accused of inappropriate selection—it is not surprising that he should wish to limit his political exposure by refraining from the use of any kind of headline or lead.[24] By doing this, the news writer restricted himself to being a purveyor of news rather than acting as both its communicator and interpreter. As Bell says, "[a lead] is a *directional* summary, a lens through which the point of the story is focused and its news values magnified."[25] In dispensing with introductory orientation both

---

[23] For a comparison of news reports in the English coranto of 9 July 1621 with the original extant Dutch coranto of 3 July 1621, see Brownlees, *Corantos and Newsbooks: Language and Discourse in the first English Newspapers 1620–1641*, pp. 51–3. The analysis shows that in the few occurrences when literal translation does not occur in the English text it is because the translator either omits or glosses a proper name in the source text.

[24] In relation to the interpretative potential provided by a non-chronological structure, see Friedrich Ungerer, "When news stories are no longer just stories: the emergence of the top-down structure in news reports in English newspapers," in Andreas Fischer, Gunnel Tottie and Hans Martin Lehmann (eds), *Text Types and Corpora. Studies in Honour of Udo Fries* (Tübingen, 2002) pp. 91–104. He writes that such interpretative potential "appears as an instantiation of the sorting and weighting strategies along the scale of relative informational importance. And since sorting and weighting the objects of the world is often not a straightforward task but burdened with many choices and alternatives, the sorting and weighting approach to text structure again provides a richer strategy than merely assuming a linear top-down gradation" (p. 103).

[25] Bell, *The Language of News Media*, p. 183.

the news writer and hence the news publisher, too, ran less risk of falling foul of censorship restrictions.[26]

The absence of the directional summary in most reportage also reflected the news writer's reluctance to be seen as wanting to influence the readers' reception of the reported events. In standing aside and letting readers decide for themselves the significance of an event the writer was recognizing the complex realities encompassing the news writer-reader relationship. First of all, the writer would have been aware that some readers might well have objected to the idea that he, a mere pamphleteer, could be presumptuous enough to explain to a social superior, the reader, the importance of a piece of news. Regarding this, Schneider writes apropos epistolary news: "Primarily because news was typically sent by social and administrative inferiors, to comment or introduce one's own opinion was a presumption."[27] As exemplification of this inborn deference towards a social superior Schneider then quotes Lord Howard who in a letter to his superior, the Earl of Shrewsbury, at the turn of the seventeenth century, carefully frames his interpretation of the reported news with the words: "your most honorable favor and love that you have always shewed unto me doth make me, in the abundance of my love and affection to you, presume to write unto you my opinion."[28]

However, apart from questions of social deference, for most of the period between 1620–41 the writer of corantos abstained from providing personal opinion because he believed that what primarily interested his readers were bare facts. For example, this is implicit in the following editorial comment: "Gentle Reader, if euer you will be pleased, now is the time: for you shall not haue a word of preamble, nor circumlocution: For the Letters and Dutch Corantos are so thick into our hands this weeke, that we can spare you no wast paper, if we would."[29]

---

[26] The fact that the Crown imposed a total ban on English corantos between 1632–38 illustrates the consequences of publishing material regarded as politically dangerous. Although no clear motivation was given, it is likely that this prohibition on the reporting of periodical foreign news was the result of the English crown's displeasure with the increasingly flattering portrayal of Gustavus Adolphus, king of Sweden. The Protestant king's enthusiastically reported victories over Imperial forces in 1631 and 1632 were probably regarded as threatening in that for the domestic audience such military successes could not but be compared with the unpopular passivity of Charles I's foreign policy.

[27] Gary Schneider, *The Culture of Epistolarity: Vernacular Letters and Letter Writing in Early Modern England 1500–1700* (Newark, 2005), p. 151.

[28] Ibid.

[29] *The newes and affaires of Europe* (15 January 1624). A similar view is expressed in *Coppies of letters sent from personages of Accompt vnto divers Personages of Worth in London* (22 June 1622), where in the introduction to the publication the publisher writes: "To the courteous Reader. Courteous Reader; ... I haue not prefixed any long preamble to the ensuing

The coranto author also sometimes claimed that his decision to distance himself from the news he was providing and thereby avoid the role of interpreter of the outside world was based on his realization that it was this very impartiality that his readership wanted. The writer accepted this reduced role even if as we see in the following address to his readers he was aware that in so doing the reader would in turn have greater difficulty in understanding the full complexity of the world around him. In the address the writer begins by referring to the complaints he has had from customers who have accused him of relying excessively on news originating in Dutch publications:

> I find some, that would as it were pull me back by the sleeue, for running too fast away with the newes, as if the Dutch-men were partiall on their side. I haue now lighted vpon other Letters, and other Authors, some in Latine, some in Spanish, and most in Italian, from whence I haue extracted the whole occurrences of the last Moneth, and to the 16. of August likewise: wherein for my part I will say no more, but let the Letters answere for themselues; onely by way of Caution let me intreat you, neither to expect an order from Prioritie of date, nor any such exactnesse, as men are tyed to in a continued Story: For in plaine tearmes for any thing I see, they that writ these Letters had them by snatches, and the whole businesse resembles a Bill of accounts, divided into severall Items, whose Summa totalis is the newes of the last July, and to the tenth of August. 1623 and so I beginne, or if you will, proceed.[30]

The pamphleteer was further aware that his readers held different political opinions. Some readers were supporters of the Catholic cause and therefore hoped to find in the news a totally different perspective from that sought by Protestant readers. What could the news writer therefore do with such a heterogeneous readership? As he states in the passage below, the obvious way to satisfy the entire political spectrum was to remain neutral:

> Gentle Readers: for there are two sorts of you I know: the one wishing well to the Emperor and his proceedings: the other, murmuring and repining that the

---

Relation, neither is it stuffed with any superfluous coniectures, but you have them printed in the same wordes and phrase in which I received them. Vale."

[30] *Ital: Gazet. Nū. Pri°. More newes from Europe* (29 August 1623). The explicit refusal to provide either interpretation or commentary is not confined to the seventeenth century. In the first number of the first English daily newspaper, *The Daily Courant*, the publisher writes in his "advertisement" to the reader (11 March 1702): "Nor will he [the editor] take upon him to give any Comments or Conjectures of his own, but will relate only Matter of Fact; supposing other People to have Sense enough to make Reflections for themselves."

Palatines cause and Bohemias businesse thriues no better: Now how can you both be satisfied with any report or newes that concerne either party: therefore to auoid partiality and take an eauen course concerning the reports abroad, and passions at home, I will directly proceed in my accustomed manner of searching and opening the Letters that came from beyond the seas, and so acquaint you with their secrets: and if any of you all either out of deeper apprehension, or quicker capacity, find fault with the newes for tenuity or small variety, or impertinent matters to expectation: blame the Letters or the Time that affordeth no more plenary satisfaction: but neither mee nor the Printer ..."[31]

To complete this survey of the default textual structure in monothematic coranto reportage mention should also be made of two other features of this narrative framework. The first concerns the suspense and dramatic effect that a narrative strategy with no initial summary can provide. If the final details in a news item are potentially as important as the first information the reader must read until the end to find out how the story unfolded.[32] This, for example, is seen in the previously quoted passage from the *Franckford* coranto where the reader has no way of knowing until the end of the report how the Swedish forces ultimately fared.[33] One last characteristic of the chronological mode of narration is its relative ease of comprehension. Regarding this, Bell says that

---

[31] *The affaires and generall businesse of Europe more particularly* (24 February 1624). The editor's recognition of his readers' heterogeneity in this passage should be read in the light of other editorial addresses where it would seem that the readership was prevalently Protestant. For example, in the 20 April 1624 number he writes regarding the plight of a Protestant prince of the Palatinate, "I am perswaded there is neuer a true hearted English, French, or Dutchman, but ardently desires the Prince *Palatines* restauration and recouery of his Honoure" (*The newes of Europe with all such particular accidents*), while on 2 September 1631 he enthusiastically comments on the victories of the Protestant king of Sweden: "God grant him the multiplication of the like victories and good successe untill all his Enemies be vanquished and a generall Peace be settled in all the parts of *Germany*, Amen" (*The continuation of our forraine occurrences*).

[32] Although this feature of suspense caused no comment among contemporary critics of print news, the early seventeenth-century poet Richard Brathwait did mock another suspense-inducing device. In his poem *Whimzies: or, a New Cast of Characters* (1631) he satirizes the tendency of the coranto writer to finish "his sentence abruptly with, hereafter you shall heare more. Which words, I conceive, he only useth as baites, to make the appetite of the reader more eager."

[33] In *News Analysis: Case Studies of International and National News in the Press*, p. 105, Van Dijk cites the German tabloid *Bild Zeitung* as an example of a newspaper which even nowadays resorts to linear narrative so as to provide tension and drama. The emotive effect of the chronological narrative style is also commented on in Iedema, Feez and White. They write that "people working in the area of media research have found that texts written in

the research of cognitive psychologists shows that in story-telling chronological order "is apparently the 'natural' order because it matches its discourse structure to the event structure."[34] The canonical linear narrative adopted by most early English newsbook writers was a strategy that therefore facilitated news comprehension.

Experimentation in Coranto News Structure

Having discussed standard narrative structure in coranto reportage, I now wish to analyze those cases where the news writer experiments with textual organization for specific communicative purposes. In general such experimentation is most frequently found between 1622 and 1624. It was during these two years that the syndicate involved in the publication of corantos employed a specific editor to oversee the presentation of the news. The editor was Thomas Gainsford and between the autumn of 1622 and his probable death from the plague in the summer of 1624 he frequently modified the standard manner of reporting contemporaneity.[35] Unlike what had occurred before news was now often presented in a continuous narrative or "continued relation"[36] rather than in short unrelated dispatches. The information still came from newsletters and foreign print news but was now collated by the editor and presented more cohesively. Gainsford himself refers to this novel mode of presentation on several occasions. For example, in one of the first corantos that he wrote in the autumn of 1622 he twice refers to this new form of reportage:

> I begin with Naples, because as neere as I can I will come orderly forward with the prouinces as they lye, and in regards the seuerall Letters beare not one date, I haue thought good to Muster the Newes, which belongs to the same place, as it were into one Armie, and so you shall receiue the occurrences altogether ...[37]

(chronological) narrative style caused more emotion and mood change responses than those presented in (fragmented) newspaper style" (p. 90).

[34] Bell, *The Discourse Structure of News Stories*, p. 94.

[35] For further information on Gainsford see M. Eccles, "Thomas Gainsford: Captain Pamphlet," *Huntington Library Quarterly*, xiv (1982): 259–70; and Michael Colin Frearson, "The English Corantos of the 1620s," Ph.D thesis (University of Cambridge, 1993).

[36] This is how the editor refers to this mode of reporting news in *Ital: Gazet. Nū. Pri°. More newes from Europe* (29 August 1623).

[37] *A true relation of the affaires of Europe, especially, France, Flanders, and the Palatinate* (4 October 1622).

You see what Method I haue used, to draw the account of Europes Businesse by items, which I am persuaded is not vnpleasing, and therefore I will continue the same: for breuities sake, and to auoide discoursing, know then, that the Letters from Vienna containe these particulars ...[38]

The author is no longer the simple purveyor of news but rather has a much more dynamic role in deciding what news to select and how best to present it. The fact that he is attempting to provide a "continued relation" and not just "a Bill of accounts, divided into severall *Items*"[39] results in changes to the structure of his news text. The most obvious difference lies in the occasional use of an editorial to preface the week's news. This, for example, is found in the coranto below, where the writer interprets and familiarizes distant news by placing it within the circumstances of everyday life:

Gentle Reader, I haue often told you, that rumour and long shadowes may bee compared together: for as a man of a meane stature running in the fields at the going down of the Sunne, supposeth some formidable apparition to follow him, as he fearfully and suddenly casteth his eye behinde him: So it is with easie, credulous, and superstitious persons, they doe not only apprehend what is told them, but a sixe foot body make a two foot shadow, and though they know it, not worthy the regarding, yet will they be astonished without cause, and draw others into the same error without occasion. And is not this most apparent at this instant, concerning the formidable reports of Spaines wonderfull preparations; the Emperours imperious proceedings, the Archdutches Tripartite Army ...[40]

However, apart from such prefatory editorials, we also need to see whether there is experimentation in the use of a summary (headline and lead) and non-chronological narrative. As regards headlines, what we notice is that although they as such are not found, what the editor does occasionally experiment with are margin captions. These, for example, are sometimes adopted in the autumn of 1622 when the editor places besides the reportage itself marginal captions indicating the main theme of the report. Thus, in *A continuation of the news of this present weeke* Gainsford includes the marginalia "Siege of Manheim," "The Grisons discontents, after the losse of the Valtaline," "The present greatnesse of the house of Austria" beside the respective news paragraphs.[41] Through such marginalia the editor is focusing the readers' attention on the news theme

---

[38] Ibid.
[39] *Ital: Gazet. Nū. Pri⁰. More newes from Europe* (29 August 1623).
[40] The newes of Europe, with all such particular accidents (20 April 1624).
[41] 5 November 1622.

rather than simply on the date and place of the news source as is the case with datelines.[42]

Under Gainsford's editorship we also occasionally see the use of non-chronological narrative and forms of leads. He occasionally provides the immediate essential details of the story and then in the rest of the report gives information regarding aspects such as the event's background, causes, and consequences. For example, his final report in the coranto of 17 May 1623 begins:

> We will for this time conclude our booke with the execution of the foure traytors, against the Prince of Orange: which were Slatius the Arminian preacher, Abraham and Iohn Blansaert, and William Party; upon Thursday last before the 5. of May, had they warning to provide themselues to die the next day. Whereupon some Preachers being sent to prepare them, they offered rather to dispute with them, then to be comforted by them: The next day the guards being set, they were brought forth about nine or ten a clocke; where having made their confessions, Slatius was tyed to an officer, and so led to the Scaffold; which when he had mounted ...[43]

The story does not follow a simple chronological framework in that the most recent chronological event is not found at the end of the text as is the case with a straightforward temporal recount but rather at the beginning since it is that event that the writer wants to foreground. Therefore, first, the writer reports the focal news, the execution of the "foure traytors" and who they were, and then, going back to the earliest temporal occurrence ("upon Thursday last") he reports the unfolding of events prior to the execution. Of course, this is not a lead in the modern sense of the term since from a graphic point of view it is not separated from the rest of the text but what it does highlight is the writer's willingness to overturn the default narrative structure of early seventeenth-century print reportage to focus more clearly on the particular theme he wishes to emphasize.

A similar structuring device, that is, the use of what can be called a proto-lead,[44] is also found in the passage below from a 1622 coranto. This time Gainsford is reporting news from Prague, though as with the previous coranto the news item is neither preceded by dateline nor highlighted by summarizing margin caption.

---

[42] For other examples of marginal annotation see *Newes from most parts of Christendome* (25 September 1622); *A continuation of the affaires of the Low-Countries, and the Palatinate* (22 October 1622); and *The continuation of the former news* (21 November 1622).

[43] *The continuation of our former newes from Aprill the 8. until the 17. relating these particulars* (17 May 1623).

[44] In using the expression "proto-lead" I am borrowing a term used by Elisabetta Cecconi in her presentation on the structure of seventeenth-century broadside news at the Conference on Historical News Discourse in Zurich in September 2007.

> There are (it seemeth) in Prague two Lutheran Churches of the Confession of Auspurg, where they stand in great feare, that their Churches shall be taken from them, & the free exercise of their Religion forbidden them, for so they write from Lipsich in Saxony, the 30. of Octob. And so two seuerall Letters from Prague it selfe, the eighteenth of October, and the two and twentieth, relate that Maximilian Landtgraue of Lichtenstein, Lord Deputie of Bohemia, came from the Emperor (as you have heard in some former Newes) with two Commissions: one for the examination and execution of some Lords, with confiscation of their Estates, which goes on very eagerly: and the other with power to shut up the two Dutch Protestant Churches, and to vrge the Citie and Country to a Reformation ...[45]

Once again the temporal order of events is reversed since the most recent event (the news of 30 October) is reported first since it is that which acts as proto-lead to the two other related news items. Therefore, as with the previous passage, we see an exception to the default reportage textual structure. In his desire to move beyond the role of simple chronicler of the contemporary world the editor is not only acting as an information gatekeeper and thereby deciding what news to include in his coranto but also in conjunction with his objective of providing a "continuous narrative" of events he also occasionally, and paradoxically given the supposed continuity of narrative, overturns the traditional temporal order of natural narrative. While in most coranto news the recount is temporally organized along the chronological principle in Gainsford's reportage we find him sometimes modifying this standard narrative framework so that in true modern-day journalistic fashion he can foreground the story's news value.[46]

---

[45] *The Continuation of the former Newes* (21 November 1622).

[46] Although distinct from reportage, so-called "narrations" or "relations" also occasionally reflect a non-chronological narrative structure. The text types, that within the coranto were marked out graphically as separate features, and frequently ran to more than 500 words, were typically framed by an initial brief summary of the ensuing story. One such narration is that describing the fall of the city of Maghdenburg in 1631. Appearing in a 1631 coranto, the narration begins with the contents summary and continues with a proto-lead before reverting to the standard chronological recount:
> A true Narration of the dolefull losse of the City of Maghdenburgh, taken by General Tilly the 20. of May. Written from Leypsich the 26. of May. // No pen is able to write, or tongue expresse, the wofull and lamentable tragedy lately happened at the taking of the City Maghdenburgh; and indeed so pitifull a relation very fearefull with teares for Christian eares to heare, and a subiect so vnpleasing to a religious heart, so much as to thinke of so bloody a massacre, almost vnheard of in the memory of man. I will therefore be briefe in the particulars. The 20. of May the General Tilly ... (*The continuation of our forreigne newes*, 10 June 1631).

Newsbooks 1641–1660

Newsbooks replaced corantos as the principal form of periodical print news in late 1641.[47] Following the breakdown of royal government and censorship that year these 8–16 page news pamphlets started coming out ever more frequently, providing a forum for a hitherto unimaginably large number of writers and opinions. Although newsbooks had the same format as the small quarto folio corantos of most of the previous 20 years they differed from their predecessors in two very important aspects. First and above all, the news they printed included not only foreign events but also domestic affairs; secondly, their publication was much more constant in that each newsbook came out more or less regularly on its own weekly publication day.

Given the explosion of news print during this period and in particular during the Civil War years, an overview of news structure such as I am attempting in this chapter can only hope to provide a broad identification of the main characteristics of the myriad news texts. Bearing in mind this premise, my analysis would suggest that newsbook reportage can be divided into two main categories. In the first we can group news stories relating to highly charged ideological topics such as national politics and religion, which during this twenty-year period and in particular during the 1640s, tore apart British society. The other category instead comprises such conventional non-politicized hard news stories as crime, court reports, natural events, and foreign news, especially where such news probably amounts to the translation of foreign news publications.

Ideology and Text Structure

As my focus is on monothematic hard news, I shall only briefly mention the kind of continuous narrative which so often appears in periodical pamphlets of these years. This narrative style which in form reminds one of what Thomas Gainsford first developed in the 1620s in that it lacks a dateline and runs on from one subject to another often presents the reader with a highly personalized, ideologically-charged commentary of the previous week's news. For example, in the following paragraph the news writer's voice is ever present in this recount of Civil War news:

---

[47] For monographs on newsbooks see Joseph Frank, *The Beginnings of the English Newspaper 1620–1660* (Cambridge, 1961) and Joad Raymond, *The Invention of the Newspaper. English Newsbooks 1641–1649* (Oxford, 1996). In a following volume, *Pamphlets and Pamphleteering in Early Modern Britain* (Cambridge, 2003) Joad Raymond also analyses newsbooks but in this work he places the publications within a general study of the context and production of pamphlets in early modern Britain. The role of newsbooks in the diffusion of propaganda is examined in Jason Peacey, *Politicians and Pamphleteers: Propaganda during the English Civil Wars and Interregnum* (Aldershot, 2004).

Narrating Contemporaneity: Text and Structure in English News   245

You see how active the Newarkers are to play their game. We heare that besides this they have committed many other outrages in that Countrey, the particulars whereof I shall give you as they come to my hands: the cause wee fight for is truth, and therefore I hope it will not be malignancy to speake it. The Spaniards reward those Messengers best who bring worst tidings, whereby their losses being timely redressed, seeme rather slips then falls, they are no sooner downe then up againe. I doubt not but in this we shall shortly immitate them by taking the more speedy course against these pestilent Newarkers, and make their strength and these their proceeds rather as Whetstones to our courage then Grave-stones to our resolutions ... [48]

Regarding instead monothematic news reports which though not devoid of personal voice are nevertheless classifiable as hard news, what one notices is experimentation in the structure of the news text and in particular in the use of a summary and non-chronological narrative. For example, *Mercurius Britanicus*, one of the most important parliamentarian publications, often makes use of margin captions which in form reflect the quintessential features of headlines.[49] Thus, in the news items below what we find is not a simple dateline but instead topic-focusing margin captions that correspond in syntax to what Turner says of headline syntax: "the syntax of ... headlines is analyzed on the assumption that a headline is an abbreviated message, summarizing the following text and labeling it."[50]

Table 12.1   Margin captions in *Mercurius Britanicus* (10–17 June 1644)

Oxford hast.	I must remember you of his Majesties hast from Oxford with about foure or 5000. horse and foote, with the Prince, and divers Lords, and many Ladies, who because they were something lighter of carriage then ordinary, did not much clog their train of Artillery ...
A visit.	His Majesty tis thought took horse to visit the Queen, and returned as soon, she lies sick it seemes of her disease and affaires at once ; onely the bloody execution and massacre at Bolton, on the godly party there, hath little refreshed her ...
Persons left in Oxford.	There are now in Oxford divers of quality, Cottington, Littleton, Banks, Foster, &c. these stay in Oxford, not out of any love to the University, or situation, for it was never worse seated they think, then at this time, now that our forces are drawing neere, and that there is a noise of Colonell Brown advancing ...

[48]   *Mercurius Civicus* (31 July–7 August 1645).
[49]   *Mercurius Britanicus* (1643–46), like other parliamentarian newsbooks, was published in London.
[50]   G.W. Turner, "The Grammar of Newspaper Headlines Containing the Preposition *On* in the Sense 'About,'" *Linguistics*, 87 (1972), p. 72.

Consisting of noun phrases the captions reflect both the grammatical succinctness and summarizing function characteristic of a headline. Admittedly, these marginal annotations are placed beside the body of the text rather above it as is the case with conventional headlines but this does not reduce the functional value of the information. The margin captions still summarize the contents of the dispatch and the fact they were in this position on the page rather than above the news item was simply the consequence of the high cost of paper. Had they headed the report rather than being placed beside it they would have taken up more space and hence their inclusion would have led to a greater cost.

Although it would be mistaken to assume all margin captions in *Mercurius Britanicus* possess the quintessential qualities of modern-day headlines—for they were often considerably longer than headlines today[51] and furthermore lacked the wordplay and phonological foregrounding of much modern headline writing—what one needs to realize is that *Mercurius Britanicus*'s aim was just to underline the essential focus of the news item. And it is this fact that is important in the present discussion. With the use of such marginalia, what the news editor is doing is providing explicit, immediate interpretation of the reported event.[52]

This use of margin captions and proto-headlines during the Civil War years also coincides with the occasional presence of proto-leads at the beginning of extended news reports. The passages below are from *Mercurius Aulicus*, the most influential royalist newsbook, and both contain in the first part of the report the summary of the nucleus of the story. Neither of the stories therefore follows the straightforward chronological principle since after the initial summary the narration goes back in time to recount what led up to the final event which in the news report is placed at the beginning of the text. As with the relationship between margin captions

---

[51] Examples of longer margin captions in the same number as the above shorter captions include: "What prodigious service Aulicus did for their party in his life time," "A Message from the Lords concerning Greenland house," "A description of a picture taken amongst others in the Dunkirk Ship at Arundell."

[52] As I am focusing on reportage in this chapter, I have not sufficient space to consider the form and function of title-pages in corantos and newsbooks. However, as between 1620–60 there is some degree of experimentation in the language and contents of such pages, research into the topic could be interesting. For example, in many numbers of the newsbook *Certaine Informations* the editor makes use of either block language or, at most, very simple declarative sentences on the title-page to focus on stories in that particular number. Thus, in the issue of 29 May–5 June 1643 we see on the first page, top left-hand corner, the words: *Robbing by the knowme* [sic] *Laws. Treachery will raise Houses. The Scots sent for. Plots against the parliament and City.* Placed on successive lines such captions draw the reader's attention to the outcome of some of the most important stories in the publication. Likewise, the short-lasting but nevertheless interesting newsbook *The Welch Mercury* also has first-page proto-headlines, while *The Scotish Dove* often highlights its news through the use of simple front-page top verse.

and present-day headlines, one cannot speak of an exact correspondence in form between modern-day press leads and those found in these mid-seventeenth century newsbooks. There is not the clear textual and graphic demarcation in the proto-leads below that is found in their modern-day counterparts but notwithstanding this what one sees in the following passages is the writer's foregrounding of the story's central event at the beginning of the report.

> TUESDAY. Aug. 13.
> These Rebels perceiving Wingfield Mannour not hastily gained, drew off their Horse and Dragoones (14 Colours) leaving their foot to goe on with the siege; but their horse were so well met with the Governour of Lichfield, that they quickely returned to their fellowes at Wingfield; The particulars were thus: Colonell Bagot marched from Lichfield towards Stafford with 400 Horse ...[53]
> SUNDAY. Aug. 18.
> The first newes of this weeke, is of a sharpe difference betwixt the Conquerour and the Woodmonger (commonly called Sir William Waller and Colonell Browne) who have broken out into such unbrotherly language, as if one were an Independent, and the other a Presbyterian. The quarrell grew about their superiority in Oxford-shire and Berkeshire, where Sir William having sent his Commands to Browne, was strangely disobeyed. Hereupon the Conquerour posted up to Westminster ...[54]

In determining why this should be the case, that is, why the above proto-leads and proto-headlines should be found in the Civil War newsbooks one cannot ignore the role of these news publications. The fact that Civil War newsbooks frequently revert to such reader-orientation devices in their reportage exemplifies what Iedema, Feez and White generally refer to as the "pressure of practical social demands on both the grammar and text structure of news reporting."[55] In those Civil War news pamphlets that were particularly politicized the writer and reader felt the need to get to the heart of the news at once. The years between 1642–46 were dramatic times and in the reporting of such drama some of the more fervent news writers looked beyond standard forms of narration. This was certainly the case with *Mercurius Aulicus* and *Mercurius Britanicus* since with both these newsbooks the news writer wanted to emphasize the news focus, especially the positive news as soon as possible, and the readers too wanted to find this information immediately.

---

[53] *Mercurius Aulicus* (10–17 August 1644).
[54] *Mercurius Aulicus* (17–24 August 1644).
[55] Iedema, Feez and White, p. 104.

Text Structure in Non-Ideological News

In the reporting of non-ideological news such as natural events, accidents, human interest stories, as well as foreign news, Civil War and Interregnum newsbooks emulate corantos in their tendency to follow a chronological narrative structure in longer news reports. This default narrative paradigm is not surprising since to a large extent the various reasons that had prompted the use of such a narrative principle for corantos were still applicable for newsbooks. After all, this was the textual organization to which writers and readers were accustomed, it did provide a positive element of suspense, and as regards specifically the reporting of foreign news much of such information was still based on the translation of foreign print publications or newsletters, and these latter continued to follow the temporal structure of news reporting where the news writer was required to supply basic fact with the onus or right of interpretation of such news left to the reader.

However, as exception to this general tendency one needs to mention the reporting of court trials. The reporting of this aspect of the contemporary world stands out for its frequent use of a lead. In the first of the reports below we see a summarizing lead at the beginning followed by a chronological narration of what preceded the event, whereas, in the second passage there is a particularly complex temporal narration since the story proceeds from court trial to sentencing and execution, and then back again to the context and description of the act that led to the trial of the two men.

> At the Sessions in the Old bayley on Thursday, Fryday, and Saturday last was tried one Mistris Beard, who upon Evidence, was cast for bewitching a child: the manner thus: About fifteen weeks ago, the child was struck lame on the left leg then in the right Arm ...[56]
>
> Munday, January, 27.
>
> From Plymonth 18 Ianuary, came thus. The last Saturday and Monday, a Court-Marshall was held here where two souldiers Iohn Story, and Robert Stone, and a Gent. of Armes were tried for their lives, being accused for killing of Iohn Moreshead of Inplecomb in the Country of Devon, a master of a ship: The one of them, Story who committed the Fact was sentenced to death, and yesterday executed accordingly ... The quarrel whereupon this lamentable accident fell out, was very trivially grounded, and indeed upon a jest, the mischief suddenly committed in a rash humour, without any time for consideration which may make every one the more cautious ...[57]

---

[56] *The Weekly Post* (21–28 February 1654).
[57] *A Perfect Account of the Daily Intelligence* (22–29 January 1651).

Why the reporting of court cases should have followed a non-chronological structure is difficult to ascertain but the fact that it did not has led Ungerer to suggest that this particular subgenre of the news story may have played a significant part in the diffusion of the non-chronological story structure in the latter half of the nineteenth century.[58] He argues that as this mode of narration already existed in this sub-genre, as it did by the nineteenth century in other sub-genres such as accidents and political news reports, what happened was that this non-chronological story telling gradually became for various technical and commercial reasons increasingly common until in time it represented the norm for all kinds of hard news writing.

Conclusion

In this chapter I have investigated what the narrative structure of monothematic hard news can tell us about how the contemporary world was reported and understood in English periodical news publications of the first half of the seventeenth century. In relation to the structure I have focused on two particular features that have been described and explained by leading contemporary news analysts including in particular van Dijk. The two aspects in question, the summary consisting of headline and lead and the non-linear narrative are an integral part of modern-day news narration and set the news story genre apart from other forms of story narration. Through the headline and lead which in itself imply a non-temporal narration the reader is provided with immediate orientation as to how the news should be interpreted. The writer is assuming the role of guide in the cognitive processing of the reported event. Rather than offering a simple-structured tale based around a straightforward temporal recount of the piece of news whereby each separate occurrence is presented in the text as it occurred in real life the writer is rearranging the world so as to make more sense of it or at least to give it the sense that he or she wishes it to have.

This way of reporting contemporaneity is very different from what occurred in the early seventeenth-century periodical press. What we find in corantos of the 1620s and 1630s is a hard news structure that instead distances the writer from the event that is being reported. The default structure involves neither headline (nor anything corresponding to its functional significance) nor lead which would have involved the writer extracting from the morass of fact what was most important so as to shape the story for the reader's benefit. Furthermore, in those relatively few cases where the news item develops beyond that of a simple

---

[58] Ungerer, p. 94.

dispatch towards something more textually elaborate the temporal organization of the event as recounted on the written page is very simple with little or no attempt being made to rearrange textually the temporal succession of events in order to highlight any particular part of the story, be it the background, consequences, reaction, or whatever within the body of the text. The reasons for such a mode of news narration were various and incorporated both what was generally preferred by the reader as well as what was most expedient for the writer and publisher. However, within this normal framework of recounting contemporaneity we also find exceptions and in such circumstances we see the coranto writer experimenting with conventional forms of hard news structure in an attempt to emphasize what that reportage meant for his readers.

In the case of newsbooks between 1641–60 the text structure of hard news varies considerably as is only to be expected with such an outburst of pamphlet publication. However, even within this enormous mass of print news, it is possible to identify two strands of text structure regarding the presentation of hard news. In the first grouping we find the highly politicized newsbooks where the news writer sometimes experiments with the reporting strategies of news so as to emphasize the political focus of the event whilst in the second category consisting mostly of non-ideological news stories we usually find the traditional form of news narration whereby the news writer provides the facts but little guidance as to how these facts should be understood in relation to one another and indeed the reader's own world.

CHAPTER 13

Historical Text Mining and Corpus-Based Approaches to the Newsbooks of the Commonwealth

Andrew Hardie, Tony McEnery and Scott Songlin Piao

Introduction

A key component in the study of emergent contemporaneity in the early modern press is the interrelationships between various publications which reused one another's text. In so doing they established a form of consensus on the noteworthy contemporary events at any one moment. At the same time, variations in the redaction of reused text afford us an insight into ideological stance and editorial practices of early journalists.

In this study, we apply techniques from the field of corpus linguistics[1] to the study of text reuse in the English Newsbooks of the Commonwealth period. We describe the process of this research from construction of the electronic data resource, through development of analytic tools, to the final outcomes. Our results suggest that these techniques are useful on a macro-level to quantify the level of text reuse in a collection of documents, and also at a micro-level to describe in greater detail the relationships that exist between particular documents and particular periodical series.

To accomplish our purpose it was necessary first to create a collection of Newsbook text in machine-readable electronic form. We drew the texts for inclusion in our dataset from the Thomason Tracts, an extensive collection of documents published in London between 1640 and 1661, compiled by George Thomason, a London bookseller (c. 1602–66). The collection is substantial—the Tracts consist of over 22,000 individual documents, over 7,000 of which are Newsbooks. We wished to explore a subset of the Newsbooks in the Tracts to look for evidence of text reuse using a corpus-based approach to the problem. As large-scale quantification of text reuse, is an otherwise almost impossible task, establishing a methodological framework within which this can be achieved

---

[1] See Tony McEnery and Andrew Wilson, *Corpus Linguistics* (Edinburgh, 2001) second edition.

may allow historians to better explore text reuse itself, and also consider how text reuse impacts upon issues of wider interest such as the emergence of contemporaneity in the early modern period.

In exploring text reuse we were interested in four broad questions. Firstly, can corpus methods provide evidence of text reuse on a scale that is difficult for human analysts working with eye and hand alone to achieve? Secondly, are we able to usefully quantify the scale and nature of that text reuse using these techniques? Thirdly, can the automated analysis assist us to isolate instances of ideologically-motivated variation within units of reused text (for example, variation indicating royalist sympathies)? Finally, does the analysis corroborate, extend, or challenge similar analyses undertaken by human analysts, notably Joseph Frank's study,[2] or is it undermined by such earlier work? These questions are addressed in the discussion section of this chapter.

Before applying the automated analytical techniques in question, a significant obstacle to their use had to be removed—the provision of suitable machine-readable texts. While the documents of the Thomason Tracts are widely available in image form, these versions were not of use for this research, as the text of the documents could not be read by a computer. To submit the Newsbooks to corpus-based methods of study, an electronic version of some of the Newsbooks in the Thomason Tracts was necessary. While other parts of the Thomason Tracts have already been subject to transformation into machine-readable form, notably through such sources as the Lampeter Corpus,[3] no source had converted the Newsbook material in the Tracts into machine-readable form. In the following section we will briefly describe how we made an electronic edition of the Newsbooks. Following this, we will introduce the methods employed in analyzing the texts, using a specially-developed piece of software (named *Crouch* after one of the journalists of the period).

---

[2] Joseph Frank, *The beginnings of the English newspaper 1620–1660* (Cambridge, MA, 1961). Consider also C. John Sommerville, *The News Revolution in England: Cultural Dynamics of Daily Information* (Oxford: Oxford University Press, 1996), and the articles in Joad Raymond, ed., *News Networks in Seventeenth-Century Britain and Europe* (London: Routledge, 2005).

[3] Rainer Siemund and Claudia Claridge, "The Lampeter Corpus of Early Modern English Tracts," *ICAME Journal*, 21 (1997): 61–70.

Methodology

The Corpus

In order to pursue this research we built the Lancaster Newsbooks Corpus. This is a one million word collection of English Newsbooks from the 1650s.[4] It consists of two bodies of text. The first is the full run of one highly anomalous Newsbook title, *Mercurius Fumigosus*.[5] The second, which forms the dataset for the present study, consists of a complete collection of every Newsbook published in London between the middle of December 1653 and the end of May 1654.[6] All the documents in the corpus were transcribed from the copies of the Newsbooks preserved in the Thomason Tracts (catalogued by Fortescue et al.;[7] bibliographical details on these periodicals are also available through EEBO–Early English Books Online[8]). Table 13.1 gives further details on the documents in the dataset analyzed in this study, including the short codes that will be used together with issue numbers when citing examples from the data in this paper. Further references in this chapter to "the corpus" refer to this subset of the corpus, excluding *Mercurius Fumigosus*.

In building the corpus we decided to construct a comprehensive snapshot of the news in a short period of time, across six months in 1654. We chose 1654 as a time of historical interest, representing the tail end of a period which saw a relatively liberal attitude to the press by the Commonwealth government. It also contains a number of historical events of note, such as the Glencairn Uprising (see Graham, 1820).[9]

---

[4] The construction of this corpus was supported by two grants from the British Academy, grant references SG–33825 and LRG–35423. The corpus is available through the Oxford Text Archive. See also http://www.ling.lancs.ac.uk/newsbooks.

[5] For discussion of Mercurius Fumigosus, see Tony McEnery, *Swearing in English: bad language, purity, and power from 1586 to the present* (London, 2006), p. 79.

[6] All dates given in this chapter assume a calendar year beginning on 1 January.

[7] G.K. Fortescue, assisted by R.F. Sharp, R.A. Streatfield and W.A. Marsden, *Catalogue of the pamphlets, books, newspapers, and manuscripts relating to the Civil War, the Commonwealth, and Restoration, collected by George Thomason, 1640–1661* (London, 1908), vol. 2.

[8] See http://eebo.chadwyck.com/about/about.htm#tracts, http://eebo.chadwyck.com/about/ped_list.htm.

[9] See J. Graham of Deuchrie, *An Account of the Expedition of William the Ninth Earl of Glencairn, as General of His Majesty's Forces in the Highlands of Scotland, in the Years 1653 and 1654*, In *Miscellanea Scotica* (Glasgow, 1820), vol. 4.

Table 13.1 Details of the Data

Title of periodical	Short title	No. documents for this title	Word count for this title
The True and Perfect Dutch-Diurnal	DutchDiurn	9	21,687
Every Day's Intelligence	EveryDayIntell	24	67,618
The Faithful Scout	FScout	19	64,677
The Faithful Scout (imitation by G. Horton)	FScoutHorton	7	22,662
Mercurius Politicus	MPol	23	118,667
The Moderate Intelligencer	ModIntell	13	40,490
A Perfect Account	PerfAcc	21	55,967
Perfect Diurnal Occurrences	PerfDiOcc	6	16,946
The Perfect Diurnal of some Passages and Proceedings	PerfDiurn	24	133,381
Proceedings of State Affairs	ProcState	23	138,980
The Weekly Intelligencer of the Commonwealth	WIntell	26	68,225
The Weekly Post	WPost	19	55,876
Periodicals running for only a small number of issues (11 different titles)	Various	25	63,790
Total word count			868,966

Note that in the original newsbooks, titles are lengthy, often extending across several lines, and frequently changing over the lifespan of a periodical. In the interests of economy and to give each series of newsbooks a consistent label, the "titles" given here contain the most salient, unique, and consistent elements of the full original titles.

The texts were created by a process of manual transcription. While it would have been ideal to scan in the texts using an optical character recognition system and then to correct the resulting text, the poor quality of the originals we were working from meant that this process was in fact much more time consuming than wholly manual transcription. Figure 13.1 shows an example page from an original Newsbook, demonstrating just how poor the quality of the Newsbook texts could be and why wholly manual transcription proved necessary.

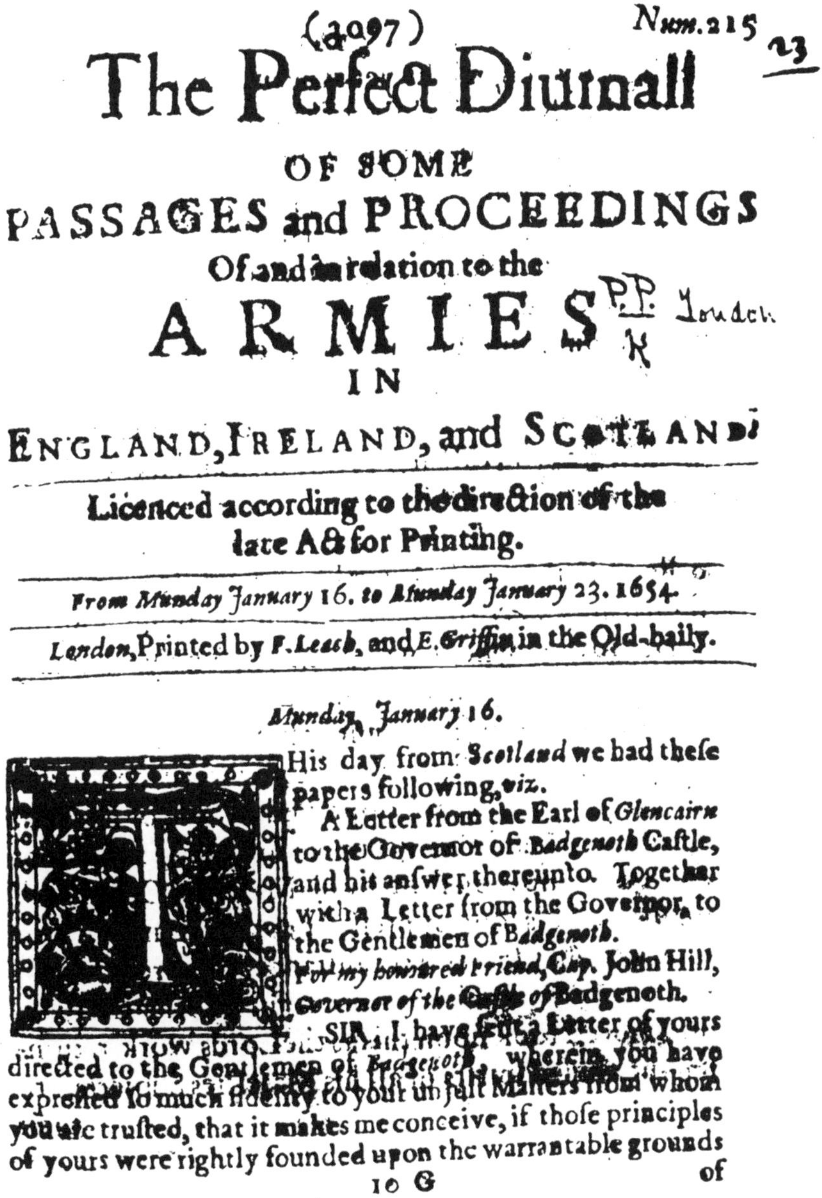

Figure 13.1   An original page from *The Perfect Diurnal*. British Museum.

Once a text had been typed into a word processor, the transcriptions were checked for errors. During the process of transcription XML codes were introduced into the texts, which indicate major formatting features of the text. The XML codes used were: `<p>` (paragraphs); `<h1>`, `<h2>` and `<h3>` (a three-way categorization of headings); `<i>` and `<go>` (typeface variants italic and gothic, respectively); `<em>` (contrastive italicization used in this period for significant words in the sentence, for instance, proper nouns); `<table>`, `<tr>`, `<td>` (tabular layout); `<poem>`, `<stanza>`, `<line>` (verse); `<hr>` (lines across the page); and `<img>` (placeholder for an illustration). Two further tags proved necessary. The first was `<unclear>`. It was not possible to read all of the text in the Newsbooks reliably, hence the need for this tag to denote an area of illegible text in the original. The final tag was `<reg>`. While the transcribers faithfully rendered the texts in their original spellings, the `<reg>` tag was used by them to encode the modern standard form of any archaic or variant spellings that they encountered. This ensured that the integrity of the original text was maintained, while regular spellings were made available for use by text processing software where appropriate. For example, if the form *Cromwel* appeared in the original text of a Newsbook, then the transcriber rendered it as `<reg orig="Cromwel">Cromwell</reg>` in the corpus. Software which is aware of XML markup can be ordered to display only the original text—nothing but *Cromwel* would be shown. However, the regularization markup links *Cromwel* to any other variant forms which are regularized in the markup as *Cromwell*. In this way, the integrity of the text is retained, while the ability of the machine to process the text is maximized. The page in Figure 13.1 would appear as follows when the transcription is viewed without the XML codes being hidden:

> `<p>`This day from `<em>`Scotland`</em>` we had these papers following, `<em>`viz`</em>`.`</p>`
> `<p>`A Letter from the Earl of `<em>`Glencairn`</em>` to the Governor of `<em>`Badgenoth`</em>` Castle, and his answer thereunto. Together with a Letter from the Governor, to the Gentlemen of `<em>`Badgenoth`</em>`.`</p>` `<p><i>`For my `<unclear>`honoured`</unclear>` Friend`</i>`, Cap. `<em>`John Hill`</em>`, Governor of the Castle of `<em>`Badgenoth`</em>`.`</p>` `<p>`SIR, I have sent a Letter of yours directed to the Gentlemen of `<em>`Badgenoth`</em>`, wherein you have expressed so much `<unclear><!--approx. 5 characters--></unclear>` to your un just Masters from whom you are trusted, that it makes me conceive, if those principles of yours were rightly founded upon the warrantable grounds of[...]

Automated Analysis of Text Reuse

Our approach to identifying reused text is predicated upon the assumption that relations between texts can be examined by testing relations between text subunits. While a range of subunits might be selected for analysis (for example, individual word tokens or short sequences of words), the *Crouch* system is based on the mapping of related sentences via an alignment approach. Alignment is a technique that is traditionally used in the corpus analysis of multilingual text.[10] Given a written text in one language and the same document translated into another language, the aim of alignment is to indicate which sentences in the translation correspond to each sentence in the original.[11] This alignment information then assists in further analysis. While it is possible to analyze alignment manually, the task is frequently automated.[12] In principle, the same means can be employed in the detection of similarity between two sentences in the same language as are utilized in the detection of similarity between two sentences in different languages. We are in effect asking the same question in either case: what sentences in text A are similar or identical to what sentences in text B?

The *Crouch* system is based on this insight: that the techniques used in automated alignment can also be applied to two texts in the same language where text reuse is suspected—whether in the form of one text copying another, or in the form of both relying on a common source. *Crouch* is based on a prototype tool developed by the METER Project at Sheffield University.[13] In the METER Project the text reuse under investigation was the reuse of press agency wire service text by different modern newspapers, often in slightly different forms. This problem is directly parallel to the problem we face in identifying text reuse in the

---

[10] William A. Gale and Kenneth W. Church, "Identifying word correspondences in parallel texts" in *Proceedings of the Fourth DARPA Workshop on Speech and Natural Language* (Pacific Grove, CA, 1991), pp. 152–7.

[11] Cross-linguistic alignment may also be done at the word level, but the *Crouch* tool is based on techniques for sentence alignment rather than word alignment.

[12] See Scott S.L. Piao and Tony McEnery, "Multi-word unit alignment in English–Chinese parallel corpora," in *Proceedings of the Corpus Linguistics 2001 Conference* (Lancaster, UK, 2001), pp. 466–75. See also Scott S.L. Piao, "Word alignment in English–Chinese parallel corpora," *Literary and Linguistic Computing*, 17/2 (2002): 207–30.

[13] See Paul Clough, Robert Gaizauskas, Scott S.L. Piao and Yorick Wilks, "METER: MEasuring TExt Reuse," in *Proceedings of the 40th Anniversary Meeting for the Association for Computational Linguistics* (2002), pp.152–9. See also Paul Clough, Robert Gaizauskas and Scott S.L. Piao, "Building and annotating a corpus for the study of journalistic text reuse", in *Proceedings of the 3rd International Conference on Language Resources and Evaluation (LREC-02)*, (2002), vol. V, pp. 1678–91.

Newsbooks Corpus. In this section, we will describe the algorithm originated by the METER Project and adopted and extended in the *Crouch* tool.

The technical and mathematical details of the algorithm are reported at length by Piao and McEnery;[14] only a brief non-technical overview will be presented here. The process begins with two texts which are being tested for relatedness, the candidate source text and the candidate derived text. First, both texts are divided into sentences. Then, each possible pair of sentences is compared to see whether or not they are similar or the same. That is, the first sentence in the candidate source text is compared in turn to each sentence in the candidate derived text; then that process is repeated for the second sentence in the candidate source text; and so on for all the other sentences in the candidate source text.

The similarity between pairs of candidate source and candidate derived sentences is quantified by combining together a number of different measures. The factors that are calculated for each, contributing to the relations between candidate sentences, include:

- the lengths of the two sentences,
- the number of words that occur in both sentences,
- the number of n–grams (sequences of two or more words) that occur in both sentences.

When calculating the number of identical words in a pair of sentences, around 200 very frequent words are not taken into account, namely grammatical function words such as *is*, *the*, *in*, *of*, amongst others. These words are so common that they cause noise in the results, making sentences that are actually independent appear to be related. Filtering out these words prevents this problem, and does not hamper the analysis because function words typically contribute very little to the meaning of a sentence. On the other hand, function words are taken into account when they occur as part of an n–gram.

One other factor taken into account is the number of words in the candidate source sentence which are very similar (but not identical) to a word in the candidate derived sentence. It was necessary to add this measure because of the issue of spelling variation. While most archaic spelling variants in the corpus have been tagged and regularized according to the system outlined above, some have not—especially in the case of proper names, where the transcribers may not have been familiar with the modern standard spelling of the names of historical

---

[14] Scott S.L. Piao and Tony McEnery, "A tool for text comparison," in *Proceedings of the Corpus Linguistics 2003 Conference* (Lancaster, UK, 2003), pp. 637–46.

persons such as the Earl of Glencairn (or Glencarn, or Glencarne ...). Words whose spellings differ in minor ways from text to text are brought within the analysis by this means.

Different permutations of these factors are used to produce three different scores that quantify the relationship between the two sentences. These scores are then combined together into a single quantitative metric, which indicates the strength of the relationship between the candidate source sentence and the candidate derived sentence. This process is then repeated for all the other candidate source sentences; ultimately the candidate source sentence with the highest score is determined (that is, the most likely match for the candidate derived sentence) and this pair of sentences is determined to be aligned. *Crouch* also makes allowance for the fact that sequences of source sentences may relate to a single target sentence.

This process of sentence alignment must then be repeated for each remaining sentence in the candidate derived text. When *Crouch* compares a single pair of texts the process stops here. In this mode, the software can present the sentence-by-sentence alignment and comparison interface in a range of graphical formats that allow further investigation of similarity; some examples of these outputs will be presented below.

However, when more than two texts are being compared, it is necessary to summarize the sentence-alignment scores into a single statistic which characterizes the relationship between a pair of texts (allowing direct comparison of the strength of the relationships between each pair of candidate source and derived texts). A summary statistic is calculated which weights together the strength of each sentence pairing, the lengths of the paired sentences, and the overall length of the texts. The final score ranges from 0 to 1. A score of 0 indicates that the candidate derived text is completely dependent on the candidate source text (that is, they are identical). A score of 1 indicates that the candidate derived text is completely independent of the candidate source text (that is, there is no overlap at all). The score can be considered as representing the probability that the candidate derived text is *not* actually derived from the candidate source text (and thus, (1 – score) would represent the probability that the candidate derived text *is* actually derived from the candidate source text).

When a number of texts are compared in this way, the result is a matrix of scores, as shown in Table 13.2. (The sample matrix shown here is a subset of the matrix for the whole corpus.)

Table 13.2 An Example Text Comparison Matrix

Text Label	DutchDiurn09	EveryDayIntell$08	EveryDayIntell$09	FScout168	FScoutHorton169
DutchDiurn09	0	0.998	0.999	0.727	0.984
EveryDayIntell$08	0.998	0	0.978	0.837	0.998
EveryDayIntell$09	0.999	0.978	0	0.995	0.991
FScout168	0.85	0.899	0.996	0	0.998
FScoutHorton169	0.986	0.997	0.981	0.993	0

As can be seen, when a text is compared with itself the score is always zero. However, the comparison of text A to text B does not necessarily generate the same score as the comparison of text B to text A. In many cases the figures are reasonably similar, but not in all—as some examples examined in the following section will demonstrate. This asymmetry is due to the differing ways in which candidate source and candidate derived texts are treated during analysis. Most of the figures in the matrix in Table 13.2 are not low enough to be suggestive of a large amount of text reuse (although the cells scoring 0.727 and 0.85 might be worthy of following up).

It should be clear from the description above that the procedure of generating a matrix is very computationally intense. Every given sentence in the candidate derivation text must be compared to every sentence in the candidate source text. Then, every text must be compared to every other text. Depending on the size and number of texts, a full *Crouch* analysis such as those which will be presented below can take days or weeks to run on a standard desktop computer.

Once a matrix has been generated, the next step is the creation of a clustergram automatically grouping the texts into a hierarchy of similarity. First, the most closely related pairs are placed together, and then pairs of more distantly related texts are added to create, in effect, a "family tree." The algorithm used here is Ward's approach[15] as used by Phillips.[16] The cluster that is generated from the matrix shown in Table 13.2 is given in Figure 13.2; Figure 13.3 is a manually-constructed visualization of the relationships that the cluster hierarchy encodes.

---

[15] Joe H. Ward, "Hierarchical grouping to optimise an objective function," *Journal of the American Statistical Association*, 58/301 (1963): 236–44.

[16] Martin Phillips, *Aspects of Text Structure—An Investigation of the Lexical Organisation of Text* (Amsterdam, 1985), pp. 72–84.

Historical Text Mining and Corpus-Based Approaches 261

```
{ n=3
    { n=2
       { n=1  DutchDiurn09  FScout168 }
       { n=1  EveryDayIntell$08 }
    }
    { n=2
       { n=1  EveryDayIntell$09 }
       { n=1  FScoutHorton169 }
    }
}
```

Figure 13.2   Clustergram Output for the Matrix shown in Table 13.2

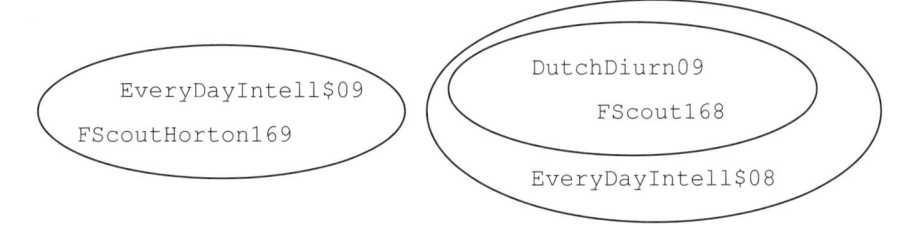

Figure 13.3   Visualization of the Clustergram in Figure 13.2

We would normally assume that the texts in the bottom layer of the hierarchy are the most useful pairs for further analysis, especially where two bottom-layer texts are within an { n = 1 } in the cluster hierarchy. These would normally coincide with the numerically low values in the matrix—as is indeed the case with DutchDiurn09 and FScout168. Examples of the types of further investigation of such pairs that can be undertaken will be given in section three below.

In the course of the development of *Crouch*, it was necessary to test the system's precision. This was done as follows: 33 texts from the Newsbooks Corpus, those published in December 1653, were clustered using *Crouch*. The 16 text pairs in the bottom-layer clusters were selected for evaluation. These 16 text pairs were compared using the graphical interface in *Crouch*, producing 594 sentence alignments. 555 of these sentence pairs were true matches, i.e. 93.4 percent precision. The 16 pairs of texts were also manually checked; two of them were judged not to be truly related, resulting in 87.5 percent precision. As a larger test of precision, a 500,000 word subset of the corpus was clustered, and the 59 text pairs from the bottom-layer clusters were collected for evaluation. These 59 text pairs were again compared one at a time using *Crouch*, producing 2,463 sentence alignments of which 217 pairs were mismatches, resulting in 91.2

percent precision. The 59 pairs of texts were manually checked, and none were found to be spuriously linked, indicating 100 percent precision. Taken together, these two tests suggest that precision at the sentence level is consistent and acceptable, being in the range 90–95 percent. The greater precision at the text level in the larger test is easily explained by the increased size of the corpus: with more texts to compare and thus more relations to evaluate, it is not surprising that the strongest relationships identified are all real relationships. Due to the difficulty of manually finding all of the true sentence alignments contained in the data, no attempt was made to examine recall in this evaluation. This will become possible only when and if a testbed corpus with all of the true sentence alignments in the Newsbooks explicitly marked-up becomes available. However, the high level of manual annotation that would be needed to produce such a testbed corpus is prohibitive, to say the least.

The analyses of the subsections of the corpus that were examined to test the precision of the *Crouch* tool will not be presented in detail here. Rather, in the following section we will present the results of applying *Crouch* to the entire corpus.

Approaches to the Data

The most straightforward way to input the corpus data into *Crouch* is simply to run the cluster analysis on the entire 239 documents in the 870 thousand word dataset. However, the sheer size of the resulting whole-corpus matrix (239 x 239 = 57,121) and clustergram makes the results difficult to interpret on a large scale. For this reason, a broader-brush procedure was also employed. The documents of the corpus were combined together according to the series of periodical to which they belonged. That is, all issues of *Mercurius Politicus* were merged into a single document; all issues of *Proceedings of State Affairs* into another; and so on. Newsbooks which either did not become ongoing series (for example *Mercurius Poeticus*) or which did not run for the full period of December 1653 to May 1654 (for example *True and Perfect Dutch Diurnal*) were simply dropped from this part of the analysis. The aim here was to assess whether there exist particular large-scale patterns of interrelation between different periodicals. Thus, a matrix was constructed for the interrelationships of eight large blocks of text, which between them constitute 83.6 percent of the words in the corpus. These blocks contain roughly the same number of documents, and are roughly similar in extent—except in the case of the double-length titles *Mercurius Politicus*, the *Perfect Diurnal*, and *Proceedings of State Affairs*.

The mode of the following analysis will be to move from an initial examination of the broad-brush matrix and clustergram for the major series of periodicals, to attempts to characterize the whole-corpus matrix in general terms, to detailed examination of particular text-pairs within that matrix. Thus, the overall thrust of the analysis is to move gradually from macro- to micro-level. At the micro-level as well as *Crouch* we make use of a web-based concordance tool to search for individual passages of text.[17] At each stage the findings of this study will be linked to that of Frank wherever possible. This year by year history of the Newsbooks from 1620 to 1660 is based upon an exhaustive reading of some 7,500 of the approximately 8,000 Newsbooks published before the Restoration,[18] and touches on many issues of text reuse and ideological bias. This manual analysis therefore provides a useful point of reference against which to evaluate the findings that emerge from our large-scale automated analysis.

Analysis

Comparing Major Series of Newsbooks

The matrix for the combined periodical titles is given in Table 13.3, and the related clustergram in Figure 13.4.

It is difficult to make overall conclusions about all eight titles; however, some points do emerge. The three 16 page periodicals, *Proceedings of State Affairs*, *Mercurius Politicus*, and the *Perfect Diurnal*, appear from the matrix to be more similar to one another than any of the three is to any other title. Surprisingly the clustergram only groups the second and third together, but looking at the two lowest scores on the three relevant rows of the matrix makes the link clear. Two reasons might be posited for this pattern: firstly, the extended length of these titles would mean that their editor-journalists could leave less news out and would thus necessarily have more overlaps; and secondly, according to Frank's account,[19] all three relied to a large degree on official government documents and presented the government line.

---

[17] This tool was based on an SQL database of the corpus with a PHP front-end. It is freely available on for use over the internet: see http://juilland.comp.lancs.ac.uk/hardiea/newsbooks.
[18] Frank, p. vi.
[19] Frank, pp. 199–252.

Table 13.3 Matrix for Major Series of Periodicals

	EveryDayIntell	FScout	MPol	PerfAcc	PerfDiurn	ProcState	WIntell	WPost
EveryDayIntell	0	0.81	0.796	0.79	0.774	0.738	0.677	0.893
FScout	0.85	0	0.838	0.828	0.795	0.758	0.888	0.632
MPol	0.88	0.879	0	0.871	0.593	0.764	0.912	0.927
PerfAcc	0.751	0.738	0.754	0	0.519	0.738	0.789	0.887
PerfDiurn	0.887	0.874	0.654	0.798	0	0.698	0.921	0.924
ProcState	0.868	0.845	0.792	0.876	0.688	0	0.902	0.897
WIntell	0.654	0.859	0.851	0.81	0.845	0.818	0	0.923
WPost	0.862	0.394	0.842	0.866	0.816	0.761	0.888	0

```
{ n=3
   { n=2
      { n=1    EveryDayIntell    WIntell     }
      { n=1    PerfAcc           ProcState   }
   }
   { n=2
      { n=1    FScout            WPost       }
      { n=1    MPol              PerfDiurn   }
   }
}
```

Figure 13.4 Clustergram for Major Series of Periodicals

Three points characterize the remaining series of periodicals. Firstly, there is a strong relationship between the *Weekly Post* and the *Faithful Scout*—both Newsbooks usually attributed to one editor-journalist, Daniel Border, and put out by two printers (Robert Wood and George Horton) who either collaborated or competed over both these titles and other, shorter-run Newsbooks (such as the *Moderate Intelligencer*). The reuse between Wood and Horton will be explored in one of the specific examples to be examined later in this section.

Secondly, there is a similar link between *Every Day's Intelligence* and the *Weekly Intelligencer*. This is more surprising as there is no known connection between them—according to Frank and the EEBO catalogue they had separate editor-journalists and different printers, and *Every Day's Intelligence* was actually produced by the editor of *Proceedings of State Affairs*; while there is an overlap here, it is not so extensive as that with the *Weekly Intelligencer*.

Thirdly, the *Perfect Account* appears to copy text from everywhere (with the possible exception of the *Weekly Post*). Frank reports[20] that "[e]ven the paper's fillers were derivative, and the editor borrowed freely from most of his colleagues ... [and was] less original than most ...." The matrix, which gives low scores for the *Perfect Account* as a candidate derived text compared to any other periodical, would seem to confirm this. But it tells us, as Frank's (admittedly brief) report does not, that the borrowing was most extensive from the *Perfect Diurnal* and least extensive from the *Weekly Post*. If we were to speculate on why this might be, we might refer to the weekly publication schedules: the *Perfect Account* came out on Wednesdays, the *Weekly Post* and *Weekly Intelligencer* (which has the highest score on this line of the table after the *Weekly Post*) on Tuesdays, and the *Perfect Diurnal* on Mondays: the others came out on Thursdays and Fridays. Possibly a two-day lag gave greater opportunity for copying than did a one-day lag, whereas Newsbooks from the end of the previous week would contain less of current relevance. But this is a very great deal of speculation to build on very broad-brush data. Further investigation of this point at the level of stories occurring in multiple individual documents would be required to address this question.

Distribution of Scores across the Whole-Corpus Matrix

As a first step towards a micro-level analysis, let us look now at the matrix for the entire corpus—that is, 239 documents each compared to every other document. It is unfortunately quite impossible to present a table of this matrix, or even a representative extract of it, in paper form. In this section, we will attempt to summarize the contents of the matrix by indicating the distribution of scores in the matrix and exemplifying pairs of documents with scores from different ranges.

Table 13.4 summarizes the frequencies with which scores in different bands of similarity occur in the overall matrix where every document in the corpus was compared to every other document. Note that approximately 97 percent of the comparisons yield extremely high scores (0.9 or higher) which represent little or no similarity. This is to be expected: any given document is extremely distant in time from the majority of other documents and thus will not be expected to have any text in common with those documents, except in some cases start and end boilerplate text.

---

[20] Frank, p. 241.

Table 13.4 Distribution of Scores across the Whole-Corpus Matrix

Score	Number of comparisons
1	17,210
0.9 to 0.999	38,152
0.8 to 0.899	843
0.7 to 0.799	376
0.6 to 0.699	147
0.5 to 0.599	73
0.4 to 0.499	48
0.3 to 0.399	19
0.2 to 0.299	10
0.1 to 0.199	2
0.001 to 0.099	2
0 (= comparison of each text to itself)	239

Note that, since each pair of texts is compared twice, the "number of comparisons" must be halved to approximate the number of pairs of texts that are actually found to be related. To make sense of these scores, let us look briefly at four example comparisons, which were examined in detail using *Crouch* as detailed in 2.2 and exemplified below.

Table 13.5 Sample Comparisons at Different Levels of Scoring

Candidate texts	Score	% word overlap	Description of overlap
Derived: DutchDiurn09 Source: WPost169	0.99	1%	One matched date–line, one matched location–line ('From Uppsala'), one *false* match of a content sentence
Derived: WPost$127 Source: PerfAcc157	0.98	2%	One short story (two sentences); rest do not match
Derived: ProcState234 Source: FScoutHorton171	0.956	4%	One very short story and one moderate length; rest do not match.
Derived: PerfDiurn215#2 Source: MPol190	0.802	20%	Two stories near the start and a one–paragraph letter near the end; rest do not match.
Derived: WPost152 Source: FScout157	0.601	40%	Three very lengthy stories (inc. text of the Instrument of Government); rest do not match
Derived: ModIntell166 Source: FScoutHorton167	0.402	60%	Two large blocks of identical sentences (each with multiple stories) surrounded by smaller blocks of unshared sentences

It should be clear from these examples that any score that is noticeably below 1 can indicate real text overlap (which in most cases means text reuse as the term is employed here: that is, copied or with a common source). However, chunks of matching text that are both multiple and substantial in extent—the ones that are most likely to indicate that the actual source document being tested has been reused—seems to occur with scores of around 0.8 or less. Given that 1,520 comparisons in the entire matrix score less than 0.9, there are therefore unlikely to be many more than about 760 pairs of documents with extensive overlapping text, and each document probably overlaps extensively with, on average, six to seven other documents. Text reuse is clearly rampant in the corpus, as was observed by Frank and Watson[21] on non-quantitative grounds.

This quantitative conclusion is, however, obscured by the distribution in Table 13.4, which is clearly skewed by the very large number of completely unrelated pairs of documents. A more meaningful approach to the distribution of scores across the corpus may be to look at the minimum score for each text. This is here defined as the lowest score derived when that text is treated as the candidate derived text for any other text in the corpus. That is, the minimum score of a text represents the similarity of that text to the other text to which it is *most* similar. Figure 13.5 shows the distribution of the 239 minimum scores.

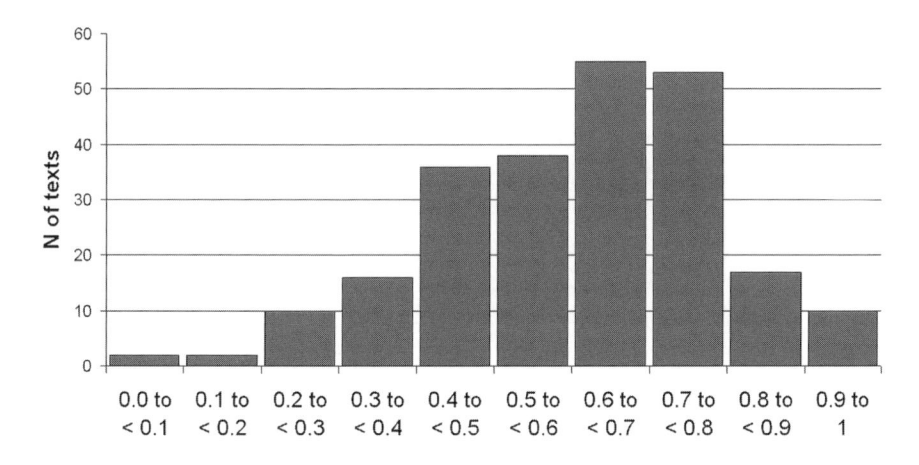

Figure 13.5   Distribution of Minimum Similarity Scores for Candidate Derived Texts

---

[21]   George Watson (ed.), *The New Cambridge Bibliography of English Literature* (Cambridge, 1974), vol. 1, pp. 2093–4.

What Figure 13.5 demonstrates is that the vast majority of texts in the corpus (182 out of 239, or 76 percent) have a minimum score between 0.4 and 0.8. By comparison, far fewer have minimum scores outside this range, and particularly there are very few texts (only four) with a minimum score below 0.2. To interpret this: most texts show a moderately strong match to at least one other text in the corpus (probably indicating at least three or four very similar or identical stories); rather few show a strong match (very extensive overlap) to another text, and only four show an extremely strong match; and similarly, rather few appear to be mostly independent of all other texts in the corpus.

The true power of the *Crouch* program is that it allows us to investigate in depth particular pairs of texts. This was how Table 13.5 was generated; in the following section, the process will be presented in detail for the most closely-linked pair of texts in the corpus, and the other documents that form this pair's immediate temporal context. Although other pairs of texts could have been selected, looking at the smallest minimum—the most extreme case in other words—gives us the opportunity to map the limits of the phenomenon of text reuse in this initial micro-level analysis.

The Minimal Score: WPostWood171 and ModIntell171#2

The very lowest scores in the whole matrix were two scores of 0.011 for both directions of comparison between two texts that were actually the same text, included in the corpus twice due to transcriber error. Excluding this known error, the lowest score is 0.188, for the comparison of ModIntell171#2 (published Wednesday 5 April 1654) as candidate derived text to WPostWood171 (published Tuesday 4 April 1654) as candidate source text. This is equal to an 81.2 percent probability that the former text is derived from the latter. The inverse comparison scores 0.222, the fourth lowest in the matrix. It is pleasing that *Crouch* produces the result that it is more likely for the later text to be derived from the earlier text than the other way around—this is what we would hope to happen if the procedure works as it should.

If we use *Crouch*'s two-way comparison function to examine this pair of texts, we get a number of different outputs. In Figure 13.6 we see the Summary Output from *Crouch*, which summarizes how much of the text of ModIntell171#2 is matchable to WPostWood171. It shows that a very large proportion of the text matches in some way.

Analysis on Matched Items in the Suggested Derived Text

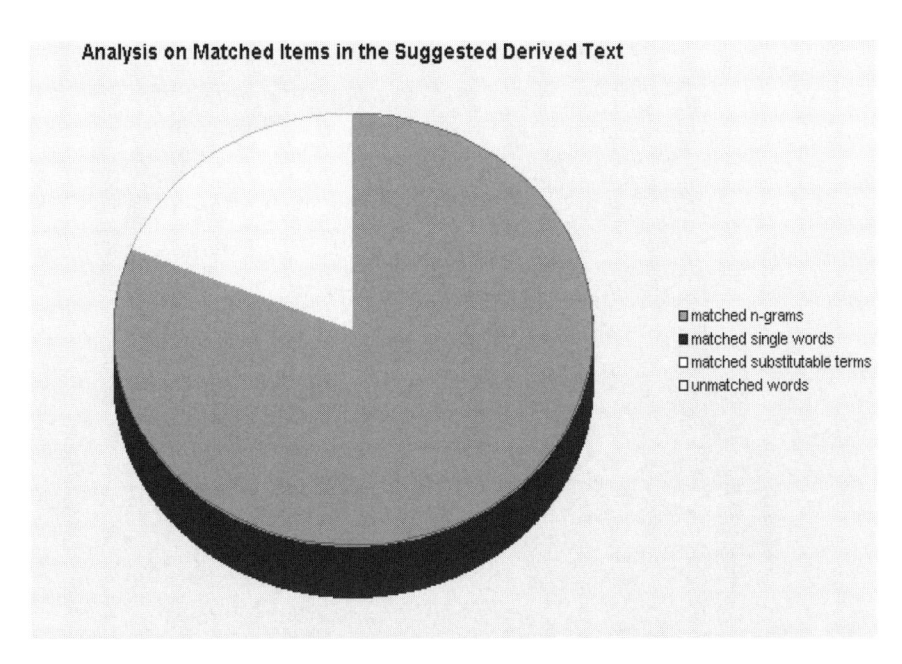

- matched n-grams
- matched single words
- matched substitutable terms
- unmatched words

Figure 13.6   Crouch Summary Report for ModIntell171#2 as Candidate Derived Text, WPostWood171 as Candidate Source Text

Another important output is the Weighted Score graph. This presents the likelihood of each sentence in the candidate derived text corresponding to some part of the candidate source text. The X-axis of the graph represents the sequence of sentences in the candidate derived text. So the Weighted Score graph for the comparison we are dealing with (shown as Figure 13.7) shows that the initial sentences of ModIntell171#2 do not correspond to anything in WPostWood171 but that in the middle of the text there are a very large block of sentences which are either completely or almost completely matched in WPostWood171. Finally, ModIntell171#2 ends in another set of sentences that cannot be matched.

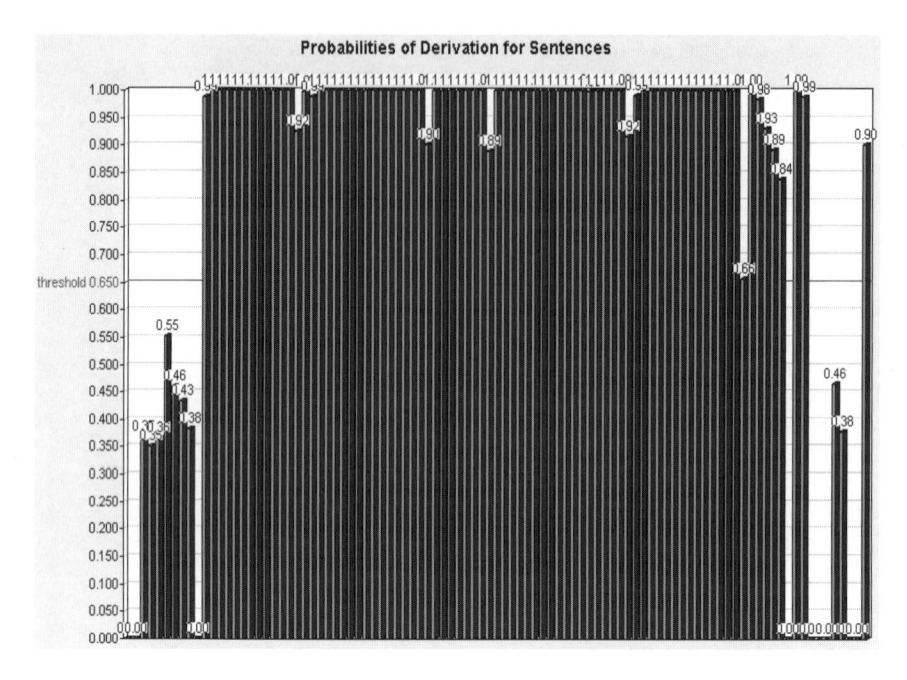

Figure 13.7   Crouch Weighted Score for ModIntell171#2 as Candidate Derived Text, WPostWood171 as Candidate Source Text (overall score: 0.188)

While this display gives us a reasonable idea of the distribution of the reused text, it is also useful to manually examine the matches, to see whether they are valid; the *Crouch* output called Alignment Table, a sample of which is shown in Figure 13.8, allows us to do this. It is clear that, in the case of the sample of sentences shown, the text is far too similar for the alignment to be the result of chance and we have indeed observed a genuine instance of text reuse.

Historical Text Mining and Corpus-Based Approaches 271

Similarity Scores	Suggested Derived Sentence(s)	Suggested Source Sentence(s)
PSD=1.0 PS=0.766 PSNG=1.0 WS=0.988	Taxes and Oppressures and 11) to his Highnesse the Lord Protector, professing much affection to his Highnesse and the late change of Government.	40) A Petition Congratulatory hath been presented from the Town of Newcastle to his Highnesse the Lord Protector, professing much affection to his Highnesse and the
PSD=1.0 PS=1.0 PSNG=1.0 WS=1.0	12) From Scotland our Post is inform'd that Middleton hath summoned in all the Gentlemen of Sutherland and Ross, and prohibited the sheriffs to act any more in the name of the Lord	41) From Scotland our Post is inform'd that Middleton hath summoned in all the Gentlemen of Sutherland and Ross, and prohibited the sheriffs to act any more in the name of the
PSD=1.0 PS=1.0 PSNG=1.0 WS=1.0	13) He brought over above 60 Officers, the least of them a Captain; there is since another Vessel landed in Caithness with more arms and	42) He brought over above 60 Officers, the least of them a Captain; there is since another Vessel landed in Caithness with more arms and

Figure 13.8 Crouch Alignment Table for ModIntell171#2 as Candidate Derived Text, WPostWood171 as Candidate Source Text

One of the interesting things that can be ascertained from the Alignment Table is that, while all the stories in the middle part of ModIntell171#2 are derived from WPostWood171, they do not appear in the same order in the two texts. The final important *Crouch* output, the Text Output, is a copy of the original text marked up with sentence tags as follows:

```
<s n="12" corresp="41" score="1.0"> From Scotland our Post
is inform'd that Middleton hath summoned in all the Gentlemen of Sutherland
and Ross, and prohibited the sheriffs to act any more in the name of the Lord
Protector, saying he will give them a new commission to act by.</s>
```

This indicates that sentence # 12 of ModIntell171#2 has been aligned to sentence # 41 of WPostWood171 (which is shown in an adjacent window). A manual analysis of this output produces the text analysis shown in Table 13.6.

Table 13.6 Sentence-by-Sentence Breakdown of Correspondences between ModIntell171#2 and WPostWood171

Section of ModIntell171#2	Content	Corresponding section of WPostWood171
S1 to S10	Opening boilerplate, summary, news from French court	None
S11 to S17	Middleton and the war in Scotland	S40 to S46
S18 to S22	Dutch Freebooters	S39, S35 to S38
S23 to S25	French Ambassadors; Queen of Sweden	S32 to S34 (out of order)
S26 to S47	Prizes taken by English frigates	S10 to S31
S48 to S58	The war in Scotland; French pirates; Poland/Muscovy; Diet at Regensburg	S50 to S60
S59 to S64	Cromwell bans cock–fighting	S85 to S90
S65 to S66	News relating to Ireland, Sweden	S83 to S84
S67	War in France	S80
S68 to S70	English navy	S77 to S79
S71 to S81	Letter from the Hague	S61 to S71
S82 to S86	Treaty with Netherlands; Charles Stuart; the war in Scotland; storm in the Thames; Portuguese Ambassador's riotous party	S71 to S74 and S76 (but in the inverse order)
S87	The war in Scotland	None
S88 to S89	Naval conflict with the Dutch	S8 to S9
S90 to S96	Treaty with Netherlands; other miscellaneous news from Europe and the sea	None
S97	End boilerplate	S91

A close study of Table 13.6 demonstrates why the probability of derivation is greater when ModIntell171#2 is treated as the candidate derived text: whereas nearly all the text of WPostWood171, with the exception of its opening boilerplate, is found in ModIntell171#2, the converse is not true—there is one substantial block (S90 to S96) which is unique to ModIntell171#2. Interestingly, that section begins as follows, with direct reference to other publications (regularized spellings are shown):

> <p> Though I had not the happiness to lead the Van, give me leave to bring up the Rear, and though I have been anticipated in this Intelligence, yet good news cannot be unpleasing in the Reiteration; the precedent Mercurians

have all certified you that the Articles are fully concluded and firm peace agreed upon between England, Holland, and Denmark, which yet goes for current; but if it be heralded, and not speedily confirmed by the supreme Authority of both Commonwealths, I will never believe we shall have peace till I hear it proclaimed at the Crosse.</p>

It is this news, which the author explicitly says he is late in reporting, which has been added to the text copied from WPostWood171—the latter Newsbook concluded with the account of Cromwell's order banning cock-fighting.

The Context of the Minimal Scoring Pair

Why does this pair of Newsbooks give the lowest score of any comparison in the corpus? A careful inspection of the metadata for the two documents suggests an explanation. First, it should be noted that both were printed by Robert Wood (as indicated in the opening boilerplate of each text) but that the series to which they belong (or purport to belong) were both more usually printed by George Horton. Furthermore, both had the same issue number as, and appeared simultaneously with, numbers of the same titles printed by Horton (see 11.7). In his description of London news publications in this period, Frank describes Horton as Wood's "sometime rival, sometime collaborator."[22] A concordance search for the two men's names in the corpus indicates that both the *Moderate Intelligencer* and the *Weekly Post*,[23] along with a third title, the *Faithful Scout*, were printed by both Wood and Horton in different issues during the span of time covered by the Newsbooks Corpus—according to Frank, all three were in probability actually written/edited by Daniel Border. However, it is only on the 4/5 April 1654 that this competition and/or collaboration over the *Moderate Intelligencer* and the *Weekly Post* resulted in four Newsbooks—one of each title from each printer—appearing near-simultaneously, as shown in Table 13.7.[24]

---

[22] Frank, pp. 247–9.

[23] The *Weekly Post* went through several name changes; after being *Great Britain's Post* and the *Grand Politique Post*, *Weekly Post* is the name it eventually settled on later in April 1654.

[24] The system for labelling documents in the corpus may cause some confusion here. WPost171 and WPostWood171 are labelled as issues of separate series, whereas ModIntell171 and ModIntell171#2 are labelled as separate issues of the same series (albeit with the same issue number). This inconsistency arises because variant issues by different printers were only labelled as different series in the catalogue of the corpus when there was a noticeable difference in the page-one header. Wood successfully simulated Horton's layout of the *Moderate Intelligencer*, but (due to a variant spelling) not that of the *Weekly Post*.

Table 13.7   Extract from Corpus Metadata

Label	Published	Attribution
WPost171	4 April 1654	George Horton
WPostWood171	4 April 1654	Robert Wood
ModIntell171	5 April 1654	George Horton
ModIntell171#2	5 April 1654	Robert Wood

We may note that Wood and Horton's production of the *Moderate Intelligencer* and *Weekly Post* is responsible for some of the other very small minimal scores in the corpus. For example, the smallest minimal score after the ModIntell171#2/WPostWood171 comparison is 0.199: it is found for the comparison of WPost168/ModIntell168 (both published by Horton on the 14 and 15 March respectively). Rather than look at earlier or later pairs of periodicals, however, we will remain with the ModIntell171#2/WPostWood171 pair and attempt to get a broader picture of how it relates to other Newsbooks published at the same time—both Horton's alternative versions, and the other documents published that week.

Frank describes ModIntell171#2 as a counterfeit;[25] but what the text reuse analysis makes clear is that its similarity was to a closely contemporaneous text also printed by Wood, not the text by Horton that (according to Frank) it counterfeits. In fact, we find it hard to accept this as a straightforward case of counterfeiting, since this incident came at the end of a period when Horton and Wood had been printing alternate issues of the third title they shared/competed over, *The Faithful Scout* (by late April, they settled on it being published with the attribution "printed by Robert Wood, for G. Horton"); they also went on to alternate their publication of the *Moderate Intelligencer* and *Weekly Post*. The precise motivations of the two printers are probably not now recoverable in full, although amusingly, both Horton's and Wood's versions of issue 171 of the *Weekly Post* carry the attribution, "Printed by [name of printer]; to prevent all false copies."

However, we must ask, if Wood's two publications within this two-day period produce the most closely-similar pair of documents in the corpus, what of Horton's two parallel publications, namely ModIntell171 and WPost171? The similarity matrix for all four documents (extracted from the overall similarity matrix) is shown in Table 13.8.

---

[25] Frank, p. 249.

Table 13.8   Matrix for Wood and Horton's Newsbooks of 4 and 5 April 1654

	WPost171	WPostWood171	ModIntell171	ModIntell171#2
WPost171	0	0.961	0.414	0.964
WPostWood171	0.967	0	0.908	0.222
ModIntell171	0.364	0.872	0	0.884
ModIntell171#2	0.97	0.188	0.893	0

Apart from the very high similarity of the two Newsbooks published by Wood— already commented on extensively—two points are of note here. First is that there is also a high degree of similarity between the two Horton publications—the score of 0.364 corresponds to a very high level of overlapping text, as shown in Figure 13.9, although not as high as that observed above between the two Wood publications.

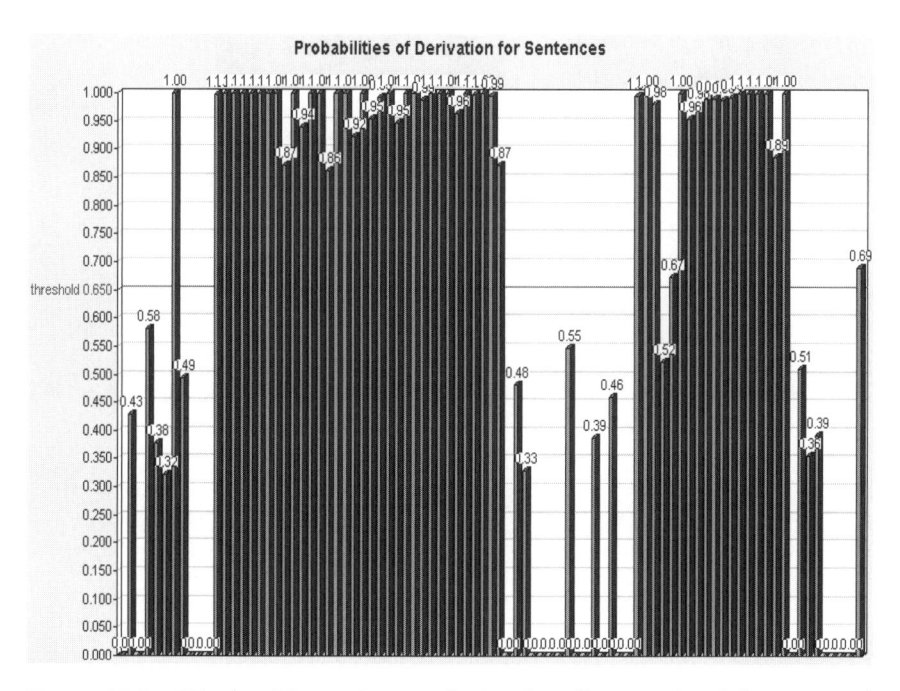

Figure 13.9   Weighted Score Output for ModIntell171 as Candidate Derived Text, WPost171 as Candidate Source Text (overall Score: 0.364)

The second point of interest is that there is much less similarity between the Wood titles and the simultaneous Horton titles. For example, ModIntell171 only scores 0.872 compared to WPostWood171. The weighted score output of this comparison is given in Figure 13.10; examination of the alignment table shows that the similarities here consist of: some identical items in a list of naval prizes; identical wording of the *verbatim* quotation of Cromwell's decree banning cock-fighting; and two identical news items from Scotland, suggesting a shared newsletter as the source—although note that even in this case there are substantial differences. As the differences are illustrative, they are quoted in full.

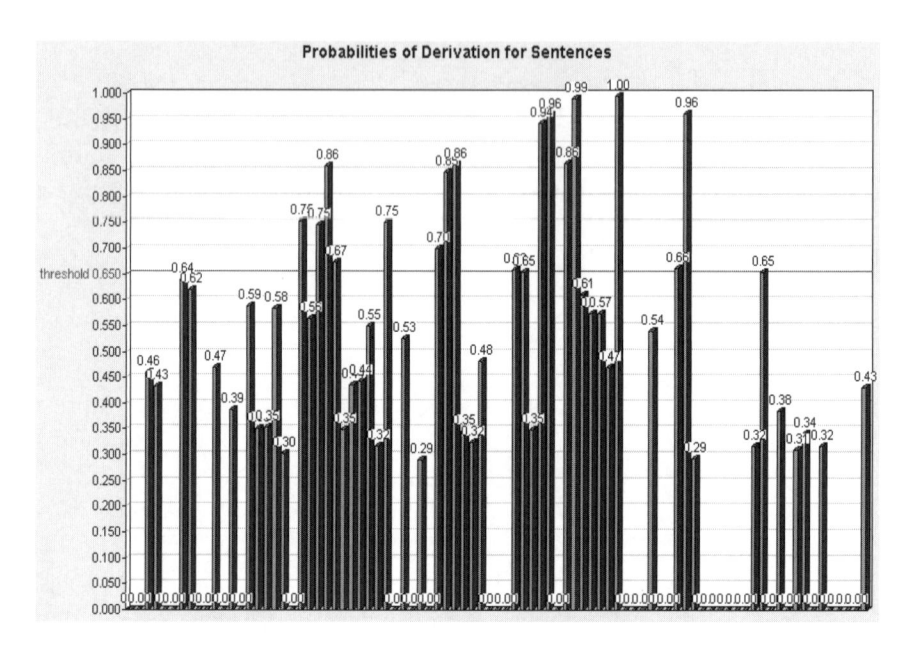

Figure 13.10 Weighted Score Output for ModIntell171 as Candidate Derived Text, WPostWood171 as Candidate Source Text (overall score: 0.872)

From WPostWood171 (printed by Wood):

<s n="50"> From Scotland our Post received intelligence, That the Commander in chief having issued forth a Proclamation requiring all Burgesses and others to secure all suspicious persons, or otherwise to give intelligence of them to the next adjacent Garrison or Quarters under pain of being deemed Enemies to the present government, and proceeded against accordingly: Several towns have been lately found guilty of the breach of that Proclamation, and have been fined by a Court-Marshal for the same.</s>
<s n="51"> The last week the Parish of Liberton, two miles from Edenburgh for harbouring 15 of the Enemy by the space of a night and a day, and neither

securing them, nor giving intelligence of them, and the Tories at their going away stealing 15 horses, the Parish was for that offence fined 200 l. sterling, the person in whose house they were concealed, sentenced to imprisonment during pleasure, and the house where they were harboured to be raced to the ground, and a pair of Gallowes to be built there.</s>

<s n="52"> There are divers other Parishes who are summoned in to Court Marshals upon the very same account, who will suffer for it.</s>

<s n="53"> It is hoped this course will in time compell the Scots not to give any Entertainment unto the Tories, but give notice of them where ever they shall come, otherwise they will suffer for it.</s>

<s n="54"> The 21 instant Col. Cooper with a party of Horse and Dragoons from Glascow and another party at the same time falling into the Isle of Leven, where about 300 of the enemy quartered (about 4 in the morning) took Mac-Naughtons Trumpet, and 35 other prisoners, and narrowly missed Mac-Naughton and Newark, who were both there; they killed 12, whereof one of them (as the enemy confess) was a Lieutenant of Horse, and took about 60 Horse and some Armes and totally scattered and routed the whole party, returning without any loss at.</s> [Followed by one further story]

From Scotland from ModIntell171 (printed by Horton):

<s n="65" corresp="50 51" score="0.661"> From Edenborough our Post bringeth intelligence, That the Commander in chief hath issued forth a Proclamation, requiring all Burroughs and Parishes to secure all suspitious persons, and enemies to this Common-wealth Several Towns have been found guilty of the breach hereof, the persons confined, and their houses level'd with the ground, and a pair of Gallows erected in the same place.</s>

<s n="66" corresp="54" score="0.962"> The 21 instant Col. Cooper with a party of Horse and Dragoons from Glascow, and another party at the same time falling into the Isle of Leven, where about 300 of the enemy quartered (about 4 in the morning) took Mac-Naughtons Trumpet, and 35 other prisoners, but Col. Newark escaped.</s>

<s n="67" corresp="0" score="0"> In this Conflict many a stout Spirit saluted the ground, and the whole part was totally routed, with very little.</s>

The spelling variations have been preserved here as they are illustrative: see, for instance, *suspitious* vs. *suspicious*. Clearly there is no word-for-word reproduction here. In fact, overall it is clear that the text has not here been reused in the very strict sense that was observed when comparing the two Wood texts to one another, or the two Horton texts to one another. Rather, the reuse appears to be two different, possibly rather free adaptations of a common source, with the adaptation in ModIntell171, published a day later, being the more abbreviated one. Checking the other documents, ModIntell171#2 contains the same account as WPostWood171, although it opens with "From Scotland we have received intelligence"; and WPost171 follows ModIntell171 although this part of the text in WPost171 is actually damaged so that the first half of the opening paragraph could only be partially transcribed.

The differences between the two versions appear to be at least partially ideological in motivation as well as motivated by length. Note in particular the contrast between "they killed 12, whereof one of them (as the enemy confess) was a Lieutenant of Horse" and "[i]n this Conflict many a stout Spirit saluted the ground." To put this in context, let us consider how this incident is reported by other Newsbooks. A simple concordance search for the word "Cooper" suffices to determine that a total of seven other Newsbooks refer to this encounter on 21 March 1654. This constitutes every Newsbook published in the week beginning Monday 3 April, except the final issue of the short-lived *Mercurius Aulicus* (which, since it followed up most stories with lengthy comment in verse, could presumably therefore print correspondingly less news than other publications). All eleven, except for *Mercurius Politicus* begin their accounts with the words "Col. Cooper with a party of Horse and Dragoons," suggesting a common source newsletter right across the board; in *Politicus*, the account is much abbreviated, but shows signs of being derived from the same correspondent in Scotland, whose letter *Politicus* labels as coming from Dalkeith on 25 March. Table 13.9 lists all eleven documents, each together with its author (according to Frank 1961), its publication date, and the section of text referring to the death of Cooper's foes.

The most common phrasings are two essentially minor variants, differing only in capitalization and spelling, one used by Pecke, Walker, and B.D. (and presumably copied from Pecke's *Perfect Diurnal*, which was first to print: there is no reason to think that these editor-journalists shared a printer), and the other used by Border-printed-by-Wood. *Politicus* gives an abbreviation of one of these two, or—perhaps more likely—of their common source. The *Weekly Intelligencer* has a rephrasing unique to itself but not different in substance from the former Newsbooks. It is only the Newsbooks printed by Horton which contain the potentially ideologically motivated variant, which stands out even more clearly against this general background than it does against the background of the Border-printed-by-Wood titles alone.

Let us assume that the four variants other than Horton's between them give us a reasonably close picture of the wording of the original letter from Scotland. If so, Horton's phrasing represents a deliberate deviation from the source material that demands an explanation. We might posit a number of such explanations.

Table 13.9 Variation in the Discussion of Scottish Deaths in the Battle against Cooper

Text label	Author	Published	Description of deaths of Cooper's foes
PerfDiurn225	Pecke	Mon 3 April	They killed 12, whereof one **of them** (as the **Enemy confesse**) was a Lieutenant of Horse …
WIntell325	Collings	Tue 4 April	They killed 12 **of the enemy**, one **of them** [gap] was a Lieutenant of Horse
WPost171	Border (Horton)	Tue 4 April	**In this Conflict many a stout Spirit saluted the ground** …
WPostWood171	Border (Wood)	Tue 4 April	they killed 12, whereof one **of them** (as the **e**nemy confess) was a Lieutenant of Horse …
ModIntell171	Border (Horton)	Wed 5 April	**In this Conflict many a stout Spirit saluted the ground** …
ModIntell171#2	Border (Wood)	Wed 5 April	they killed 12, whereof one **of them** (as the **e**nemy confess) was a Lieutenant of Horse …
PerfAcc169	'B.D.'	Wed 5 April	They killed 12, whereof one **of them** (as the **e**nemy **confesse**) was a Lieutenant of Horse
MPol199	Nedham	Thur 6 April	killed 12, whereof one (as the ene**mies** confess) was a Lieutenant of horse …
ProcState236	Walker	Thur 6 April	They killed 12 whereof one **of them** (as the **e**nemy **confesse**) was a Lieutenant of Horse …
FScout173	Border (Wood)	Fri 7 April	they killed 12, whereof one **of them** (as the **e**nemy confess) was a Lieutenant of Horse …
EveryDayIntell$12	Walker	Fri 7 April	They killed 12, whereof one **of them** (as the **e**nemy **confesse**) was a Lieutenant of Horse …

Firstly, it might be irony. Secondly, it might be a genuine expression of royalist sympathy. If so it would be hard to ascribe this with certainty to Border, since Border-printed-by-Wood does not have this version. It might be ascribable to

Horton (Frank notes that Border was a "hired hand" for his publishers[26]). Horton is described by Frank as an "energetic" publisher,[27] one who was apparently new to news publication in the early 1650s, and one who frequently innovated with the use of illustrations and large-text proto-headlines. No mention is made of royalist sympathies on his part, although a more detailed investigation of Horton's output might throw light on this point. If this variant cannot be attributed to Horton then we must reconsider the attribution of editorship of the Horton, Wood Newsbooks. Border was not necessarily the editor of every single issue of all the titles ascribed to him by sources such as Frank and the EEBO catalogue, and a period when Horton and Wood were putting out multiple publications that clashed with one another is perhaps the *least* likely time for Border to be writing all the news published by both printers.

Another indication that traditional authorship summaries miss crucial details is the somewhat mysterious case of the editor-journalist known only as B.D. Frank speculates[28] that this attribution is a reference to Border (initials: D.B.); but ultimately argues that there are differences in the character of their output and considers them separate individuals, describing B.D. as "Border's former rival and partner."[29] On the other hand, the EEBO catalogue attributes all B.D.'s work to Border. However, the publisher of the *Perfect Account* and B.D.'s earlier *Perfect Weekly Account* was neither Wood nor Horton but one Bernard Alsop. Certainly, PerfAcc169 shows, in the analysis above, no especial similarity with either Wood or Horton's titles. So the attribution of the *Perfect Account* to Border is also dubious on the basis of this analysis. Obviously a wider range of data would be needed to make an overall judgment on this point.

One final question is the relation of these texts to the third Border/Horton/Wood title, which as mentioned above was *The Faithful Scout*. The immediately preceding issue of this was FScoutHorton171 (published by Horton on 31 March 1654), and the immediately following issue is FScout173 (published by Wood on 7 April 1654). Tables 13.10 and 13.11 list all the scores below 0.9 achieved when FScoutHorton171 is the candidate *source* text (Table 13.10) and when FScout173 is the candidate *derived* text (Table 13.11); the scores for the inverse pairings are given as [I = …] and are similar in all cases.

---

[26] Frank, p. 248.
[27] Frank, pp. 235, 240.
[28] Frank, p. 128.
[29] Frank, p. 215.

Table 13.10 Scores < 0.9 from the Matrix Column for FScoutHorton171

Text label as candidate *derived* text	Published	Compared to FScoutHorton171 (31.3.1654) as candidate *source* text
WPost170	28.3.1654	0.689 [I = 0.731] [S = 24/88]
WPost171	4.4.1654	0.342 [I = 0.366] [S = 49/88]
ModIntell171	5.4.1654	0.645 [I = 0.682] [S = 36/88]

Table 13.11 Scores < 0.9 from the Matrix Column for FScout173

Text label as candidate *source* text	Published	Compared to FScout173 (7.4.1654) as candidate *derived* text
PerfDiurn225	3.4.1654	0.855 [I = 0.923]
WIntell325	4.4.1654	0.879 [I = 0.87]
WPostWood171	4.4.1654	0.785 [I = 0.836]
EveryDayIntell$12	5.4.1654	0.804 [I = 0.763]
ModIntell171#2	5.4.1654	0.698 [I = 0.758]
PerfAcc169	5.4.1654	0.846 [I = 0.828]
ProcState236	6.4.1654	0.488 [I = 0.769]

All three texts to which FScoutHorton171 bears any especially marked similarity were also printed by Horton. Using *Crouch*, a rough count has been made of how many sentences (out of the total in FScoutHorton171) are replicated. This is given as the [S = ...] measure; it is a much less precise measure than the probability score, but gives a more easily conceptualized illustration of how extensive the overlap is. By contrast, the overlap between WPost170 and WPost171 is minimal: the pair scores 0.928 and 0.937 depending on which is the candidate source. How is this to be interpreted? We have already seen that the overlap between WPost171 and ModIntell171 is very great (see Table 13.8). So the overall picture that emerges is that the text of the Newsbooks of

Border-printed-by-Horton gradually changes over the week, so that his Friday title, the *Faithful Scout*, overlaps about half of the text of both the preceding and following issues of his Tuesday title, the *Weekly Post*; but successive issues of his Tuesday title do not overlap with each another at all; in this particular week, when Horton publishes both the *Weekly Post* (Tuesday) and the *Moderate Intelligencer* (Wednesday), they overlap extremely prominently; and finally there is rather less overlap in Horton's titles with text from other printers.

Table 13.11 shows a rather different picture for Wood's *Faithful Scout* of the following Friday 7 April. There is, as with the Horton titles, a moderately strong relationship to Wood's version of the Tuesday and Wednesday titles (WPostWood171 and ModIntell171#2, which have already been discussed at length). However, there is also a strong overlap with titles not printed by Wood. Indeed, the strongest relationship is with ProcState236, which is not a Wood publication.

Let us consider why this link should be so strong. Firstly, ProcState236 was published immediately prior to FScout173, so the temporal overlap is very great. Secondly, both texts include the letter from Scotland that describes *inter alia* Cooper's victory, in closely parallel form. Thirdly, both give in full the text of two of Cromwell's decrees, which other Newsbooks do not do (it is for this reason that in Table 13.11, no [S = ...] values are given, as sentences in *verbatim* decrees are frequently much longer than other sentences). Most importantly, the length of ProcState236 (*Proceedings of State Affairs* was 16 pages long, whereas the *Faithful Scout* was eight pages) simply means that it is more likely to contain the things that the editor of FScout173 happened to select for publication—which is, incidentally, why the inverse score is much higher.

These four reasons do not constitute reason to ignore the link, however. After all, MPol199 was also published on 6 April 1654 and was also 16 pages long—but the scores for the comparisons of MPol199 and FScout173 are both above 0.9. The link to ProcState236 is real: perusal of the material would suggest that both were based on common sources—since close examination shows that the decrees from Cromwell are identical but other shared stories have some variation of phrasing, capitalization, or spelling, as shown in the penultimate two rows of Table 13.9 for the story of Cooper's victory.

In fact, the match between Tables 13.9 and 13.11 is generally remarkable. The Newsbooks that share, more or less, "Border"-printed-by-Wood's description of the deaths of Cooper's foes are *also* the Newsbooks that score less than 0.9 when compared with FScout173. The strong similarity score of FScout173 to the other seven texts cannot be accounted for solely by the similarity of this one report. A close examination shows that other reports are in common as well—though there are in some cases substantial elements of variation in presentation. For example, PerfAcc169 and FScout173 overlap in the letter from Scotland already discussed, but also in stories on Henry Cromwell, the *Sapphire* frigate, the *Newcastle* frigate, and the Highlanders, leading to an overall score in the range 0.8–0.9; but PerfAcc169 contains many instances of editorializing on news that other publications present straightforwardly (of which space unfortunately does not permit the quotation of any examples). So in short, FScout173 repeats *verbatim* text from other titles printed by Wood, and the text of Cromwell's decrees; but stories from other sources often, albeit not always, vary in presentation.

The hypothesis which we might formulate on the back of this evidence is that when a given pair of Newsbooks start to correspond closely, they are liable to continue doing so—as noted, and as the examples in Table 13.5 show, multiple overlaps are necessary to explain these scores. This in turn might suggest that at some stages, at least, what is being copied is actual published Newsbooks—as suggested by Frank (1961: 241)—rather than common source documents, although the latter clearly happens as well, as with Cromwell's decrees and some newsletters.

What can be concluded from this extensive analysis of the first week of April 1654? Firstly, we may conclude that the printer-publisher of a text may be as important for variation in text reuse as the editor-journalist. Whereas Horton's titles do not overlap strongly with any Newsbooks but his own in this week, Wood's titles overlap with several titles from other printers, albeit more loosely than with his own titles. Of course further investigation would be needed to see if this is a generalizable pattern over time. Word-for-word text reuse appears to be most common across different Newsbooks published by the same printer—whereas, assuming the traditional view that Border did indeed write/edit the text for both Wood and Horton, he *did not* reuse his text for Wood in his Horton Newsbooks. What Frank calls a "counterfeit" *Weekly Post* created by Wood, which produces the strongest similarity score in the corpus, did not replicate text from the Newsbook it was counterfeiting, but rather replicated text used elsewhere by the same printer. This is, on reflection, not surprising: indeed, we may easily suppose that a counterfeit *could not* reuse text from its target publication, since the counterfeit's target would not have been published when the counterfeit was being typeset. Finally, subtle variations of case, phrasing, and spelling can be used to track patterns of variation across different titles—or lack thereof, in the case of printings of Cromwell's decrees.

Conclusion

The aim of this analysis was to use *Crouch* to assess the extent of text reuse in the Lancaster Newsbooks Corpus collection of documents from late 1653/early 1654. The macro-level answer to this question is that most documents have moderate overlap (say, at least three or four substantial, very similar, or identical stories) with at least one other document in the corpus; rather few have very extensive overlap; and similarly, rather few appear to be independent with no reused text. Also at the macro-level, we have found that text reuse measurements group certain series of periodical together (for example *Proceedings of State Affairs*, *Mercurius Politicus*, and the *Perfect Diurnal*).

What the micro-analysis contributes to this assessment is the repeated demonstration that low scores in a *Crouch* matrix really do represent lots of reused text (scores of less than about 0.8 indicating multiple, substantial overlapping stories): this was true in every individual comparison we looked at in depth. Again at the macro-level, this means that every document in the corpus probably overlaps extensively with, on average, six to seven other documents.

Some points which emerged at the macro-level were underlined and cast in sharper relief by the micro-level analysis. For example, the macro-analysis showed a strong relationship between the *Weekly Post* and the *Faithful Scout*, but it was the micro-analysis which brought out the subtleties of what this might mean in terms of text being reused among and between Horton's texts and Wood's texts.

At the micro-level, we were also able to illuminate the text reuse practices of individual printers. For instance, both Horton and Wood's Newsbooks in the first week of April 1654 reuse text from other titles produced by the same printer in identical or near-identical form, but unlike Horton, Wood's titles also reuse, in very similar form, text from other printers' publications. The practices of other printers—and of other editor-journalists—remain to be examined. But we were very easily able to identify an example of text reuse across virtually all the Newsbooks published in the first week of April 1654, and to find within that example both potentially ideologically motivated variation and also the more subtle variations of case, phrasing, and spelling that can be used to track patterns of text transmission. This suggests that examples appropriate for examining the practice of other editor-journalists and printer-publishers will be straightforward to acquire using *Crouch* and the techniques outlined in this chapter.

As noted, we also sought wherever possible to relate the findings of the text reuse analysis to claims made by Frank on the basis of his own extensive reading of the Newsbooks. This has been achieved; in some cases we were able to confirm Frank, and put his claims on a quantitative footing (for example, the macro-analysis substantiated Frank's assertion that the *Perfect Account* was a prolific reuser of other Newsbooks' text, but we were able to go further and say which titles its editor borrowed most from). In some areas (for example, Border's authorship of Horton and Wood's titles in the week examined, or the status of ModIntell171#2 as a counterfeit) it has been possible to use the outputs from *Crouch* to problematize Frank's views.

But the most notable novelty of this study has been the ability to use corpus searches to find and quickly compare, in the example case of Cooper's victory, the same story across 11 Newsbooks, identifying both minor typographic or phraseological variation and significant differences that are potentially ideologically motivated. The usefulness of *Crouch* for our original purpose— namely the identification of ideologically motivated variation in the manner of reporting of a given news event—has clearly been substantiated.

It should be noted that the incident of Cooper's force killing twelve Scots (one of them, as they confessed, a Lieutenant of Horse) was not known to us before we commenced the investigation that has been outlined here. Indeed, we know no more of the incident now than has been presented in the foregoing account. The incident was not selected for whatever historical significance (if any) it may have. Our attention was directed to it purely because:

a. it is referred to in the most strongly-matching pair of Newsbooks in the corpus and
b. on further investigation it was observed that its presentation varied in a complex way across the eleven documents that mentioned it.

In a like manner, it was purely quantitative considerations that led us to considering the relation between Wood, Horton and Border and their (collective?) stable of Newsbook titles: this was not a planned part of the analysis either. It is one of the strengths of the methods that this study has employed that they are capable of leading researchers to things that they didn't know in advance were interesting.

What this study has not accomplished is an assessment of the relative proportions in the corpus of ideologically interesting variations in reused text, as opposed to differences of phrasing/spelling only, as opposed to absolutely *verbatim* reuse. This is something which cannot be quantified at the macro-level, but only via micro-level analysis of many, many document pairs to identify dozens or hundreds of stories that recur across many documents. These relative proportions would, furthermore, be difficult to quantify on the basis of any sample of the corpus or of the alignments within it, since the corpus is not sufficiently variegated for us to trust in the representativeness of even a random sample. Thus this particular issue has been, thus far, too prohibitively labor-intensive to address: it is work for the future. But undertaking this effort will allow further insights to emerge from the study of text reuse: in particular in how news from sources from different parts of the world is processed and presented, how this varies, and what this can tell us about how the Newsbooks conceive of events in (successively) London, England, Britain, Europe, and the world as their sphere of contemporaneity.

The existence of this corpus opens up other avenues of future research as well. Of course, the corpus is not perfect, primarily due to the limited time that could be invested in its creation (which for the collection of 1654 Newsbooks was on the order of a thousand person-hours for the typing alone). In particular, there are typing errors and, occasionally, lines left un-transcribed due to poor legibility of the original; and some preliminary investigation of the transcribers' spelling regularization has shown that it is patchy with regards to proper names of people and places unfamiliar to the transcribers, such as "Uppsala" or General "Monck." Some of the irregularities are interesting in themselves—for example, the use of *Hamborough* for *Hamburg* and similar examples may well say something interesting about how foreign and local spaces are conceptualized by the journalists and readers of these Newsbooks. Further investigation would be required here.

However, even a corpus resource which falls far short of the perfectionist ideal can still produce useful results, as exemplified by the analysis presented here, because the quantitative nature of many corpus results mean that individual errors in the corpus construction are drowned out by any strong overall trends. This is the case for the alignment algorithm used by *Crouch*, and by the same principle we could easily use a quantitative keyword or key concept analysis (see Baker for an overview[30]) as a means of investigating ideological stances, preoccupations, and biases of the editor-journalists of different sections of the corpus. A step in a similar direction has already been taken by Prentice and Hardie,[31] who use a partially-quantitative analysis of concordance data from this corpus to investigate the discourses (in the sense of Critical Discourse Analysis[32]) surrounding the Earl of Glencairn and other figures associated with the Glencairn Uprising.

The primary point which we would emphasize from the foregoing analysis is that applying corpus-building and corpus-analytic techniques to the Newsbooks of the Thomason Tracts provides us with new options in the exploitation of this key resource for the history of journalism. Our hope in making the data widely accessible is that others will use the Lancaster Newsbooks Corpus for purposes we have probably not even thought of ourselves, and will thus extend this new field of research at the intersection of historical inquiry and the methodologies of corpus-based and computational linguistics.

---

[30] Paul Baker, *Using corpora in discourse analysis* (London, 2006), pp. 121–49.
[31] Sheryl Prentice and Andrew Hardie (*forthcoming*), "Empowerment and Disempowerment in the Glencairn Uprising: a corpus-based critical analysis of Early Modern English news discourse."
[32] See Teun van Dijk, *Racism and the press* (London, 1991).

Epilogue

If the terms "globalization" or "knowledge society" have any real meaning as characterizations of our world, surely the reporting of foreign news and the flow of information concerning international affairs must be regarded as key components. No wonder Jürgen Wilke pointed out already in the 1980s that "no subject in communication research in recent years has stimulated greater interest on a world-wide level."[1] And what was true for the news media of modern times, according to Wilke, held equally for that of the past, although social scientists sometimes forget that the characterizations of our world derive from a world that existed before. Can we responsibly utilize the term "globalization," for instance, without a full knowledge of the emergence of the means of communication when the world became one place? Indeed, Wilke added, "as is the case with many other questions in which communication research is interested, no study has been made up to now of the long-term, historical dimension of foreign news coverage and international news flow." Since he wrote these words, much has happened to illuminate international news flows in the earliest days of printed journalism, as we have seen in this book.

Wilke's conclusion, on the basis of the first quantitative studies of this problem, was that international news flow increased immensely across the three centuries covered by his study, so that, at least in the German case, foreign news far outweighed German news already by 1674. The preponderance of foreign news in the earliest journalism was hardly surprising, since to a certain degree the earliest journalism emerged precisely in order to convey information about matters that were not commonly known by the usual word-of-mouth sources in the public streets and squares. In spite of the increasing importance of local news, which some scholars have attributed to the inward-looking preoccupations characteristic of incipient nationalism, foreign news remained a long-term staple. What changed significantly over time was the scope and origin of this foreign news. In the earliest periods rather strict "regionalism" was the rule—in other words, the coverage available in a particular place tended to focus on contiguous places, or the contiguous region. German papers expressed curiosity about France, England, Holland, Italy, to a lesser extent, Spain. Focus might also be on places "functionally" contiguous—so that German news focused more on areas to the east, west and south than on areas to the north. The Scandinavian region tended

---

[1] Jürgen Wilke, "Foreign news coverage and international news flow over three centuries," *International Communication Gazette* 1987: 39, 147.

to remain rather marginal—and the same went for areas beyond the Habsburg empire: for instance, Russia. However, the Ottoman empire was "functionally" contiguous to many European countries because of Ottoman activity in the Mediterranean and expansion on the continent. Only, between the Ottoman area and Europe, news coverage mainly went one way. Reciprocity: that is giving two places equal coverage in each of news about the other, thus hardly existed between the Ottoman area and Europe. Reciprocity was nonetheless the rule between the countries of Europe.

Even today, we are far from living in a thoroughly "connected" world. The "digital divide" between those who have access to modern communications and those who do not, may indeed be narrowing; but there are few signs that it will disappear any time soon.[2] Where the "digital divide" is most deeply felt, censorship of standard media is still able to silence the spread of knowledge. Elsewhere, as soon as new methods of communication are developed, new methods of censorship emerge (with the strange complicity of Western businesses), for instance in China, to prevent their free and unfettered use.[3] Because of education, literacy, and available media, people living in the industrialized countries are inevitably better informed than others. On the other hand, information in the industrialized countries where there is no official censorship may be selective too; and the selection applies not only to the kinds of stories, but to the places whence the stories come. For instance, news coverage of almost anything happening in Africa is sporadic. A recent survey of US newscasts between 2002 and 2004 had this to say: "The results indicate that despite the fact that African nations faced many newsworthy events such as controversial elections in Zambia and Zimbabwe, an ethnic cleansing campaign in the Sudan, wide-scale famine in the West African nations of Mali, Mauritania, Cape Verde, Gambia and Senegal, a widespread AIDS epidemic in sub-Saharan Africa and numerous civil wars, American television newscasts do not view the African continent to be newsworthy."[4] That the "functionally" contiguous (to the US) continents of Europe and Asia, major trading partners with strong cultural ties to the US, should receive more coverage, can hardly be surprising.

Coverage alone, of course, is not enough; nor, for that matter, is contemporaneity. Even supposing that news coverage of the developing world

---

[2] Ming-te Lu, "Digital divide in developing countries," *Journal of Global Information Technology Management*, 4, no. 3 (2001), pp. 1–4; also note Deborah Carr, "The Global Digital Divide," in *Contexts*, vol. 6, no. 3 (2007), p. 58.

[3] Clive Thompson, "Google's China Problem (and China's Google Problem)," *New York Times Magazine*, 23 April 2006.

[4] Guy J. Golan, "Where in the World Is Africa?: Predicting Coverage of Africa by US Television Networks," *International Communication Gazette* 70 (2008), p. 53.

and especially Africa were to become greater, what might be the consequence? Would this significantly alter the world distribution of power and resources? Would lives be improved? When does information lead to remedial action? The question cannot be answered on the basis of the historical data alone. We have seen cases where information about events in one place inspired action in another—take, for instance, the circulation of news concerning the revolt of Palermo in 1647, which encouraged what could in part be designated as a copy-cat phenomenon in Naples. Other cases abound; and in order to be convinced that news inspires action one only has to look at the English Civil War.[5] However, the concept of contemporaneity only refers to the sharing of information, and about the sharing of some sentiments. It says nothing about how information is internalized and incorporated into patterns of behavior.

Information may also accompany indifference to human suffering. Not simply because the aestheticization of violence may turn attention away from what violence does, as in Giovanni de' Medici's comment about the routing of the enemy from the field before Ostend: "a thing well worth seeing, as it was carried out with such elegance and regularity that it seemed to be painted."[6] A simple statement "1000 died and 4000 were wounded" supplies enough to the imagination concerning a brutal event. Data of this sort, repeated day by day, week by week, year by year, must give some idea of the realities of war. Now, a surfeit of words and images describing the pain of others may not necessarily inure us to suffering; but as Susan Sontag points out, it also does not necessarily inspire action to alleviate suffering. Indeed, it may reinforce our sense of helplessness, or even give us an impression of having fulfilled our duties as global citizens merely by paying attention.

The instruments of communication are only one, albeit an important one, among the several structures born and developed during the early modern period that have built the modern way of life. Their history reminds us that the structures themselves do not make a world—their content does, and more importantly, what individuals do with that content. In our own age, we have seen the emergence of highly advanced technologies for producing, conveying and storing information of every type; and yet, achieving a more responsible use of knowledge still seems as elusive a goal as that of achieving a just world.

---

[5] Joad Raymond, *The Invention of the Newspaper: English Newsbooks 1641–1649* (Oxford, 2005).

[6] ASF, MdP, filza 5157, f. 120r, 27 May 1604, Giovanni to Ferdinando: "Arrivato così con S. A. alla piattaforma dalla sommità di essa si vedde la ritirata fatta dall'inimico, la quale certo è cosa degna di esser vista essendo fatta con tanta pulitezza, et tanto ben finita che par dipinta."

Index

A Perfect Account of the Daily Intelligence 248, 254
Acapulco 47
Acconzaicco, Hieronimo 177
Acuña, Josepe de 31, 32
Adreß-haus in Berlin 217
Advertiser 212, 213, 214, 218, 219, 220, 222
Africa 288
agents 30, 35, 36, 41, 42, 49
Ágoston, Gábor 155
Alba, duke of 90
Albert, archduke of Austria 104, 107, 111, 112, 104, 193, 195, 196
Alcazar, Cayetano 25, 27
Aleppo 142
Alessandria 30
Alexandria in Egypt 5, 52, 142, 145
alignment 257, 258, 259, 262, 269, 270, 271, 272, 275, 276, 286
Allen, John B. 37
Almási, Gábor 168, 169
Alonso, Gascón de 12, 23
Alsop, Bernard 280
Alvar Ezquerra, Alfredo 34, 35
America, 42
Amsterdam 17, 26, 53, 59, 119, 140, 143, 182, 194, 198, 200, 202, 203, 229, 235
Anatolia 46
Andaman 44
Anderson, Benedict 2, 208
András, Dudith 168
Andreas, Georgius 168
Angelelli, Paolo 56, 59
Angerville 29
Anjou, Philippe duc d', *see* Philip V 181

Anne of Austria 185
Antwerp 13, 18, 28, 29, 53, 100, 102, 104, 108–13, 171–4, 193–205, 235
Aragón, 24, 30
Arblaster, Paul 1, 18, 193, 195, 196
archives 83, 85, 93–4
Arditi, Bastiano 88, 92, 93
Ares, J.M. de Bernardo 39
Aresi, Lucio 58
Arias Roca, Victoria 95
Ascandoni, Jaime 25
Ashkenazi, Nathan 147, 139
Assarino, Luca 58
Assonitis, Alessio 16, 138
astrology 90
Augsburg 30, 71, 172, 176
Avignon 26
avvisi 84, 86, 158, 159, 164, 165, 171, 172, 174, 175, 176, 177

Bächtold, Hans Ulrich 170
Bacon, Antony 54
Bacon, Francis 17, 54, 207, 208
Badajoz 46
Baetens, Roland 199
Baghdad 142
Baillie, Laureen 120
Baker, Paul 286
Balbano de León, Mateo 32
Bálint, Ilia 167
Barbari, Jacopo de' 7
Barbarics-Hermanik, Zsuzsa 17, 51, 159, 163, 167, 169, 176, 177
Barbiche, Bernard 91
Barcelona 26, 29, 31
Barducci, Roberto 52

Baron, Sabrina Alcorn 1, 2, 137, 138, 230, 234, 195
Baroncelli, Cosimo 105, 108, 110, 113
Barth, Gerda 73
Basadonna, Pietro 59
Bastl, Beatrix 168, 172
Batiffol, Louis 93
Baumann, Michael 170
Baumanns, Markus 129, 132, 133, 134
Bavaria, elector of 127
Bayona, 29
Behringer, Wolfgang 138, 160, 201, 217
Belgrade 142
Bell, Allan 225, 228, 236, 239, 240
Bellocchi, Ugo 10
Bender, Klaus 72
Bensheimer, Jan 147
Benz, Josef 168
Benzing, Josef 122
Berecz, Mátyás 155
Berger, Peter L. 208
Berkvens-Stevelinck, Christiane 1
Berlin 71, 74, 217, 233
Berniero, Giovanni Battista 175
Bethencourt, Francisco 51, 156, 157, 159
Bethlehemsdorf, Georg Thurzo von 163
Beyrer, Klaus 128
Beza, Theodore 172
Bild Zeitung 239
Blindow, Ulrich 163
Blois 27
Blome, Astrid 17, 209, 221, 213, 214
Blotius, Hugo 160, 161, 162, 166, 167, 168, 169, 171, 176, 177
Bluche, François 116, 119
Blühm, Elger 75, 77, 121, 122, 149, 155
Bogel, Else 74, 75, 121, 122, 149
Bohemia 13, 74, 77, 239
Boileau Despreaux, Nicolas 119
Bologna 11, 30, 168
Bongart, captain 130
Bongi, Salvatore 157

Böning, Holger 1, 69, 74, 137, 151
Bonn 130, 132
Bordeaux 202
Border, Daniel 264, 273, 279, 280, 282, 283, 285
Borreguero Beltrán, Cristina 15, 23
Boullion, cardinal of (Emmanuel-Théodose de La Tour d'Auvergne) 128
Boumans, René 198
Bourbon 124, 126
Bourgogne, duke of (Louis, Dauphin of France) 191
Boyd, Andrew 226
Brabant 204, 205
Bradley, Susan 116
Brandenburg 232
Brathwait, Richard 239
Braubach, Max 115, 125, 132, 133
Braudel, Fernand 3, 5, 158, 159
Brazil 13, 200
Bremen 74
Brixen 30
Brownlees, Nicholas 18, 229, 236
Bruges 29, 52, 100, 104, 195
Brulez, Wilfrid 199, 200
Brunn, Gerhard 209
Brunot, Ferdinand 179, 181
Brunswick, prince of 56
Brusoni, Girolamo 57
Brussels 18, 25–30, 32, 104–6, 111–12, 119, 165, 176, 193–205
Buck, August 117
Buda 142
Buisseret, David 7
Bull, golden 196
Bullinger, Heinrich 161, 163, 165, 166, 167, 169, 170, 172, 173, 175, 176, 177, 178
Bullinger-Zeitungen 160–62
Bünger, Fritz 5
Buonsignori, Stefano 95
Burdeos 29

Bureau d'adresse, 212, 213, 216, 217 *see also* Office of Intelligence
Burger, Thomas 78
Burgos 27, 28
Burgundy 30
Burgundy, house of 24
Burkart, Roland 208
Burke, Peter 9, 117, 166, 188
Burkhardt, Johannes 164
Bužek, Vaclav 159

Cadiz 47
Cairo 142
California 47
Cambrai 29
Caneva, Caterina 90
Cantagalli, Roberto 88
Canterbury 29
Capefigue, Jean-Baptiste Honoré Raymond 91
Cappello, Bianca 84
Caracena 205
Carmona, Michel 91
Carolus, Johann 69–82
Carr, Deborah 288
Casteleyn, Abraham 149
Castets 29
Castile 25
Catalonia 24, 30
Cateau–Cambrésis, 29
Cattarini Léger, Elena 91
Cauwenberge, G. van 201
Cecconi, Elisabetta, 242
censorship 230, 237, 244
Certaine Informations 246
Chambery 30
Chamillart, Michel 186
Chantonnay, Thomas Perrenot de 37
Chappell, Miles 91
Charles IV, emperor 196
Charles II, archduke of Inner Austria 171
Charles V, 24, 25, 26, 47, 195, 198
Charles VI, emperor, and archduke of Austria 181
Chartier, Roger 116, 119, 156
Chaworth, George 196
Chiavenna 173, 175
Chmel, Joseph 157, 168
Christ, georg 52
Church, Kenneth W. 257
Cicero 204
Ciliano, Michaelo 177
Cisneros, Antonio de 42
Civil War (England), 225, 228, 244, 246–8
Claridge, Claudia 252
Clarisse, Louis 199
Clemente VIII 105
Clercq, Leo de 201
Clough, Paul 257
Coenen, Thomas 147
Colbert, Jean Baptiste 117
Colletet, François 181
Cologne 13, 53, 55, 71, 72, 129–34, 169, 173, 174, 197, 200–203
Colonna, cardinal Marcantonio 86
Comenius, Johann Amos 77
Comensky, Jan 77
communication infrastructure 208ff
Concino, Giovan Battista 89
Condé, Armand de Bourbon-Conti, prince of 205
Constantinople 5, 11, 32, 46, 140, 142, 150
consumers of news 138–9, 142–4, 146–52
Continuation of our Forreigne Newes, The 243
Continuation of the Affaires of the Low-Countries, and the Palatinate 242
Continuation of the Former Newes, The 243
Cooper, colonel 282, 285
Cope, sir Walter 210
Coppens, Maarten 201–3
coranto 225, 229–44, 249–50
Corfu 174
corpus (linguistics) 251, 252, 253, 262, 285, 286

correspondence networks 141–4, 150, 152
Cosimo I, duke of Tuscany, 83, 90, 95, 96, 97
Costa, Julián de 44
Costo, Tommaso 60, 61
couriers 32, 37, 38, 40, 45, 46, 87–90
court 23–5, 27–31, 33–9, 41–5, 49
Coventry, sir Henry 121
Cromwell, Oliver 256, 282, 283
Cruz, Jorge Antonio de la 45
Curiel, Jerónimo de 42
Cuvelier, Joseph 203

D'Arco, conte Prospero 174
Dahl, Folke 229
Daily Courant, The 238
Dallmeier, Martin 128
Danti, Ignazio 95
Dantziger Ordinari Zeitung 147
Dantziger Ordinari Zeitung 147
Danzig 146, 150, 203
Daston, Lorraine 152
Datini, Francesco 51
Degryse, Karel 200
Dei, Benedetto 52
Delfino, cardinal Zaccaria 86
Delft 202
Delgado, Juan 40
Della Rovere, Francesco Maria II 88
Delorme, Philippe 91
Denia 35
Depezay, Charles-Henri 17, 179
Deuchrie, J. Graham of 253
Deursen, Arie Th. van 125
Deutsche Presseforschung (Bremen) 137
Diarium, 219
Diaz, Furio 83
Diet of Regensburg, 187
Dietz, Alexander 220
digital divide, 288
Dijk, Teun A. van 225, 227, 229, 239, 286
Dilbaum, 73
Doering-Manteuffel, Sabine 221

Dolfin, Biagio 52
Dolfin, cardinal Giovanni 65
Donà, Pietro 58
Donegal, 27
Dooley, Brendan 1, 2, 8, 138, 137, 156, 159, 163, 195, 230, 234
Dornberg, Balthasar 174
Dornberg, Veit von 174
Dover 29, 101, 201
Drake, sir Francis 35, 98, 100, 101, 104, 103, 158
Dresden 217
Dresler, Adolf 157, 165
Drury, John 17
Dubreuil, Jean Tronchin 18
Duchhardt, Heinz 124–5
Duerloo, Luc 199
Dülmen, Richard van 211
Dumschat, Sabine 148
Dunkirk 29, 100, 101, 195, 201
Duranton, Henri 187
Dury, John 207, 208, 219, 221
Dutch 13
Dutch War 124, 129, 131

East Indies 46
Ebben, Maurits Alexander 199
Eccles, Mark 240
Effingham, Charles, lord Howard of 103, 104, 237
Egli, Tobias 172
Egmond, Florike 51, 156, 157, 159
Elizabeth I, queen of England 103, 105
employment 211, 213, 214, 217, 218
Engelsing Rolf 155
England 7, 124, 181, 183, 190, 202
English 13
English Civil War, *see* Civil War (England)
Enkemann, Jürgen 119
Erasmus, Desiderius 167
Eraso, Antonio de 36
Ernuszt, Johanna von 168, 171

Escorial, San Lorenzo del 34
Essen, Leon van der 97
Etényi, Nóra G. 171
Ettinghausen, Henry 1, 138
Evans, Florence M. Grier 120, 121
Everaert, John 200
Every Day's Intelligence 264, 265
Exclusion crisis 124

Fairclough, Norman 225
Faithful Scout, The 254, 264, 274, 282, 284
Farnese, Alessandro, duke of Parma 29, 30, 32, 37, 38, 98, 99, 97, 100, 101
Faulstich, Werner 117
Feez, Susan 225, 227, 228, 247
Felsecker, Eberhard 121, 122, 123
Ferdinand I, emperor 169
Ferdinand Charles, duke of Mantua and Montferrat 58
Ferdinand IV, emperor 13
Fernández Bayo, Juan Ignacio 38, 27
Ferreira, Godofredo 46
Feuille du Bureau d'adresse 118, 212
Feyel, Gilles 67, 179, 182, 183, 210, 211, 212
Finot, Jules 199
Fiorani, Francesca 95
Fischer, Andreas 236
Fitzler, Mathilde Auguste Hedwig 71, 157, 168, 172, 173, 174, 177
Flanders, *see* Low Countries
Flomarino, Ascanio, cardinal 9
Florence 26, 30, 83–94
Florio, John 54
Fohrmann, Jürgen 164
Ford, Caroline 151
Fortescue, George Knottesford 253
fortifications 107
Foscarini, Antonio 65
Fox, Adam 8
France, 5, 24, 115, 202
Franche-comté 30
Francis I, king of France 26

François, Etienne 117
Frank, Joseph 244, 252, 263, 265, 274, 280, 283, 284
Frankfurt 53, 71, 74, 123, 140, 220
Frankfurter Frag- und Anzeigungs-Nachrichten 220
Fraser, Peter 119, 120, 121
Frearson, Michael Colin 240
Frederick William i, king of Prussia, 217
Fredericq, Sigismund 168
Fronde, the 185
Frugoni, Francesco Fulvio 66
Fuchs, Martina 167
Fuchs, Ralf-Peter 209
Fuenterabbía, 28
Fugger, family 176
Fugger, Oktavian secundus 167, 169, 177
Fugger, Philipp Eduard 161, 167, 168, 169, 171, 172, 174, 177
Fuggerzeitungen 157, 159, 160, 162, 166, 171, 174
Funck-Brentano, Frantz 159
Fürstenberg, Wilhelms von 17, 129, 130, 131, 132, 133, 135, 181

Gaden, Daniel von 148
Gainsford, Thomas 229, 240–44
Gaizauskas, Robert 257
Galatowski (Galiatovs'kyi), Ioannikii 146
Galatowski, Ioannikii 146
Gale, William A. 257
Galluzzi, Jacopo Riguccio 92
Garay Unibaso, Francisco 48
Garrett, Peter 225
Gaza 142
Gazette d'Amsterdam 17, 180–85, 188, 189, 190, 191
Gazette de Leyde 18, 180, 182, 184, 185, 188, 189, 191
Gazette of Paris 1, 115, 117, 128, 129, 131–3, 179, 183, 185, 187, 190, 191, 210

gazettes (handwritten) *see also* handwritten newsletters 51, 54–67, 77
gazettes (printed) *see also* individual titles 77, 115, 133
Gelderen, Martin van 97
Gelpke, Clara 217
Genoa 14, 26, 29, 30, 46
Geppert, Alexander C.T. 209
Germany xiv, 1, 5, 53, 199, 202, 233
Ghent 29, 111–12, 195
Gibraltar 35
Gier, Helmut 163
Giesecke, Michael 156
Gilles de la Tourette 118
Giraffi, Alessandro 8
Giuliani, Benedetto 59
Gloucester, duke of 205
Goa 43, 46
Golan, Guy J. 288
Goldfriedrich, Johann 123
Goldthwaite, Richard A. 51
Gómez de Santillán 36
Gorges, Arthur 210
Govea, Manuel de 39
Grana, duke of 130, 133
Granada 27
Granvelle, Antoine Perrenot de, cardinal 172
Grasshoff, Richard 157, 165
Gravesend 29
Graziani, Françoise 91
Greenwich 29
Gregory XIII, pope 5
Grimmelshausen, Hans Jakob Christoffel von 122
Groof, Bart de 97
Gross, Lothar 177
Groth, Otto 157, 165
Grotius, Hugo 188
Gryse, Piet de 201

Haarlem 150
Habermas, Jürgen 8, 78, 180, 186

Habsburg emperors 167, 168, 169, 170, 176
Habsburg family 124, 126, 156, 198
Habsburg, Albrecht von 112
Haeghsche Post-Tydingen 149
Haeghsche Post-Tydingen 149
Haerlemse Courant, 152
Haffemayer, Stéphane 186
Haffemayer, Stéphane 211
Hagner, Michael 211
Hague, The 202
Halberstadt 217
Halle 217
Hamburg Wochentliche Zeitung 149
Hamburg 7, 13, 71, 75, 96, 143, 144, 200, 202, 203
Handover, Phyllis M. 121
handwritten newsletters 155, 156, 157, 158, 159, 160, 161, 162, 163, 164, 165, 166, 167, 168, 169,
Hardie, Andrew 18, 251, 286
Harline, Craig 156
Harms, Wolfgang 137, 156
Harris, Bob 1, 121
Härter, Karl 219
Hartlib, Samuel 207, 215, 219, 221
Hartnack, Daniel 2, 77
Hatin, Eugène 116, 118
Hausmann, Guido 148
Hayez, Jérome 51
headline 225–9, 233, 236, 241, 245–7, 249
Hegel, Georg Wilhelm Friedrich 2
Heinscheidt, Anton 220
Hemels, Joan 203
Hemmeon, Joseph Clarence 120
Henday, 29
Henry IV, king of France 64, 90, 92, 112
Henry VIII, king of England 98
Herald, The 228
Heyde, Hendrik Jacobsz van der 203
Hirsch, Kaspar 176
Holland 115, 203
Holland, Abraham 230

Honacker, Karin van 204, 205
Honacker, Karin van 204
Honselaar, Wim, 152
Horn, Ildikó 171
Horton, George 264, 273–5, 277–85
Hörwart, Marx 177
Hottinger, Johann 140, 143
Hottinger, Johann 140, 143
Houben, Birgit 204
Huguenots 189, 217
Hungary 169
Hunter, Paul 2
hybridism 178

ideology 251, 252, 263, 278, 279, 284, 285
Idiáquez, Francisco de 32
Idiáquez, Juan de 33
Iedema, Rick 225, 227, 228, 247
imaginary news 139–40, 144–7, 150–52
India 42
Infelise, Mario 2, 16, 51, 58, 159
Innsbruck 25, 27, 30
Intelligenzwesen 215, 216, 221
Interregnum 225
Ireland 101
Irsigler, Franz 209
Irún 28
Isabella, Infanta of Spain (Isabel Clara Eugenia) 111–12, 194–6
Isacker, Karel van 201
Italy 5, 25, 26, 29, 31, 32, 33, 34

James II of England VI of Scotland 103, 181, 183, 190
James I 195, 210
Jan III Sobieski, king of Poland 125, 126
Janota, Johannes 163
Jensen, Uffa 209
Jerusalem 142
Jesuits 46
Jewish communities, Jews 139–42, 146–7, 151–2, 199, 218

Joad Raymond 1, 229, 244, 252, 289
Jobin, Thobias 70
Jöchner, Cornelia 209
Johanna of Austria, grand duchess 83, 84, 85, 88, 90, 92
John II Casimir, polish king 147
John, Alfred 196
Jonisch, Gottfried 144
Jonson, Ben 234
Jordan, Claude 18, 182, 184, 187, 188–91
Jovane, Enrico 10
Jubert, Gérard 216
Jucker, Andreas H. 225

Kamen, Henry 26
Kapp, Friedrich 123
Kauffmann, Georg 117
Kelbitsch, Friedrich 171
Kempter, Kaspar 157, 173
Kenderessy, István 174
Kermina, Françoise 91
Kern, Stephen 3
Khmelnits'kyi uprising, 147
Kinsale, battle of 6
Kintz, George 69
Kitchin, George 120
Klaits, Joseph 117, 119
Klarwill, Viktor 157
Kleinpaul, Johannes 157, 159
Knoblauch, Hubert 211
Kolster, Brigitte 75
Koopmans, Joop w. 196
Koßmann, Gilles 118
Kral, Pavel 159
Krasser, Jeremias 177
Kretschmann, Carsten 211
Kurpfalz, elector of 176
Kutsch, Arnulf 1, 69, 74–6

L'vov (Lemberg), 142
La Font, Jean-Alexandre de 184, 189, 191
Labrosse, Claude 116

Lancellotti, Secondo 58
Landolfi, Domenica 97
Landwehr, Achim 209
Lankhorst, Otto 1
Lavergne, Gabriel-Joseph de, comte de Guilleragues, 119
Lavisse, Ernest 117, 125
Lawrence, Frederick 78
Le Mayre, Marten 193
lead, 225–9, 236, 242, 246–9
Lefèvre, Joseph 203
Lehmann, Hans Martin 236
Leibniz, Gottfried Wilhelm 215, 216, 218, 219, 221
Leipzig 75, 123
Lengyel, Tünde 171
Lentulus, Scipio 173, 175, 177
Leopold I, emperor 181
Lesperon 29
Leti, Gregorio 67
Lettres persanes 190
Leuzzi, Maria Fubini 84
Levis, Helga 75
Liège, 202
Lindemann, Margot 158
Linden, James van der 201
Liner, Mans 175
Lionne, Hughes de 182
Lisbon, 36, 201
Lisola, Francis Paul baron of 131
Liszthi, János 171
Livorno, 142, 150
Lloyd News 214
Lnchay, Hnri 203
Lobkowitz, prince 56
London 5, 7, 11, 15, 29, 38, 55, 59, 105, 115, 119–21, 143, 145, 198, 201–3, 210, 213, 230–31, 251, 253, 273, 285
London Gazette, The 115, 120, 121, 125, 126, 127, 129, 131, 132, 134, 134, 135
London Intelligencer, The 202

López Gallo, Juan 42
Lorraine, charles V duke of 125–6
Louis de France, Dauphin 128
Louis XIII, 113
Louis XIV 17, 117, 128, 131, 179, 180, 186, 188, 189, 191
Louthan, Howard 169, 170, 171
Louvois, François-Michel le Tellier, Marquis de 182
Low Countries 5, 24, 26, 29, 30, 31, 34, 42, 16, 53, 104
Lu, Ming-te 288
Lucangelo, Nicolo 177
Lucar, San 35
Luckmann, Thomas 208
Luxemburg, 109
Lyon, 26, 27, 30

MacPherson, Harriet Dorothea 117
Madrid 35, 36
Magedeburg 217
Maier, Ingrid 141, 146, 148, 152
Majia, Agustin 105
Malacca 44
Malettke, Klaus 117
Malta 14, 32
Mančal, Josef 163, 221
Mandrou, Robert 117
Manila 47
Mantua 30, 60, 140
manuscript news 137–42, 145, 147–8, 150–52
Marie Thérèse of France, queen 128
Marino, John 9
Marma, Margaret of 30, 31
Marranos 200
Martelli, Camilla 84
Martin, Henri-Jean 116–19
Martinengo 56
Martínez Ruiz, Enrique 25
Masaniello 9
Mather, Increase 140

Mathesy, Stephan 176
Matthieu, Jean-Baptiste de 92
Mauelshagen, Franz 168
Maximilian Heinrich of Bavaria, 56
Maximilian II, emperor 83, 169, 176
Maximilian of Poland 33
Mazarin, cardinal 185
McCarthy, Justin 161
McElligott, Jason 230
McEnery, Tony 18, 251, 253, 257, 258
McKenna, Antony 187
McLuhan, Marshall 79
Mecatti, Giuseppe Maria 92
Medici, Alessandro de' 86, 88
Medici, Anna de' 85
Medici, Cosimo I de' 93, 98
Medici, Don Giovanni de' 16, 96, 98, 99, 100, 101, 105–14
Medici, Eleonora de' 85
Medici, Ferdinando I de' 86, 92, 98, 100, 101, 105, 108, 114
Medici, Filippo de' 93
Medici, Francesco I de' 83, 85, 86, 87, 89, 92, 98
Medici, Isabella de' 85
Medici, Lucrezia de' 85, 90
Medici, Maria de' 16, 83, 87, 89
Medici, Romola de' 85
Medina Sidonia, duke of 100–102
Meijer, Jaap 141
Mejia, Agustin 105
Melgarejo, Juan 48
Melis, Federigo 158
Mello, Martín Alonso de 45
Melun 30
Melzi, Lodovico 108, 109, 113
Mencsik, Ferdinand 168, 171
Mendle, Michael 1
Mendoza, Bernardo de 32, 103
Menéndez, Diego de 48
Meneses Vello, Fernando 44
Meneses, Duarte 43, 45, 48

Mercurius Britanicus 245, 246, 247
Mercurius Politicus 278
Mercurius Aulicus 246, 247
Mercurius Civicus 213, 245
Mercurius Fumigosus 253
Mercurius Librarius 213
Mercurius Poeticus 254, 262, 263, 284
Merlin, Hélène 185
Messerli, Alfred 156
Messina revolt, 124
methods, 1
Meurrens, Marc 202
Meyer, Ingrid 18
Milan 26, 30, 62
Millen, Ronald 93
millenarianism (chiliasm) 144–6, 148, 151–2
Miller, John 120
Minden 5
Minummi, Antonio 60
Miranda de ebro 28
Miranda del Castañarmiranda, Juan de Zúñiga y Avellaneda, count of 32, 33, 36
Mirandola, duke of 56
Miscellanea Scotica 253
Mitelli, Giuseppe 3, 8
Modena 30
Moderate Intelligencer, The 254, 64, 273, 274, 282
modernity (modernization) 138–9, 151–2
Montaigne, Michel de 210, 221
Montanus, Fabricius 172
Monte, Juan de 38
Montesquieu, Charles de Secondat, baron de 190
Montoya, Phiippe 29
Montpellier 26
Morales, Francisco Javier de Carlos 42
More Newes from Europe 241
Morel, Bernadino 31
Morgan, Hiram 6

Morgues, Mathieu de 92
Morosini, Alvise 52, 99
Moscow 141, 150
Moureau, François 187
Mozambique 44
Muddiman, Joseph George 120
Mueller, Reinhold C. 51
Mulay Hassan 195
Müller, Arnd 123
Muscovite Russia 141, 146–9, 151
Muscovy, emperor of 33
Musi, Aurelio 9

Nadasdino, Tomas 163
Nádasdy, Tamás 161, 162, 165, 167, 169, 175, 176, 178
Nádasdy-Zeitungen 160, 161, 166
Namur 30
Nancy 64
Naples 9, 25, 26, 27, 30
Narbonne 26
narrative 240
Navarre 30
Navascués Palacio 39
Nedham, Marchamont 213
Nelson, Carolyn 213
network 23, 24, 26, 27, 29, 34, 42, 45, 49
Neuhoffer, Theodor 157
Nevitt, Marcus 234
Newburg, John William duke of 125
Newes and Affaires of Europe, The 237
Newes From Most Parts of Christendome 242
newsbooks 225, 240, 244–8, 250, 254
newsletter writers 99, 104, 106, 162, 164, 165, 166, 167, 174, 175, 177, 178
Nice 32
Nieuwpoort 195
Nîmes, 26
North, Michael 5
Nouvelles ordinaires 115, 118, 126, 127, 128
Numan, Philip 197
Nuremberg 17, 122, 128, 176

O'Donnell, Hugh 42
Offenberg, Adri K. 145
Office of Intelligence 207ff
Ogg, David 120
Oldenburg, Henry 215
olivares, count of 32
Oparina, Tatyana A. 148, 151
Oprechte Haerlemse Courant 142, 145, 148, 149, 150
Oprechte Haerlemse Courant 141–2, 145, 148–9, 152
oral transmission of news 138–9, 147
Ordinari Dienstags Zeitung 149
ordinary post 28, 29, 30, 31, 33, 36, 41, 44
Orkney Islands 8
Orleans 29
Ormus 44
Ostend 29, 97, 103–11, 195, 289
Ott, David 173
Ött, Hans Georg 174, 177
Ott, Jeremias and Christoph 173
Ottoman Empire 124, 139–42, 144–5, 148, 155, 167, 169, 170, 174
Overvoorde, Jacobus Cornelis 202, 203
Ovieto, Paolo 52
Oxford Gazette 115

Pálffy, Géza 171
Paller, Matthäus 176
Papal States, 183
Paris 7, 10, 13, 17, 26–32, 37, 53, 55, 63–5, 115–16, 181, 183–4, 191, 197–8, 201–3, 210–12, 216–17
Park, Katharine 152
Parker, Geoffrey 39, 49, 97, 199
Parma 30
Pauser, Josef 168
pawn phop 211, 217
Peacey, Jason 244
Pecke, Samuel 278
Pérez Bustamante, Ciriaco 30
Pérez de Guzmán, Alonso 98

Pérez de Herrera, Cristóbal 34
Pérez, Antonio 33
Perfect Account 265, 280, 284
Perfect Diurnal 254, 262, 263, 265, 278, 284
Perfect Weekly Account 280
Perger, Johann Georg 128
Persia, king of 46
Persico, Panfilo 60
Petercsák, Tivadar 155
Peuter, Roger de 197
Philip II 15, 23, 24, 25, 27, 30, 31, 33, 36, 37, 38, 39, 41, 42, 43, 44, 45, 46, 47, 49, 84, 105, 195
Philip III 45
Philip IV 202
Philip V 191
Philip V 181
Philippines 47
Phillips, Martin 260
Piacenza 30
Piao, Scott Songlin 18, 251, 257, 258
Picchena, Curzio 105
Pieper, Renate 51, 158
Pieraccini, Gaetano 92, 97
Pilger, Wouter 141, 146, 152
pilgrimage 85, 90
Pirożińska, Czesława 158
Pirożiński, Jan 158
Pisa 26
Pius V, 83, 84, 89
Place of Knowledge 211, 215, 219
Plomer, Henry R. 121
Poitiers 29
Poland 141, 146–8
Pölnitz, Götz, freiherr von 167
Polo, Baltasar 35
Popkin, Jeremy 116
Portugal 13
Pory, John 202
postal networks 148
postal service 24, 25, 26, 27, 28, 29, 30, 34, 36, 37, 39, 41, 44

Powell, William S. 202
Prague 63, 126, 140
pranks 88
pregnancy 83–90
Prentice, Sheryl 286
Proceedings of State Affairs 254, 262, 263, 265, 282, 284
Prosperi, Adriano 158
Protestants 199
Prussia 5
Pubens, Peter Paul 93
Publick Adviser 213
Puerto Rico 48
Pym, Anthony 193

Quorli, Filippo 55
Quorli, Giovanni 57–9, 60, 61, 62

Racine, Jean 119
Ragusa 174
Rainaldo III d'Este, duke of Modena 60
Rauschenbach, Sina 211
Raymond, Joad 234
Reggio 30
Reinhauser, 30
Relations véritables 204
Renaudot, Eusèbe 179, 181, 186, 187, 188, 190, 191
Renaudot, Théophraste 17, 66, 116, 118, 119, 186, 210, 211, 213, 214, 216
rentería 28
reportage 226, 227, 231–3, 236–7, 239–44, 246–7, 250
Rétat, Pierre 116, 182, 184
Rhete, David Friedrich 146, 147, 150
Rhete, David Friedrich 146–8, 150
Richelieu, Armand Jean du Plessis, cardinal de 116, 210
Ridder, Paul de 197
Robinson, Henry 213
Roche, Daniel 117
Rochester 29

Roelants, Jan-Baptist 201
Rogers, Everett M. 213
Roloff, Hans-Gert 158
Roma, Pompeo 177
Romana, Julio Felipe 49
Rome 25, 26, 27, 30, 32
Römer, Claudia 170
Roos, Hans 125
Rosen, Mark S. 95
Rossi, Bernardino 174
Rovito, Pier Luigi 9
Rowland, Daniel B. 151
Rudolf II, emperor 167, 169
Rühl, Edith 177
rumor 87–8, 93
Rustemeyer, Angela 148

Sabbatai Sevi (Shabbatai Zevi), Jewish pseudo-messiah 18, 137, 139–52
San Clemente, Guillén de 33, 34
Sandl, Marcus 209
Santa Sruz, Don Alvaro de Bazán marquis of 97, 98
Sardella, Pierre 5, 158
Sarego, 56
Sasportas, Jacob 143
Sasportas, Jacob 143–4, 150
Savoy, duchy of 10
Scala, Ercole 60
Scala, Ettore 60
Schepper, Hugo de 204
Schieder, Thomas 125
Schiffle, Jeremias 177
Schilling, Lothar 219
Schilling, Michael 137, 158
Schneider, Gary 237
Schneider, Maarten 203
Schöffer, Ivo 125
Scholem, Gershom 139–47, 151
Schottenloher, Karl 157
Schrauf, Karl 214
Schröder, Thomas 1, 156, 157, 219

Schröder, Wilhelm von 215, 216
Schultheiß-Heinz, Sonja 119, 120, 122, 123, 124, 126, 127, 128, 129
Schumacher, Winfried 141, 144, 146
Schumann, Jutta 137
Schwendi, Johann Wilhelm 171
Scotish Dove 246
Scudamore, John 202
Seccombe, Matthew 213
Senn, Matthias 168
separates (broadsides, pamphlets) 137, 140–41, 144–8, 151
Serbelloni, family 56
Serrarius, Petrus 143
Serrarius, Petrus 143–4, 145–6
Seville 35, 47, 201
Sgard, Jean 1, 116, 118, 119, 120, 184
Shamin, Stepan M. 147, 151
Sherman, Stuart 234
Shrewsbury, earl of 237
Sicily, 14, 30, 46
siege of Ostend 105
Siemund, Rainer 252
Siena 26, 30
Sieveking, Paul 120
Simoni, Anna E.C. 104
Sittig, Wolfgang 169
Sittingbourne 29
Smyrna 142, 150
Soeffner, Hans-Georg 211
Sola Castaño, Emilio 23
Solinas, Francesco 90
Solomon, Howard M. 113, 118, 211
Sommerville, C. John 1, 252
Sommi Picenardi, G. 97
Sontag, Susan 289
Sotillo, José de 40
Spahr, Blake Lee 117
Spain 23–50, 139, 158, 181, 188, 191, 195, 200–202, 241, 288
spelling variation 256, 258, 259, 277, 278, 282, 286

Spinelli, Riccardo 91
Spinola, Ambrogio 106
Spooner, Frank C. 159
Sporhan-Krempel, Lore 71, 165, 122
St. Gallen 175
Staple of News, The 234
Steinhausen, Georg 157
Stepney, William 193
Stieler, Kaspar von 77, 78
Stöber, Rudolf 1, 69, 74, 76
Stollberg-Rilinger, Barbara 209
Stols, Eddy 199, 200
Stradling, Robert A. 41
Strasbourg 16, 74
Strossi, Francisco 175
Strozzi, imperial count 130
Styrian estates 160, 162, 167, 168, 169, 171, 175, 176, 177
Sumaran, Leopold Wilhelm 214
supernatural, belief in 138, 140, 143–6, 148, 151–2
Supino, Raphael 145
Sutter-Fichtner, Paula 169
Sweden, 131
syncretism, 178
Szakály, Ferenc 174

Tabacchi, Stefano 83, 84
Tänzler, Dirk 211
Targone, Pompeo 106
Tarragona 35
Tartars 44
Tassis family (hereditary imperial postmasters) 18, 24–9, 30, 34, 36, 38–40, 42, 56, 197, 201–5
Tassis, Bautista Mateo de 25
Tassis, Simón de 25
Tassis, Charles de 201
Tassis, Juan Bautista de 29, 30, 201
Tejeda, Antonio de 35
Tengnagel, Sebastian 160, 161, 167, 170, 168
Terence 27

Teutsche Kriegs–Kurier, 115, 121, 122, 123, 126–35
text reuse 251, 252, 257, 263, 264, 265, 267, 268, 274, 277, 278, 282, 283, 284, 285
Thijs, Alfons K.L. 198
Third Anglo-Dutch War, 124, 129
Thirty Years War 229, 234
Thøfner, Margit 196
Thomas, Werner 199
Thomason Tracts 251, 252, 253, 286
Thomason, George 251
Thompson, Clive 288
Thuillier–Foucart, 93
Thurn und Taxis, 71
Thurzó family 162, 169
Thurzó, György 167, 169, 171
Thurzó, Szaniszló 161, 167, 169, 175
Thurzó-Zeitungen 160, 161
Tishby, Isaac 143
Toledo 27
Toledo, Eleonora di 90, 93
Tolosa 28
Tottie, Gunnel 236
transcription 254, 256, 286
transit times for news 142, 144–5, 148, 150
translation, 229, 233–6, 244, 248
Trent 30
Tripoli 32
Tronchin Dubreuil, Jean 184
True and Perfect Dutch Diurnal 262
Tubize 29
Tunis 145
Turin 10, 30, 63, 65
Turkish emperor 7
Turks 14, 45
Turner, George William 245
Tuscany 6
Tuxaxa, king of 49
Twelve-Year Truce 104

Ughi, Gabriello 107

Ukraine 142, 150
Ungerer, Friedrich 236, 249
United Provinces 185, 188

Valencia 24
Valenciennes 29
Valladolid 25
Várkonyi, Ágnes R. 158
Vasari, Giorgio 95
Velasco y Tovar, Juan Fernández de 112
Velez, Los, marquis of 9
Vendosme, Louis 118
Venice 5, 7, 11, 30, 53, 58, 65
Veracruz 47, 48
Vermeir, René 204
Vernon, James 121
Verona 25
Versatz- und Fragamt 218
Verstegan, Richard 197
Vesti-kuranty, translated Muscovite news compendia 141, 144, 147–8
Vienna 123, 126, 130, 132, 142, 145, 217
Villari, Rosario 8
Villeroy 189
Villota 37
virtual marketplace (of information) 210, 221
Vitelli, Vincenzo 98
Viterbo 26, 30
Vitoria 28
Vittu, Jean-Pierre 1, 180, 183
Voeten, P. 201, 202, 204
Voss, Jürgen 117
Vries, Jan de 198

Wagner, Fritz 125
Walker, Henry 213, 278
Walker, R.B. 120
Wall, Ernestine G.E. van der 143
Walravens, Hartmut 119
Walter, Éric 119
War of the League of Augsburg 181, 190

Ward, Joe H. 260
Warsaw 126
Watson, George 267
Waugh, Daniel Clarke 18, 141, 144, 146, 148, 150
Weber, Johannes 1, 2, 16, 69, 76, 77, 78, 128
Webster, Charles 207
Wee, Herman van der 197, 198, 199, 200
Weekely Newes from Germanie, and Other Places of Europe 38, 231, 234
Weekly Intelligencer, The 254, 265
Weekly Post, The 248, 264, 265, 273, 274, 282, 284
Weinhold, Jörn 209
Welch Mercury 246
welfare 211, 221
Welke, Martin 2, 69, 75
Werner, Theodor-Gustav 158, 165
Westphalia 5
White, Peter 225, 227, 228, 247
Wick, Hans Jakob 163, 167
Wick, Johann Jakob 162, 165, 166, 169, 173, 177
Wickiana 160, 161, 162, 166
Wiedemann, Conrad 117
Wienerisches Diarium 218
Wijk, Jetteke van 141
Wijk, Yetteke van 149, 152
Wilhelm V Wittelsbach, duke of Bavaria 85
Wilke, Jürgen 157, 287
Wilkins, John 215
Wilks, Yorick 257
William III, prince of Orange, King of England 125, 181, 190
Williams, Joseph 120, 121
Wilson, Andrew 251
Windisch–Graetz, count of 62
Winkelbauer, Thomas 161
Winkler, Karl Tilman 121
Wintermonat, Georg 155, 156
Witt, Johan de 125
Wochentliche Zeitung (Hamburg) 149n39

Wolf, Robert 93
Wolfenbüttel 74
Wolfgang, Reinhard 158
Wood, Robert 264, 273, 274, 275, 277, 278, 279, 280, 282, 283, 284, 285
Woodward, David 7
Woolf, Daniel 8
Wunder, Bernd 220
Württemberg, prince of 176
Wüst, Wolfgang 219, 221
Wyss, Arthur 161

XML 256

Yard, Robert 121
Yemen 142
York, duke of 205

Zamora, Fernández de 42
Zara 174
Zarnack, Joachim August Christian 217
Zimmermann, Walter 121
Zinho Mudafar, king 44
Zittel, Claus 211
Zöllner, Erich 160
Zürich 140, 143
Zwierlein, Cornell 159